Suzan-Lori Parks

ALSO EDITED BY PHILIP C. KOLIN

The Influence of Tennessee Williams:
Essays on Fifteen American Playwrights
(McFarland, 2008)

Suzan-Lori Parks

Essays on the Plays and Other Works

Edited by PHILIP C. KOLIN

McFarland & Company, Inc., Publishers
Jefferson, North Carolina, and London

LIBRARY OF CONGRESS CATALOGUING-IN-PUBLICATION DATA

Suzan-Lori Parks : essays on the plays and other works /
edited by Philip C. Kolin.
p.   cm.
Includes bibliographical references and index.

ISBN 978-0-7864-4167-9
softcover : 50# alkaline paper ∞

1. Parks, Suzan-Lori — Criticism and interpretation.
2. African Americans in literature.   I. Kolin, Philip C.
PS3566.A736Z89   2010   812'.54 — dc22   2010024881

British Library cataloguing data are available

©2010 Philip C. Kolin. All rights reserved

*No part of this book may be reproduced or transmitted in any form
or by any means, electronic or mechanical, including photocopying
or recording, or by any information storage and retrieval system,
without permission in writing from the publisher.*

Front cover: Suzan-Lori Parks "smiling photo in front of diner on
Great Jones Street, New York City," ©peter sumner walton bellamy 2010

Manufactured in the United States of America

*McFarland & Company, Inc., Publishers
Box 611, Jefferson, North Carolina 28640
www.mcfarlandpub.com*

Table of Contents

Preface 1

Puck's Magic Mojo: The Achievements of Suzan-Lori Parks 7
    PHILIP C. KOLIN

Everything and Nothing: The Political and Religious Nature of
    Suzan-Lori Parks's "Radical Inclusion" 20
    RENA FRADEN

"Jazzing" Time, Love, and the Female Self in Three Early Plays
    by Suzan-Lori Parks 34
    JACQUELINE WOOD

"You one of uh mines?" Dis(re)membering in Suzan-Lori Parks's
    Imperceptible Mutabilities in the Third Kingdom 45
    PHILIP C. KOLIN

Sampling and Remixing: Hip Hop and Parks's History Plays 65
    NICOLE HODGES PERSLEY

"For the Love of the Venus": Suzan-Lori Parks, Richard Foreman,
    and the Premiere of *Venus* 76
    SHAWN-MARIE GARRETT

"A Full Refund Aint Enough": Money in Suzan-Lori Parks's
    Red Letter Plays 88
    JON DIETRICK

Does Reshuffling the Cards Change the Game? Structures of
    Play in Parks's *Topdog/Underdog* 103
    JOCHEN ACHILLES

Suzan-Lori Parks's *365 Days/365 Plays*: A (W)hole New
    Approach to Theatre 124
    JENNIFER LARSON

Parks and the Traumas of Childhood 140
    CHRISTINE WOODWORTH

Demeter, Persephone and Willa Mae Beede: Suzan-Lori Parks
    Gets Mother's Body 156
        GLENDA DICKER/SUN

The Unconscious and Metaphors in Suzan-Lori Parks's
    Screenplays of *Girl 6* and *Their Eyes Were Watching God* 169
        CHARLENE REGESTER

An Interview with Suzan-Lori Parks 181
        SHAWN-MARIE GARRETT

A Parks Remix: An Interview with Liz Diamond 191
        FAEDRA CHATARD CARPENTER

A Production History of the Works of Suzan-Lori Parks 203
        RICHARD E. KRAMER

About the Contributors 207

Index 211

Preface

Suzan-Lori Parks has transformed the American theatre with her mythic plays about black history and identity in contemporary America. The acclaimed heir of Adrienne Kennedy and Ntosake Shange, Parks has produced provocative dramas that capture the nightmares of African Americans endangered by a white establishment determined to erase their history and eradicate their dreams. Inspired by these earlier dramatists' works, Parks has created haunting characters whose identities change rapidly and who use a new stage language based on the poetry of spoken black English. Her disarming sets and dislocating narratives deconstruct a linear, ordered sense of history. Parks's plays exist in a world where time, space, and consequence slip and slide away from the strict obligations of logic. Her characters are displaced versions of themselves, trying to find their identity — in a family, a city, a nation, a continent, the universe.

Since the 1980s, Parks's plays have won the acclaim of dramatists, critics, and audiences worldwide. Frequently anthologized and performed at large professional and regional theatres alike, her works have won her recognition as a provocative and influential playwright. She rivals almost every other American dramatist in terms of the "firsts" that she has pioneered. She was the first African American woman playwright to win the Pulitzer Prize for *Topdog/Underdog* in 2002. She was the first to receive the Master Writer Chair at New York's prestigious Public Theatre. With *365 Plays/365 Days* (in 2006–2007) she became the first dramatist to have her works staged/premiered at 700 theatres across the nation and the globe. Her innovative scripts have created a new black theatre/stage, breaking conventions and establishing a provocative epistemology of performance. Excluding Tennessee Williams, Parks may also be the most prolific and diverse playwright America has ever produced. Her genius has led her into many other genres as well — she is a novelist, a screenwriter, a poet, a musician, an actor, a lecturer, and so on. The 12 original scholarly essays plus two new interviews — with Parks and with her longtime friend and director Liz Diamond — included in *Suzan-Lori Parks: Essays on the Plays and Other Works* explore almost all of her multi-layered and provocative plays up to 2010, in addition to assessing her other achievements in the arts.

The first two essays in this collection supply necessary background information and theory for understanding and appreciating Parks's evolutionary works. In "Puck's Magic Mojo," I discuss Parks's biography, her themes, her characters, her dramatic strategies, and her role as both a performer and a creator of performances. Like Shakespeare's Puck, she has transformed the stage as she recreates and recasts African American history. Throughout her canon she works through spells, magic, and spirits. Whether her plays are set in an indeterminate location or in a ghetto, whether they take place in the present or in a murky past, the element of postmodern performativity is common to them all, as it is to her own life. In the next essay, Rena Fraden explores the religious and political ideas that undergird Parks's creative principle of "radical inclusion." Arguing that Parks rejects philosophical essentialism as "insidious," Fraden argues instead for a religious universalism that accounts for and illuminates Parks's experimentation. In reading Parks's major works, Fraden finds that her politics refuse to be narrowly nationalistic while her religion seems to be a blend of eastern New Age mysticism. She concludes that Parks's creative identity overflows not only national borders but racial and gender ones as well.

Not surprisingly, race and gender also play a major role in the following two essays that turn to Parks's early works. Concentrating on three neglected Parks scripts — *Betting on the Dust Commander*, *Pickling*, and *Devotees in the Garden of Love* — Jacqueline Wood acknowledges the power of her frequently used "Rep & Rev" techniques. But Wood finds that jazz also allows readers to interrogate the constructions of African American female selfhood in relation to time and money, black men, and social traditions in these three plays. Labeling them black women's plays, since they center on the black female experience, Wood examines how these dramas unpack romantic views of love and marriage to reveal the detrimental impact of traditional expectations on the black woman's mental health and identity. In "jazzing" the black (1989) female subject, Parks began her career as she has continued it — with provocative experimentation. Turning to another early play, Parks's first work, *Imperceptible Mutabilities in the Third Kingdom*, I trace the evolution and execution of her psychic/anatomical pun on "(dis)membering," symbolizing the attacks on black memory and black bodies. *Mutabilities* problematizes memory of a black past that has been lost in the "Third Kingdom," a terrifying place where Africans find themselves dislocated after a harrowing journey through the Middle Passage. Black bodies, whether they belong to young contemporary black women or to the ghosts of slaves, are repeatedly being "dis-membered," disfigured, extracted, and amputated, a physicalization of the mental tortures blacks have suffered. Tragically marked for dismemberment, Parks's characters in *Mutabilities* share a horrific plight over the centuries.

Looking at Parks's history plays (*Death of the Last Black Man in America*; the *America Play*), Nicole Hodges Persley continues this collection's investigation of Parks's use of music to structure her work. While "Rep & Rev" jazz techniques form a major part of Parks's dramaturgy, Persley believes that Hip Hop may provide a more useful lens through which we examine Parks's dramatic processes. She argues that the Hip Hop DJ's strategies of sampling and remixing are reflected in Parks's remixing representations of blackness in American history. Connecting Hip Hop to the writing of history, Persely identifies the sampled figures and themes Parks has selected from various sources in constructing her narratives.

Examining one of Parks's most celebrated plays, Shawn-Marie Garrett explores the premiere of *Venus*, directed by Richard Foreman, in one of the seminal theatrical productions of the 1990s. Drawing a distinction between the director's aims and aesthetics and those of Parks, Garrett argues that Foreman's production, which influenced many prominent interpretations of *Venus*, elided crucial aspects of Parks's play, namely, the dynamics of empathy and love. While scholarship has ably parsed the play in terms of its politics, Garrett maintains that very little has been said regarding the dynamics of emotion in *Venus*, and what Parks means when she says, as she has repeatedly done, that the play is about love. Garrett's essay, firmly grounded in the performance culture of the decade, invites critical consideration of the neglected topic of emotion in *Venus* and, by extension, in all of Parks's work.

Among the narratives that Parks has remixed are sanctified white canonical literary texts, which Jon Dietrick looks at in Parks's Red Letter Plays (*In the Blood* and *Fucking A*) as he illuminates how Parks recreates African American history by deconstructing Hawthorne's *Scarlet Letter*. Ironically, Hawthorne, like Parks, expresses the same desperate need for fixed signs and self-evident identities. Dietrick claims that in both *Scarlet Letter* and the Red Letter Plays, money and economic thinking are bound inextricably together. In studying the centrality of money in contemporary American life, with a concomitant concern — the slipperiness of verbal and visual signs — Dietrick reads Parks's works in the context of an American realist/naturalist tradition deeply rooted in economic thinking. But, he contends, Parks transforms this tradition by conceiving identities that transcend naturalism's rigid distinction between language and action, "hard" and "soft" currency, the essential and the mimetic.

In his essay on Parks's *Topdog/Underdog*, her Pulitzer Prize–winning play, Jochen Achilles analyzes this signature work in light of contemporary game theory. He argues that the play is dominated by two exploitative performative scenarios, or commodified forms of play — the simulated arcade shootings of a Lincoln impersonator and the performance of the three-card monte con game. In the interaction between the two black brothers, named Booth and Lincoln by their father for fun, these two scenarios partially overlap and transform each other before they tragically converge in the lethal restructuring of the brothers' family history. Looking at Parks's play in terms of these performative scenarios in *Topdog*, Achilles finds that postmodern realities belong to a universe of the playful where the distinction between virtuality and reality collapses.

Unwaveringly anti-mimetic, Parks's theatre is postmodern, self reflexive, and unstable, a theatre full of black holes. Viewing her *365 Plays/365 Days* as a meditation on the evolving significance of the "Great Hole of History," Jennifer Larson's essay studies the *365 Plays* as a text about writing and taking audiences on a daily journey that is simultaneously circular, temporal, spatial, personal, and communal. Seen as many texts made into one, *365* stands as a fitting metaphor for its revisioning Parks's "Great Hole of History" at the center of her *America Play*. For Larson, the diverse *365* plays not only describe the convergence of art and text, but they enact and embody it. These *365* plays do not exist in a bitter dichotomous battle for Larson, but in symbiotic harmony, since the written text provides the "whole." The pun on "hole"/"whole" extends the Parksian concept of radical inclusion beyond the stage to the page and to the writer as well. While the "Great Hole of History" in Parks's earlier plays was characterized by its inability to represent identity, Larson claims that Parks supplies "holes" in *365* designed to create rather than destroy, to include rather than to exclude. On these grounds, *365 Plays/365 Days* embodies a Parksian creation mythos.

But as the inheritors of such a mythology, children are almost always at risk in Parks's plays, and since they play such a powerful role in the dismemberment and dislocation of her other characters, they deserve a separate essay. Accordingly, Christine Woodworth examines Parks's children and how they reflect the larger dramaturgy of Parks's canon. Typical of Parks's overall sense of theatre, children embody troubling contradictions — their innocent playfulness is undercut by darker adult overtones. In many of Parks's works, Woodworth argues that children are estranged from parents, must grapple with war, poverty, and murder. They bleed because of ruptured families. Yet in spite of these bleak circumstances, Parks's children strive for a sense of connection, searching for their familial legacy. Reading six of Parks's plays, ranging from *Mutabilities* to *365* to *Topdog*, Woodworth divides Parks's theatrical offspring into various categories in which child characters function as performative genealogies of their respective family history or of an even larger history that highlights the cyclical nature of Western literary traditions that Parks interrogates and invents.

Though Parks's skill as a novelist has been trumpeted, few extended essays have focused on her *Getting Mother's Body* (2003) and how it relates to the plays. Renowned dramatist and performance artist Glenda Dicker/sun provides such a needed essay. She explores the mythic analogues and foundations of Parks's heroine, Billy Beede, who hopes to find her wealth inside her mother's coffin, another Parksian hole. Labeling Billy a Parks "bad girl," Dicker/sun boldly asserts that this iconoclastic character is "thinking with her vagina." Deftly explaining the numerous mythological figures with whom she convincingly compares Billy and her deceased mother, Dicker/sun claims that Billy recalls Parks's Hester from *Fucking A*. Like Hester, Billy can "bear the unbearable."

In the following essay, Charlene Regester evaluates Parks's skill as a screenwriter to illuminate how her plays have been informed by her achievements in film productions. Analyzing two of Parks's screenplays, *Girl 6* and *Their Eyes Were Watching God*, Regester insists that Parks's knowledge of cinematic techniques and popular culture emanate from and return to her work for the stage. In *Girl 6*, the script Parks wrote for the Spike Lee film, Regester finds that the protagonist, a phone sex operator, responds to her male customers based on her own psychodynamics and inadequacies and recreates fantasies to fulfill both her clients' desires and her own. As Regester argues, the protagonist in *Girl 6* has much in common with Parks's other abused women. In her adaptation of Zora Neale Hurston's *Their Eyes Were Watching God*, Parks introduces a series of linked metaphors that Regester claims can also be found in the plays. As seen in earlier essays in this book, Parks's plays are often foregrounded in a series of key metaphors, be they great holes or acts of (dis)membering, or bloodletting. In this essay, Regester productively traces such important metaphors as fruit, windows/doors, water, and eyes/vision, through which Hurston's novel and Lee's film dissolve into Parks's screenplays.

Following these essays are new two new interviews with Liz Diamond and Parks herself. Having these interviews extends and enriches the scholarly assessments which precede them. Shawn-Marie Garrett's interview with Parks is instructively wide ranging, covering Parks's comments on her new play *Father Comes Home from the Wars*, yoga, religion, Lincoln, directing, the Pulitzer Prize, and influences on her work. As always, Parks is dynamic, perceptive, and ready to discuss the contexts of her plays. Twenty years after the playwright-director duo of Suzan-Lori Parks and Liz Diamond came on the scene with *Imperceptible Mutabilities of the Third Kingdom* in 1989, Faedra Chatard Carpenter interviewed the celebrated director to discover how Diamond envisions Parks's impact on contemporary theatre — on and beyond the stage. Carpenter asked Diamond to revisit past performance events for her commentary and to evaluate more recent ones to see how and why Diamond's understanding of and approach to Parks may have changed. Carpenter also turned to questions about how young directors can understand Parks's work as a "musical score" and if there is a "Parks Effect" among up-and-coming playwrights. "A Parks Remix" discloses Diamond's practical and philosophical insights as an artistic educator.

Suzan-Lori Parks: Essays on the Plays and Other Works concludes with Richard Kramer's helpful production chronology, a valuable listing of where and when Parks's plays premiered or saw major revivals, beginning with her first play written at Mt. Holyoke.

In editing and writing for this collection on Parks, I became the beneficiary of much help and goodwill. Straightaway, I want to thank my contributors for their cooperation and zeal, and for sharing their insights on Parks with me and the large audience of those who see, read, teach, and/or write about her plays. I also thank the administration of the University of Southern Mississippi for their continuing support of my work, particularly Provost Bob Lyman, Denise von Herrmann, Dean of the College of Arts and Letters. I am also grateful to Danielle Sypher-Haley, PennyWhite, and Cecily Hill in the Department of English. Finally, my love and gratitude go out in abundance to my family for their many acts of kindness and their prayers. As the good Benedictines say, "Ora et labora."

Puck's Magic Mojo:
The Achievements of Suzan-Lori Parks

Philip C. Kolin

For his in-depth article in *The New Yorker* on her *365 Days/365 Plays*, Hilton Als acclaimed Suzan-Lori Parks as a "Show-Woman," a title that resonates with multifaceted meanings for her career and her canon. Tellingly, the expansive ambiguity of "Show-Woman" may be the most profitable way to enter Suzan-Lori Parks's world. "Show" is her shibboleth. In an interview with Deborah Behrens, she declared, "I don't tell people anything; I show people what's there" (20). A *magistra ludi*, Parks is the creator/conductor of shows, fables, and spectacles with self-alienating characters with bizarre names and an even stranger language; her plays amaze and alarm, and defy and dismantle the linear, the static, the predictable. She remains unchallenged as the *primum mobile* of American theatre today. But she herself is also a one-woman show, the performer, the cultural icon who in the last twenty-five years or so has changed and challenged the American theatre. Writing is performance for her. The multiple photos of Parks sitting in a fire-engine red convertible on the cover of her *365 Days/365 Plays* broadcast her charisma; she is the auteur of alterity.

Undeniably, the indwelling spirit of Parks's shows, her art, is acting, performativity. As she told Una Chaudhuri, "The idea of someone getting up on stage pretending they are someone that they are not ... that can be so much fun — and so I wanted to give these actors the opportunity to play lots of characters and change roles a lot. Because it is all about Show" ("Posterior's Sake" 28). The métier of acting — pretending, assuming a role, adopting multiple identities, donning costumes, engaging with an audience — is at the heart of Parks's canon. She agreed with Kevin Wetmore who claimed, "You've become one of your own characters" (133). Shortly after graduating from Mt. Holyoke College in 1985, she went to the Drama Studio in London to study acting in the hopes of improving her writing. Providentially, she starred as Puck in a student production of *A Midsummer Night's Dream* at the Studio (Als 78). No role could have been more proleptic, more symbolic. Like Puck, Parks uses spells, fantastical shapes, and frightful pageants to express and probe the collective unconscious of her characters, and of her audiences as well. Like Shakespeare's master showman-storyteller Puck, she speaks a magical, incantatory language unheard on the American stage before. Puck-like as well, her fictions elicit laughter with their broad comedy, but also sting with their nightmarish shapes and sights. Like

Puck, too, she presents shadows, but they are the offended shadows of a harrowing racial past. As she confessed, "Being a playwright of any race is difficult, and Lord knows it gets more difficult the further you get from the middle of the road. I don't know what kind of magic my mojo is working, but it is working" (Williams C:1). Parks's mojo, like Puck's, is irresistible, comic, frightening, mystical, all at once.

Though her career is still in the making, Suzan-Lori Parks herself has played many diverse roles, all spectacular shows, performances. As the headline of a *New York Times* story says, "Suzan-Lori Parks: Whatever She Does, She Creates a Buzz" (Guinn). As Erick Jackson graphically describes her, "Clearly, Parks possesses an omnivorous creative appetite — with the drive to pull it off." She is prolific, ironic, complex, brilliantly experimental. Fellow dramatist Han Ong declared: "She sits all alone amongst her generation, peerless" (qtd. in Garrett, "Possession" 24). With their heightened theatrical, haunting language, satirically historicized sets, and surreal characters, her plays interrogate black cultural memory and contemporary black identity. Resisting and subverting white exclusionary history, Parks writes from her gut about the racial outrages directed against the black body and spirit. Black bodies in her plays become the site where colonialism, discrimination, and self interact. She has radicalized America's sense of history as much as she has the theatre. As C.W.E. Bigsby observed, Parks "deliberately dislocates the supposed fixities of identity and history alike" through her "disturbing metaphors and metamorphoses" (310). Her transformations of characters, language, and place have liberated African Americans from a compulsory sense of selflessness.

But her talents extend to other media, other shows. She is an original and highly respected novelist who illuminates in prose narratives the search for black self and heritage found on her stage. Her novel, *Getting Mother's Body*, in fact, can serve as a gloss on her plays. As a screenwriter for Spike Lee's *Girl 6*, she energized the film adaptation of Ruthie Bolton's novel through her own past performances as a phone sex operator. "Yes, I actually was really good at phone sex. I have a good phone voice and a very good imagination. That's why Spike asked me to write the screenplay. I knew I could do it. My experience wasn't tragic [though]" (Morgan 74). In June 2009, she starred in her own *Father Comes Home*, staged at the Public Theater, contributing a framing shamanic voice to the production.

Inseparable from these shows — literary and dramatic — are Parks's successes as an engaging public speaker/lecturer/teacher. With her dreadlocks and beguiling smile, she is well known as a lively performer on college campuses and before theatre audiences nationwide. Delivering a spirited talk at Wabash College in March 2008, for instance, she elicited this response from student Gary James: "Fraught with attention-grabbing physical gestures, humor and unusual sound effects, Suzan-Lori Parks uses her own story and creative mind to offer suggestions and deliver lessons learned throughout her life" ("Parks Entertains, Offers Advice"). Those lessons, plus her passion for writing, have made her a highly respected teacher — at the California Institute of the Arts and elsewhere. Adding further to her repertoire of performances — public shows — Parks has earned a brown belt in karate, has won victories as a long distance runner, and plays the guitar, though not well by her own reckoning. Even so, she is recognized for her musical talents, e.g., writing for her *Father Comes Home from the War* and the libretto for *Ray Charles*

Live—The Musical! Her interest in performance and shows includes the exotic, too. On a recent trip to India, she became fascinated with snake charming. "I do have a strange fondness for snakes. I mean, in my mind it'll be snake handling. That's where I'm going. Snake handling. That's the next thing" (Chen, "Interview & Ticket"). Coincidentally, her play *Snake* (retitled *The Book of Grace*) premiered at the Public Theater in 2010.

Parks's life has been filled with creative accomplishments/performances that bear the stamp of her genius. Opening herself to limitless creative energies, she lives a life devoted to radical inclusion. At age 5 (she was born in Fort Knox, Kentucky, in 1964), Parks began working on a novel (Garrett, "Possession" 22); and by age 9 she and her brother launched their own newspaper, the *Daily Daily* (Miller and Cotliar 143). Moving to Germany while in grade school, after her father, a career army officer, was transferred there, Parks became fluent in a second language and absorbed another culture, accounting for her fascination with the history and politics of words. While in college she studied under James Baldwin, who predicted that "this beautiful creature ... may become one of the most valuable artists of our time." Graduating Phi Beta Kappa from Mt. Holyoke in 1985, she wrote her first play, *Sinner's Place*, for her English honors thesis. Foreshadowing some of her later, provocative works, the play was rejected for performance by the Theatre Department at Mt. Holyoke because of its raw ("dirty") language and subject matter. Parks staged her first play, *Betting on the Dust Commander*, in a small, dingy New York City bar in 1985. At the age of 28, she finished the mesmerizing quartet of scenes grouped under the intriguing title *Imperceptible Mutabilities in the Third Kingdom*, which began a collaboration with director Liz Diamond. *Mutabilities* won Parks her first Obie and kudos from Mel Gussow, who welcomed her as "the year's most promising playwright." Her first screenplay, *Anenome*, was written for an independent film company in 1990. That same year, she received her second Obie for *Venus*, directed by the celebrated playwright/manager George C. Wolfe at the New York Public Theater.

Repeatedly acknowledging her astonishing creativity, *The New York Times* hailed her in 1993 as one of "30 artists under 30 most likely to change the culture for the next 30 years," and in 1999, *Time Magazine* numbered her among the "100 Innovators for the Next Wave." In that same year, *In the Blood*, the first of her Red Letter plays, was a finalist for the Pulitzer Prize. Because of her work with the Public Theater, Parks has been playfully called "the Belle of Off-Broadway" (Bryant 45). In 2000, she received a Guggenheim Fellowship, and the following year, she was awarded a MacArthur Foundation "Genius" Grant with a stipend of $500,000 to further her art. But, as she confesses, "My plays are much larger and more intelligent than I am" (Bornstein). As a further sign of her artistic performances, the Signature Theater devoted its 2008-2009 season to a celebration of her works. And in October 2008, Parks again made history by being named the first Master Writer at the New York Public Theater, where *Venus* premiered, for "setting the standard for the highest level of achievements in theatre."

Her plays have recast and reconfigured the American theatre. Winning a Pulitzer Prize for *Topdog/Underdog* in 2002, Parks became the first black woman to receive the honor for drama. Moreover, *Topdog/Underdog* was "the only play by a black woman ... to make it to Broadway since Ntozake Shange's *For colored girls who have considered suicide when the rainbow is enuf.* Additionally, *Topdog* is an extremely rare example of a woman writing a drama featuring only male characters" (Rasbury). Perhaps her most daring accomplishment came in 2005-2006, when Parks began writing a play each day for a year to produce the marathon cycle *365 Days/365 Plays*. This cycle challenged the way theatre is created and performed, subverting such hallowed conventions as premieres, seminal productions, acting spaces, and even a dramatist's privilege to decide how his/her play should be staged. In what was called "the largest multi-city premiere of a live theatre event ... since the Federal Theatre Project" of the 1930s (Beach 649), the *365* plays were coordinated in 52 hubs in the United States and abroad that included more than 800 theatres and diverse acting troupes and individuals — which amounted to "a nationwide theatre festival." "In all probability, Parks had surpassed any other playwright, including Tennessee Williams and possibly Shakespeare, in having his/her works produced across the U.S. in 2006-2007" (Kolin, "Redefining" 66). Creating the cycle of *365* scripts was relatively easy for a playwright who told Tom Sellar that she could imagine "what it would be like if five Greek plays were running simultaneously in [her] head" (39). Reflecting her amazing creativity, Parks gingerly rattled off her accomplishments when asked about her memory of winning the Pulitzer: "I finished my novel on April 6th, my play opened on Broadway on April 7th, and I won the Pulitzer on April 8th" (Marshall, "A Moment with Suzan-Lori Parks, Playwright").

Is it possible to characterize Parks's plays? She strongly denies that there is anything like "a Suzan-Lori Parks play," insisting that with each new work she does something different — "I've got to go into uncharted waters to write it" (Wetmore 127). Reinforcing the importance of self-discovery, she claimed, "I have no idea what kind of writer I am. I don't. I find out with every play" (Sellar 39). There is no doubt her canon is compellingly experimental, unsettling. It is at once comic and cosmic, absurd and tragic, erotic and fervent, historical and iconoclastic. As a whole, her plays might be read as phantasmagoric fables that mime diasporic fragmentation; they depict and deplore dismemberments simultaneously (Geis 11; Thompson 172). Intriguingly, Sara Warner has labeled Parks's plays "the Drama of Disinterment"; but they also participate in a theatre of resurrections. With postcolonial fervor, Parks portrays blackness as a symbol of subjugation, but even as she deconstructs the fantasies of white power, she converts the black body into a theatre of trauma. August Wilson aptly described her as "an original whose fierce intelligence and fearless approach to craft subvert[s] theatrical conventions" (qtd. in *Suzan-Lori Parks*, 66). Rejecting the naturalism of earlier dramas, with their desire to be encapsulated in verisimilitude, Parks has created a new type of theatre, one that has transmuted and transcended conventions by radicalizing (re-imagining, re-figuring, subverting) them. Her work is "disturbing, funny and poetic, but never literal" (Weinberg 14). She has challenged both periodicity and performance.

The vestigia of numerous sources lie scattered across her canon. Identifying several traditions that Parks has deployed, Carol Schafer, for instance, claims that *In the Blood* is "a classical tragedy" where Hester's infanticide clearly links her to Medea, while *Venus* is comparable to an epic whose hero "becomes the African version of Helen of Troy." Throughout her canon Parks testifies to the traumas inscribed in slave narratives, the writings of Frederick Douglass, and especially in works of Zora Neale Hurston; in fact, she wrote the screenplay for Oprah's production of *Their Eyes Were Watching God* (1937).

Minstrelsy, Broadway musicals like *Old Man River*, and vaudeville skits are also part of the mix out of which she conceived *The Last Black Man*. In her Red Letter Plays — *In the Blood* and *Fucking A* — she recasts Hawthorne's Hester Prynne, who has been famously romanticized and mystified, and insists we consider her again "through the lens of our cruel and continuing histories of oppression" (Geis 140). Re-inscribing and contemporizing Hawthorne through *In the Blood*, Parks turns Hester into a welfare mother battling the system, including race traitors, but in the process she murders her son; in *Fucking A*, Parks's heroine tragically becomes an abortionist, a crime which replaces Hawthorne's "adultery" as Hester's "A" sin. Other white male canonical figures in Parks's dramas include Bertolt Brecht, with his alienation effects and epic theatre; James Joyce; Samuel Beckett; and particularly William Faulkner, whose *As I Lay Dying* became a prominent text as she worked on *Getting Mother's Body*. Gertrude Stein, as well, has been an inspiration for Parks.

Her plays also look back to, but refashion the techniques, characters, and ideologies of, the Theatre of the Absurd, represented through Pirandello, Chekhov, Genet, and Sartre. Even though she raves about Shakespeare, her panoptic *365 Days/365 Plays* absurdly turn such classics as *Macbeth* and *Hamlet*, as well as *Oedipus* and *The Sea Gull*, upside down, just for "Derridian fun" (Kolin, "Redefining" 70). Closer to home, Parks gracefully acknowledges she has been powerfully influenced by the surrealistic nightmares and haunting, lyrical poetry of Adrienne Kennedy's plays, and also by the unconventional language and dramaturgy of Ntozake Shange's choreopoems. As in Shange's plays, Parks's unconventional spelling reflects the ways African Americans are re-figuring language. Indebted to Kennedy and Shange, Parks also writes about black female identity and agency in a culture that stigmatizes African American women as mindless, crude, expendable. The legacies of these two modern dramatists are essential to Parks's theatre of shadows, and together with them she forms a triumvirate of African American women playwrights whose works have most radically transformed the American theatre in the last 50 years. But however many texts lie embedded/commingled in Parks's theatre, her distinctive vision and spirit emerge with show-woman charisma and conviction.

In fact, an intense spirituality is at the core of Parks's life and canon. As she declares, "I write for God," the "God without limitations" (Wetmore 132), the energy behind the principle of "radical inclusion" that pulsates throughout her life and works. Grounded in her study of Eastern religions, Yoga, and Sanskrit, Parks enthusiastically admits, "The Spirit says 'Write the next thing.' And I write it." In doing so, she also follows the advice of her mentor James Baldwin. "The most important thing Mr. Baldwin taught me was how to conduct myself in the presence of the spirit — the writing comes from the spirit" (Parks, "Suzan-Lori Parks on James Baldwin"). As she told Shawn-Marie Garrett in the interview included later in this volume, "The more I do, the more God is there." Embodying such beliefs is a distinctive Sanskrit mantra tattooed/inscribed around her forearm — "Follow God Follow God Follow God" (Roach; Garrett interview). Raised a Roman Catholic, she credits the Oberammergau Festival for her early inspiration. "I did some of my growing up in Germany. There is this town, Oberammergau. Once every 10 years the whole town gets together and puts on a religious pageant. My plays are very much like that — the community gets together and creates this pageant.... So the idea of pageant is intrinsic to [my canon]" (Wetmore 139). Earlier, she told Han Ong, "My plays are like these passion plays where the community comes together to reenact the passion [of Christ]. They're a guide book to who we were or how we are, or what we should be" (49). Deborah Geis and others have identified the Stations of the Cross, the sacred ritual memorializing the road to Golgotha read on Good Friday, as foundational to understanding *Last Black Man*. *Venus*, too, reveals the subtext of sacred drama for Parks — "It's more like a miracle play than 'Look at her, she's a black woman with a big butt'" (qtd. in Chaudhuri 32). The sanctity of heritage and family in the ritual performances of one's identity are central to Parks's history plays as well as to *Topdog/Underdog*. Responding to her *365* plays, the coordinator for the Atlanta Hub, Danielle Mindess, described them in religious terms: "Parks's book [of *365* plays] is like a daily devotional of plays" (qtd. in Kolin, "Redefining" 71).

True to the spirit behind religious pageants and precepts, Parks's dramas probe an ancestral past, an atavistic world of black myths, to unearth and emancipate racial identities that have been stolen from her characters and to discover what they (and the audience!) should be doing about it. As she declares in the prefatory material to *The America Play and Other Works*, her job as dramatist is "to locate the ancestral burial grounds, dig for bones, find bones, hear bones sing, and write it down" (4). The "Great Hole of History" found in *The America Play*, for example, contains the bones of the sacred but obscured black dead. Their remains are both a talisman and an indictment of how history has robbed African Americans of their spiritual connections to a past that is far different from that fabricated for them by the "Blonde Bone Man" who, through enslavement, tried to erase the spiritual essence from their souls. How African Americans search for an ancestral home is at the heart of *Imperceptible Mutabilities*, but the characters are unable to find their indigenous landscape or names to restore their sense of self and dignity. Their humanity, and any pretense about it, has been stripped away. Shamans who possess sacred knowledge about life and death are replaced in *Mutabilities* by figures with orphic sounding names — Shark-Seer, Soul-Seer — but who cannot recall or restore. In her *365* cycle plays and in many others (e.g., *Last Black Man*, *Venus*, *Topdog*), Parks explores and reenacts events with immense spiritual meaning — deaths, rebirths, and resurrections.

Consistent with her pervasive and eclectic spiritual beliefs, it is not surprising that the dead — their re-animated corpses — return frequently through rituals, the cycles around which Parks's dramas spin. By creating scripts — show places — in which the dead speak, Parks becomes an intercessor for them. Commenting on the *Last Black Man* in a 1996 interview, Parks emphasized, "We see him die several times, and he comes out with a rope around his neck, and it's all really horrible, but it's a kind of play that's more like a religious experience, you know, like at Oberammergau where they parade Christ through the streets and reenact his story" (Chaudhuri, "Posterior's Sake" 36). The Resurrectionist in *Venus*, though far from being an ideal, exemplifies Parks's interest in the supernatural, death and afterlife. In her *365* plays, "Parks's Hindu spirituality gives audiences ... a feeling that they are watching the excavation of souls, their transformation, reincarnation, and return in a seamlessly endless cycle" (Kolin, "Redefining the Way Theatre is Created" 71). "A Play for the Day of the Dead" solemnly, symbolically comes near the end of the *365* cycle, while, more comically, "A Person of Great Compassion is resurrected from the dead" in the earlier "A Play Written on a Piece of Packing Paper" (132). Fascinated by Abraham Lincoln, Parks has incorporated the mythology surrounding his life and death in *365, The America Play, Topdog*, and *Father Comes Home*. Yet as she explained in a 2006 interview in the *Austinist*, "I bought a kids book about Abraham Lincoln, a picture book. There he was, looking skinny and worried. But the plays have less to do with Lincoln and more to do with the memory of Lincoln.... It's the past in the present moment. It's not just looking back. It's the past as it explodes into the present. When we remember, we're literally putting the members back together, putting our bodies back together" (Chen, "Interview & Ticket Giveaway"). Parks's spiritual odyssey has shaped her sense of history as well as her theatre of anatomies.

While still reflecting Parks's spiritual beliefs, many of the characters and events in her plays center on popular entertainments, whether they be staged at a theatre, arcade, circus, theme park, or sideshow. But, as in Adrienne Kennedy's *Funnyhouse of a Negro*, amusement sites become toxic for her characters. True to her postmodern sensibilities, Parks's theatre is recursively self-reflexive, always theatricalizing, unabashedly reminding audiences they are watching a play or a play/show-within-a-play. Parks creates metatheatre, a theatre in search of itself, but one that invites the disruptions out of which it springs. Her plays are filled with commentary by characters who announce, exaggerate, or undercut the trappings of their performativity; the artifacts of disguise — costumes, beards, masks, hats, make-up, and even holes — are crucial to her aesthetics of traumatized history. Her characters slip into and out of elusive, protean identities, like actors appearing in two or three different plays being performed simultaneously. Gifted with double, even triple, consciousness, Parks once again demonstrates her skill as show-woman. By participating in these entertainments, or what Cote calls "surreal sideshows," her characters strive to (dis)cover who they are, were, or should be, thus freeing themselves from circumscribed roles. When asked if she intended to add more "sideshows and low culture" in her plays, Parks revealed why such performances intrigued her:

> Well, I think that the sideshow really chooses me. There's something exciting about it. First of all, it's a show, and I love plays that have plays in them, you know? I just love that, when it's a play-within-a-play, and I used it in *The America Play* and then again in *Venus* and now in *Topdog/Underdog*. There's something exciting about — I mean, especially with Abraham Lincoln, who was shot while watching a play, so it can't get any more fun than that [Conan].

But Parks's sideshows are not just anti-mimetic, metatheatrical amusements; they are central to her discourse, her theatre, the terrifying world of a racialized culture.

In *The America Play* and *Topdog*, a black man impersonates Abraham Lincoln to amuse a fictive audience in an arcade or theme park, but also to discomfort the larger theatre audience before which Parks shows play. In *The America Play*, a character called Foundling Father "was told he bore a strong resemblance to Abraham Lincoln," the germ for Parks's show-within-a-show. This "Lesser Known," to distinguish him from Lincoln, "the Great Man," "had several beards which he carried around in a box. The beards were his although he himself had not grown them on his face but since he'd secretly bought the hairs from his barber and arranged their beard shapes and since procurement and upkeep of his beards took so much work he figured that the beards were completely his. Were as authentic as he was so to speak" (159–60). Because his resemblance to Lincoln was so strong — the genesis of Parks's dark humor, of course — "someone remarked that he ... ought to be shot" and so instead of just "speechifying," the Lesser Man's "act would now consist of a single chair, a rocker, in a dark box" where "the public was invited to pay a penny, choose from the selection provided of pistols, enter the darkened box and 'Shoot Mr. Lincoln'" (164). But the fabrication is palpably absurd, just like the authenticity that white history claims for and promulgates about itself when it has excluded or demonized blacks.

In play after play, Parks keeps emphasizing that history is representation/show and that the costumes/props used to project an image have a crucial role in identity formation. "My imagination is very excited about Lincoln because of his costume. What he did in history is coupled with his costume" ("The Author's Voice: Parks and Landau" 1). Ironically, Lincoln's "costume" both hides and identifies at the same time. Thus Parks travesties the exclusivity and legitimacy of an icon of white history. Through her entertainment(s), then, she asks searing questions about where identity resides for the black man caught in the pernicious "Great hole" of that history. The stage for Parks is both the emptiness (blackness) of space in history as well as a new and (re)claimed acting area for African Americans. Her theatre deploys space to re-enter and re-figure white sacred ground. Shawn-Marie Garrett insightfully comments on how Parks writes in "a space of simultaneity" ("Possession" 25), where time and place collapse, yet expand. As Andrea J. Goto convincingly argues, in Parks's dramaturgy, where "markers of 'blackness' and 'whiteness' are ambiguous," then "the Lincoln myth belongs to African-Americans at least as much, *if not more* than, to white Americans" (120). Because of her "partiality toward universalism," Parks has thereby opened up "an unconventional space" for blacks (121).

Similarly in *Topdog/Underdog*, a character named Lincoln dresses like the famed white president for his job in an arcade, where audiences, for a fee, get to "Shoot Mr. Lincoln" with a cap gun, re-enacting the crime of a nation in an arcade sideshow. As in *The America Play*, Parks elucidates the traumas of black history through a show-within-a-show. But surrounding this performance is another entertainment, the fatal card game — 3-Card Monte — that Lincoln plays with his younger brother Booth, who, like his white namesake, kills his president-acting brother. As the cards go back and forth, deals, like identities, fold and unfold (Larson 194–95). Filled with the traffic and props of theatre, *Topdog/Underdog* is metatheatre, stripping away the levels of illusions inherent in history/performance/acting/shows. As in *The America Play*, Lincoln's arcade impersonation of the president depends on costume, fake beards, whiteface, and customers who fantasize that they are in Ford's Theatre in April of 1865. Yet through this show Parks daringly revises white history as she did in *The America Play*, but adds another level of acting/representation, the fatal card game (gamble) with Lincoln's brother Booth. As Robert Faivre points out, "On the one hand, the character's narrative 'fate' is preordained by their names; on the other hand, they have a 'choice' ... to rewrite the historical narrative of Booth (killing Lincoln) in their personal lives" ("Review: *Topdog/Underdog*"). Converting her stage into a new type of historical pageant (or show), Parks destroys the audience's desire/need for white historical authenticity, showing how fickle, flawed, and skewed it is.

Even more deconstructively theatrical are the sideshows in *Venus*, which focus on the exhibition/spectacle of a woman's posterior — its exposure on stage, in a freak show and at a doctor's laboratory. Dissecting Venus on stage, or taking her apart to put her back again, as Parks claims, this young black woman becomes the object of curiosity/

lust, a commodified black body. According to the Chorus of 8 Human Wonders, "Shes thuh main atrtraction, she iz / Loves thuh sideshows center ring. / Whats thuh show without thuh star" (13). The loathsome Mother-Showman orders Venus to disrobe and reveal her naked anatomy for gluttonous white spectators. As in *The America Play*, Parks stages a range of shows to chastise white history for its cruel enslavement of blacks in the grotesque identities that have been central to a performance of race. Venus, "star" of this sideshow, undergoes a process which Parks labels as "Devolution" (*Devotees*), transforming her from a majestic Hottentot woman to a freak of nature whose physical shape is judged as being so outrageously abnormal that it is displayed for amusement or dissected for a despicable medical curiosity. On one level, then, we watch Venus as a performer/eroticized black body in a sideshow atmosphere, and that show foreshadows her debasement and eventual dismemberment in another white forum, the laboratory. But how she presents herself in these sideshows/performance arenas also, paradoxically enough in Parks's theatre, defines who she is as a human being. Speaking of how various individuals tell Venus's story — the Docteur, the Negro Resurrectionist, or even Venus herself— Parks takes audiences through the levels of performance (shows) in her play. As Tom Sellar astutely points out, "So you have these three people trying to tell the story, and it goes backwards and forwards. It also has a play-within-the-play, since — among many other things — it's about show business, showing yourself, being in a show" ("Making History," 39).

As *Venus* demonstrates, Parks's shows are punitive scopic events. Watching becomes an important part of identity (de)formation in history/performance. Historically, watching a black body was the right/privilege of the white master/overseer on antebellum (colonial) plantations. Slaves could not look their masters directly in the eye for fear of a whipping, or worse. In the film *Sally Hemings: An American Scandal*, for example, a rebellious black man is told by a young white master, "Take your eyes from me." In *Imperceptible Mutabilities*, a bigoted Naturalist concocts a large roach to spy on three black girls as if they were wild beasts or insects to be exterminated. This is not an instance of simple voyeuristic titillation. Surveillance is tantamount to documenting criminal activity; it is the opposite of the necessary witnessing/testifying to racial horrors. But in Parks's theatre, she interrogates (white) spectatorship, empowering audiences to see truths once hidden by masks. Further deconstructing the fantasy of the white world's control of representation, we watch Lincoln wearing his white face which (dis)covers a black one beneath. Similarly, in Kennedy's *Funnyhouse of a Negro*, we see Queen Victoria and the Duchess of Hapsburg played by black actors wearing whiteface. Their performance underlines the cruel deceptions/illusions the white world forces upon African Americans. Watching shows in Parks, then, as in Kennedy, is essential to identity (de)construction. According to Parks, "All that [pretending] makes for a hall of mirrors or a wave pattern. The characters perform and they're aware that they are being watched. They're each other's audience and their awareness of audience somehow makes them aware of us" (Wetmore 135).

Watching dangerous racialized spectacles forms a vital part of Parks's sideshows, plays-within-plays, theatricalized entertainments. Her stage is constantly in motion with outrageous sights to watch or sounds to hear. In *Imperceptible Mutabilities*, an old slave woman's teeth are extracted on stage. As we saw, in the *Last Black Man* a character rushes on stage with a lynching rope around his neck, visually reminding those who watch him of the countless black bodies that were staged for lynching parties and grotesquely captured on racist art and put on postcards to display these entertainments. *The America Play* restages the Lincoln assassination with a black man in whiteface. *In the Blood* is also rife with racialized spectacles. Among the most horrific sights are the cruel street doctor crawling under Hester's skirt to check her private parts as if he were a mechanic and she an impaired vehicle and, of course, Hester's murder of her own son, Jabber. Among Parks's most spectacular works, *365* is filled with alarms, executions, gun fights, bleeding hearts ("Revolver Love") and bloody hands ("Live Free or Die"), wailing voices ("Blackout"), races, and dancing. Though it contains only two characters, *Topdog*'s fast-paced card game and the violent eruptions of the players' passions offer dangerous spectacles. Booth watches Lincoln and Lincoln watches Booth and we watch them both.

No less than her dramaturgy, Parks's language is performance, a spectacle for the eye as well as the ear. It incorporates the elements of a show — myth, fantasy, history, pageant, theatre — from which she creates her scripts. In fact, one of her greatest achievements is making the visual and verbal work together. As Richard Zoglin aptly summed up, to accompany her "dislocating stage devices," Suzan-Lori Parks has created a "stark and poetic language, [with] fiercely idiosyncratic images [that] transform her work into something haunting and wondrous" (62). Inventing a new stage language, Parks has her characters speak an African American vernacular — a street-smart, rap-like at times, lingo — which she records in phonetic and subversively unconventional spellings. As C.W.E. Bigsby observed, "She develops her own language, based on a black demotic which, ironically, she glosses as 'foreign words and phrases'" (310). It becomes the language of the fragmented, the dispossessed, the disjointed. As Louise Bernard accurately emphasized, Parks's language is a "counter discourse to the dominant historical record" ("The Musicality of Language"). Here, for instance, are the frenzied words of Black Man with Watermelon from *Last Black Man* as he tries to find his place in time:

> We sittin on this porch right now aint we. Uh huhn. Yes. Sittin right here right now on it in it aintthuh first time either iduhnt it. Yep. Nope. Once we was here once wuhduhnt we. Yep. Yep. Once we being here. Uh huhn. Huh. There is uh Now and there is uh Then. Ssal there is. (I bein in uh Now: uh Now bein in uh Then. I bein, in Now in Then, in I wil be. I was be too but that's uh Then thats past. That me that was-be is uh me-has-been. Thuh. Then that was-be is uh has-been-Then too. Thuh me-has-been sits in thugh be-me: we sit on this porch. Same porch. Same me. Thuh Then that's been somehow sits in thuh Then that will be: same [126].

Syntactically and semantically, characters like Black Man with Watermelon are lost in a white world that has politicized time and space to occlude them. In what amounts to a Parksian stream of consciousness speech, Black Man's words tumble over each other searching for a logical history of his existence, a justification for who he is, was, and will be. Yet, ironically, through Parks's linguistic inventiveness, her characters do voice their desire for their own space and time, their own freedom, while simultaneously recognizing that they have been in bondage, deprived of selfhood.

Like Black Man with Watermelon, Shark-Seer and Kin-Seer in *Imperceptible Mutabilities* speak the language of absence; theirs is the speech of the displaced. After they have been taken from their homeland, carried across the Middle Passage on a slaver, and had to endure the privations of self and dignity in a strange land called the Third Kingdom, Shark-Seer and Kin-Seer chant: "And I whuduhnt me no more and I whuduhnt no fish. My new Self was uh 3rd Selfe made by that space inbetween" (55). Their language reflects their loss, their dejection in a terrorizing land. Parks's raw imagery, jarring sentences, and mythic darkness immerse us in the frenzy and fear of the Third Kingdom. In her later plays, as well, characters speak a language of limitations, oppression. History has cast them adrift and their words and sentences search for some unity, union. Her *Father Comes Home* sequences further show her characters living in a world that is unstable, unknowable, laughable and treacherous at the same time.

A trademark of Parks's style, of course, are her spells, or the repetition of a character's name, without any dialogue, "to express their pure and simple state." These provide the "impetus for various acts of dismantling, breaking up the linear succession between historical past and historical present," according to Jennifer Johung. She insightfully adds that Parks's spells "initiate a constant negotiation back and forth—flickering between the absent subjectivity of the historical figure and the present substance of the figure in [the] play, between the absent subjectivity inherent in the figurative presence and the material presence of the body of the performer" (49).

Distinctive of Parks's plays, too, is their musical origin and form. Music flows through her life and work. Married to bluesman Paul Oscher, she wants to be a better singer and guitarist. She has compared scripting plays to writing a score. Her poetic language owes a debt especially to jazz and to the blues, the two art forms historically rooted within the African American community ("Elements" 10). Bernard persuasively labels *Last Black Man* a "quintessential blues experience"; and the folding and unfolding of the dialogue and the cards in *Topdog/Underdog* might be seen as the theatrical equivalent of an improvisational jazz session. In fact, the imagery and syntax of her plays can be likened to poetic jazz stories, filled with the betrayals, abandonments, and heartaches characterizing these musical forms. Emphasizing their jazz roots, Parks has repeatedly described her plays in terms of "Rep & Rev," the repetition and revision of jazz scores and themes. As she acknowledges, "Rep & Rev" is "a central element in my work" ("Elements" 8). "Rep & Rev" is at work in her stagecraft and in her language. *Betting on the Dust Commander* (1986) most obviously exemplifies a "Rep & Rev" pattern as Parks repeats the first half of the play verbatim in the second, dramatizing the way "time, history and memory" are recorded in an "African American oral tradition" (Kolin, "Cultural Memory" 9).

Like a jazz artist, too, Parks improvises linguistically, fine tuning a keyword or idea through various characters, sets, and times. As Tom Sellar observed, "Her characters speak in tropes that form and reform endlessly to articulate and accommodate events on stage" ("Making History" 37). Some of Parks's most poignant "Rep & Rev" tropes can be heard in such haunting signifiers as *digging, holes, figuring, mines, (dis)member*, etc. Each time we hear one of these words it acquires a further, deeper meaning. She (con)figures identities and places through such tropes. Of course, other musical forms and genres have infused Parks's style. "The theatre I loved before I started writing plays was musicals. I still do" ("Why I Write" 83). Certainly that influence is evident in her lyrics for *Ray Charles Live—the Musical!*

Another achievement of Parks's language is that she has distinctly recorded a multitude of voices, some of which she has in her head speaking to her (Garrett, "Possession").

We hear con artists in *Topdog*; sideshow barkers in *Venus*; pseudo-scientists in *Imperceptible*; a street-smart mother in *In the Blood*; the dead and soon-to-be toothless old slave Aretha in *Imperceptible*; and a host of mythic characters speaking contemporary African American vernacular in the *365* plays. But, ultimately, we may ask, where is Suzan-Lori Parks's own voice? In a discussion between Parks and her longtime friend and director, Bonnie Metzgar, she answered that question head on: "Where is the playwright. Everywhere and nowhere. The characters speak for me but also beyond me. They know much more than I do. They speak from a deep well of knowledge—the intelligence of the Jungian collective consciousness. The voices of the characters are much larger than the voice of the playwright" ("Alien Baby" 52). Entering the "collective consciousness," Suzan-Lori Parks has opened the show world created by Puck, and brought us inside.

Works Cited

Als, Hilton. "The Show-Woman: Suzan-Lori Parks's Idea for the Largest Theatre Collaboration Ever." *The New Yorker*. Oct. 30, 2006: 74–81.

"The Author's Voice: Parks & Landau." *Inside the Public Theater* (Fall 1999): 1.

Beach, Maria. *365 Days/365 Plays*. *Theatre Journal* 59 (2007): 649–51.

Behrens, Deborah. "Suzan-Lori Parks: Connecting to the River of Spirit in *365 Days/365 Plays*." *LA Stage* 6.34 (Nov./Dec. 2006): 16–20.

Bernard, Louise. "The Musicality of Language: Redefining History in Suzan-Lori Parks's *The Last Black Man in the Whole Entire World*." *African American Review* 31 (Winter 1999): 687–98.

Bigsby, C.W.E. *Modern American Drama, 1945–2000*. Cambridge: Cambridge University Press, 2000.

Bornstein, Lisa. "Parks Again Bringing Her Voices to Denver." *Rocky Mountain News*, Nov. 12, 2005.

Bryant, Aaron. "Broadway, Her Way." *Crisis Forum* 109 (March-April 2002): 43–45.

Chaudhuri, Una. "For Posterior's Sake." *Public Access* (the program for the production of *Venus* at the Public Theater/New York Shakespeare Festival) 2.6 (April 1996): 26–32.

Chen, Allen Y. "Interview & Ticket Giveaway." *Austinist* [Austin, TX]. 15 May 2006.

Conan, Neal. "Interview: Suzan-Lori Parks Discusses Her Pulitzer Prize–Winning Play *Topdog/Underdog* and Her Career as a Playwright." National Public Radio's *Talk of the Nation*, April 25, 2002.

Cote, David. "Putting on the Dog: The Singular Suzan-Lori Parks Takes Her Black Lincoln for Another Spin in the Sibling Drama." *Time Out New York*, July 12–19, 2001: 161.

Faivre, Robert. "Review of Topdog/Underdog." *The Red Critique* (July/August 2002). http://www.RedCritique.org.

Garrett, Shawn-Marie. "An Interview with Suzan-Lori Parks." In *Suzan-Lori Parks: Essays on the Plays and Other Works*. Edited by Philip C. Kolin. Jefferson, N.C.: McFarland, 2010.

_____. "The Possession of Suzan-Lori Parks." *American Theater* 17.8 (October 2000): 22–26; 132–34.

Geis, Deborah R. *Suzan-Lori Parks*. Ann Arbor: University of Michigan Press, 2008.

Goto, Andrea J. "Digging out of the Pigeonhole: African-American Representation in the Plays of Suzan-Lori Parks." In *Suzan-Lori Parks: A Casebook*. Edited by Kevin J. Wetmore, Jr., and Alycia Smith-Howard. New York: Routledge, 2007. 106–23.

Guinn, Jeff. "Suzan-Lori Parks: Whatever She Does, She Creates a Buzz." *New York Times*, July 13, 2003.

Gussow, Mel. "Review/Theatre: Identity and *Imperceptible Mutabilities*." *New York Times*, Sept. 20, 1989: C24.

Jackson, Erick. "Suddenly Susan." WEYE 32.3 (March 2003): 318. www.wmagazine.com.

James, Gary. "Parks Entertains, Offers Advice." *Wabash College News*. March 25, 2008. http://www.wabash.edu/news/displaystory.cfm?news_ID=5668.

Johung, Jennifer. "Figuring the 'Spells'/Spelling the Figures: Suzan-Lori Parks's 'Scene of Love.'" *Theatre Journal* 58 (March 2006): 39–52.

Kennedy, Adrienne. *The Adrienne Kennedy Reader*. Minneapolis: University of Minnesota Press, 2000.

Kolin, Philip. "Cultural Memory and Circular Time in Suzan-Lori Parks's *Betting on the Dust Commander*." *Notes on Contemporary Literature* 39 (May 2009): 8–11.

_____. "Redefining the Way Theatre Is Created and Performed: The Radical Inclusion of Suzan-Lori Parks's *365 Days/365 Plays.*" *Journal of Dramatic Theory and Criticism* 32.1 (Fall 2007): 65–86.
Larson, Jennifer. "Folding and Unfolding History: Identity Fabrication in Suzan-Lori Parks's *Topdog/Underdog.*" In *Reading Contemporary African American Drama: Fragments of History, Fragments of Self.* Edited by Trudier Harris and Jennifer Larson. New York: Lang, 2007. 183–202.
Marshall, John. "A Moment with … Suzan-Lori Parks, Playwright." *Seattle Post Intelligencer*, May 26, 2003.
Metzgar, Bonnie. "Alien Baby." *Public Access/Stagebill* [*In the Blood* program, Public Theater/New York Shakespeare Festival] 6.2 (December 1999): 50, 52, 54, 58.
Miller, Samantha and Sharon Cotliar. "Best in Show." *People*, June, 3 2002: 143–44.
"A Moment with Suzan-Lori Parks, Playwright." *Seattle Post Intelligencer*, May 26, 2003.
Morgan, Joan. "Wondering Who Flipped for the 'Girl 6' Script: Meet Playwright Suzan-Lori Parks." *Essence* 26 (April 1996): 74.
Ong, Han. "Interview with Suzan-Lori Parks." *BOMB* 47 (Spring 1994): 47–50.
Parks, Suzan-Lori. *"The America Play and Other Works.* New York: Theatre Communications Group, 1995.
_____. *Devotees in the Garden of Love.* In *The America Play and Other Works.* New York: Theatre Communications Group, 1995. 133–56.
_____. "Elements of Style." In *The America Play and Other Works.* New York: Theatre Communications Group, 1995. 6–18.
_____. *Getting Mother's Body.* New York: Random House, 2003.
_____. *Girl 6.* DVD. Starz/Anchor Boy, 2006.
_____. *Imperceptible Mutabilities in the Third Kingdom.* In *The America Play and Other Works.* New York: Theatre Communications Group, 1995.
_____. *The Red Letter Plays.* New York: Theatre Communications Group, 2000.
_____. "Suzan-Lori Parks on James Baldwin." *Variety*, Feb. 12, 2009: A7.
_____. *365 Days/365 Plays.* New York: Theatre Communications Group, 2007.
_____. *Topdog/Underdog.* New York: Theatre Communications Group, 2002.
_____. *Venus.* New York: Dramatists Play Service, 2000.
Rasbury, Angeli R. "Pulitzer Winner Parks Talks about Being a First." *Women's eNews*, April 11, 2002. http://www.womensenews.org/story/arts/020411/pulitzer-winner-parks-talks-about-being-first.
Roach, Joseph. "Interview with Suzan-Lori Parks and Bonnie Metzgar." *World Performance Project at Yale* (hosted at the Yale University Web site). Nov. 14, 2006. http://wpp.research.yale.edu/wpp_events.php?id=2.
Schafer, Carol. "Staging New Literary History: Suzan-Lori Parks's *Venus, In the Blood,* and *Fucking A.*" *Comparative Drama* 43.2 (Summer 2008): 181–203.
Sellar, Tom. "Making History: Suzan-Lori Parks: The Shape of the Past." *Theatre/Forum* [University of California, San Diego], Summer-Fall 1996: 37–39.
"Suzan-Lori Parks." *Writer* (January 2004): 66.
Thompson, Debby. "Digging the Fo'-fathers: Suzan-Lori Parks's Histories." In *Contemporary African Women Playwrights.* Ed. Philip C. Kolin. New York: Routledge, 2007. 167–84.
Warner, Sara. "Suzan-Lori Parks's Drama of Disinternment: A Transitional Exploration of *Venus.*" *Theatre Journal* 60 (May 2008): 181–99.
Weinberg, Sydney. "Venus Envy." *Time Out New York*, April 17–24, 1996: 14.
Wetmore, Kevin J., Jr. "It's an Oberammergau Thing: An Interview with Suzan-Lori Parks." In *Suzan-Lori Parks: A Casebook.* Edited by Kevin J. Wetmore, Jr., and Alycia Smith-Howard. New York: Routledge, 2007. 124–40.
Williams, Monte. "From a Planet Closer to the Sun." *The New York Times*, Living Section, April 17, 1996: C:1.
Zoglin, Richard. "Marginalized Characters to Center Stage." *Time*, February 19, 2001.

Everything and Nothing: The Political and Religious Nature of Suzan-Lori Parks's "Radical Inclusion"

Rena Fraden

> No one was as many men as that man — that man whose repertoire, like that of the Egyptian Proteus, was all the appearances of being. — Borges

How to define the political and religious world view that will delimit Suzan-Lori Parks, frame her work, her life, her projects, her moment in time? On the one hand, there is a kind of odd futility that we ought to acknowledge, since she is still so very much alive and well and writing, her life anything but fixed, her future uncertain as all futures are. All we can do is look retrospectively *in medias res* and fix our sense of her past from where we are right now, in the middle of things. On the other hand, looking back from this point in time in (presumably and we hope) her middle, it is not so difficult to find recurring obsessions that make a Parksian kind of writing recognizable, midway as we are. She's been digging dirt since the very first play she wrote. History will be mentioned, the way she makes fun of it, the way she rewrites it. African American history, in particular, can't be ignored, both in the way she resists it and reimagines it, and for the way she insists, as an artist, that she cannot be defined by normative views of it. Her artistic precursors are no secret; she has paid homage to the great modernist novelists, Woolf, Faulkner, Joyce, and the playwrights, Beckett and Brecht, and also to Shakespeare and Adrienne Kennedy, and everyone else in between. Her musical ear conjures the blues, jazz, and Brecht-like songs. These are all recognizable SLPisms, touchstones, wellsprings, along with that metaphor and activity of digging the dirt, dishing the dust, troping and trouping chiasmically backwards and forwards across time and desire, punning her way through the hole of a whole, poking fun at serious business, making a joke of everything, a title of fucking anything, taking on the bigshots of literary history, from A to F (and H and S and so forth and so on).

I would say we know her and her style, at least so far, pretty well. She gives interviews; she tells the same stories in them (thank god, she is consistent); she gives talks at colleges; she takes her show on the road; she appears on Charlie Rose; she is quoted in reviews, in newspapers, in scholarly articles. She is present. On-stage. At the Public. In public. She is wholly here. In this, she is very much *not* like Shakespeare, who left us no manifestoes of belief or art, outside his art. And yet, like Shakespeare, or like the Shakespeare that we figure now, Borges's Shakespeare, a Shakespeare who emptied whatever private self there was into his public creations, she is, like him, everywhere (if not nowhere). Boundless in her ambition, she ranges across artistic genres — from the early, experimental plays, like *Betting on the Dust Commander* and *The Death of the Last Black Man in the Whole Entire World*, to the later, more realistic, Pulitzer Prize–winning play *Topdog/Underdog*; she has written the screenplay for Spike Lee's film *Girl 6*, the script for Oprah Winfrey's television adaptation of *Their Eyes Were Watching God*, and a Faulknerian novel, *Getting Mother's Body*, her take on *As I Lay Dying*; and she writes songs too, for her play, *Fucking A*, and for her most recent project, *Father Comes Home from the Wars, Part 1, 8, and 9*, songs which she sang herself on stage at the Public Theater in 2009. She refuses to adhere to a single artistic path. Her work has ranged from the highly experimental to the utterly commercial. And her ambition is Proteus-like in reach and complexity as she conjures up the world on stage and on screen and in print, mixing tragedy and comedy together, slang with formal poetics, folk songs for the people and references to the canon for the learned, writing a beginning and a middle, with no end in sight.

I believe that Parks can be identified not only by her style, humor, obsessions, and themes, but also by the ways in which she practices creativity — for the "radical inclusion" that structures her work, from beginning to end. So here, I will ponder creation with her, the politics and religion of creation, since her notion of politics and religion inflect, I believe, the sorts of creations she engenders. Or one might argue that the creations engender a particular form of politics and religion. They are each rooted in the other. In her essay "Elements of Style," Parks writes that she spends a lot of time reading the dictionary. "The word 'grammar' is etymologically related to the word 'charm.' Most words have fabulous etymologies. Thrilling histories. Words are very old things" (*America Play* 11). Indeed, politics, religion, and creation *are* old, human things. And certainly one of the most charming things about Parks on a page and in person is the way she goes back there, to old words and their meanings, and investigates them, their sounds haunting her utterly contemporary voice. Her juxtaposition of great learning and idiomatic expression produces a voice of easy familiarity that knows far more than one might expect, at first. She lets a whole lot in.

In my own digging into roots of the words "politics" and "religion," I see how their etymological histories haunt her creations. Digging down to the root of politics —*polis*, a citizen, and *ics*, a body of knowledge — we find Parks's practice of politics generates art in which she interrogates what it means to be a citizen in the broadest sense, a person with a particular tradition, but a citizen, too, of the world. From the root of religion — *re*, back, and *ligare*, to bind — we see the ways she finds to connect and to embrace all sorts of spiritual practices, traditions, histories. From the root of creation —*kreas*, flesh — we see words on a page become sounds on a stage, a something (or everything) made out of nothing. Her notions of politics and religion are as capacious and as concrete as their earliest root histories. Her practice of politics and religion transcends the individual city state or single god. She holds dual and triple and quadruple forms of citizenship and is eclectic in her faith. That generosity, what she calls Radical Inclusion, drives her creative work.

Duality and Inclusivity are principles she insists upon, as the most important creative principles under which she operates. This may be biographically driven: her father in the Army, the family wandering, going to school in Germany where she didn't know the language; the DuBoisian African American double consciousness of looking at oneself through the eyes of others. Raised Roman Catholic, she invokes more often now a sort of mélange of New Age/Far Eastern practices (yoga, meditation, Zen, dance) that she relies on to stay creative. James Baldwin, her teacher in college, became a model for her of an artist bound to his discipline of writing, and through writing, bound to a more capacious, inclusive self:

> It does have to do with having faith in your voice. It does. Sticking to your guns. Believing in yourself. Realizing that your "self" isn't — let me see if I can spell it right — "y-o-u-r, *little* s-e-l-f*.* " It's not that. It's "y-o-u-r — capital S e-l-f." Your Self includes everybody. You're part of the huge universal community at all times, even when you meet somebody you don't like, who isn't like you. I was telling the honor delegates today that the concept of radical inclusion means you have to include even folks you don't like, which is hard. Having faith in your Self, having faith in your own voice, things like working hard.... Service, the idea of service, the idea of being there for the people. Not just maybe your own people — you know, African American women under the age of 44. No. Your people are, again, the entire people, entire world [Academy].

Parks, from the beginning then, had this model of writing in which you write not just for your self or about your self, or others like your self, but rather a model in which you write to and for the many, that is, for all.

In her suggestive essay, "Possession," Parks describes her process of writing as a giving up, a canceling out, and at the same time, as a physical manifestation: "Writing I dance around spinning around to 'get out of the way' like Zen sort of, the self simultaneously disappears *his bones cannot be found* and is revealed" (*America Play* 3). Her self has to get out of the way in order to open herself up to ... whatever ... whatever comes.... It isn't definitive, it isn't ever precise, her descriptions of the creative process; it is "Zen like, sort of," this opening up to a New Age sort of spirit. She physically and determinedly is there and not there. In that space, other voices come. As she got older, the notions of self, service, and love became more overtly tied to Eastern religious traditions: "I owe my Self, my great Self, my big Self." This tattoo — and if anybody speaks Hindi or reads and speaks Sanskrit — it's from the Yoga Sutra, sutra number 123. The sutra is by Patanjali, and it says, '*Ishvara-pranidhanad va*,' which basically means, 'Your life is an offering to God.' The big S, your big Self. So it's a love for your big Self, that's what discipline is. It's just a devotion to the greater beautiful thing that allows us all to be here. It sounds a little 'woo-woo,' but basically, it's manifested in me because I'm a writer" (Academy). She mentions this tattoo again, in an interview with Joseph Roach at Yale, translating it somewhat differently, as: "Follow God, the inner spiritual guide," but it essentially means the same thing. As she explicates in that interview, for her, The Spirit (or God) and Religion are very different things. Religion is about rules, but the spirit is bigger, she says, than any rules. The spirit "is this great coursing thing through which songs, screenplays, novels, plays" all come forth (Roach).

Writing, she has said, "is more about listening than creating.... [It is] more about grace, less about will.... I get out of the way and let the story speak. I'm not passive. I do active listening" (Lecture, Pomona). She may stress the role of grace (and luck), but the exercise of discipline cannot be underestimated. There's no mistaking her own intense discipline and drive; it surely, as much as grace, propels Parks and the fecundity of her work. Parks, I believe, thinks of the discipline of writing as a kind of sacred grace. The act of writing for her, an active listening and imagining, becomes the central practice of what I would call Parks's religious universalism. The discipline of writing binds her and also ties her to communities of other writers, and their imaginations, to citizens from all cities, states, and nations.

365 Days/365 Plays, the tour de force project where she decided to do just that and write a play a day for a year, of all her works to date, best demonstrates the way in which the discipline of writing is a religious and political act — an act of grace that is sacred and also communal. I start here with *365 Days* because it encapsulates so many of her themes, and because it is the most ambitious of her works, not so much because it is theatrically great (it isn't), but because in its genesis and its exfoliation, it performs the Parksian spirit in its purest form. It performs a private kind of religious binding and then a public political binding of communities.

She describes her inspiration for writing *365 Days* in many places, including the opening of the printed edition of the plays:

> I got this notion to write a play a day for a whole year. "I'm going to write a play a day for a whole year! I'll call it 365 Days/365 Plays!" I told my husband, Paul. "Yeah, baby, that'd be cool," Paul said. And so I started writing. It was November 13, 2002. I thought about waiting until January 1 to begin, but I wanted to keep it real, so I started right where I was, working with whatever I had at the moment.... Every day for the next year I would wake up and ask myself, "Ok, so what's the play?" and I wrote what came. The plan was that no matter what I did, how busy I was, what other commitments I had, I would write a play a day, every single day, for a year. It would be about being present and being committed to the artistic process every single day, regardless of the "weather." It became a daily meditation, a daily prayer celebrating the rich and strange process of a writing life [*365 Days/365 Plays* i].

In 2007, at Mount Holyoke College, her alma mater, she told the same story with slight variations. "Ready to receive.... You develop a set of skills every day of your life. You open up your arms and receive what comes." She went on to call this "radical inclusion," opening the door and welcoming whoever comes. Somewhat inflected by her college audience, she framed her efforts as a kind of disciplinary act of faith. You begin with high hopes, you panic, you keep going:

> So I wrote, "Start Here." I was full of joy, promise ... like when you graduate college. Then you wake up the next day. I panicked. [Laughter. Recognition. College students get it.] But I wrote, "Father Comes Home from the Wars." And I felt then I had a place to stand. I woke up every morning tickling the balls of God. What's the play? You tell the bouncer of your mind to take off for a year. And then a few months in ... the plays kept coming [Lecture Mount Holyoke].

It's that bouncer Parks needs to get rid of, that voice that says, "No, you can't write *that*. That's unacceptable, inappropriate, not serious enough, not 'protest' enough, not black enough, not great enough." She's going to play around — tickling the balls of God —

howsoever she pleases, and she tickles us as she tickles God in doing so. And look who shows up. Krishna, a god-child, a supreme being, a prankster, and Arjuna, his friend, a great archer, who needs to be persuaded that taking part in war is justified. In the first short play of *365 Days*, "Start Here," it isn't clear where they're going or why, they just start here ... or there.

> KRISHNA: ... At the start theres always energy. Sometimes joy. Sometimes fear. By the end, youll be so deep into the habit of continuing on, youll pray that youll never stop. Happens all the time. But don't take my word for it. Lets go and youll see for yrself. (*Rest*) Get up. There you go. Breathe. Ok. Come on.
> ARJUNA: Where to?
> K: For me to know and for you to find out.
> K. & A.: Hahahahahahahahahah.
> K: Come on. Not to worry. Walk with me. Keep the feet moving. And, with any luck, we'll get there [4].

Parks didn't know on that first day of writing in November where she was going and she didn't care. The point was not to map out the satisfying ending (tragic or comic), but rather to get "deep into the habit of continuing on" and to see where she would land. The 365 plays range all over the map, quite literally. Some of them are deliberately unperformable. Some of them are unperformable *and* without dialogue, such as Day 29:

> "(Again) Something for Mom"
>
> Stage directions. A Kid (you could even cast an actual child), holding a bunch of flowers, runs toward Mother. Mother is surprised and happy. Kid presents flowers. Mother admires the flowers. Then, lifting Kid, Mother showers love. This happens several times, with other Mothers and other Kids. And "Mothers" and "Kids" are mutating and expanding to include all of us, filling the stage, the theater, and the world, as the action continues and repeats forever. Even during peacetime [163].

She was interested, in *365*, in stretching herself, as she took on stretching the boundaries of the stage and the conventions of drama. What Parks says about *365* is that it "is experimental theatre. Aristotle's *Poetics* don't apply. There is no fifth act like Shakespeare; no third act; it's more about process. *365* is a devotional act. A way of saying thank you to theatre. These 365 plays; they define the form. It was a play. But what *is* a play? We should answer that question with every play we write" (Lecture Mount Holyoke). At Mount Holyoke, she mentioned one boy in Texas who asked her where the second act of the play was that he was trying to figure out how to stage, and "then he realized he didn't *need* a second or third act. The windows of possibility are open" (Lecture, Mount Holyoke). In writing *365 Days*, Parks presented herself with a disciplinary exercise. Could she do it? Could she devote herself to the task, consistently, every day for a year to write a prayer, to devote herself to the task of being open to inspiration, and when that failed, to write anyway, until the act became a habit she could not break? Writing, during this experimental stage, was a private devotional, religious act of faith, a way of tying her ligament to a chair every day, of tying her physical self down to the act of creation, of making it habitual, whether good or bad.

There is no doubt that her interest in Hinduism, that tattoo on her arm, finds its way into the content of *365 Days* as well as its form. There are those Hindu gods, of course, but there is also the way in which the very public production of *365 Days* metamorphosed formally into what has been called "yoga drama" in which audiences all over the country were "'breathing together, observing together, giving attention'" (Swanson, quoted in Kolin 71). The idea of a public production was secondary to Parks, although it reveals, in its purest form, the symptomatic Parksian qualities of her political creative spirit. Some theatres expressed interest in staging the whole, but she felt "it didn't match the spirit of the play. I was sitting with Bonnie Metzgar in Denver, where she is Associate Director. And I had finished and I said, 'I did them.' And she said, 'Yeah, but now girl, you got to *do* them.' And we decided then to do them all over" (Lecture Mount Holyoke). In another gesture of radical inclusion, Parks and Metzgar decided to co-produce a *365 Days/Plays* National Festival, involving hundreds of theatres around the United States, lasting an entire year, leasing out the rights for a dollar to theatres to put on a week's worth of plays from Nov. 13, 2006, to Nov. 12, 2007. This effort, as Parks and Metzgar write in the printed edition, created "a testament not only to the daily artistic process, but also to the incredible diversity and richness of the American theatrical landscape" (401). And beyond that, it testified to Parks's belief that the arts are at "the very center of life — not as a monument but as a commonplace necessity like fire, water, bread or shoes" (401).

The earliest testimony of the arts — images painted on a cave wall, Dionysian choruses — may be seen as acts of devotion and homage, the artistic and the religious impulse both, at root, expressions of need and desire and wonder, as necessary (as necessarily human) as bread and water and shoes. At this point in Parks's career, she doesn't talk about the importance of words, but rather of energy and light. "All I do now is create energy. Then the words come.... I'm actually a scary person who behaves in a happy way. The plays are energy coiled. Like when you write, you release a lot of energy. People can be cleansed when it's out there" (Lecture, Pomona). The individual plays that make up *365 Days/365 Plays* are like energy coiled. Since they are so anti-theatrical, so grand in their designs, they can be produced a thousand and one different ways. The light comes only if someone turns on the switch to imagine these plays onto the stage. Staged over the 2006-07 calendar year, it felt (I think) to those of us who watched different weeks performed in different venues by different companies, or produced/performed in them ourselves, that the single play or individual event gained weight, "energy," because we knew we were part of something more. I don't know if we were cleansed or purged by what we saw, but there was an undeniable *frisson*, an energy, of being part of something larger, some idea grander than the single performance. It was clear there wasn't a "right" way to do Day/Play 29; multiple productions got thrown up on YouTube; you could see multiple versions almost immediately, in real time. But then, also, you could experience the whole in virtual pieces, or, what Philip Kolin in his essay on *365 Days* calls "digital theatre, a theatre of virtual performance(s)" (81). Some productions used videos and elaborate staging; others had people stand on a corner and read the words. It was all an experiment, all multiple and exponential attempts at uncoiling the energy from the words on the page. The important thing was that it was multiple and various and inclusive. It tied people together and made them aware not only of the state of their own small city/community, but of others, everywhere, interrogating their own borders.

"Stay open. Don't get hardened into high art, low. Go with the flow. Brilliant. Sanskrit. Yoga. Follow God" (Lecture Mount Holyoke). And, indeed, looking backwards, that is what Parks has consistently done. From her earliest plays, she has stayed open, resisted writing exclusively "high" art or "low." She has resisted too, vigorously and with distress, the expectation that she write "a black way." She has always been intensely interested in creation myths, and when she is asked whether she believes that American literature lacks a unifying creation myth, with writers writing white creation stories and black black ones, she dissents: "But we *do* have a creation myth.... I do think that the Pilgrims coming over in 1620, taking the land from the Indians, and then come the slaves, and *blah blah blah di blah blah*—I think that *is* our creation myth. I don't see us as a pocket of special interests at all.... We have so many different types of people, but we have decided to be American, and when we go abroad we're recognized as Americans. When I was in Canada on 9/11, I wasn't a 'sister,' I was an American" (Morris).

When she rejects philosophical essentialism as "insidious," she does so vehemently because she refuses to be trapped in narrow definitions of the self that can only legitimately truly behave fundamentally one way. That completely stops her flow — of experimentation, of inclusion, of following many gods. Her politics refuses to be narrowly nationalistic; her creative identity overflows not only national borders, but race, and gender too. In her essay "An Equation for Black People Onstage," Parks describes what she means by "insidious essentialism" and its relationship to black identity:

> As a Black person writing for theatre, what is theatre good for? What can theatre do for us? We can "tell it like it is"; "tell it as it was"; "tell it as it could be." In my plays I do all 3; and the writing is rich because we are not an impoverished people, but a wealthy people fallen on hard times. I write plays because I love Black people. As there is no single "Black Experience," there is no single "Black Aesthetic" and there is no one way to write or think or feel or dream or interpret or be interpreted. As African Americans we should recognize this insidious essentialism for what it is: a fucked-up trap to reduce us to only one way of being. We should endeavor to show the world and ourselves our beautiful and powerfully infinite variety [*America Play* 21–22].

Rejecting essentialism is to embrace the idea of identity as socially constructed, and for Parks, this allows for a kind of freedom to compose new and different pasts, presents, and futures. Is this post-racial? Perhaps, though she never denies her black personhood either. In an hybrid essay/performance/manifesto written ten years after "An Equation for Black People" called "New Black Math," Parks performs blackness which, characteristically, morphs into a dynamic universal creation beyond color. In the idiom of American blackness, we learn that "A black play is deep"; "A black play makes do if it got to / fights / screams / sings / dreams / WORKS IT / talks in code and tells it like it is ALL UP IN YA FACE" (576). But also, and then, "A black play is a white play when the lights go out"; "A black play keeps you up at night"; "A black play is very intellectual"; "A black play is such things as dreams are made on" (577–78). A black play is black in that it is tough and strong and smart and deep into language, so that if it is *really* black, it could be written by a black person or a white person: "Im saying *The Glass Menagerie* is a black play.... Cause the presence of the white suggests the presence of the black. Every play that is born of the united states of America is a black play because we all exist in the shadow of slavery. All of us. *The Iceman Cometh* is a black play. *Angels of America* is a black play and Kushner knows he's a brother" (580).

Parks is always investigating identity, refusing to see it a certain way, or a single way. Like Toni Morrison, she will claim that no piece of great American literature escapes the darkness and legacy of slavery. All great American authors are playing in the dark, existing in the shadows. In the beginning, she tells her truth, but tells it slant. Stylistically, her earliest plays resist altogether the form of protest and realism, which had been the norm for black writers, what may still be expected, and which she has always refused. Most especially in the earliest of her produced plays, *Imperceptible Mutabilities in the Third Kingdom* (1986–1989), *The Death of the Last Black Man in the Whole Entire World* (1989–1992), and *Venus* (1990), which are also her, to date, most experimental plays, Parks deals directly with perceived African American stereotypes, African American history, and American creation myths. These early plays are much more difficult to read on the page than her later efforts and more difficult to imagine in performance than even the most outlandish of any of the *365 Days* plays. They are dense, the language dream-like, allusive. Rhythmically, the plays flow from scene to scene, rather than build in monumental Acts. Parks creates a third space on stage, where everything real becomes someone else's dream:

> SHARK-SEER: I dream up uh fish that's swallowin me and I dream up uh me that is then becamin that fish and uh dream of that fish becamin uh shark and I dream of that shark becamin unshore. UUH! And on thuh shore thuh shark is given shoes. And I whuduhnt me no more and I whuduhnt no fish. My new Self was uh third Self made by thuh space in between. And my new Self wonders: Am I happy? Is my new Self happy in my new–Self shoes? [*America Play and Other Works* 39].

Selves metamorphose into other selves, species evolve, and it is unclear whether happiness trails any of the beings, masters or slaves, fish or foul. History is dynamic; the world turns. In *The Death of the Last Black Man in the Whole Entire World*, history is divided between Before Columbus (a character in the play) and After.

> BEFORE COLUMBUS: The popular thinking of the day back in them days was that the world was flat. They thought the world was flat. Back then when they thought the world was flat they were afeared and stayed at home.... Them thinking the sun revolved around the earth kept them satellite-like. They figured out the truth and scurried out. Figuring out the truth put them in their place and they scurried out to put us in ours" [*America Play and Other Works* 103].

Parks refuses to be put into place. Now that The Last Black Man has died, a newer Negro comes into being. And after that newer Negro, no doubt some other post-racial Someone will follow. "Where he gonna go now that he done diedid? Where he gonna go tuh wash his hands?" (*America Play and Other Works* 102). In Parks's plays, the last Black Man, the newer Negro, and the post-racial Someone all co-exist as mutual ghosts, haunting our reading of the other.

Venus is in some ways the hardest of all the early plays to imagine staging. The story of the Hottentot who is made into a theatrical spectacle in the nineteenth century and then again in the twentieth on stage is painful to read, and Parks's version created a furor when it was first staged at Yale, directed by Richard Foreman. She was accused of performing the same kind of commodification and objectification that imprisoned the first

Venus (Young). And there is no doubt that Parks is intensely interested in the subject of objectification; one might argue that is what all these early plays are about. In *Venus*, everyone speaks for the Hottentot; witness upon witness comes forward to say what it is the Venus means and how she is seen. Witness #1 sees her "clothed in a light dress, a dress thuh color of her own skin. She looked, well, naked, kin I say that? The whole place smelled of shit" (68). Another recounts her husband saying, "'This is a sight which makes me melancholy!'" ... And then he walked away from me, deep in thought, and then, totally forgetting his compassion, shouted loud: 'Good God what butts!'" (69). An abolitionist, Witness #3, is offended to see a human being exposed as a curiosity, while Witness #4 believes she has a right to exhibit herself, just as any other freak does in a circus show (72). And when Venus gets to speak, as she does throughout the play, she shifts what she believes she means as well. She is never "just me" (76). Sometimes she figures herself as a victim, sometimes as an actor who wants to make money, who is in love, who wants to see the world.

Debby Thompson argues that Parks is always "performing an archeology of race," in which race is "not a pre-existing biological category which then accrues historical meaning and political valence" (173) but instead a category that is there to be dug into, turned inside out, examined, played with. In rejecting naturalism, these early plays turn instead to a politics that exposes the natural as an idea that is variously ridiculous, when not dangerous, dehumanizing, or just plain nasty. The spirit, if it is to be found here, exists in the rests that punctuate this play, the rests that are Parks's pauses or silences, what she calls "spells." In those seconds of silence, she writes in her essay, "Elements of Style," the characters on stage "experience their pure true simple state.... A spell is a place of great (unspoken) emotion" (*America Play and Other Works* 16–17). What is Venus thinking in those pauses sprinkled throughout the play? We cannot be sure of her meaning then, and that becomes the dramatic moment of reckoning for both the actor and the spectator. What does she mean? It is our choice. The spirit enters us as we imagine meaning.

In an interview that took place in 1995, Parks is pressed to explain what her plays *mean*, but she refuses, grows exasperated, laughs:

> PARKS: I'd rather talk about the "reading" of my plays than the "meaning." Every time I talk about meaning to people it sounds like they're trying to substitute something else for what I've written.... [When people ask what I mean] that's basically saying, "you're being obscure and why don't you tell us what you want, what you really mean," thinking the writer has some sort of agenda that hides somewhere behind or underneath the text or behind the production somewhere.... Well, one meaning or reading is the fact that there are all black people in the play. And that's something I feel very strongly about, but it's not about just that. But then it's "oh, so the play's about black-on-black violence." That's what I mean about meaning. It's like, oh shit, that's the little limit we get [*Laughs*] ...
>
> DRUKMAN: I'm not quite sure why that is, what this resistance is of critics to seeing you as a formalist, or as formally experimental.
>
> PARKS: I can't figure it. I think it has something to do with what we allow ourselves — we, meaning the world, black people included — what we allow black people to do and one of them is not theory.... You can get away with it if you are in an academic setting, and they're beginning to get away with it in the visual arts. Or if you're Houston Baker.... In theatre it's still ... theatre's like the lag behind.... In theatre we still have more simplistic forms of representation that are still held up as examples of the best kind of theatre that

black people can involve themselves in. [*Laughing*] It's just a long road, a long dumb road [Drukman "Interview," 61].

There is no doubt that her formal experimentalism in the early plays and beyond is, at least in part, generated out of her fierce resistance to political and social essentialism, to being told she must play a certain role, be a certain type. With the callout to theory, she replays the older debate by black critics between realism/protest on one side and theory/formalism/experimentalism on the other. But she slips the yoke of this sort of dead-end binary opposition by refusing to go down *either* one side or the other — of this means *this* or *that*, of following one road only:

> ... I think I provide the map, but I think the map is the map of — you know — I'm not going to say the map of the world, but the map of, say, New Jersey. I mean it's the map of a piece of land. And what I try to do is say there are 10 roads, 20, 50 roads — take one.... I think that the playwright provides the map. But I think a bad play only has a one-way road. Yes, I think the bad play has one road; one idea, one message, one way of doing it.... And everybody walks out of the theater going, "Yeah, homelessness is bad," for example. That's not a map; I don't know what it is. It's bad art [Jiggets 312].

Constitutionally, then, Parks's practice of creative radical inclusion and her refusal of political essentialism (even strategic essentialism) allows her to transcend the one way streets of a restrictive identity politics which, in turn, she believes produces "bad art." Her politics and her religion swerve from the particular to a sort of universalism. "My life is not about race, it's about being alive" (Solomon 74). And part of being alive is, for Parks, about race and how race comes to *mean* what it does. Her politics are bipartisan; her faith lies in embracing multiple gods. She rejects a restrictive equation of identity with race or gender or experience in general. Imagination trumps all. And a generous Borgesian/Shakespearean imagination is best of all; certainly, according to Parks, it produces the best art.

She embraces all roads, all traditions — religious, philosophical, and certainly literary. She suffers no anxiety of influence. Her interest in engaging with Great Authors, the sacred literary canon — which organizes the next few plays and her first novel — is similarly driven by a desire to exercise artistic freedom. She loves the Great Authors. She does not find them alien figures, but rather Ancestors, who ought to be honored, enjoyed, digested, *used*. Every person alive now exists *in* the womb of the ancestor: "Inside every great work of literature, inside every theatrical production that has moved and amazed us, there we all were and are, conceived within its every line and gesture, as part of the Next New Thing" ("Tradition" 27). Wisdom is to be found everywhere. People can claim as family heritage any piece of the literary or religious tradition. One needn't be biologically related to claim creative ancestry. Parks refuses a simple equation of experience to creation. The whole idea that one ought to "write what one knows," she dismisses:

> There is a rule that one should write only about "what one knows," which is often interpreted to mean that, if the writer has never been married, but has just broken up with her beau, broken beauing, and not marriage, is the suitable subject for her. Well. We "know" much more than our conscious minds think we know.... There is a truth that undercurrents most writing, regardless of situation or subject matter. While there are many fine poets who fought a duel a day, many playwrights who slept with all the men in the state of Texas, many

novelists who rode motorcycles helmetless at high speeds, remember too that Phillis Wheatley was a slave, Anton Chekhov worked as a simple country doctor, and Marcel Proust and Emily Dickinson both hardly ever went out of the house ["Tradition" 27–28].

Humanity's creativity is grounded in a combination of the conscious and unconscious and the physical — the spine, or the gut, or the balls. Truth, for Parks, (a different register from the essential) underlies most of her writing. But truth is not biologically determined; it has nothing to do with race; or predeliction (riding motorcycles helmetless) or circumstance (working as a country doctor). Truth lies elsewhere: in an imagination alive to more than chance or fate. No one sort of life guarantees access to an imaginative truth, but a certain kind of practical openness might.

When Parks turns, then, to rewriting the canon, she does so not because she is doing battle with Great Dead White Male Authors; there is no Oedipal complex at work, nor a political clearing off of the oppressive traditions, or of politically incorrect authors, so she and other sub-alterns can have their turn. None of that. If there's any anxiety at all, it is thoroughly masked behind the way she insists engaging the Tradition as funny, a joke. She is boating with a friend and has the idea of the title, *Fucking A,* and starts to laugh, and from there ... sits down to write a new story of Hester (Hannaham). Humor, she says more than once, allows her the space to get to the bottom of things. "I mean, humor's a great way of getting to the deep shit, isn't it? Humor is a very effective way of saying something that you probably could never say ordinarily. And, you know, we do it everyday. I say all kinds of bizarre things with a little laugh, or as a joke" (Drukman 73). In the Hawthorne/*Scarlet Letter* Hester plays, *In the Blood* (1999) and *Fucking A* (2000), and in her Faulknerian novel, *Getting Mother's Body* (2003), sort of mid-career within her career at mid-point, she makes a joke out of canonical works in order to play with fate, the constraints of genre and plot and power.

Making a tragedy out of Hawthorne's *Scarlet Letter* and a great romance out of Falkner's semi-comic *As I Lay Dying,* Parks twists and turns the undercurrents from the ur-text to chart a different course. The topsy turvy quality — the joke of what she does — is a kind of investigation into fundamentals. Hawthorne's Hester only imagines, at one dark point in the novel, killing her child and then herself, but does not do so, and there are even intimations of Hester's daughter's finding great happiness and riches in Europe when Hester returns to the New World; but both of Parks's Hesters end up killing their son, their ending starkly circumscribed and awful. The spirit of Parks's Hesters are diminished, brought low by their poverty, boxed in by society, and by their own imaginations. The Hester of *In the Blood* is an illiterate mother of five children, all of whom have different fathers. They live under a bridge, homeless. She sells herself for food. When she sees a shadow passing over the sky, her world goes dark. The Reverend tells her it must have been a cloud or an airplane. She insists it was an *E*-clipse: "It was a big dark thing. Blocking the sun out. Like the hand of fate. The hand of fate with its 5 fingers coming down on me. (*Rest*) (*Rest*) And then the trumpets starting blaring. (*Rest*). And then there was Jabber saying 'Come on Mommie, Come on!' The trumpets was the taxi cabs. Wanting to run me over. Get out of the road" (*Red Letter Plays* 77). Those 5 fingers *will* come down on her at the very end of the play, as her son taunts her and she beats him to death, and stretches her bloody hands upwards, "Big hand coming down on me." She repeats that line and the play is over. No cloud, no airplane: it is the hand of fate which comes after her. There is no possible escape, no redemption possible, no spirit to help her, no inner self with the strength or skill or belief to guide her: she is fated to be cast out. This is a play of radical *exclusion* and it is relentless in its drive to a fated tragic end.

The Reverend of *In the Blood* is a complete and utter hypocrite, who screws Hester and lies to her and leaves her. The Reverend Roosevelt Beede in Parks's novel, *Getting Mother's Body,* has also lost his calling as the novel opens, and just about lost his wife, but in the course of the novel's journey, in stark contrast to the Hester plays, people do find their true spiritual calling. "Some men are called by God to lead the people. But that's rare. A man of the people thinks the people are calling him but it's just his own voice, overly loud, shouting his own name and hearing it echo back to him through the open mouths of the people, mouths open in awe and wonder watching a man shout his own name loud. A man of God has his mouth shut until God opens it, forces it open sometimes. And sometimes forces it closed" (151). There is a spiritual grace in this novel, a presiding spirit which bequeaths redemption and love and understanding to its main characters. The dead are forgiven and the living start anew. Parks and Faulkner end their novels with a marriage, but Faulkner's is complicated by the character of Anse's survivalist, cunning motives, that make for a bitter, funny, disgusting ending, a marriage of convenience that takes all of a few seconds to secure; while Parks's Billy Beede finds, through the leisurely run of the novel, true love and unalloyed happiness. The joke of Parks's rewriting allows her to change the course of Faulkner's plot and tone, and thereby create a whole new version, making even the original, different, nothing quite like it was.

Finally, in the next stage of her career, in which she wrote the two Lincoln plays, *The America Play* (1990–1993) and *Topdog/Underdog* (2001), the latter the play that won the Pulitzer and took her to Broadway, in which she decided she would "write live people now" (Lecture Pomona), Parks most clearly and fundamentally fools around with how those live people deal with the dead. Quoting John Mbiti's *African Religions and Philosophy*:

> A person dies and yet continues to live: he is a living-dead, and no other term can describe him better than that.... The living dead are bilingual ... and speak in nasal tones.... The state of possession and mediumship is one of contemporarizing the past, bringing into human history the beings essentially beyond the horizon of present time [*America Play and Other Works* 5].

Is it the case that when people pretend to be someone else long enough, that they may become that person in fact? The Foundling Father in *The America Play* recounts how the Lesser Known grows a beard like Lincoln, wears a false wart like Lincoln, begins to declaim Lincoln, and goes west to play Lincoln in small towns: "And when someone remarked that he played Lincoln so well that he ought to be shot, it was as if the Great Mans footsteps had been suddenly revealed" (*America Play* 164). As with essential notions of blackness, or a literary canon that seems fixed and unapproachable, Parks now undoes history to make it work for her. She opens it up, turns white into black, and black into white. A black man named Lincoln dresses up as Lincoln and offers himself up to be shot. Animating history, engaging it, she shows us how made up it is, how much a performance, though for all that it is, no less potent for that. "I take issue with history because it doesn't serve me—it doesn't serve me because there isn't enough of it. In this play, I am simply asking, 'Where is history?,' because I don't see it. I don't see any history out there, so I've made some up" (Pearce 26).

In *The America Play*, as with *365 Days*, she opens up her spirit to include pageants of historical souls, who parade all around the Great Hole of History. Lucy and her husband honeymooned there: "He and Her would sit on thuh lip and watch everybody who was ever anybody parade on by. Daily parades! Just like thuh Tee Vee. Mr. George Washington, for example, thuh Fathuh of our Country hisself, would rise up from thuh dead and walk uhround and cross thuh Delaware and say stuff!! Right before their very eyes!!!" (179). And when we're reminded that it wasn't *really* George Washington, but just his "lookuh-like," we recognize how everything around us—including the actors we're watching, or conjuring up in our mind's eye as we're reading—are all lookuhlikes, but still, in that moment, as real as they're ever likely to be. The expanse of *The America Play*, with pageants of historical figures described, and an East and a West to get lost in, narrows dramatically in *Topdog*, another take on the Lincoln story. Here the two brothers, Lincoln and Booth, tangle in a one-room apartment, their historical hole not only created by their familial history, abandonment, disappeared parents, but also, of course, by their names, and the fate their historical names forecast. In *The America Play*, the Foundling Father threw himself into the role of Lincoln; he *became* Lincoln. But in *Topdog*, Lincoln is only pretending at his job, and not so wonderfully that he isn't afraid of being fired from it. He resists the conflation of identities: "I would make a living at it. But it dont make me. Worn suit coat, not even worn by the fool that Im supposed to be playing, but making fools out of all those folks who come crowding in for they chance to play at something great. Fake beard. Top hat. Don't make me into no Lincoln. I was Lincoln *on my own* before any of that" (my italics, 28). It's perhaps understandable that he resists the part he has to play to make a living. But it is a foolish thing, in Parks's world, to think one is ever really ever completely on his own. Her characters inhabit names that belonged to others; their names are attached to characters who reside in someone else's novel; there, they meant something different to someone else. They are all figures embedded in a matrix of other traditions and histories and spirits. To ignore all the ways in which they are connected, and therefore all the ways in which meanings swirl around them, is to risk great loneliness, but it is also clearly dangerous. Those who cannot embrace a spirit of radical inclusion, or resist it, will get stuck, fixed, and fucked. Those who act out radical inclusion—who let it in, play with it, engage it, perform it, reimagine it—get to have some fun, and sometimes, hard-earned wisdom and a day's worth of love.

Parks makes up history and characters, who strut and fret and sing and murder and love upon the stage. "Like Shakespeare," she says, "one of my favorite writers, he was everywhere and nowhere at the same time. When you look at his plays, he was everywhere. That's the reason I love his plays so much. In other plays, you see one character who is the voice of the author. In Shakespeare, there is no one character, he's everywhere. He's in every character, which is what I strive to do. I want to be in all the characters at the same time" (Academy). Parks, like God, or Shakespeare, creates worlds and characters to people them. She loses her self in all of their selves. Parks's politics and her faith are that in such conjurations, she might create other opportunities, and alter history, our past, and therefore the present, and so, the future. We shall see.

WORKS CITED

Borges, Jorge Luis. "Everything and Nothing." Translated by Andrew Hurley. In *Collected Fiction*. New York: Penguin Books, 1999: 319–320.
Drukman, Steven. "Suzan-Lori Parks and Liz Diamond Interview." *TDR* 39.3 (1995): 56–75.
Hannaham, James. "Funnyhouse of a Negro." *Village Voice*, November 3–9 (1999).
Jiggets, Shelby. "Interview with Suzan-Lori Parks." *Callaloo* 19.2 (1996): 309–317.
Kolin, Philip. "Redefining the Way Theatre Is Created and Performed: The Radical Inclusion of Suzan-Lori Parks's *365 Days/365 Plays*." *Journal of Dramatic Theory and Criticism* 22.1 (2007): 65–83.
Morris, Steven Leigh. "The CEO and the Lynch Mob: Suzan-Lori Parks is rewriting the American." *LA Weekly*, July 4–10, 2003.
Morrison, Toni. *Playing in the Dark: Whiteness and the Literary Imagination*. Cambridge: Harvard University Press, 1992.
Parks, Suzan-Lori. "Academy of Achievement Interview." www.achievement.org. 2007.
_____. *The America Play* in *The America Play and Other Works*. New York: Theatre Communications Group, 1995: 157–199.
_____. "An Equation for Black People Onstage." In *The America Play and Other Works*. New York: Theatre Communications Group, 1995: 19–22.
_____. *Betting on the Dust Commander*. In *The America Play and Other Works*. New York: Theatre Communications Group, 1995: 73–90.
_____. *The Death of the Last Black Man in the Whole Entire World*. In *The America Play and Other Works*. New York: Theatre Communications Group, 1995: 99–131.
_____. "Elements of Style." In *The America Play and Other Works*. New York: Theatre Communications Group, 1995: 6–18.
_____. *Fucking A* in *The Red Letter Plays*. New York: Theatre Communications Group, 2001: 113–225.
_____.*Getting Mother's Body*. New York: Random House, 2003.
_____. *Imperceptible Mutabilities in the Third Kingdom*. In *The America Play and Other Works*. New York: Theatre Communications Group, 1995: 23–71.
_____. *In the Blood* in *The Red Letter Plays*. New York: Theatre Communications Group, 2001: 1–112.
_____. "Lecture, Reading." Pomona College, Claremont, California. March, 23, 2005. www.pomona.edu.
_____. "Lecture, Reading." Mount Holyoke College, South Hadley, Massachusetts. March 4, 2007. www.mtholyoke.alumni.edu.
_____. "New Black Math." *Theatre Journal* 57.4 (2005): 576–583.
_____. "Possession," in *The America Play and Other Works*. New York: Theatre Communications Group, 1995: 3–5.
_____. *The Red Letter Plays*. New York: Theatre Communications Group, 2001.
_____. *365 Days/365 Plays*. New York: Theatre Communications Group, 2006.
_____.*Topdog/Underdog*. New York: Theatre Communications Group, 1999
_____. "Tradition and the Individual Talent." *Theater* 29.2 (1999): 26–33.
_____. *Venus*. New York: Theatre Communications Group, 1990.
Pearce, Michele. "Alien Nation: An Interview with the Playwright." *American Theatre* 11.3 (1994) 26.
Roach, Joseph. "Interview with Suzan-Lori Parks and Bonnie Metzgar." *World Performance Project at Yale* (hosted at the Yale University Web site). Nov. 14, 2006. http://wpp.research.yale.edu/wpp_events.
Solomon, Alisa. "Signifying on the Signifyin': The Plays of Suzan-Lori Parks." *Theater* 21.3 (1990): 73–80.
Thompson, Debby. "Digging the Fo-fathers: Suzan-Lori Parks's Histories." In *Contemporary African American Women Playwrights: A Casebook*. Edited by Philip C. Kolin. New York: Routledge, 2007.
Young, Jean. "The Re-Objectification and Re-Commodification of Saartjie Baartman in Suzan-Lori Parks's *Venus*." *African American Review* 31.4 (1997): 699–708.

"Jazzing" Time, Love, and the Female Self in Three Early Plays by Suzan-Lori Parks

Jacqueline Wood

For Suzan-Lori Parks, time, and history as its derivative, is the overarching prism through which she examines human experience in her early plays. And she is not hesitant about infusing her drama with the influences of great playwrights whom she admires precisely for their interrogations of time, history, and the real. The creative strategies of Samuel Beckett and Bertolt Brecht, in particular, inform her early dramatic techniques, which lay foundations for her later dramatic confrontations with history and time. In three of her early plays, *Betting on the Dust Commander*, *Pickling*, and *Devotees in the Garden of Love*, her permutations of time are paradoxical examinations of temporal fluidity and stasis as incomprehensible, all-consuming, and inevitable in the experiences of human beings. These are further nuanced by complications of racialized and gendered alienation and suffering. Heavily informed by Beckett's interrogation of time and its domination of the human psyche, her dramas also challenge traditional forms of theatre through Brechtian staging and action.

Such strategies are a part of her larger project of rewriting Africana history. Beckettian reconfigurations of time and Brechtian alienation of audience evolve into Parks's strategies of signification — appropriation and revision or "jazzing" of the dramatic project; she jazzes these European experimentalists' dramatic strategies as parts of formal and linguistically signifying texts to provide room for liberating black self-perception and self-representation. In so doing, she interrogates the idea of fixed historiography, exploring the possibilities of rewriting the "history of literature ... [and] the history of history," particularly as reviewing history can sustain new African American realities. A play for her is a

> blueprint of an event: a way of creating and rewriting history through the medium of literature. Since history is a recorded or remembered event, theatre, for me, is the perfect place to "make" history — that is, because so much of African-American history has been unrecorded, dismembered, washed out, one of my tasks as playwright is to — through literature and the special strange relationship between theatre and real-life — locate the ancestral burial ground, dig for bones, find bones, hear the bones sing, write it down ["Possession" 4].

Parks's advocacy of a "special strange relationship" that exists between the real and theatre mirrors her view of interaction between reader/spectator and the dramatic text, an occasion for "new history" to act on "real-life" ("Possession" 4–5). Her drama, a performative "incubator to create 'new' historical events..., re-membering" history in its remembering and in its "staging of historical events," engages the present conditions of African Americans through an African-centered (re)vision of the past. As she contends, "the bones tell us what was, is, will be; ... their song is a play — something that through a production *actually happens*" (4–5). Her works survey the experience of Black Americans as a community, but she also devotes certain of her works toward the specific questions of black women's experience. *Pickling, Betting,* and *Devotees* are examples of such interrogations of African American female selfhood in relation to time and memory, black men, and social tradition.

Jazzing these early texts using repetition and revision as investigative strategies of black womanhood operates as an example of Parks's neologism *re-membering,* the reconstruction of history and representations of black consciousness through new ways of seeing and recording. To re-member female African American racial and historical consciousnesses, Parks's dramatic form employs poetic and cumulative repetition through changeable dramatic sequences. She thus establishes a dramatic strategy for re-membering which she calls "Rep & Rev" (Repetition and Revision), a rewriting of African-inspired call-response steeped in the more recent complex musical formulations of jazz aesthetics ("Elements" 8–9). "Rep & Rev" is in itself "a literal incorporation of the past" in Parks's drama ("from Elements" 10). In addition, while "Rep & Rev" buttresses the re-membering of history and Black selfhood, this dramatic strategy challenges as well any reader who lacks familiarity with the function of jazz/blues in its "patiently incremental, not to say heavily repetitious form" (Cooke 22). The impact of the polymorphous jazz form is tied closely to the level of understanding of the audience. This audience response is in itself necessarily subjective. As Langston Hughes argues in his "Jazz as Communication," "with you in the middle — jazz is only what you yourself get out of it" (494).

If, as Parks's textual practice seems to suggest, she is creating a reversal of the dynamic of othering through alienating textual devices, then the cultural complexities of jazz as a foundation for her plays seems a most apt frame for challenging readers. Parks is, in fact, othering the mainstream reader/spectator unschooled in the language and culture of jazz. She iterates the querulous moment described by Louis Armstrong who is purported to have said, "Lady, if you have to ask what it is, you'll never know" (qtd. in Hughes 494). The outcome of this distancing is an interesting repositioning of the reader into a suspension of time and memory much like that of the black female characters in these plays, a way of experiencing the alienating yet revelatory repetitive accumulation of meaning as the real. And, since meaning in jazz, as in Parks's drama, is extended in the manner of musical performance "by repetitions and virtuoso musical interludes," it does "contain a wealth of unique and transitory features" (494). As a result, the thrust of Parks's Rep & Rev is for many readers a relative textual inaccessibility, which in these early plays becomes a structural iteration of alienated black female social presence.

Because of Parks's insistence on the derivation of form from content, it is not surprising that the deep structure of her plays is informed by the revising, repetitive forms of jazz, forms, according to Philip Kolin, that "destabilize the way a naturalistic theatre conceives of and represents time, history, and memory through linear plots that lead to irrevocable climaxes" (9). Parks argues that history or time "has a circular shape" ("from Elements" 10), a perspective in itself reminiscent of the ideological feminine. In her early plays examining black women's experiences, such circularity is clearly privileged, as, for example, in *Betting on the Dust Commander*, first produced in 1987. In *Betting*, a "cyclical history" (Kolin 10) or circular structure, works through Parts A, B, C. Part A begins with a slideshow of a married couple, Mare and Lucius, in wedding outfits, while the couple provides commentary off-stage about replacing the fresh flowers at their wedding with plastic ones. Part B is an argumentative conversation about body functions like stuck crossed eyes, "hung" cries, stuffed up noses, blotting, snotting, blowing, sniffing — all allergic responses to dust, horse races, Lucius's threats to leave for the races, and Mare's pleas for him not to go.

The play is circular because Parts A and C are identical in language. Such limited action and content that come full circle both reflect Parks's sense of the historical and, specifically, allow for a Rep & Rev analysis of the strangled moments in the couple's marriage. Parts A and C are exact re-iterations of the couple's plans and preparations for their wedding day, which has actually occurred "One year long ago" (82). The characters' repeated discussion of replacing fresh flowers with plastic ones reveals their desire to preserve their memories and, ultimately, characterizes Lucius's aversion, or his allergic reaction, to real flowers and to some of the real demands of marriage.

As in so many of Parks's plays, we see these two characters' comments as "signifyin'" re-presentations of Beckettian negotiations of time and memory. For Park's characters here, time and memory are revealed through repetition and recycling of recollections. Lucius's and Mare's interlocution ultimately addresses the often confusing aspects of facing past and present and how these construct the self. As Mare observes,

> You wanted plastics — I got plastics — mm telling you so. Ssgood luck.... I replaced em all with plastics. It costed. I got every last one.... Expensive plastics got the real look to em, Lucius. Expensive plastics got uh smell. Expensive plastics will last a lifetime but nobody'll know, Lucius. Nobody knows [75].

This notion that plastic is somehow more valuable over time than the real characterizes the struggle of these two figures to aptly comprehend the fluid nature of the present, the transitory quality of life represented by fresh flowers. The most jolting language in this quote is Mare's insistence that the plastic is so close to the real that "nobody'll know." Everyone will be fooled by the fake history instead of the real, even if the plastic replacements smell strange or last forever in a state of horrid perfection, a perfect stasis. Key here, too, is the revelation in the quote that, in fact, it is Lucius who asks for plastic flowers. He claims he is allergic to the real, "Throats getting scratchity. Mare. Throats getting scratchity tight" (75). Mare demonstrates her devotion to Lucius in attempting to assuage his attacks: "Got em all, Luki.... Ain't nothing to flare your fit —" (76). And Lucius acknowledges her attention, asking her, "Uhchoo choo choo! Bless, me Mare" (76). But Lucius's allergic condition, nonetheless, influences how the memory of their wedding will be expressed and preserved. By the end of Part A, Lucius even seems to be allergic to Mare herself, a manifestation of his unease with certain strictures of his marriage demonstrated by his repeated threats to leave Mare and go to the races.

As Part B unfolds, it becomes increasingly clear that Parks is closely examining the relationship between these two characters, specifically the often domineering nature of Lucius and the submissive, self-sacrificing response of his wife Mare. For example, traditionalized marital roles of women are exposed through naming. The name *Mare*, as Lucius calls his wife, while an obvious derivation of Mary (the ultimate Western ideal of womanhood), is certainly reminiscent of Zora Neale Hurston's representation that the black woman is "de mule uh de world" (29), carrying implications of breeder, beast of burden, commodity. *Mare* takes on added implications as it connects with the numerous references in the play to racetracks ("Churchill"), racehorses, and gambling. Parks conflates Lucius's fascination for betting on horses, or going to "Church," with his notions of betting on his choice to marry Mare (78).

The great winning horse of Lucius's life is named Dust Commander, and Mare is quite easily signified by the phrase in her capacity as a waitress, feather-dusting tables and, later, as a housewife, a literal dust commander. The fact that in the play Parks shifts the sex of the actual stallion Dust Commander (who won the Kentucky Derby in 1970) to a "filly" (81) who "goned forth n multiplied.... So many Dust Commanders these days" (81) suggests further that Mare and the female Dust Commander are parallel representations of the "many" domestically challenged housewives. Lucius when he was young betted on the long shot Dust Commander and won. His odds were "100:1 or something like that" (81). It is significant that his win occurs because Mare gives him a tip, a fact that he only obtusely acknowledges in his description of the other woman, who he says is like Mare "in every respect" and "Gived me uh tip" (82). Lucius's strident language and behavior towards Mare suggest that he does not feel as lucky in his gamble with marriage. Even as he shows some care by fussing and worrying about Mare's stuck eyes and hung cries, he still observes that his wager here has resulted in a payoff that is less than exciting. He describes her as "uh old biddy" (76, 83).

In the middle of Part B, the characters repeat verbatim its first half. The turning point is when Mare suggests that Lucius wear something different to the "Church." He without fail wears his Bermuda shorts and his hat; he never takes them off: "Sharp as uh blade da grass, right? They know me by my Bermudas they know me by my hat" (77). He does not take his shorts off to bathe or even to urinate, "pee rolls up the leg I says" (82). Mare's suggestion that he change seems to rattle Lucius deeply; it bodes an alteration of their relationship and threatens his sense of security derived from repetitive predictable behavior. When Mare observes that he could "Go tuh thuh Church in long pants. Surprise em. Sspecial Day," they arrive at an ultimate sticking point in their relationship (82). Mare attempts to "unstuck thuh zipper," and Lucius cries, "AAAAW! Stop that Mare!" and reverts immediately to the exact language that begins and develops Part B. Mare follows his lead.

From this moment on in the play, all the dialogue is identical to what has gone before. The characters rehearse the next six and a half pages verbatim. There is a false, in fact decomposing, safety in this predictable, repetitive behavior that both characters turn to in their greatest instance of instability in the play. While Deborah Geis observes that Mare and Lucius seem "frozen in time, trapped ... in a cycle of repetition, a kind of life in death" (27), in fact, there is an almost imperceptible movement in the feel of these characters. Like a jazz ensemble returning to the beginning constitution of their performed piece, where both musicians and listeners have been changed by the revisions or riffs that have occurred, audience and characters also evolve in the last repeated elements of *Betting*.

With its alienating effects of the slideshow reminiscent of Brechtian Verfremdungseffekt, and the slow, deliberate circularity of form and language, *Betting* distances the reader/spectator much as Mare is distanced from Lucius, through slight shifts and revisions that reframe the meaning of the first part, A, and the last part, C. For the reader/audience what is exactly the same in dialogue has now irrevocably changed in meaning through the slight forward progression and climax of Part B. Knowledge of the cycling, complex emotional nature and interaction in Mare's and Lucius's relationship now adds a new, nuanced layer of meaning. Circling back to the slideshow and to the repeated offstage comments in part C reveals to a previously unschooled audience a jazz-like progression, a new meaning evoked from the intense repetitive interaction between Mare as an older, unfulfilled married woman and Lucius as a critical and domineering husband, both grappling with the complexities of married life.

Their marital reality is, thus, startlingly re-memebered through a distilled combination of circular repetitive action and language. In fact, circle images abound in the play: rounded race tracks, ellipses, a "wreath," a "winning circle," a quarter, dimes, and nickels (81). In addition, Mare identifies herself with her beloved golden budgie, "gold" like "thuh undersides" of her eyes that strain toward new positions. She, like the bird, is flying "Round n around round n around looking for a way out" (80) for a relationship that often suffocates her as much as the plastic bag constricts her dead bird. Actually, Mare's psychological struggle within the bonds of matrimony with a domineering husband is somewhat like the real physical death of her bird. She exclaims, "Shouldn't put no animal in plastic. Animal should breathe free" (80). She even reclaims the bird's life by seeing it breathe in her dreams, which Lucius immediately ridicules, "In your dreams. Whoever heard of that" (81). It becomes obvious that Mare's sense of suffocation is due to Lucius's repetitious criticism, warnings, and demands that she "Blot! ... Wipe!" (85), and "Blow" (84). She suffers from his accusations of "smearing the sky blue" to "sky grey" because she "Aint never understood the little things" (79) and his threats to leave, "Warned you. Shore own fault. Hand me my hat mm gone" even when she cries "Don't leave me wrong-side by the way side, Luki, please" (83).

Lucius's responses aggravate Mare into an emotional state, causing her to be afraid of getting "STUCK!" (76). Yet when she is faced with the repeated demand by Lucius to replace real flowers with plastic flowers strewn "Roundin around thuh altar," she aids him in his effort to remedy his allergic reaction to the sacrificial altar of marital commitment and to Mare herself. Mare braves a "hung" cry in order to entreat Lucius to stay and love her: "He huh he huh he huh — love me — he huh he he he huh huh" (77). And in Part B Lucius does attempt to soothe her, "Mare. There there, Mare," in response to her cry (77). In this instance we see that there are some redeeming moments in this relationship; they have after all been married for 110 years. Yet the recycled memories of Parts A and C seem to throw them back into a continued struggle to reconcile their present with their past, causing Mare and Lucius to repeat and in rare instances revise versions of their relationship and their memories. An excerpt of a Gertrude Stein quote is an epigraph of this play: "Slowly everyone in continuous repeating, to their minutest variation, comes to be clearer to someone" (qtd. in Parks, *Betting* 75). Through this quote the reader might infer that perhaps in another 110 years Mare and Lucius will be able to circle back to their "fresh" relationship. In this they would demonstrate Parks's larger paradigm of re-membering history and the self rather than recycling them, so that Rep & Rev realizes "the symbolic, recurring multiplicities of cultural memory and representation" (Kolin 10). Form and content thus can meet effectively in *Betting* as one of Parks's foundational plays, a text that establishes a jazzing of the black female subject, particularly in terms of male/female relationships.

A similar technique of jazzing form and content in an effort to realize black female consciousness is demonstrated in *Pickling*, first performed as a radio play in 1990 (Geis 29). Again this is a play structure that proffers limited plot development and no dynamism in character. These repeated strategies suggest that recreating or signifying on black women's experience is not feasible for Parks via "those structures [that] could never accommodate the figures which take up residence inside me;" instead it is necessary for her to "explode the form," since radicalized content requires configurations which are both independent and unruly ("Elements" 8).

Pickling is a cautionary tale against the perils of idealizing the past, especially as it can reify the roles of women. Miss Miss, the only character in the play, while speaking in the present, seems only to concern herself with the past. Development of meaning is accomplished through repetition and revision of images, actions, and moments divulged by the character through a streaming monologue. Miss Miss reveals herself to be an agoraphobic old maid who is experiencing an increasingly alarming sense of misplacement and alienation as an isolated black female. She is determined to remain at home: "Ssgood Ive got everythin I need right here at my fingertips never need to go outside is overwhelming sstoo much. Havent been out since. Synce uh comedinlass. Hee!" (9). She is also determined to safeguard her remembrances because "there are people starving you know. People going without" (94). Her agoraphobia emerges wildly, even more and more troubling as Miss Miss wanders through her ostensibly rambling conversation about pickling jars, souvenirs, preserved body parts, containers for the past, and protecting her "juicy." Parks's bizarre yet carefully crafted metaphors resonate literally, sexually, and psychically in terms of Miss Miss's threatened black female personhood and her obsessive, conflated notions of memory, love, and reality.

Miss Miss's one brief, healthy love encounter is itself irrevocably affected by her obsessions. Charles, her brave, athletic, life-guard lover, whom she calls her "professional savior" (97), balks when he finds that in addition to photographs as mementos, Miss Miss has preserved in pickling jars a number of interesting items: sand and a condom from their first encounter, nuts and bolts from her old refrigerator, the smile of her dead mother in the form of her gums, which were red but have "gone a little black now" (96), and pieces of her mother's hair which when dyed changed from black to red. She had "Pickledem." Miss Miss mentions that Charles "didnt understand thuh jars. Didnt get it. Them. Thuh jars. Showed him mother. What I saved. Her photograph went over well enough. Didnt find fault with her picture but did mind her parts isnt that always thuh way" (95–96). Miss Miss begins to ask "Something to remember you by?" (97) as Charles accuses her of Voodoo, signaling a shift in their interaction. She begins to suspect that Charles comes only to eat the pickled beets Miss Miss continually prepared with her mother when she was alive, and that Charles comes only to enjoy "the juicy.... Emptying my jars. Mines" (97). Subsequently, her question permutates to "something tuh re-member you by" (97–98). If she has not actually destroyed him through this re-membering, Miss Miss wishes him dead:

> Voodoo? Damn right. Eat one beet uh day. Dont wanna waste nothing.... Now. Begin: I told him to do it in here. Save it. Now begin. Put it in here. Now begin:..... Oh. Like steel he was. Hee! Begin: Steal away. Glide-it uhcross. Oh. Warm steal. Oh Warm. Warm. Oh: To thuh worms. To thuh worms. To thuh worms [98].

Final libidinal observations of Miss Miss leave unclear how Charles has departed, but either literally or figuratively he is out. Again with jazz-like circularity, the play ends where it begins, Miss Miss reminiscing, illustrating each point by showing her jars and beginning again. We come to see that she is a woman hobbled by her personal fears; she is the one who cannot get out. Her consistent repetition of "Now begin" suggests that she is stuck in present time, outside of, but unable to break free of, her past.

Yet again, as in jazz, the audience is changed by the shifts and revisions in Miss Miss's commentary. And we are left to contemplate the stasis of Miss Miss as she wrestles with the complexities of her failed love relationship and her inability to move beyond repetitive beginnings or to function in the real world. The image of a paralyzed Miss Miss is an iteration of the impossible position of many black women who face difficulties in American social economies that are often unrecognized but nonetheless real. Black women are confronted with the challenge of "interlocking structures of race, class, and gender oppression while rejecting and transcending those same structures" (Collins 124). As a result of such an ominous outside world, Miss Miss has retreated inward. Her agoraphobia seems an answer to an oppressive society within which she cannot safely maneuver.

Miss Miss's mother, another black woman evading the harsh realities of the present, seems to have only emphasized Miss Miss's skills of pickling, preserving what has gone before. And these skills seem enough while her mother is alive, "there were no empty jars you had your beets and no empty jars" (97). But her mother's death, where she "just—crumbled—" in a "puddle of her own pickling" (97) leaves Miss Miss alone and unable to cope. Miss Miss's vulnerability is further exacerbated by the appearance of Charles in her otherwise closed life. After the fact, Miss Miss is accusatory, claiming that Charles

> spied the juicy. Had tuh have him some. Lived next door. Close. Steal away. Gobblin the beets on his Thursdays. Smackin lips wipin lips on his wrist. He was sleeveless. Muscle shirt. With arms. On thuh back of his wrists. Eighteen Thursdays of slobbering beet juice back wrists use a napkin please he had hisself developed uh long red beet smear stain. Emptying my jars. Mines [97].

Miss Miss's jealous regard for her beets, her full jars, "her juicy," constructs implications that go beyond the obvious. Charles has violated not only her cupboard, but her body, her safe place, and her trust. Her inability to cope with his manipulation and rejection leaves her further entrapped in her closed world, further away from personal salvation. Offering little hope for those who have not developed the skills to meet racial, sexual, and social challenges head on, Parks presents here the devastating effects of parasitic relationships on black women. And she seems ultimately to emphasize through Miss Miss's tribulations that African Americans should have a healthy regard for the dispossessing effect of overemphasizing the power of the past, but must also have a necessary connection to those in the present community, as well as in history, who offer wisdom in the struggle to survive. Miss Miss's reified veneration of history, brought on by the difficulties extant in life as a black woman in the present, has destroyed her capacity to live; she will always be forever beginning to go back. Parks's insight into the paralyzing nature of over-romanticizing and idealizing love relationships between black men and women tempers her emphasis on privileging memory and history. She reminds us that the past is only as important as its usefulness toward improving the present.

Jazz elements in *Betting* and *Pickling* are evident in strategies that signify directly on language as well. In appropriating standard English and its variants, Parks creates verbal "Rep & Rev" that structurally underwrites the thematic jazzing of her subjects in these plays. Iterative lines contain words that sustain shifts in their spellings, in their order, and Parks is not hesitant to coin new words or sounds. Parks here has jazzed language as well through her own neovernacular that she has derived from African American vernacular English.

In both *Betting* and *Pickling*, strange sounds, neologisms and startling phrasing are all indicators of jazzing language both to alienate the reader in a simulacrum of the characters' sense of distance and as a way of expressing what for black women has not seemed adequately communicated for or about them. Mare and Lucius both use language that is sprinkled throughout the play with sounds like "WAAAH," "HHHhhhhhhhhhhh," "Snnnnnnnch," "snucch" (77). In addition, streaming compound words creates new impressions with fairly standard words as in Mare's desperate plea "wecudbetogethernights" (78). Vernacular inspired spelling like "Aaaanuhstick em" (83), "Mmtelling Mama" (77) and clearly invented words like "fuzzicate" (79), "hunkerchip" (77), and "Riggamartin's" (88) are the newly creative language that Parks invents for tackling the project of effectively expressing the singular experiences of black people, especially in terms of racial and gender struggle.

In *Pickling*, synthesized phonetic spellings produce an almost lyrical visual as well as aural rendition of language, designed as a misleadingly simple but penetrating analysis of black female isolation and dementedness. As in *Betting*, alternative spellings and streaming compound words based on vernacular pronunciation abound in this play. Miss Miss describes singing a "Prell-yude," hearing her mother exclaim, "I-monmuhwayow. Tuh," and insisting that she "Musttellthuhtruthfirst" (95, 96, 97). Miss Miss's unique vocabulary of sounds and nonsensical words further defines Parks's early skills as an exquisite linguistic dramatist. This playwright's insistence on language as a "physical act" establishes a direct connection between the search for identity and the search for a culturally apt form of verbal expression. In awe of the impact of words, Parks observes that:

> Words are spells in our mouths. My interest in the history of words—where they come from, where they're going—has a direct impact on my playwrighting because, for me, Language is a physical act.... Look at the difference between "the" and "thuh." The "uh" requires the actor to employ a different physical, emotional, vocal attack ["from Elements" 11].

Miss Miss further delivers puns and metaphors that are both entertaining and strikingly powerful. Charles is described suggestively as steel in terms of his muscles and his manhood. Because he steals her juicy, in the final scene Miss Miss leaves us with a cold sense of her desperate loneliness, anger, and possible revenge: "Like steel he was. Hee! Begin: Steal uhway. Glide-it across. Oh. Warm steal. Oh. Warm. Warm. Oh: to thuh worms. To thuh worms" (98). In this last view of Miss Miss, repetition, wordplay, punning and vernacular spelling all culminate in a final burst of language, action, and meaning that is stunning in its exposure of this black woman's crazed anguish, and provides a riveting finality to her predicament.

Parks's jazzing of language as a revelatory strategy with characters such as Miss Miss is actually explained to some extent in her own created, selective glossary, which she entitles "foreign words & phrases" ("Elements" 17–18). A number of the words in this list are systematically used in the majority of her plays and often express otherwise un-writeable moments of stage communication. In creating this carefully wrought glossary, Parks takes an ironic dig at the complexities of language study and linguistic orthography, challenging monolithic notions of language as a science and as a regulatory system accepted as capable of rendering the experiences of the marginalized, in this case African American women. Her use of specialized words in her plays represents and champions an alternative understanding of the role of language in dramatic structure that will offer self-determination and subaltern expression in a way that replaces dominant, oppressive narratives of the self and community.

Even individuals versed in African American vernacular and music are at times hard-pressed to decipher the meaning of Parks's jazzed language and structure, particularly in the complex rendition of black male/female relationships that she presents in *Devotees in the Garden of Love*. The play evokes a struggle at first for possible meaning in discussions between George and her Aunt Lily on the art of "Love." From a high hill the women aloofly observe suitors in battle below for the fair hand of George: "They may not be peacing by morning through.... ThisOne has uh move which ThatOne counters and ThatOne has uh counter to which ThisOne always gives reply" (140). As the battle continues the two women consider the power of Love; "It could be a protracted engagement down there.... But I think thingsll wrap theirselves up nicely.... Cuz the cause of Love. Our word is 'devotion.' My match is made in heaven" (140).

Parks offers a fascinating mix of vernacular, archaic language, and battle imagery in this scene. George declares to Mama Lily that

> puss green-slimed bile and contagion may grow from thuh wounds of the wounded seep intuh thuh ground and kill and kill ... thuh sky may shake and spit fire and crack open and swallow um all up but itll all end nicely.... We will hold fast. Unto thuh death. We will not come out all asunder.... How come? Cuz thuh cause of Love [140].

Images of mortal combat and the carnage of war are mixed with language of courtly love. Furthermore, George frequently rehearses her skills in French, reciting passages in the premiere European language of love. This is followed by her spirited reaction to battle: "KERBLAM! Sweet Bejesus! Scuze my French!" (137). Parks's ambiguous representation here of the art of Love is an ironic appropriation of European constructs of courtly, romantic sexual love brought to bear in the context of African American male/female relationships. She implies here that there must be alternative, positive possibilities in moving away from traditional behaviors, assumptions, and social expectations. Traditional love or romance as presented here is a bloody, horrific war where male suitors disembowel each other while the female prize, "thuh bride-who'll-be" (152), sits at an elevated distance, emotionally detached and completely caught up in the ritual of romance. Her hope chest, her bride-head, her place settings are exaggerated symbols of her worthiness.

Ironically, George, as an eligible black female sports a masculine name, and by the end of the play, she has insisted that her name be changed to Patty. As Patty, she narrates in third person that the suitor who won her hand had only his head on a platter remaining after battle, and he won her devotion by saying the "Words of love!!" as "Thuh lips twitch" to say "Be Mine" (155). Words of love that give Patty such joy, however, are soon described in less than positive terms. Beginning with "Once upon uh time," she narrates: "After thuh marriage thuh boy it seemed soon forgot his home-own lingo. To woo her he had used thuh words 'be mine....' Although they were in love that 'be mine' got rather old rather quick. Soon even his 'be mine' dried up" (155). Patty leaves him and goes to "Gay Paree" for twelve years. Finally, we find Patty "at thuh Front" reporting that the talking head husband and his wife made another go at their relationship, "lived happily ever after and stuff like that. Talking back and forth" (156). The sardonic effects of fairy tale stock phrases and the banal tone of the ending where a bodiless lover enjoys the "stuff" of life with his wife are underwritten by the final moment when Patty as a reporter describes her own marriage in third person while on the scene of a new battle for love. The incongruous ending leaves the audience baffled by inconsistent figures, behaviors, and events that contradict each other and lack stability. Introduced and interrogated in *Betting*, and distorted in *Pickling*, representations of black female roles in love and marriage are further challenged in *Devotees* and, ultimately, beg for a refusal of the ideologically traditional toward new possibilities. The shifts in opposing structures, images, and language in this last play exercise a kind of jazz riffing on sentimental representations of the war of the sexes.

Parks determines here, as in many of her other plays, a positioning of African American culture and language in relief to dominant notions of blackness. She executes in these three early plays, *Betting on the Dust Commander*, *Pickling*, and *Devotees in the Garden of Love*, a specialized dramatic approach, an intense rendition of the chasm between expectations and experiences of black women in American society. More broadly, in each of these three plays, we see Parks accomplish a re-membering of the art of drama itself that serves her in due stead in the many plays that follow. Her overarching dramatic strategy of Rep & Rev establishes a new feel, a new terrain for the reader/spectator to come to meaning through a most convincing adaptation — verbal and structural anatomies of jazz pieces in the realm of dramatic literature. Her nuanced, layered presentation of meaning comments upon the politics of perception, revealing how subtly, yet irrevocably, language is tied to our understanding of the self and of the past. She demonstrates for us, too, how re-presentations of language, of concepts of time, and of versions of love can offer new understanding for those who have been forced to straddle the racial and gender divide.

Works Cited

Collins, Patricia Hill. *Black Feminist Thought: Knowledge, Consciousness, and the Politics of Empowerment.* New York: Routledge, 1991.

Cooke, Michael G. *Afro-American Literature in the Twentieth Century: The Achievement of Intimacy.* New Haven: Yale University Press, 1984.

Geis, Deborah. *Suzan-Lori Parks.* Ann Arbor: University of Michigan Press, 2008.

Hughes, Langston. "Jazz as Communication." In *The Langston Hughes Reader: The Selected Writing of Langston Hughes.* New York: George Braziller, 1958. 492–494.

Hurston, Zora Neale. *Their Eyes Were Watching God.* New York: Harper and Row, 1990.

Kolin, Philip. "Cultural Memory and Circular Time in Suzan-Lori Parks's *Betting on the Dust Commander.*" *Notes on Contemporary Literature.* 39.3 (2009): 8–11.

Parks, Suzan-Lori. *Betting on the Dust Commander.* In *The America Play and Other Works.* New York: Theatre Communications Group, 1995. 73–90.

———. *Devotees in the Garden of Love.* In *The America Play and Other Works.* New York: Theatre Communications Group, 1995. 133–156.

———. "Elements of Style." In *The America Play and Other Works.* New York: Theatre Communications Group, 1995. 6–18.

———. *Pickling.* In *The America Play and Other Works.* New York: Theatre Communications Group, 1995. 91–98.

———. "Possession." In *The America Play and Other Works.* New York: Theatre Communications Group, 1995. 3–5.

"You one of uh mines?": Dis(re)membering in Suzan-Lori Parks's *Imperceptible Mutabilities in the Third Kingdom*

Philip C. Kolin

Suzan-Lori Parks's *Imperceptible Mutabilities in the Third Kingdom*, her first major play, premiered on September 20, 1989, at BACA Downtown, a small (75-seat) performance space on Willoughby Street in Brooklyn, and was directed by Liz Diamond, who has worked with Parks on many of her provocative scripts, including *The America Play*. Winning an Obie, *Mutabilities* became a harbinger of Parks's later achievements, including the Pulitzer Prize in 2002 for *Topdog/Underdog*. Recognizing her talent, Mel Gussow claimed that *Mutabilities* provided "substantial evidence of the playwright's originality" and praised Parks for a "work [that] is shadowed by myth and metaphor" ("Review/Theatre"). In four thematically related scenes, or parts, Parks traces black history from slavery to the present. Predictive of her later works, *Mutabilities* explores black racial memory and how a white culture has de-historicized it to suppress African American identity. One of the choric characters in *Mutabilities*, Shark-Seer, summarizes the ontological horror that occupies Parks in this play and elsewhere in her prolific canon—"How we gonna find my Me?" (40). That "Me" was stolen through the Middle Passage when slavers brought Africans from their homeland, and a strong sense of self, and subjected them to the "rupture [and] forced migration" (Brown-Guillory 186) that dislocated their identity. The "Third Kingdom" refers to "the space of sea between the[se] worlds" of freedom and bondage (Geis 50). In fact, in the second part of *Mutabilities* Parks inventories the dimensions of and debasements in the hole of a slave ship, the *Brookes*, that carried thousands of black souls into oblivion. Bewailing the perpetuation of slavery into the new millennium, *Mutabilities* dramatizes how a dominant white culture still condemns African Americans to the margins of society, pushing them over the precipice into a forced cultural schizophrenia.

Because they have been stereotyped and thereby erased, black characters in *Mutabilities* find themselves repeatedly fragmented and disconnected from a past, their heritage, that has been written out of white revisionist history. Victims of racial amnesia, they are adrift in time, space, and consciousness. Their history is scattered, confused, lost. On his journey through the Middle Passage, Kin-Seer, another choric voice, articulates the trauma of black memory—"Last night I dreamed of where I comed from. But where I comed from diduhnt look like nowhere like I been" (37). White history has expunged black roots. Blacks are, consequently, forced to dig in "The Great Hole of History," as Parks describes their tragedy in *The America Play* (1995), in order to reconstruct their racial past. As she claims, "History—the destruction and creation of it through theatre pieces and how black people fit onto all this—is my primary artistic concern" (qtd. in Haike Frank). Further, Parks maintains that her job is to "locate the ancestral burial ground, dig for bones, find bones, hear the bones sing, write it down" ("Possession" 4). Excavating those holes, or the "absence of blacks in history" (Brown-Guillory 184), Parks often includes dead characters in her plays. Among the 25 roles in *Mutabilities*, several are played by characters who are dead, while all twelve characters in *The Death of the Last Black Man in the Whole Entire World* are deceased. "I keep going back to the dead speaking from the grave," Parks confessed (qtd. in Smith 37).

Reconstructing a stolen past, a lost history, is an inevitable trauma for Parks's characters in *Mutabilities*, and also in *The America Play* and *The Death of the Last Black Man*, where, again, a white culture stands at the doorway to memory, blocking their traveling back and forth freely, confidently, knowledgeably. The quintessential white man in *Mutabilities*, Charles Saxon ("Mr. Charlie" and his tribe referred to as "Bleach Bones Man" [38]), informs an old black woman, Aretha (who may have been his slave, nanny, or widow), about the function of memory in the white superclass culture of America: "Memory is a very important thing, don't you know. It keeps us in line. It reminds us of who we are, memory. Without it we could not be anybody. We would be running about here with no identities" (48). Who controls memory controls power in white America. Memory determines who and what history records, codifies, preserves, and empowers. But according to Charles, memory upholds white, not black, history and values. While memory privileges white identity, it strips blacks of theirs. Black history, in the process, has to be measured in loss, not in sums. Without a clear memory of historical events and times, Parks emphasizes, black identity becomes confiscated, or fabricated. In the "Afterword" to *The Book of Laughter and Forgetting*, Milan Kundera aptly notes: "What is the self? It is the sum of everything we remember." Without a memory, there can be no self. Dressed all in white in a production of *Mutabilities* at the MIT Dramashop in February 2007 (Dupuis), Charles assumed a deific role in condemning Aretha to a self-less hell of obscurity along with other African Americans who have been assimilated through stereotype: "We won't be able to tell you apart from the others. We won't even know your name" (53). For Charles, as well as for his racially-christened progeny, Anglor and Blanca Saxon, Aretha and other black characters have become a "fabricated absence" (Drukman 67). Depending on one's racial identity, then, memory can be protection or punishment in white America.

The production of memory is at the heart of *Mutabilities*, as it is in Parks's other works. In every sense, *Mutabilities* is a black memory/morality play that stages how black recollections of the past have been fragmented and disconnected. In a 1994 interview, Parks claimed, "My plays are like these passion plays [those at Oberammergau, Germany] where the community comes together to reenact the tragedy.... They're like a guide ... to who we were, or how we are, or what we should be" (Ong 49). Digging back in racial time/memory, Parks uncovers narratives beneath narratives, voices deep inside her characters' subconscious: "You know, sometimes when you dig, and you just open the door, which is what eavesdropping is, hearing stories as they come into your head" (qtd. in Sellar 38). As Parks stressed in a 2007 interview, "Writing is not just about writing but it's actually more about becoming more familiar with the great enormous unconscious, the thing that underlies all things" (qtd. in Hansen). As she pointed out, "I'm working theatre like an incubator to create new historical events. I'm re-membering and staging historical events, which through their happening on stage, are ripe for inclusion in the canon of history" ("Possession" 4–5). Parks incubates history by inserting her "re-membering" into reality, creating plays that map black memories holding events, people, and times that have been hidden or lost.

As the depository of memory, the mind holds center stage for Parks, as it did for Adrienne Kennedy, whose surrealistic plays of the 1960s — such as *Funnyhouse of a Negro* and *The Owl Answers*— have compellingly influenced her. "She inspired me to take weird riffs and shifts of character," Parks declared (qtd. in Solomon 75). As Kennedy did thirty years earlier, Parks has radicalized theatre in her "re-membering." Through nontraditional staging reminiscent of Kennedy's plays, she creates characters who flow in and out of identities and names, travel across landscapes that shift, and exist in times that swing back and forth over 300 years. The past is not separated, blocked off, from the present; the two are fused. In the process of representing memories, Parks resists following sequential, white Cartesian logic and chronology in *Mutabilities*. She hears the same types of tortured voices that spoke to Kennedy through her doomed young black women (Johanna Frank; Kolin). Like Kennedy's haunted women, too, Parks's characters are "obsessed and possessed by representations of blackness" (Elam, "Remembering" 8). As Kennedy's heir, then, Parks takes audiences on a nightmare tour of a memory-embattled black America. Time and space, life and death, consciousness and unconsciousness collide in *Mutabilities*, as they earlier had in *Funnyhouse of a Negro,* leaving black memory in "the abyss of a history that disappears before it can be written and then reappears only as performance" (Roach 307).

Essential to Parks's performance of race and memory in *Mutabilities* are the "Rep & Rev" techniques ("Possession" 9) she borrows from jazz musicians; that is, repeating signifying phrases and words but varying the context and chronology to challenge spectators' expectations. Heidi Holder usefully points out that the function of "Rep & Rev" in Parks is to "unmoor images and sounds from their expected contexts. The repetitions and revisions are frequently nonsensical or impossible" (19–20). As in *The America Play, Venus,* and *The Death of the Last Black Man,* Parks's "Rep & Rev" signifiers look in many directions at once — white and black, past and present, inside and outside, life and death. An essential part of these techniques are the puns they carry, encouraging audiences to see double or triple around the edges of white fictions that have enshackled African Americans. For instance, a pun on "Fo'-fathers" in *The America Play* attests to both the sorrow and the resistance of black consciousness in white America. The "Fo'-fathers" alludes to the white forefathers enshrined in history but, inseparable from this paternalistic image, is their also being "foe fathers," or "faux fathers" (Diamond 86), who oppressed blacks through slavery. Similarly, "Foundling Father," another pun in *The America Play*, suggests an orphan, a leader who is without roots, as well as his offspring, the antithesis of the benevolent patriarchs (e.g., Washington, Franklin, Jefferson) promoted in white discourse. These puns reveal what Sanja Bahun-Radunovic labels as the "chasms and fissures of language, the historicity of semantic structure in the process of their emergence, varied configurations, and dissolution" (460). Through her "Rep & Rev" signifiers, Parks opens up space and time; she has us descend into a black mine. She forces us to read backwards in racial time to feel the smarting wounds of slavery and then to jump forward to see how blacks are still excluded in contemporary America. As Sterling Plumpp has so poignantly expressed it, "Language is geography" ("Territory"). Thanks to her polyvalent, multidirectional puns, we travel over many miles and years, seeing and hearing suppressed black memories. We hear the bones sing, and wail.

Parks's puns are subversive, explosive. Commenting on her style, Shawn Garrett claims that they "wrench apart sentences, upset order, pull words apart by phonemes" (12). But her puns — her language — do more than upset syntax and semantics. They shake up language, memories/identities, as well as the human anatomy. For Parks, language "is a physical act. Language is performance. It is something which involves your entire body — not just your head" ("Elements of Style" 11). Consistent with her views on a muscular theatre language, Parks defined a "black play" in anatomical terms as one that "had its language ripped out of its mouth, the family torn asunder" ("New Black Math" 579). But what is done linguistically in Parks's plays has repercussions in what is done physically. She recognizes that while language can oppress black bodies it can also resist and subvert the white colonial dominance that has subjugated blacks. In an interview with director Bonnie Metzgar, Parks declared that "the language of the play should come from people's gut — what they want, what they don't want, what they're going through, what they're not going through, what they're thinking" ("Alien Baby" 52). Similarly, *Village Voice* critic Alisa Solomon graphically describes how Parks "stages [her characters'] consciousness itself, pulling apart language and image, pointing at their innards, and sometimes, reconstituting them anew" (74). Through her repetitive, performative language, her puns, Parks re-enacts on stage the violence done to black bodies over time, thus inscribing their "innard" history of oppression, but also their opposition to such indignities. According to James Freize, "In Parks's hands, repetition/compulsion metastasizes from a psychic into a semantic and then into a social disturbance" (530).

In *Mutabilities*, Parks's most radical semantic/anatomical/psychic disruptions occur through puns on *mine/mind* and *dis-* and *re-member* which she "Reps & Revs" into each of the four parts of her play, as she has done in other plays (Geis 11; Thompson 172). These puns are evocatively illustrated in the last section of the play, "Greeks (or the Slugs)," where black Marine Sergeant Smith, hungering for distinction in white America, catches a man who falls from the sky and, stepping on a mine, has his legs blown off. Discussing the hardships his family endures, one of his twin daughters, Buffy, complains that the white censors have cruelly blotted the name of his children in the letters the sergeant sends home. "We say 'Muffy' every day but for Sergeant Smith saying your name would be gravely dangerous." To which her twin sister Muffy answers, "Muffy's not gravely dangerous." But their mother, Mrs. Smith, retorts, "Muffy-Muffy-Muffy sounds like a minefield. What's uh mine, Mufficient." The child then replies, "A mine is a thing that dismembers. Too many mines lose the war" (64). Later when the legless sergeant comes home, Muffy announces, "A mine is a thing that remembers. Too many mines lose the war" (70). Black *mines* lie between dis-membering and re-membering in *Mutabilities*.

The Parksian slant puns on *mine/mind/minefield* express her multi-layered view of how black memory and bodies have been tragically linked — semantically and anatomically — for dis-memberment, destruction, in white America. Words are traumatically made flesh in Parks. The black *mind/mine* (signifying memory, identity, and possession) has been metastasized, in Freize's words, into a weapon (a land mine or other explosive device) to eradicate black memory. Reverberating with further significance, the word *mine* also suggests digging into the earth, that is, searching for and finding a deep interiority, the "innards," or "guts" of the submerged consciousness of black history. Ironically, the word for the black self — *mine* — is the same word used for the eradication of that self. Relevant to the combustible power of other *mines* in her plays, Parks believes that her "characters ... often explode into silence" and that "the words lead up to silences, or the silences burst open into language" (qtd. in Wishna 186). Moreover, David Cote describes Parks herself as an "animated storyteller with smart-bomb precision" ("Putting on the Dog" 61). Once the black mind is stigmatized as hostile territory, regarded as a *mine/mine(d)field*, a white culture feels justified in shattering, exploding black identity, heritage, and destiny into confusion and forgetfulness in the *mine-fields* (or *mindfields*) of America. An ad for the Negro College Fund from the 1970s proleptically spoke to the central issues that interrogate Parks in *Mutabilities*: "A mind is a terrible thing to waste." Through these puns, Parks physicalizes the destruction of black memory. Her characters' history and identity, like their minds, are shattered, exploded, horrifically transformed in *Mutabilities*.

In the process of dramatizing *mines* and *minefields* in *Mutabilities*, Parks deconstructs black bodies to bring black history to life, to "incubate" it on stage, or to "right and rewrite history in a postmodern culture that has dismantled the idea of history," according to Harry Elam and Alice Raynor (191). Looking ahead to Parks's later plays, black bodies in *Mutabilities* undergo a series of harrowing infestations, extractions, amputations, metamorphoses. In what Alisa Solomon calls Parks's "allegorical absurdism" (qtd. in Geis 45), her characters mutate into ruptured, fragmented bodies. As elsewhere in her canon, the dismemberment and disfiguration of black body are inseparable from the semantics in which these anatomical ruptures are described/expressed. What Geis says about *Venus* is true of *Mutabilities*: "The play invokes the merged images of remembering and re-membering (i.e., putting the pieces back together), of dis-re-membering (forgetting, or disrespecting), and dis-membering (taking apart)" (92).

In Particular, *Venus* centers on the postmortem of a black woman's body, especially her private parts, making them the subject of grotesque spectacle. Words are an essential part of a white culture's transformation of black flesh into a commodified sexuality. The black woman's name, Saartjie Baartman, is stripped away and replaced by a new exploitative title, "the Venus Hottentot." Under that name, her body is paraded around as a circus freak. Bodies are also littered throughout *The America Play*, as characters dig up bones to find a record (the written word) of their history, equating the physical with the semantic, one becoming the other. Similarly in *Devotees in the Garden of Love* (1992) suitors on a battlefield are maimed with/because of one word. As Odelia Pandahr, the panderer of women's eyes, remarks:

> There is one word that, I guess you could say, sums up this brilliant display this passionate parade of severed arms and legs, genitals and fingertips, buttocks and heads, the splatterment the dismemberment, the quest for an embrace for the bride ... has, for many, ended in an embrace of eternity, and that one word I think we could say that one word is "Devotion" [144].

Ironically, "Devotion," which signifies love and respect, becomes the simulacrum of the destruction of the body. Parks's later two Red Letter plays—*In the Blood* and *Fucking A*—are also filled with destroyed bodies coupled with the semantics of decay. *In the Blood*, for instance, links the inflictions visited upon Hester's body, and her children's, with the corrupted dissolution of kinship terms ("husband" or "father").

The "splatterment the dismemberment" Parks's characters endure in these and her other plays recall the horrors of Reconstruction lynchings, where black bodies were burned, gouged, strangled, and mutilated and the anatomical parts were given to spectators as trophies and souvenirs, remembrances of a festive occasion (Young). Most of Parks's plays are rooted in the horrors of lynching. At the center of a lynching was a punishment, an execution of an offending black person whose identity was altered, erased. His (or her) corpse/remains were then left hanging, a sign of justice/civil order and as a sign of transformation. Building upon lynching scholarship, Harvey Young observed that the lynching spectacle "stages the transformation of the living body into a set of lifeless parts to be collected; the spectacle becomes materially ... [a black person's] lynching enacts his disappearance" (655). Analogously, black punishments in Parks become spectacles to confirm white power, and black bodies become texts she asks audiences to read. The most obvious manifestation of a lynching in Parks occurs in *The Last Black Man*, where the title character, Black Man, appears on stage with a rope around his neck and Black Woman with Fried Drumstick tells him, "Let me loosen your collar for you" (118). But the lost body parts in *Mutabilities* can also be equated with lynching, re-membered spectacles designed to disempower blacks and to eradicate their memory and history. The dis-membering and re-membering of lynching infamies occur on a *mine(d)field* in America, the Mutable. It is little wonder that black characters cannot find their "Me." Dis-remembering leads to dis-membering, a salient characteristic of lynching. In this light, *Mutabilities* might be read as Parks's postmodern lynching play.

The "Rep & Rev" of *minds/mine/mines* that closes the play with Sergeant Smith opens it with a section entitled "Snails," where the white world sets traps/mines for young black minds. Molly, a black woman in her early twenties, has been expelled from school because she has been unable to pronounce words, white fashion. For example, when she says "ax," instead of "ask," as the white world insists, she is stigmatized, excluded. She lacks the shibboleth necessary for success in the white world. Commenting on her teacher's reaction, Molly declares, "Failed every test he shoves in my face." Apropos of Molly's dilemma, Parks frequently comments on one of her high school teachers who cautioned her not to be a writer because she could not spell words correctly, the way the white world demanded ("Suzan-Lori Parks Commencement Speech"). Unlike her characters, Parks turned such criticism into profitable theatre through her symbolic orthography. In addition to her spelling, Molly is cruelly doomed to fail because she cannot recite the mantra of white folklore/education — "The little lamb follows closely behind at Mary's heels as Mary boards the train." Exclaiming that she has never seen a lamb follow a woman on a train, Molly concludes that the "Whole idea uh talkin right now ain't right no way. Aint natural" (25). Adding to her misery, she loses her job because her "phone voice" is unacceptable in the white world of work. Again, she is threatened: "Talk right or youre outta here!" and she adds, "They tell me get Basic Skills call me breaking protocol hhhh!" (26). Distraught, she confesses to her roommate Charlene that she is considering suicide and wonders if after jumping off a building she will "splat." Staying alive, all she can expect is the degradation of searching for a job in the white world. "Only thing worse n workin ssloookin for work" (26). Sadly, Molly concludes, "Stuff like this happens every day I know. This isn't uh special case mines iduhnt uh uhnnn" (25).

Her "*mines*," that is, her identity, her psyche, inevitably point to her vulnerability/her undoing/her "splatterment the dismemberment," evoked through Parks's political pun on *mine* (self) and *mine* (explosive). In the "Rep & Rev" of this opening scene, the African American *mine*—the "Me"—and the *mind*—are transformed. Disremembering white pronunciations and grammar plus school nursery rhymes, that is, the stuff of white folklore, the protocols a dominant white society insists she commit to memory, Molly's mind leads her into the minefields of expulsion and unemployment. "A mine is a thing that dismembers," as Muffy put it. Like other African Americans, too, Molly has been excluded into otherness, without an identity (a "Me") created by a job or education. Like one of her ancestors, Aretha in Part Two of *Mutabilities*, Molly becomes a victim of white memory/history. Enfolding the past in the present, Parks links a contemporary young African American woman with an old slave woman whose memory, like her body, is scheduled for extinction. *Mutabilities* dramatizes the contradictions of white America that insist on the dis-remembrance of an Africanist experience while demanding strict remembrance of the icons and ideologies of white memory, lambs and the proper way to pronounce "ask." White memory wants to keep Molly in line. As Charles decreed, "Without it we cannot be anybody." In such a context, then, the verb "ask" retrospectively becomes the fiat of black compliance with and subordination to white history, white memory. Molly has to ask — beg, petition, seek approval — to be heard, even to exist, in a white world.

But what is natural in a white world is not always natural in a black one. When the teacher "makes" Molly recite, he is demanding that she forget (dis-remember) any African (American) reality she brings with her. He wants her "me," her "mind," to undergo an identity explosion — "He makes me recite my mind goes blank." This teacher then bristles at her resistance — "Ain't never seen no woman on no train with no lamb. I tell him so." Yet every time she is called upon to recite/repeat/valorize white codes and symbols, Molly's mind goes "blank" because she cannot comprehend or accept the racial fetishization of the totem animal of white purity and salvation. There is no record in Molly's deep racial memory of white icons, but her teacher insists that she dis-remember her black heritage to obliterate any black voices inside her. Carol Lee, co-founder of the Betty Shabazz International Charter School, aptly asserts that "the preponderance of recent research in cognition shows students learn best when they can connect what they're learning to what they already know" (33). Because Molly cannot connect to white codes, she becomes a victim of a culturally irrelevant and punitive educational system. As a consequence, she finds herself at the point of suicide, "splatterment and dismemberment," making her one of the countless cases of imperceptible mutabilities in American public education. Despite George W. Bush's promise, she has been left behind. Her fate illustrates how the contemporary white world punishes the "dis-remembrance" of African Americans whose bodies suffer the horrors afflicting their minds/mines.

Charlene, Molly's roommate, recounts an analogous story about the language-less robber Mokus who just walks into apartments and steals, never uttering a word. "He didnt have no answers cause he didnt have no speech ... he had that jungle air uhbout im that just off thuh boat look tuth his face" (26). In white America, blacks without the right speech — acceptable white parlance — are demonized as speechless/wordless robbers whose silence/blankness is a sign of their ghettoization, transforming them into primitives who inhabit urban jungles. But, as Parks mockingly notes, America's bigotry is rooted in redundancy. Without the right speech, though, Mokus could not give the right (or any) answers. Moreover, his "off-the-boat look" connects Mokus with his slave ancestors like Aretha, all stereotyped as less than human. The victim of racial profiling, Mokus had "his picture on file at thuh police station. Ninety-nine different versions. None of um looked like he looked." Yet he, like the black roommates, found out that white America "could point us out from pictures that whuduhnt us" (28). Mokus is faceless in a sea of black faces. Molly's "blank" mind and Mokus's speechlessness and looks, then, are the physical mutations of deep semantic and psychic disruptions in African American "mines." Prevented from articulating their past, they cannot tell their own "burdened story of time" (Plumpp, "Mississippi Griot" 64).

If the opening section ("A") of Part One of *Mutabilities* dramatizes how the white world attacks the black mine/mind, then the later sections reveal the process by which this has been accomplished. In these sections, Parks creates a Kafka-esque, surreal allegory revealing what it means to be black in contemporary America; that is, how blacks look at themselves (the "Me," the "mine") and how they are expected to look in front of a white audience. Going by a different name, Molly, now calling herself Mona, raises crucial questions about identity, "dis(re)memberment," and the scopic power of a white superclass. "Once there was uh me named Mona who wondered what she'd be like if no one was watchin" (27). And later she reveals, "once there was un me named Mona who wondered what she'd talks like if no one was listenin" (28). But the terrifying truth in *Mutabilities* is that white authority figures are always watching and listening in order to dismember Molly/Mona and her two roommates who also have double first names, Veronica/Verona and Charlene/Chona, as if they themselves were in the very process of mutation. White spectatorship and the exploitation of fetishized black bodies, reminiscent of cruel overseers who managed plantations, occur in almost all of Parks's works, especially in *Venus*, *America Play*, and *In the Blood*. As in a lynching, too, the white overseers in *Mutabilities* inscribe their meaning, interpretation, onto black bodies through the "splatterment [and] dismemberment" process ongoing in the play.

In comes the Naturalist, Parks's satiric portrait of the quintessential white spectator, a behavioral scientist who wore outlandish eyeglasses in the BACA premiere, the better to spy on Mona and her roommates (Dupuis). To do so, he hides inside the "fly," a large cardboard mechanical roach that blends "in with the environment under scrutiny" (27), so he is able "to conceal himself and observe the object of study—unobserved," which seems almost a parody of Hamlet, the "observed of all observers." The Naturalist characterizes the girls as "subjects" to be "monitored" in "their own world (*mundus primitivus*)" (29), but in his convoluted soliloquy he blurs distinctions between species, demonizing blacks as primitives or, worse yet, insects. In effect, this loathsome overseer infests the girls' apartment with bugs. Justifying his experimentation in white monumental (stilted and clinical) language, he declares, "I ask us to remember that our founding fathers went forth tirelessly crossing a vast expanse of ocean in which there lived dangerous creatures of the most horrible sort tirelessly crossing that sea jungle to find this country and name it" (29). Here he voices the punishing credo of white memory/history which remembers and associates patriotism with conquests and slaving. In conflating "sea" with "jungle," he links the two symbolic landscapes responsible for the forced black diaspora through the Middle Passage. In the Naturalist's perverted biological politics, "creatures of the most horrible sort" can simultaneously refer to animals and to blacks, both grouped as monstrous. Alarmed by an unjust society he helped to create and now perpetuates, the Naturalist fears "the great cake of society is crumbling." At the end of his soliloquy, he orders, "Watch closely," as the undercover fly reports on the girls' activities as their apartment teems with "Thousands Thousands [roaches] creepin in through the cracks" (30). The scientist's scopic intrusion, like his eugenics, is racist.

Not surprisingly, Molly/Mona screams, "Splat! I can't even talk. I got bug bites bug bites all over!" (28). Later, Verona yells, "Monas got bug bites on her eyelids" (34). She then shouts, "Down, Mona, bites! Oh my eyelids! On-her-heels! Down Mona down" (34). The bites on Mona's eyelids signify a cruel dis-membering—her vision of self has been distorted thanks to a dehumanizing white culture. Moreover, her self-commands of "Lie Mona lie Mona down" and "Down Mona down" depict her as a leaping animal. Her "eyes" (*I/mine/me*) have been infested by a white world depriving her of self-esteem, even personhood. Metaphorically, she is being transformed (dis-membered) into a grotesque-looking creature, a monstrous picture of how the black body is depicted in white history, the strange fruit on the lynching tree. To remedy the roach situation, Charlene decides to hire "Wipe-um-out-Lutzsky with uh Ph.D." (28), "Dr. Wipe-em-out Extraordinaire, Sir" (33). Lutzsky, who doubles with the Naturalist, is "a company man," an absurdly comic figure of white punishment familiar with insecticide bombs and other explosive weapons to rid homes of pests. He presents a toxic portrait of the racist who uses pseudo-scientific terminology and jingoistic language (he makes a living "from the vermin that feed on the crumbs which fall from the table of the broken cake of civilization") to underwrite his prejudices.

Through Lutzsky's outrageous actions, the girls are morphed into grotesque primitives, "savages" (34), "horrible creatures," slated to be exterminated for being black. Throughout this section Parks attacks the white rhetorical custody of black bodies. Dismembering them through language that turns them into pests, Lutzsky squirts the girls with his gun but, confused, cannot tell them apart and asks: "You're the one aren't you, Molly? Wouldn't want to squirt the wrong one. Stand up straight. The line forms here"

(33). He then aggressively hoses Charlene/Chona down as if she were also one of the "vermin." Throughout Parks's surrealistic horror comedy, Mona mouths an onomatopoeic litany of "Splatsplatsplat" that connects her contemplated suicide ("jumping off a tall building-splat") in Part A with the sound of Lutzsky's squirting/exterminating roaches in Parts D and E. Treating the girls as if they all looked alike, he exclaims: "There goes my squirt gun. Did you feel it?" "Hold still, Charlene," he says, "I'll hose you down." Verona recoils, "*HE'S SHOOTIN THUH WILD BEASTS,*" really the three black roommates (35).

In punishing Molly/Mona, Lutzsky can be linked to the white teacher who expelled Molly for not remembering the correct way to pronounce words and to recite folk sayings. Though evocative of a sitcom, the Lutzsky stage business more seriously points to the ways white language dis-members, and ghettoizes, the three black roommates, stripping them of identity and dignity. Decades earlier, Adrienne Kennedy's *Rat's Mass* (1965), a play demanding comparison with *Mutabilities*, even more graphically dramatized how black children were cruelly metamorphosized by a punitive white society into rodents with a *"rat's head, ... a rat's belly, a tail"* and with *"rat's blood"* and *"gnawing"* everywhere (Sollors, *Kennedy Reader* 47, 48). Appropriately enough, the final part of *Mutabilities* about the black Smith family is entitled "The Slugs," another example of black bodies being refigured, recast. Repeatedly, Parks laments that black bodies in a white world are unstable, mutable. A dominant white society thus constructs an identity for the girls that dis-members them as black women in order to re-member them as insects. As a result, they have lost their "Me," their self definition.

There is a further dis-memberment of the black *mine/mind* in Parks's allegory. Broadening her satiric attack on racism, she takes audiences from Lutzsky to Dr. Marlin Perkins, the host of *Mutual of Omaha's Wild Kingdom*, a popular television program in the 1960s and 1970s that featured a soft-spoken, grey-haired Perkins in a pith helmet, carrying his rifle, and tracking down exotic beasts in the wilderness (he "petted a rhino once") and then displaying them before the camera to entertain a white colonizing audience. Ironically, Veronica/Verona keeps a picture of him close by: "I had to have Marlin by my bed at night" (36). Hailed as a daring naturalist, Perkins was often filmed hacking his way through "darkest Africa" and communicating with the natives who looked and acted as if they just had emerged from the bush — "Black folks with no clothes" (36). However hilarious the prospect of Verona having a bedside photograph of Perkins, the incident reveals the racist undercurrents in white society and television in the 1950s and beyond. By exoticizing (and dehumanizing) Africa and Africans, *Wild Kingdom* left "profound lingering ramifications" that adversely affect Verona's "sense of personal identity, culture, and history" (Elam, "Remembering" 8). The great white naturalist/adventurer Perkins, rifle in hand, watches/oversees Charlene/Chona whose apartment, by metaphoric extension, becomes a jungle in darkest Africa — the wild kingdom — as she herself is transformed into one of his primitives, or worse yet, one of the wild animals he "targeted and put ... into zoos for their own protection" (36).

In a stroke of genius, Parks fuses the eminent Perkins with the foolish Lutzsky. On the surface the two figures could not be more dissimilar, but Parks's message is that both misrepresent and thus dis(re)member blacks. Evoking our just seeing Lutzsky with his squirt gun, Verona cries out, "Marlin Perkinssgot uh gun" (33). But through the gun symbolism, Lutzsky embodies the absurd but dangerously real extension of Perkins's racially-colored reporting. Seeing the girls as primitives, savages, Lutzsky does fire his gun but calls the police for backup, screaming into the phone, "Hello. This is Dr. Lutzsky. Send ten over. Just like me. We've got a real one here. Won't even grunt" (34). According to a bigoted white memory and representation of Africans, the girls are expected to act ("grunt") like the subjects from the *primitivus mundus*. Behind such absurdity lies the message of *Wild Kingdom*. Perkins's most dangerous weapon, though, was not his rifle but the lens of his camera that portrayed blacks as savages, part of the jungle landscape in which he identified and defined them. Verona's comment that "Marlin loved and respected all wild things" (36) drips with irony. In Parks's ontology, Perkins was a part of the mock realism of the white media's presentation of Africa and blacks.

Lutzsky's antics still carry ominous consequences for contemporary black characters. Fearfully, they believe that "Lutzsky-is-shooting ... for real [because] We diduhnt pay our taxes" (35), that is, they are in trouble for non-compliance with white law, a type of *mind/mine* washing promulgated by an overseeing, punitive white world. As Mona/Molly was under suspicion for her verbal offenses in Part A, she and her roommates again fall under the strict jurisdiction of a white authority. Using another Parksian pun, Verona warns, "Don't touch the phone. It's bugged" (35). Through her ingenious puns, Parks moves from the comic antics of Dr. Lutzsky's pesticide to a pervasive institutional surveillance to censor blacks. Throughout *Mutabilities*, then, Parks alludes to a multitude of white power figures who terrorize black *mines/minds*—teachers, cops, naturalists, researchers, television stars, military brass, and, in Part F, public housing authorities. These so-called order figures dis(re)member blacks to uphold white codes of behavior, white canons of justice.

The Albee-like comedy in *Mutabilities* explodes with the horrors blacks confront in America because of stereotypes imposed by a colonialist white culture. As Charlene observes when Lutzsky takes the roaches away, "Knew us by names that whuduhnt ours" (28). Defamation leads to de-formation/dis-memberment in *Mutabilities*. Appropriately, the question of black identity, and dis-membering, are the subjects of Verona's soliloquy which ends the first part of the play. As a counterpoise to the Naturalist's soliloquy, Verona tells the story of her dog, "Namib," named after "thuh African sands," who has to be destroyed because he "told lies uhbout me behind my back" (36). A "euthansia specialist" at a veterinary hospital, Verona "wipes out" a "black dog" that someone brought in and "cut her open because I had to see I just had to see the heart of such a disagreeable domestic thing.... Nothing different. Everything in its place" (36). Verona's autopsy, another Parksian example of lynching dis-memberment, is a fitting coda to the horror comedy about the eradication of blacks (here allegorized through the dog) because of their perceived disruptive behavior. The black dog is Verona's *bête noir*. Euthanizing Namib "cuts off any relationship Verona has to this particular black representation" of self (Elam, "Remembering" 9). As Geis remarks, "Verona's actions like the many dissections and dismemberments in Parks's works, show the desperation and difficulty of remembering or understanding how these cycles of exploitation are perpetuated" (49). Metaphorically personified through roaches, snails, snarly black dogs, and "creatures of the most horrible sort," the three roommates in Part 1 are dis-membered (that is, sent down the chain of being), erased like lynched bodies. In Part 2, the chorus of men recounting the journey across, the Third Kingdom, Shark-Seer appropriately recalls, "I dream uh fish that's swallowin me and I dream up uh me that is becamin that fish..." (39). They are victims of what Parks calls "De-evolution" (*Devotees in the Garden of Love* 141). That being accomplished, "Everything is in place" in the racist world order.

Part 3 of *Mutabilities*, entitled "Open House," chronicles the fate of an old black woman, Aretha, and the nefarious ways white society has dis(re)membered her. Typical of Parks's nontraditional staging, Aretha's lifespan crosses hundreds of years in racial and psychological time until she is at last marked for extinction. But as one of Parks's speaking dead, participating in the "near historical events" performed on stage, she is given a voice which does call us to repudiate and to rewrite the white history that consigns her to non-being. As part of the "Great Shucking," Aretha learns she has to be exterminated to make room for more slaves. She is viciously "let go" by the white family she raised and loved, evicted from her home, and told "You expire along with your lease. Expiration 19-6-65 with no option to renew" (47). Ironically, June 19, or Juneteenth 1865, the date slaves in Galveston, Texas, were freed under the Emancipation Proclamation issued two years earlier, became the holiday of black freedom. For Aretha it is her day of execution.

Aretha's expiration/erasure is linked to her dis-memberment, symbolized through the extraction of her teeth. In fact, Part 3 of *Mutabilities* might be subtitled "Aretha's teeth mythology." Illustrating a slaveowner's rhetoric, a bigoted and self righteous Miss Faith orders the bed-ridden Aretha: "Bid your teeth good bye," as she *appears to extract Aretha's teeth with a large pair of pliers* (46). According to Geis, "To extract Aretha's teeth is to remove her identity, to separate her from the past, just as slaves were forced to surrender their names and families" (51). True, but much more is involved in Aretha's ordeal. Describing the production of this scene, director Liz Diamond recalled: "I wanted Aretha's bed to be just floating in space and I wanted it to be spinning around and her to be wrenched from the bed and I wanted those pliers over her head ... the shape of the pliers felt like it had to be a really a wild hallucinogenic sort of nightmare" (Drukman 70). Replacing the suspended rope, the pliers over Aretha's head signify another lynching scene. Moreover, as Kennedy does in her nightmarish settings in *Funnyhouse*, *Rat's Mass*, and *Owl*, Parks immerses her characters in landscapes that symbolize their terror physically and psychically. Consistent with other dis-memberments of black bodies in *Mutabilities*, teeth have multiple and even contradictory significance. Possibly the leading signifier in *Mutabilities*, teeth profoundly affect the way the black body is represented and erased at the same time, as in a lynching, and the way a dominant white culture has been empowered in the process. Parks's use of teeth in "Open House" adumbrates the dissections/distortions/disintegration of black bodies over time in *Venus*, *The America Play*, *The Death of the Last Black Man*, and *In the Blood*.

Doubtless the most devastating use of teeth as a symbol of lynching/racial suppression occurs in sections B and D when, transported back in time, Aretha waits for new slaves to disembark from a slaver. At first alone on stage, she tries to estimate how many arriving slaves the ship can hold. "Gotta know thuh size exact. Thup. Got people comin. Hole house full. They gonna be kin? ... How many kin I hold. Whole hold full" (42–43).

Dressed like a sadistic nun in the BACA production (Dupuis), Miss Faith declares that, "Six hundred will fit. We will have to pack them tight" (44). In terms of Parks's surrealistic allegory, Aretha must lose her teeth to accommodate these new arrivals. Justifying such heinous action, Miss Faith argues, "The old must willingly shuck off to make way for the new. Much like the snakes new skin suit. The new come in and we gladly make them room. Where would they go if we did not extract" (51). Again, the dis-memberment of the black body is inscribed with terrifying, punitive historical texts. Aretha's teeth are personified as old slaves having to be extracted/extinguished so new ones can "fit in."

In one of Parks's most caustically elastic "Rep & Rev" puns, Aretha refers to the shipload of new slaves as "Hole house full," as if they were kin arriving for a nostalgic homecoming, alluded to in the title of this part of *Mutabilities*, "Open House." Aretha's "hole" or empty mouth might also be radicalized as a womb in which her new family members — the kin — are packed and will be (re)born into slavery in America. In her novel *Getting Mother's Body* (2003), Parks references several polyphonic "holes" in connection with life, death, mothers and babies, family histories, the past and present (Smith, "Words as Crossroads" 37). Parks's multidirectional pun, of course, refers to both a "whole" family and the dreaded "hole" of a slaver. Metonymically, too, Aretha's empty mouth becomes a *hole* to be filled, a grave, signifying a piece of black oral history that has been lost, recoverable only through the history Parks recreates on stage in each performance. Black history is buried deep in the individual and collective subconscious, and Parks must dig through the ravages of memory to find it. But as Elam also argues, "As her teeth are being extracted, Aretha suffers through confused and even contradictory memories" ("Remembering" 15). Tragically, Aretha dis-remembers historical reality, coloring it in ways that are antithetical to the freedom and identity that African Americans sought. Describing the slaves' arrival in familial, nostalgic terms and ways, alongside the gruesome calculations of space and the number of bodies a slaver could hold, she omits the harrowing realities, tortures of slavery. As James Freize points out, "Aretha appears to have swallowed whole the rhetoric that validated slavery" (528). She has internalized her slavery.

Once again, through her "Rep & Rev" routines, Parks maps the black body as a *mine/mindfield* to be blown apart as a systematic expression of white domination and prejudice. Every denial of Aretha's identity in Part 3, her dis-remembering, is physicalized through the extraction of her teeth until one of the children whom she raised cries, "She has no teeth. She is out" (49). From the start of her monologue, Aretha associates teeth with re-membrance and dis-memberment. Complimenting one of the white children, Aretha announces: "You got such nice white teeth, Miss Blanca. Them teeths makes uh smile tuh remember you by" (41). Through Parks's "hallucinogenic" stage business, each of Aretha's teeth thereby becomes "scraps uh graphy for my book" (54), another brilliant Parks malapropism for the bits/pieces of racial history (the graphs both visual and verbal) through which black memory and identity have been splintered. Aretha's "graphy" can be read as her slave's memoir, her family album. Ironically, though, without her teeth, Aretha loses her smile, and once that is gone, so is her personhood, the memory of who she is and was. A toothless Aretha loses her "Me." Later, in Section G, Charles similarly warns her in "Dreamtime": "You let them take out the teeth you're giving up the last of the verifying evidence. All'll be obliterated. All's left will be conjecture.... We won't even know your name. Things will get messy. Chaos. Perverted. People will twist around the facts to suit the truth" (53). In point of fact, Aretha's teeth mythologies dramatize how white memory/pathology twists the facts to suit its truth and how blacks are dis(re)membered, made to disappear, in white society. As Aretha's teeth are extracted, a physicalization of Parks's "Rep & Rev" signifiers, we watch as parts of her are erased before us on stage, leading ultimately to her extinction.

Even in death Aretha will be unidentifiable. Forensically, a dead person's dental record is essential to determine his/her identity. Yet Miss Faith perversely tries to convince Aretha that only by extracting and photographing her teeth can she "be chronicled" (47). "An opened jawed awed will do," she reassures the old black woman. But, ironically, Aretha is excluded from the great white book of memory even as she remembers the slaver's records which are memorialized in Miss Faith's history. As her teeth are extracted, Aretha knows she is like "The woman [who] lay on the sickness bed her gums were moist and bleeding," preparing for the inevitable (46). Like Molly or Chona in Part 1, then, Aretha is at the mercy of white society that has the power to infect, infest, extract body parts, and thereby determine whose life history should be recorded and memorialized. Aretha's dental fate contrasts coincidentally with that of one of the "Foundling fathers," George Washington, whose image is recalled through the centuries by his false teeth. Teeth, then, in *Mutabilities* simultaneously symbolize black identity and the dis(re)membering/disappearance of the black body, another typology of lynching. The lynched black body signaled absence, the denial of personhood, the objectification of exclusion. Extracting Aretha's teeth, Miss Faith envisions the same fate in store for Aretha, stripping the old black woman of the right to her own body, and with it her right to sign/identify herself.

Ironically, Aretha is ordered by the adult Anglor Saxon to "Give us a grin" until Blanca reminds him she is "toothless" (51). A toothy grin/smile was part of a black person's official repertoire in the white world, a gesture of servitude in white visual culture. Teeth become the physical signature — artifact — of her slavery. In this twisted world portrayed through Parks's allegory, a black person's identity, even survival, depended on how she or he was portrayed with regard to their teeth. Pictures of minstrels and famous black faces like Uncle Ben, Aunt Jemima, Buckwheat, or the Kingfish in *Amos 'n' Andy* all display the stereotypical grin expected by white audiences from black characters. "Smiling at work. They like smiles," advises Sergeant Smith's wife in Part 4. But *Mutabilities* savagely parodies the white tradition of picturing blacks as always smiling, grinning, their teeth symbolizing compliance, submission, and (enforced) happiness. In their journey through the Third Kingdom, black characters learn about the savagery of smiling. Recounting the terrors of that sea voyage, Shark-Seer says, "Edible fish are following us. Our flesh is edible to them fish. Smile at them and they smile back," but then adds, "Jump overboard and they gobble you up" (38). As Aretha and her kin learn, smiles do not protect enslaved black characters. Anticipating the arrival of new slaves, the members of her whole family, Aretha announces, "Thump! I was gonna greet em with uh grin" (46). Throughout this section she "smiles, smiles, smiles." But, as we saw, a toothless Aretha, the grinning parent welcoming more children into servitude, symbolizes that she has lost her history and disremembers a skewed version of it. As Shawn-Marie Garrett claims, "Parks's characters always play multiple, self-alienating roles" (6).

In such a context, Parks, paradoxically, also undercuts (pun intended!) white masters with references to their having to show their teeth, to grin for the black history she is writing through the performance of *Imperceptible Mutabilities*. As we saw, Aretha remembers Blanca Saxon by her smile. She exclaims, "Wish I had me some teeths like yours, Miss Blanca. So straight and cleaned. So pretty and—white" (41). Part 3 graphically, satirically, begins with a series of slides showing Aretha with Blanca and Anglor in "an enlargement of smiles" (41). But the snapshot is indicting—smiling white children are pictured with a smiling, always available, black nanny whose trademark of enslavement they adopt. Even a white God is depicted by his teeth—"And the Lord looketh upon her with kind azure eyes and on his face ... lit a toothsome—a toothsome smile" (44). Aretha's last words to her former master are—"Mm gonna remember you grinnin" (54). In terms of her volatile aesthetics of teethology, then, Parks turns the racial tables on the traditions of grinning, attributing the servile gesture not to just slaves but to their masters and their children. Again, Parks repeats white history only to revise, subvert it.

Yet however comical Parks's satire of white America is, Aretha's dis-memberment—the extraction of her teeth—is repeatedly mandated (and justified) by white characters invoking the power of the "book," the undisputed text of empowerment and erasure. The book in *Mutabilities* ranges from being a racially sanitized Bible and slaver's manifest to the codification of repressive race laws to a policy manual from the "Division of Housing and Community Renewal" (45) explaining "the specifics of co-op apartment sales" (49). In point of fact, the book, another one of Parks's floating "Rep & Rev" signifiers, could be any text perpetuating white rule of black bodies. As we saw in Part 1 with Molly at school, the gestalt of the book in *Mutabilities* codifies and enforces the white memory of history, language, and voice even as it dis-members a black world view. "We got differin books" (15), concedes Aretha, talking to the "two Babies" she cared for. But for black characters in *Mutabilities*, white books always record the dark side of the American dream, the horror of the trans–Atlantic slave trade and the African Diaspora it engendered. The book, with its terrifying text, is their doomsday ledger. As Miss Faith cruelly informs Aretha, "The book says you are due for an extraction" (44), but, at the same time, she treacherously offers Aretha encouragement: "Find solace in the book and kiss your teeth goodbye" (44). Functioning as an official with the public housing authority, Charles likewise pontificates: "The books says you are to expire. No option to renew" (45).

Hilariously, but dangerously, Parks reveals the duplicity and self-serving circularity of the white book of history, the epistemology of the dominant rule. Asking Miss Faith "if it says anything about Retha Saxon's master Charles in the book," which would acknowledge Aretha's presence in history, the faithless white woman brusquely retorts: "She is named what her name is. She was given that name by him. The book says your Charles is dead. Sorry. Never to return. Sorry. That is a fact. A fact to accept. The power of the book lies in its contents. Its content are facts" (47). Her circuitous and bigoted reasoning insists that because Charles the master no longer exists, neither does his slave Aretha. She is so dependent on him that only he, and no one else, can bestow personhood on her. Her name, her identity, were given to her by Charles, who is not alive to vouch for or inscribe Aretha as a human being. Her presence depends upon his word and, like Molly, she is undone by the white words excluding her. Aretha's life of service to Charles and his children, therefore, is canceled, dis-remembered, since the book declares he is dead. Instead of reason or comfort, then, Miss Faith's white book relies reflexively on its contents, which, as we saw, are not synonymous with the fact that Aretha has and does exist in Parks's re-membering black history on stage.

Even so, the contents of the book spell dismemberment, disgrace, and the stripping away of Aretha's self, her "splatterment." In fact, when Miss Faith repeats that "Charles is dead. Never to return. Thus says the —," Aretha finishes the sentence with a Parksian pun emphasizing the horrors of dis(re)memberment — "Buchenwald! Buchenwald!" (52). Punning on "buch" and "book," Aretha confuses, and thereby conflates, the written records of cruel slave holders with their modern counterparts who ran the Nazi death camps. Just as the Nazis dismembered their victims, so Aretha is dismembered through the extraction of her teeth and the expiration date stamped on her life. Thanks to a privileged white history book that alienates and erases her, Aretha's life is a projected holocaust of suffering. But an African American script, *Mutabilities* offers a footnote specifying that while 6 million Jews were killed, more than 9 million Africans were forced into slavery (52), intensifying the enormity of the white attack against black bodies. In both cases — Buchenwald and the enslavement of blacks — the justification for such horrors was by and through the book which determined who should be saved and who should perish. Shockingly, Aretha remembers more white history than Miss Faith gives her credit for. This and the other footnotes in *Mutabilities*, along with the glossary of words Parks includes at the beginning of *The America Play and Other Works*, are instances of paratextuality, or those spaces "dismissed by whites as marginal, minor, as inconsequential [but which took] on great importance to African Americans" to resist white texts and to assert their own inscriptions (McCoy 159). In these traditionally unmarginalized spaces, Parks inscribes African American truths otherwise lost, discredited, or denied in the white world. As with smiles, Parks subverts white dichotomies (text is primary; paratext is ancillary) as she re-historicizes black narratives resonating with the horrors of enslavement.

In the fourth and last part of *Mutabilities*, Parks continues to explore the connections between dismembered black bodies and the loss of cultural memory and identity. This section concentrates on Sergeant Smith and his family — a wife, twin daughters and a son — all of whom await his homecoming. Of all parts of *Mutabilities*, this is undoubtedly the most autobiographical. Parks's father was a career army officer — a colonel — whose wife, two daughters, and son longed to see their husband/father who was frequently gone on a military mission. But unlike Parks's highly decorated father, Sergeant Smith is given the foolish job of guarding a rock, which amounts to little more than janitorial duties. "Our commander, the man in charge, likes a clean rock. It's my job to keep this rock clean.... My rock is the cleanest of all rocks in our island home" (61). Earning a military distinction for Sergeant Smith means getting his own desk: "Standin at thuh desk. My desk. Sssgonna be mines, anyhow. Fnot this un then one just like it" (58). But his identity — his "mines" — is invested in a white organization that will eventually dismember him in a rescue that is depicted as mock heroic. Tragically, Sergeant Smith receives his "distinction," his desk, only after he is fragmented, mentally and physically. He "stepped on a mine.... The mine blew his legs off" trying to catch "uh man as he was fallin out thuh sky" (70). As in earlier parts of *Mutabilities*, his *mine* turns into a *minefield*. The pun on *mine*, again and again, harrowingly links any memory of an African American self with traps, explosions, detonations of black bodies.

The Sergeant's disabled body symbolizes his fragmented identity in the world of white power that wants to obliterate his self, and self advancement, and replace it with a lynched (dissected, deformed) black body. As Mel Gussow smartly put it, Sergeant Smith "is all starch and polish, mimicking the white man and debasing himself as he waits for his unknown and perhaps irrelevant 'distinction' to arrive." Like Molly/Mona, Charlene/Chona, and Veronica/Verona, who were transformed into primitives and, even lower, into insects, and Aretha who loses her teeth, when Sergeant Smith loses his legs, he is stripped of a vital part of his identity, his memory. (More than a decade later Parks would write about the psychic problems of returning Vietnam and Iraqi veterans in her "Father Come Home" plays in *365 Days/365 Plays* and in the *Father Come Home* script performed at the Signature Theatre in 2010.) By losing his legs, Sergeant Smith has become the victim of a white ritualistic punishment for being black. As Alisa Solomon contends, "White culture, Western mythology, have externally crippled Sergeant Smith even as he earns his distinction ... in the white man's world" (79). Discarded by the system, he forgets his family, his "mine." "You one of uh mines?" he asks his daughter Muffy (70). Earlier, she questioned her mother, "Duhdun't he know my name? ... Duh don't he know my name" (69, 62). The Sergeant cannot even distinguish a picture of himself from that of his child. "I got pictures. Uh whole wallet full. That's me," he tells his son Duffy, who frighteningly responds, "Nope. That's me. We look uhlike" (69). But the future for the Sergeant's children looks as grim as it does for their father. Mrs. Smith tells her daughter: "Wouldnit uh named you 'Muffy,' but they hadnit invented mines when you came along." The girl replies, "They named mines after me," revealing the explosive horror behind Parks's pun on black identity and the white instrument used to detonate it.

In America, then, *mines* simultaneously refers to black bodies as well as to the weapons/traps that dis(re)member them. Mines fragment memories and displace histories. Accordingly, black memories (*mine/mind*) are judged as insignificant, imperceptible by a white society that sees any attempt to remember black identity/autonomy/community as transgressive. I cannot concur with James Frieze, who claims, "Having been dis-membered by losing his legs, [Sgt. Smith] begins to re-member himself by imposing his way of knowing" (530). On the contrary, a legless Sergeant Smith suggests an impotent, impaired man, a lynching victim. He is oppressed by an official, white book — Army protocols, regulations, orders, awards — with language that diminishes his identity, his dignity. But loss is genetic in the Smith family. Mrs. Smith loses her eyes waiting for/looking for her husband's return. "When did you lose your eyes?" asks the Sergeant (69), who is kept in the dark about his own family's dismemberment. For Parks, a legless father and sightless mother thus symbolize what has happened to *mine*—the black me and family in white America. The father cannot remember his children's faces and the mother cannot see them. These and other lynched black bodies throughout *Mutabilities* reinforce Parks's message that a "mine is a thing that dismembers" (64). Having their *mines/minds* put in jeopardy, the Smith family is caught in some timeless world outside their recollection. Their identity does more than elude them; it jeopardizes them in white punitive America.

The question of identity puzzles the Smith children as well. Earlier in Part 4, Buffy worried that "Thuh wind'll steal her [sister's] clothes and then she'll be naked ... [she] can't be outside and naked people will see her she'll be shamed" (59). Calming her daughter, Mrs. Smith voices one of the most caustic responses to black identity in a white culture: "She kin hide behind her twin. They look just alike.... Nobody'll notice nothing" (59). In white America, blacks are inseparable and invisible. They are not to be identified as individuals; they are unreportable clones of each other, their *mines* are imperceptibly mutable. Recall that Charles informed Aretha that no one will notice when she is gone and her memory is wiped out; her progeny may follow but will not know her. The Smith children's fate, of course, contrasts with Anglor and Blanca Saxon's, Mr. Charles's respectably white offspring, who will continue his legacy of bigotry. In one of the most heinous historical imperceptibilities of all, no one in white America noticed when millions of slaves died in their passage through the Middle Kingdom and their descendents were condemned to devolution in contemporary America. As Sergeant Smith teaches his children, they are not even members of the human race. "We'se slugs. Slugs. Slugs" (71). Slugs have neither legs (like Sergeant Smith) nor separate identities (his daughters, the Biloxi Twins, are inseparable and he and his son look just alike). Not surprisingly, much of the discussion in the Smith household turns to transformations, mutabilities, as in earlier sections of the play. Duffy asks, "Sergeant Smith uh mammal?" (66), because the child recalls that "He said he was uh turtle" (66). But Muffy rejoins that a turtle just "Masqeurade[s] as fish" (67). Through her savage satire, Parks shows us a contemporary black family masquerading as individuals, striving for personhood ("Me") in America. But their *minds/mines* have been dis(re)membered.

As we have seen, Parks repeatedly connects dismembered black bodies with space/time, the ever-shifting coordinates on which identity is plotted in *Mutabilities*. Her early Obie-winning play challenges the imperatives of white history by recreating, and rewriting, black history through performance. History for Parks is as much a physical place as it is a metaphorical one. In *Mutabilities*, she relates an essential part of black history to the geography of entrapment — the slave's journey from Africa across a wide, unforgiving ocean (the Third Kingdom) to an enslaving America. As Shark-Seer and Kin-Seer chant in the "Third Kingdom (reprise)": "My new Self was un 3rd Self made by thuh space in between" (55). But that new black self is diminished, dis-remembered, in the "space in between," whether that is a contemporary classroom, an office, a nineteenth-century slave ship or plantation, or a distant and desolate army post. Stationed in the middle of the ocean, across his Third Kingdom, Sergeant Smith, for instance, cannot see or connect with his family, which always was the slave's nightmare. "Next time your mother takes you to visit the ocean, Buffeena, look very far out over the water and give me a wave. I will waaaave back! You may have to put on your glasses to see me, and I expect that to you I'll look like just a little speck. But if you look very far, you'll see me and if you wave very hard, I will waaaaaaave back!" (61). But his sense of time is colonized; he is caught in the "gaps," as are the black roommates in Part 1 and Aretha in Part 3 of *Mutabilities*. Isolated out in the ocean and stationed in a different time zone from his family, Sergeant Smith shares only four hours with them. "Over here they are un whole day ahead of us. Their time ain't our time" (63). Through time and space he and his family lose their identity, their "mines." Devolving, de-creating, into slugs crawling over an American minefield, they become imperceptible mutabilities.

Works Cited

Bahun-Radunovic, Sanja. "History in Postmodern Theatre: Heiner, Muller, Caryl Churchill, and Suzan-Lori Parks." *Comparative Literature Studies* 45 (November 2008): 446–70.

Brown-Guillory, Elizabeth. "Reconfiguring History: (Re)Membering in Suzan-Lori Parks's Plays." *Southern Women Playwrights: New Essays in Literary History and Criticism*. Edited by Robert L. McDonald and Linda Rohrer Paige. Tuscaloosa: University of Alabama Press, 2002. 183–97.

Cote, David. "Putting on the Dog." *Time Out New York*, July, 12–19, 2001: 61.

Diamond, Liz. "Perceptible Mutabilities in the World Kingdom." *Theater* 24.3 (1993): 86–87.

Dupuis, Sarah. "THEATRE REVIEW: Anything but Imperceptible." *The Tech*, Feb. 17, 2007. http://tech.mit.edu/V127/N4/Imper.html.

Drukman, Steven. "Suzan-Lori Parks and Liz Diamond: Doo-a-diddly-dit-dit: An Interview." *The Drama Review* 39.3 (Fall 1995): 56–75.

Elam, Harry J., Jr. "Remembering Africa, Performing Cultural Memory: Lorraine Hansberry, Suzan-Lori Parks, and Djanet Sears." In *Signatures of the Past: Cultural Memory in Contemporary Anglophone North American Drama*. Edited by Marc Maufort and Carolyn DeWagter. New York: Peter Lang, 2008. 1–16.

Elam, Harry J., and Alice Raynor. "Echoes from the Black (W)hole: An Examination of *The America Play* by Suzan-Lori Parks." In *Performing America: Cultural Nationalism in the American Theatre*. Edited by Jeffrey Mason and Ellen Gainor. Ann Arbor: University of Michigan Press, 1999.

Frank, Haike. "The Instability of Meaning in Suzan-Lori Parks's *The America Play*." *American Drama* 11 (Summer 2002): 4–20.

Frank, Johanna. "Embodied Absence and Theatrical Dismemberment." *Journal of Dramatic Theory and Criticism* 21 (Spring 2007): 161–71.

Frieze, James. "*Imperceptible Mutabilities in the Third Kingdom*: Suzan-Lori Parks and the Shared Struggle to Survive." *Modern Drama* 41 (Winter 1998): 523–32.

Garrett, Shawn-Marie. "Figures, Speech and Form in *Imperceptible Mutabilities in the Third Kingdom*." In *Suzan-Lori Parks: A Casebook*. Edited by Kevin J. Wetmore, Jr., and Alycia Smith-Howard. New York: Routledge, 2007: 1–17.

Geis, Deborah H. *Suzan-Lori Parks*. Ann Arbor: University of Michigan Press, 2008.

Gussow, Mel. "Review/Theatre: Identity and *Imperceptible Mutabilities in the Third Kingdom*." *The New York Times*, Sept. 20, 1989: C24.

Hansen, Liane. "Interview: Writer Suzan-Lori Parks Discusses Favorite Classic Books." National Public Radio's *Weekend Edition Sunday*, June 15, 2003.

Holder, Heidi J. "Strange Legacy: The History Plays of Suzan-Lori Parks." In *Suzan-Lori Parks: A Casebook*. Edited by Kevin J. Wetmore, Jr., and Alycia Smith-Howard. New York: Routledge, 2007. 18–28.

Kolin, Philip C. *Understanding Adrienne Kennedy*. Columbia: University of South Carolina Press, 2005.

Kundera, Milan. "Afterword." *The Book of Laughter and Forgetting*. New York: Harper Perennial, 1993.

Lee, Carol. "O Pioneer!" *Northwestern University Alumni Magazine* (Summer 2008): 33.

McCoy, Beth. "Race and the (Para)Textual Condition." *PMLA* 121 (2006): 154–69.

Metzgar, Bonnie. "Alien Baby." *Public Access/Stagebill* [*In the Blood* program, Public Theater/New York Shakespeare Festival] 6.2 (December 1999): 50, 52, 54, 58.

Ong, Han. "Suzan-Lori Parks." *BOMB* (Spring 1994): 47–50.

Parks, Suzan-Lori. "Elements of Style." In *The America Play and Other Works*. New York: Theatre Communications Group, 1995. 6–18.

———. *Getting Mother's Body*. New York: Random House, 2003.

———. *Imperceptible Mutabilities in the Third Kingdom*. In *The America Play and Other Works*. New York: Theatre Communications Group, 1995.

———. "New Black Math." *Theatre Journal* 57 (December 2005): 576–83.

———. "Possession." In *The America Play and Other Works*. New York: Theatre Communications Group, 1995. 3–5.

———. "Suzan-Lori Parks: Commencement Speech to the Mt. Holyoke College Class of 2001 on May 27, 2001." www.myholyoke.edu/offices/comm/opedloriparks.shtml.

_____. *Venus*. New York: Theatre Communications Group, 1997.
Plumpp, Sterling. "Mississippi Griot." In *Blues: The Story Always Untold*. Chicago: Another Chicago Press, 1989.
_____. "Territory I Explore." *Valley Voices: A Literary Review* 9 (Spring 2009): 85.
Roach, Joseph. "The Great Hole of History: Liturgical Silence in Beckett, Osofisan, and Parks." *South Atlantic Quarterly* 100 (2001): 307–17.
Sellar, Tom. "Making History: Suzan-Lori Parks: The Shape of the Past." *Theatre/Forum* [University of California, San Diego] Summer-Fall 1996: 37–39.
Smith, Wendy. "Words as Crossroads." *Publishers Weekly*, May 12, 2003: 37–38.
Sollers, Werner. *The Adrienne Kennedy Reader*. Minneapolis: University of Minnesota Press, 2001.
Solomon, Alisa. "Signifying on the Signifyin': The Plays of Suzan-Lori Parks." *Yale Theatre* 21, no. 3 (Summer-Fall 1990): 73–80.
Thompson, Debby. "Digging the Fo'-fathers: Suzan-Lori Parks's Histories." In *Contemporary African American Women Playwrights*. Ed. Philip C. Kolin. New York: Routledge, 2007. 167–84.
Wishna, Victor. "Suzan-Lori Parks." In *In Their Company: Portraits of American Playwrights*. New York: Umbrage Editions, 2006. 186–89.
Young, Harvey. "The Black Body as Souvenir in American Lynching." *Theatre Journal* 57 (December 2005): 639–58.

Sampling and Remixing:
Hip Hop and Parks's History Plays

Nicole Hodges Persley

> You can think of sampling as a story you are telling yourself—one made of the world as you hear it, and the theater of sounds that you invoke with those fragments is all one story made of many.—Paul Miller (DJ Spooky)

Suzan-Lori Parks's history plays, *The Death of the Last Black Man in the Whole Entire World* (1990) and *The America Play* (1994), both exhilarate and confound audiences and critics. Using inter-textual references from the past and present of American history and African American life, these plays disrupt linear form and rely heavily on the embodiment of music and sound in performance. In the literary world, the written word and its sound equivalent are comparable to musical beats. These comparisons between music and Parks's dramaturgy have been the focus of much of the spirited dramatic criticism of Parks's history plays.

Mainstream critics and academics have been intrigued by and receptive to Suzan-Lori Parks's writing style since her plays began to be staged in New York in the early 1990s. *The Death of the Last Black Man in the Whole Entire World* was produced at BACA Downtown in Brooklyn, New York, in September 1990 under the direction of Beth A. Schachter. Liz Diamond, Parks's longtime collaborator, directed an interpretation of the play at Yale Repertory Theater in 1992 (Geis). Mel Gussow, in his review of *The Death of the Last Black Man in the Whole Entire World* for *The New York Times,* observes Parks's innovations in form and content to suggest "the writing becomes the spoken equivalent of a musical riff. As intended, the play is a "requiem mass in the jazz esthetic.... *The Death of the Last Black Man* is as recondite as it is elliptical." Gesturing towards Parks's abstract connections between language and jazz music, as well as her disruption of linear narratives, Gussow suggests Parks's writing has a deliberate obscurity, making it difficult to understand for most audiences. David Richards's review of the equally profound *The America Play* observes that Parks's concept of history has a non-traditional meaning which speaks to abstractions of language and music to express representations of African American life. He argues that Parks "represents the absence of black history in a society that has long defined itself by the exploits of a few select white men. *The America Play*, I suspect, wants to communicate how it feels to find yourself in this lost state, with no reliable signposts to point the way out." *The America Play* opened at the Joseph Papp Public Theatre as a co-production of the New York Shakespeare Festival, Yale Repertory Theater and Theater for a New Audience in February 1994.

Often in addressing concepts of repetition and revision through the jazz aperture, previous scholarship on Parks's works have stressed the revisionist aspect of her dramaturgy, focusing on her use of "Rep & Rev" as an act of amending text in order to correct or to improve it in some way. However, Hip Hop may be a more useful lens to examine Parks's dramaturgy. Parks's sampling and remixing of history challenges ideas of any one dominant "center" of history to propose that there is a dialectical relationship between "the one" and "the many," suggested by Meiling Cheng's theory of multicentricity (5). Carol Schafer's recent essay on Parks's dramaturgy, specifically addressing the playwright's manipulation of dramatic form and content, gestures towards the connections I attempt to make here. I offer sampling and remixing in Hip Hop as an act of historical manipulation that allows for multiple perspectives of blackness to circulate at once, overlapping, contradicting and informing one another, over time. Schafer's acknowledgment of Parks's capacity to call into question the "androcentric white European tradition" (182) through such acts of historical manipulation suggests such overlap between the dominant and the marginal.

Sampling in Hip Hop is similar to Parks's circular perspectives and writing of history. In the act of sampling, the DJ borrows part of an existing song, experience from real life, film, existing texts, television, etc., and remixes it with other sounds (manually on turntables, or using digital technologies) to create a new musical narrative. "Digging for beats" in Hip Hop is the practice of DJs searching in music archives (yard sales, record stores, personal collections, etc.) to find beats that can be sampled to *write* blackness in sound, a practice that is akin to strategies of repetition and revision in jazz. Sampling and remixing from a wide array of literary sources such as the works of Adrienne Kennedy and ntozake shange and sonic sources such as jazz music and African oral traditions, Parks remixes textual, sonic and oral sonic samples to articulate blackness in her plays.

Describing her dramaturgical process as "Rep & Rev" ("Elements" 9), Parks makes improvised connections to the *writing* of history. She argues: "The idea of Repetition and Revision is an integral part of the African and African American literary and oral tradition" ("Elements" 10). The playwright continues and improves upon a separate tradition of writing by African American playwrights that identifies sound and oral narratives as integral parts to notions of the literary. Parks's important consideration of the overlap between sonic, oral and written texts are illuminated by using Hip Hop's practice of sampling to read Parks's history plays. Hip Hop DJs and MCs continue improvised practices of repetition and revision of jazz to re-imagine notions of revision, not as acts of correcting or improving existing texts, but as acts of identifying sites for inter-textual overlap, intersection and contradiction that can be used to illuminate new imaginings of black subjectivity. Hip Hop DJs manually mixing vinyl records to produce their narratives in live performance are also similar to Parks's process of creating her plays. Parks lives in music. She is married to Paul Osher, a blues musician. She uses music to help her find the voices of her figures. She composes and plays music (such as *Ray Charles Live!* in 2007) and confesses that she does not write sitting down. By dancing and feeling, her figures come to life through her own body to the page. This may be one of the reasons why Parks does not use parenthetical stage directions. She has lived the parts before she writes them down.

Together *The Last Black Man* and *The America Play* are examples of the abstractions from jazz music that African American writers have used to self-identify within and outside of existing American sonic and literary narratives. However, Parks's works, and her dramaturgical process of creating plays, also finds kinship with Hip Hop DJs who create what Joanna Demers identifies as "lineage" (47) between the past and present of black and non-black music traditions. For Parks, the sonic (of or pertaining to sound) and oral (of, using, or transmitted by speech) are equally important acts of writing of history and equally important facets of historical memory as the literary. The intersection of these texts can be located in both black and non-black spaces and can be manipulated simultaneously to articulate multiple black perspectives. Like iconic Hip Hop music DJs of the 1970s too, such as Afrika Bambaataa and DJ Kool Herc, who sampled from blues, jazz, soul, funk and R&B records, as well as non–African American music sources, Parks scratches back and forth in history in *The Last Black Man* and *The America Play*, making connections between the past and the present to suggest the cyclical nature of history.

In this essay I explore *The Death of the Last Black Man in the Whole Entire World* (1990) and *The America Play* (1994), offering Hip Hop's strategy of sampling and remixing as an aperture to identify what Stuart Hall calls "points of identification or suture, which are made within discourses of history and culture. Not an essence, but a *positioning*" (224) that are reflected in Parks's remixing of representations of blackness in American history. Focusing on the similarity of Parks's dramaturgy to the sampling practices of the Hip Hop DJ, I identify sampled characters and themes that Parks selects from various sources in each play that are used to construct her narratives. My identification of these themes and samples show the relevance of Parks's history plays to Hip Hop and the ways that "Rep & Rev" strategies are replayed in the present discourse of sampling as it relates to Hip Hop music and culture. I focus on Parks's practices of sampling as historical manipulation of black racial stereotypes and the residual effects of slavery and make connections to similar strategies of identity negotiation in Hip Hop music and culture.

The circularity evoked by the practices of the DJ who literally and figuratively spins multiple histories suggests "it becomes imminently possible to replay and change historical events" (Kolin 9). In *The Last Black Man* and *The America Play*, Parks "cracks the mirror of history," as Trudier Harris notes, allowing shattered fragments to be reconstituted into what Harris calls "space for black playwrights that portends even more experimentation" (xvii). For Parks, these cracks are the "breaks" in history. In Hip Hop music, the break is the the part of song in which the music breaks to let the rhythm section play unaccompanied. Parks remixes her version of the past back to the beginning of the break. By remixing experiences of dominant and marginal narratives of blackness, Parks redefines what a "black" play is, was and can potentially become.

Examining the samples that Parks uses to create her figures and the recurring themes in *The Death of the Last Black Man in the Whole Entire World*, we can see kinship with Hip Hop practices of sampling and remixing. The circular overlap of Parks's sense of history and the various sources she uses to construct her representations of blackness suggest a constant state of becoming that implies a circular formation akin to African Griot storytelling and the improvised aesthetic of Hip Hop culture. Like a Hip Hop DJ, Parks requires her audience to "dig" for their own meanings in the samples she uses to remix "new historical events" ("Possession" 2). In *The Last Black Man,* Parks writes sounds of blackness that have a direct connection to the improvised narratives found in Hip Hop music. In an interview with Kevin Wetmore, Parks contends: "Well, I am known for history plays, but actually, the plays were never 'history' plays. Like Faulkner says 'History IS.' So my plays often contain historical figures. But they are all 'now' plays" (133). Parks's placing history in the active voice finds symmetry with the "now" of Hip Hop music. Scholar and DJ Paul Miller (also know as DJ Spooky) argues, "DJing is writing, writing is DJing. Writing is music" (2004).

The Last Black Man is divided into an overture, four panels that are interrupted by a chorus in Panel II, and a final chorus. The musical structure of the play is similar to Hip Hop remixes because of its constant overlap of sound. This musical quality aligns itself with Parks's dramaturgical aim "to create a dramatic text that departs from traditional linear narrative style to look and sound more like a musical score" ("Elements" 9). The repeated lines of the figures that loop throughout the narrative can be read as sonic and textual samples that are similar to the musical loops in Hip Hop remixes that connect the past and the present. Parks's characters, what she calls "figures" ("Elements" 12), are literary beats that Parks digs from the past. *The Last Black Man* begins with each figure calling its own name and gives us an introduction to the sounds from history they represent that will replay over and over throughout the play. By saying their own names, they also enter into the historical record, speaking themselves into existence. By placing these figures in conversation with one another, and surrounding them with new contexts, Parks attempts to fill in the holes of historical narratives. She argues: "The figures come from holes. It's the story that you're told goes 'once upon a time, you weren't here. You weren't here and you didn't do shit.' And it's that, that fabricated absence" (Drukman 67). For Parks, it is this "fabricated absence" that is the (w)hole of history. Sampling from characters, sounds and themes that have shaped the African American past, the play takes place in the present. Parks spins back to the breaks in history in order to show the places of suture and overlap in existing discourse on blackness. As Joseph Schloss argues, "The break beats are points of rupture in their former contexts, points at which the thematic elements of a musical piece are suspended and the underlying rhythms are bought to center stage" (32).

The Last Black Man follows Black Man with Watermelon to his final resting place, the grave. The circular narrative of the play becomes representative of a wake before the funeral where all of the figures' memories of their relationship to the last black man are presented before his burial. The wake offers mourners a chance to say goodbye to their loved one and to gather together for support. Sometimes mourners can actually touch or speak directly to the body. The remixing of the lines from figures Yes and Greens and Black-Eyed Peas Cornbread, "You should write that down and you should hide it under a rock" (102), and Lots of Grease and Lots of Pork, "This is the death of the last black man in the whole entire world" (102), are at the opening of *The Last Black Man* and are repeated by the same figures throughout the play. These repeated sounds anchor the institution of slavery to which all the figures refer. After each figure introduces him/herself in the Overture, we meet Black Woman with Fried Drumstick, who situates us within this overlapping and contradictory place Parks calls the "present":

> Yesterday today next summer tomorrow just uh moment uhgoh in 1317 diededed thuh last black man in the thuh whole entire world. Uh! Oh. Don't be uhlarmed. Do not be afeared. It was painless. Uh painless passin. He falls twenty-three floors to his death [102].

The Black Woman with Fried Drumstick narrates her husband's repeated demise through acts of violence in each panel of the play. Telling us of his fall from a window, "he falls twenty-three floors to his death" (102); his electrocution, "they juiced you some, huh?" (107); and his narrow escape from lynching, "Lightnin comed down zappin trees from thuh sky. You got uhway!" (119), she becomes representative of the "strong black woman" archetype that has been remixed throughout American history, most recently in Hip Hop culture. Parks positions Black Woman with Fried Drumstick as the narrator of story, a wife who is charged with supporting her husband and with being a leader in the community that surrounds her. Parks establishes the "now" of the play, linking the identity of black men to both violent acts and to the women who sustain them. At the end of Panel I and in the opening of Panel II: The First Chorus, Black Man with Watermelon describes his coffin, his final resting place, as a box "6 by 6 by 6" (109). Along the journey we find that Black Man with Watermelon is only capable of contemplating his existence in relationship to violence. His repeated refrain "The black Man moves his hands" (102) is used as a promise of the freedom he will experience in his final death. Many iconic Hip Hop DJs such as Jam Master Jay of Run-DMC and MCs such as Tupac Shakur and Biggie Smalls have died untimely deaths as a result of violence. Black women in Hip Hop who survive slain DJs and rappers are left with the responsibility of keeping the legacy of the artist they loved alive in the popular imagination, similar to the role of Black Woman with Fried Drumstick. As Elam and Rayner suggest, *The Death of the Last Black Man* "relates the story of a husband and wife in crisis" (449). As much as *The Last Black Man* chronicles the recurring consequences of death for African American men, it also gestures towards the impact of violence on black families that continue in Hip Hop culture.

Hip Hop is born out of depressed social conditions of neglected black communities in the United States that continue from slavery. In *The Last Black Man*, the figures Black Man with Watermelon, Black Woman with Fried Drumstick, Lots of Grease and Lots of Pork and Yes and Greens and Black-Eyed Peas Cornbread, Old Man River Jordan and Ham are all references that Parks makes to slave culture and the stereotypes and social myths it produced. The continued circulation of minstrel images of blacks with watermelon and chicken in popular culture that originate from slavery continue to denigrate black subjects in the current moment. Similar remixes of these minstrel images are rearticulated in Hip Hop iconography that both re-inscribes and subverts racial stereotypes.

The narratives of Hip Hop are also rife with intersecting and antagonistic stereotypes that are drawn from slavery. The figure And Bigger and Bigger and Bigger in *The Last Black Man* is a literary sample by Parks from Richard Wright's *Native Son* (1940). Wright's character Bigger Thomas has come to represent quests for self-determination by many African American men in popular culture who attempt to survive the social stereotype of the black "brute" ingrained in the American imagination. James Braxton Peterson suggests many Hip Hop artists share the oppressive environs of the Bigger figure in *Native Son* and represent a continuum of African American expressive culture. He argues that many popular Hip Hop rappers share a similar "cultural, racial, social and economic phenomemon" with the Bigger figure.

And Bigger and Bigger and Bigger's repeated hook in the play, "Will somebody take these straps off uh me please? I would like tuh move my hands" (110), is repeated in both lower case and capitals to suggest volume for the actor. These "straps" can be read as symbolic of various devices used to tie the hands of blacks from lynching to handcuffs. Bigger's line is remixed alternately with the Black Man with Watermelon's refrain, "The black man moves his hands" (101). In Panel I, we learn that one of the ways that Black Man with Watermelon dies is by electrocution. Describing the straps used to hold his hands before execution, he recounts their texture: "Thuh straps they have on me were leathern" (108).

Parks's inclusion of more contemporary forms of violence such as electrocution resonates with the themes of repeated incarceration narrated in Hip Hop music and culture. Many black men see Hip Hop as a space to share stories of violence and incarceration. The contemporary handcuff is to also kin to the rope used to subdue the Black Man with Watermelon. In Panel III, Black Man with Watermelon remembers his fear waiting on the platform: "Platform hitched with horses/steeds. Steeds runned off in left me there swinging. It had begun to rain. Hands behind my back" (118). The Black Man with Watermelon wants to move his hands as an act of freedom that only death can afford him. Parks's practice of naming her figures through acts of literal and figurative "incorporation of the past" ("Elements" 10) is sampled from Adrienne Kennedy in her plays such as *The Owl Answers* and *Funnyhouse of a Negro*. The figures in *The Last Black Man* are a series of generic signifiers. The naming of each figure allows us to locate the site from which they are sampled and to identify particular sounds they use to articulate blackness. Parks repeats samples of dialogue from each figure from panel to panel, allowing them to borrow speeches from one another, or to repeat particular refrains.

Similar to the "hook" in Hip Hop music, the repeated samples of themes and stereotypes incorporated into the figures of Parks's plays are essential elements to the foundation of building a powerful remix of history. The hook is similar to the chorus of a song, which is the part of the song that repeats after each verse is dropped. Many Hip Hop MCs and DJs use similar strategies of sampling to create contemporary links between the physical and psychical violence of slavery and its continued impact on African Americans. A video by rappers Eightball and MJG, "We Started This" (1999), uses a slave metaphor, showing black males being shackled and forced to rap into microphones. Saying something over and over in a rap or DJs continuously looping samples makes links that challenge traditional literary forms of writing. Parks demonstrates the overlap of varying perspectives of blackness as well as the impact historical positioning has on the life chances of African Americans over time.

Parks samples the figure Queen-Then-Pharaoh Hatshepsut from African history. Hatshepsut was the only female pharaoh of ancient Egypt and connects the other figures in the play to their African past. Parks highlights this link between the ancient kings and queens of Africa and the institution of slavery with the repeated lines of Queen-Then-

Pharaoh: "Before the Columbus the worldusta be roun they put uh /d/ on the end of round makin roun*d*. Thusly they set in motion the end" (102). Parks theorizes the "end" as the erasure of black history, a contribution to modernity after colonization of the free world. Parks follows the traditions of W.E.B. Dubois who made references to ancient Egypt in his plays and pageants as an act of challenging dominant perspectives of blacks as inferior subjects. Before Columbus is another literary sample from the book *They Came Before Columbus: The African Presence in Ancient America* (1976) by Ivan Van Sertima. Sertima's narrative speaks to the possibility of Africans in the Americas before its "discovery" by Columbus in 1492. The figure Voice on the THUH TEEV can be read as a nod to both the media and Hip Hop representations that conflate black masculinity with violence. The Voice on the TV identifies the Last Black Man in Panel II as "Gamble Major, the absolute last living Negro man in the whole known entire world" (110). Announcing his death to the world on television, Voice on the TV connects past representations of the black man to the present: "Gamble Major born a slave rose to become a spearhead in the Civil Rights Movement. He was 38 years old. News of Majors death sparked controlled displays of jubilation in all corners of the world" (110). Parks addresses the predatory nature of the media and the criminalization of black men that diminishes their life chances. From civil rights leaders such as Martin Luther King, Jr., to Hip Hop leaders such as Tupac Shakur, the lives of black men have been extinguished before they have reached their potential.

Prunes and Prisms is the only character sampled from a European literary source, James Joyce's *Ulysses*. Elinor Fuchs argues that Joyce borrowed it from Dickens (103), which confirms Parks's capacity to sample from non-black sources to articulate blackness. The figure states her name, Prunes and Prisms, throughout the play and in Panel II explains her repetition: "Say 'prunes and prisms' 40 times each day and youll cure your big lips" (113). Parks addresses the incorporation and disavowal of white relationships to blackness by highlighting the negating effects of slavery on the self-esteem of African Americans. The increased opportunities afforded to blacks with more refined or "European" features speaks to the incorporation of white ideals of beauty by black subjects. These self-effacing images are reconfigured in Hip Hop music as the music industry privileges particular racial and sexual stereotypes of African American men and women to sell music.

When Black Man with Watermelon is laid to rest in the Final Chorus after we have learned of his multiple deaths and their impact on the community and his wife, Yes and Greens and Black-Eyed Peas Cornbread tells us: "You will write it down because if you don't write it down then we will come along and tell the future that we did not exist" (130). Playing with notions of the periphery and "center," Parks allows her figures to overlap, "questioning the very history of History" ("Possession" 5). Parks's figures represent the idea that identities are "increasingly fragmented and fractured; never singular but multiply constructed across different, often intersecting and antagonistic, discourses practices and positions" (Hall 4). By magnifying the relevance of past tragedies and their connections to the present, Parks is able to link new audiences such as the Hip Hop generation, to the atrocities of racial subjugation in American history that are often forgotten by all racial and ethnic groups, including African Americans. Both humor and drama collide within Parks's frames of reference, offering conflicting strategies for her audience to deal with the ways that diverse racial and ethnic groups shape black life and the ways that black people shape the history of non-blacks.

Parks's desire to challenge what counts as American history and identity is presented in the title of *The America Play*. Parks does not name the play the "African American Play" because for her, the experiences of Africans in America are always already tied to notions of American identity. Like her predecessor, Ntozake Shange, Parks uses the body and language as a site to explore historical relationships to blackness and subjugation. Shange's "choreopoem," *for colored girls who considered suicide when the rainbow is enuf*, is an inter-textual performance piece that reflects African American women's journeys of self-definition. Similarly, Parks's *The America Play* explores the physical and psychological subjugation of black men while revealing the impact of their suffering on the lives of black women and their children. Establishing the importance of African Americans in shaping American culture in *The Last Black Man*, Parks continues her inquiry into representations of blackness and African American identity in *The America Play*. The two-act play takes place at the "an exact replica of the Great Hole of History" (159). We follow the Foundling Father, a professional gravedigger turned Lincoln impersonator, and his wife Lucy, a secret keeper for the dead. Their son Brazil is a professional mourner who learned all of his best moves from his father. Like in *The Last Black Man*, the Foundling Father and Lucy alternate positions in narrating the story, with the Foundling Father speaking in Act I and Lucy in Act II. *The Last Black Man* addresses literal acts of violence, lynching, electrocution, etc., against African American men, and their impact on the African American community. *The America Play* focuses on psychological violence, the embodiment of social values attributed to blackness and whiteness, and the "fabricated absence" of blackness in American history.

Act I begins in the replica of the "Great Hole of History," where the Foundling Father, who everyone says looks just like Lincoln, resides. The Foundling Father has created a side business where he re-enacts the assassination of Lincoln at Ford's Theatre for a penny. Parks gives Lincoln an infectious, exaggerated laugh, "Haw Haw Haw Haw" (162), which is remixed through the play as a hook when he is shot by a customer. His patrons fire at the Foundling Father, then race across the stage to shout historic words such as "Death to the tyrants!" that approximate John Wilkes Booth's utterance. Parks samples from *Our American Cousin,* the play Lincoln was watching before his assassination, with lines such as "you sockdologizing man-trap" (160), to authenticate the identification of the Foundling Father with the history of Lincoln's assassination. Within these re-enactments, we hear a long monologue in which we learn about the Foundling Father's entry into this profession, Lincoln, America and its icons. In Act I, the Foundling Father likens himself to "the Greater Man," Lincoln:

> There was once man that was told he bore a strong resemblance to Abraham Lincoln. He was tall and thinly built just like the Great Man. His legs were the longer part just like the Great Mans legs. His hands and feet were large just as the Great Mans were large [160].

The Foundling Father continues to compare his entire body to the "the Greater Man," Lincoln, throughout the play suggesting the psychological impact of whiteness and its social value on the newly emancipated African American slaves and their processes of identity negotiation. The Foundling Father uses white makeup to cover his black skin, collects pieces of hair to create his beards ("he secretly bought the hairs from his barber"[159]), and dresses in "look-alike black frock coats bought on time" (161) to complete his "look" as Lincoln. The Foundling Father has measured his self-worth against the ghost of a white Abraham Lincoln. However, the Foundling Father does reconfigure Lincoln's iconic "looks" by mixing in blond beards. "This is my fancy beard. Yellow. Mr. Lincoln's hair was dark so I don't wear it much" (163). He also uses stick-on warts and various extravagant costumes to make his impersonation a remix of the original Lincoln.

This re-enactment of Lincoln's assassination allows the Foundling Father to embody whiteness and to grapple with the value of his blackness as he dresses up in fragments of the "Greater Man's" appearance. The Foundling Father's repeated line throughout Act I is, "A wink to Mr. Lincoln's pasteboard cutout" (160). This line is repeated in remixed loops such as "A nod to the bust of Mr. Lincoln" (161) and "A wink to the Great Mans cutout. A nod to the Great Mans bust" (172). Parks highlights how gestures coupled with sound have the capacity to reinforce identifications of the body and how they are also acts of writing. By constantly having the Foundling Father wear whiteface and wink and nod to a pasteboard cutout of Lincoln, Parks comments on the role of discourse in constructing identities and the socially constructed nature of value attributed to groups identified by race, gender, ethnicity, and sexuality. Through his imitation of Lincoln, the Foundling Father begins to blur the boundaries between the original works sampled from the Greater Man, and his embodied remix of them as the Lesser Man. The Foundling Father tells us that he first began to construct his identity in relationship to "greatness" when he and Lucy took a trip to visit the Great Hole for their honeymoon. After this trip, the Foundling Father realized that he was called to "greatness": "The hole and its historicity and the part he played in it all gave shape to the life and posterity of the Lesser Known that he could never shake" (162).

In Hip Hop, many artists look to established artists in the industry, or even outside it, to give "shape" to their perspectives of greatness. Joseph Roach's analysis of the Foundling Father observes that his attempt "to emulate, to live up, to become like The Great Man (or even a rank-and-file ancestor) is to move in opposite directions simultaneously while apparently standing still" (309). Roach's connection to the tension between the Foundling Father's being and becoming (Hall 223) highlights the circularity of Parks's dramaturgy and the identity struggles between dominant and marginal discourses. The Foundling Father's remixing of whiteness through his black body in his performance of Lincoln suggests that the value of blackness is always contingent to whiteness. Many urban youth who desire to become Hip Hop DJs or MCs engage in both formal and informal acts of emulation. In order to become great, they seek to imitate those rappers and DJs that have been deemed great by society. More importantly, many Hip Hop artists want to achieve something "greater" than Hip Hop and to be compared to white artists whose works fit under classical, rock, or other "legitimate" music classifications. Some of the greatest Hip Hop albums have been deemed "Hip Hop" by mainstream music critics *because* they incorporate classic music samples, contain collaborations with white artists and/or have songs that have crossed over to mainstream white audiences. To be acknowledged as "greater" through relationships to whiteness is a key theme that circulates in Hip

Hop spoken and sonic narratives. After rehearsing his own physical death in his repeated impersonation of Lincoln, The Foundling Father dies, leaving his sampled fragments of Lincoln's identity behind in the replica of the Great Hole.

Act II encompasses the search of Lucy and Brazil for fragments of the Foundling Father in the replica of the Great Hole. Mother Lucy and son Brazil listen for the Father's voice as they dig for clues from his impersonation act in the earth. It is a musical act that spins dialogue between the mourning mother-wife and digger son that is intercut with sections of echoes. These echoes operate as samples from the Foundling Father's life and are remixed together to re-member him: to suture his various parts back together so that he can be laid to rest. Lucy, searching for sounds that she recognizes as her husband, observes: "Itsalways been important in my line to distinguish. Tuh know the difference. Not like your Fathuh. Your Fathuh became confused. His lonely death and lack of proper burial is our embarrassment. Go on: dig" (175). Lucy and Brazil dig through the Great Hole looking for the truth of the Foundling Father. They interchangeably repeat the refrain, "His lonely death and lack of proper burial is our embarrassment" (179) as they uncover his Lincoln bust, wood box, a bag of pennies, and beards: the props from his life used to sample and remix his identity.

Parks plays the breaks of *The America Play* back to the beginning of the narrative at the end of Act II. Naming each "Echo" of the past by a letter and a description, she mixes familiar beats from the first act with the digging of Lucy and Brazil to replay the fragmented sounds of the Foundling Father back to his family. The refrains B. Echo (183) and D. Echo (187) feature Parks's samples from *Our American Cousin*, the play Lincoln was watching when he was shot: "Uh Hhem. The Death of Lincoln!:—. The watching of the play, the laughter, the smiles of Lincoln and Mary Todd, the slipping of Booth in the presidential box unseen, the freeing of the slaves..." (188). In his death, the Foundling Father is finally able to inhabit the play as the "Greater Man" Lincoln.

In one of the last sonic loops of the play, named "D. Spadework" (189–194), Lucy and Brazil unearth a television set on which appears the face of the Foundling Father in "The Lincoln Act." Lucy reminisces about her husband—"All my good jokes. All my good jokes that fell flat. Thuh way I walked, cause you liked it so much" (194)—as Brazil sits in awe of his father's image. His coffin awaits him as they prepare to put him to rest. As in *The Last Black Man*, the Foundling Father must have a proper burial in order to place him in the hole of history. Lucy asks her husband to perform for their son Brazil. He samples from various famous quotes of Lincoln, locating the places of suture between his life and the life of his greater self: "Uh Hehm. 4 score and & years ago our father—ah you know the rest. Lets see now. Yes. Uh house divided cannot stand! You can fool some thuh people some of the time!" (197). After a gunshot echo, the Foundling Father "slumps in his chair" (198). Lucy and Brazil lay him to rest in his coffin. Brazil has the final speech of the play. Following in the footsteps of his "foefather" (178), he creates his own act, soliciting mourners to observe the great hole: "Note the death wound: thuh great black hole—thuh great black hole in the great head.—And how this great head is bleeding.—Note thuh last words.—And thuh last breaths.—And how the nation mourns." Brazil is left with his father's memory, his mother and the "hole and its historicity" (162).

By sampling and remixing past tragedies in the present, Parks is able to link new audiences to the atrocities of racial subjugation in American history that are often forgotten. The conflicting and intersecting representations of blackness that Parks uses in *The Death of the Last Black Man in the Whole Entire World* and *The America Play* circulate in popular culture today, specifically in Hip Hop. Her concept of time as circular, and thus repetitive, incorporates both the cultural role of the African Griot and the Hip Hop DJ as oral and sonic storytellers. Creating a call and response between characters, sampling and remixing their lines like musical loops, these history plays establish both archive and repertoire of blackness (Taylor). Parks creates a sonic remix of American history that challenges African Americans to define their own positions within and outside dominant discourses in order to shape new imaginings of blackness in the future.

Works Cited

Cheng, Meiling. *In Other Los Angeleses: Multicentric Performance Art*. Berkeley: University of California Press, 2002.
Demers, Joanna. *Sampling as Lineage in Hip-hop*. Diss. Princeton Univerity, 2001.
Drukman, Steven: "Suzan-Lori Parks and Liz Diamond: Doo-a-diddly-dit-dit." *TDR* 39.3 (1995):56–75.
Eightball and MJG. *We Started This*. Universal Records, 1999. Video.
Elam, Harry J., Jr., and Rayner, Alice: "Unfinished Business: Reconfiguring History in Suzan-Lori Parks's 'The Death of the Last Black Man in the Whole Entire World.'" *Theatre Journal* 46.4 (1994):447–462.
Fuchs, Elinor. *The Death of Character: Perspectives on Theater After Modernism*. Bloomington: Indiana University Press, 1996.
Geis, Deborah R. *Suzan-Lori Parks*. Ann Arbor: University of Michigan Press, 2008.
Gussow, Mel. "Review/Theater: Dangers of Becoming Lost in a Culture." *The New York Times*, September 25, 1990.
Hall, Stuart. "Cultural Identity and Diaspora." In *Identity: Community, Culture, Difference*. London: Lawrence & Wishart, 1990: 222–37.
———. "Who needs identity?." In *Questions of Identity*. Thousand Oaks, CA: Sage, 1996. 1–17.
Harris, Trudier. *Reading Contemporary African American Drama: Fragments of History, Fragments of Self*. New York: Peter Lang, 2007.
Kennedy, Adrienne. *Adrienne Kennedy in One Act*. Minneapolis: University of Minnesota Press, 1988.
Kolin, Philip C. "Cultural Memory and Circular Time in Suzan-Lori Parks's *Betting on the Dust Commander*." *Notes on Contemporary Literature* 39 (May 2009): 8–11.
Miller, Paul D. *Rhythm Science*. Cambridge: MIT Press, 2004.
———. *Sound Unbound*. Cambridge: MIT Press, 2008.
Parks, Suzan-Lori. *The America Play and Other Works*. New York: Theatre Communications Group, 1995.
Peterson. James B. "The Hate U Gave (T.H.U.G.): Reflections on the Bigger Figures in Present Day Hip Hop Culture." In *Richard Wright's Native Son*. Ed. Ana María Fraile. New York: Rodopi, 2007.
Richards, David. "Review/Theater; Seeking Bits of Identity in History's Vast Abyss." *The New York Times* (Theatre), March 11, 1994.
Roach, Joseph. "The Great Hole of History: Liturgical Silence in Beckett, Osofisan and Parks." *The South Atlantic Quarterly*, 100: 1, Winter 2001. 307–317.
Schafer, Carol. "Staging a New Literary History: Suzan-Lori Parks's *Venus*, *In the Blood*, and *Fucking A*." *Comparative Drama*, Volume 42, Number 2, Summer 2008. 181-203.
Schloss, Joseph. *Making Beats: The Art of Sample Based Hip Hop*. Middletown, CT: Wesleyan University Press, 2004.
Sertima, Ivan. *They Came Before Columbus: The African Presence in Ancient America*. New York: Random House, 1976.
Shange, Ntozake. *For colored girls who considered suicide when the rainbow is enuf*. New York: Collier Books, 1977.
Taylor, Diana. *The Archive and the Repertoire: Performing Cultural Memory in the Americas*. Durham, NC: Duke University Press, 2003.
Wetmore, Kevin J., Jr. "It's an Oberammergau Thing: An interview with Suzan-Lori Parks." In *Suzan-Lori Parks: A Casebook*. Edited by Kevin J. Wetmore, Jr., and Alycia Smith-Howard. New York: Routledge, 2007. 124–140.

"For the Love of the Venus":
Suzan-Lori Parks, Richard Foreman, and the Premiere of *Venus*

Shawn-Marie Garrett

"What else is love but understanding and rejoicing in the fact that another person lives, acts, and experiences otherwise than we do?"—Friedrich Nietzsche (229)

"I was drawn to her as a subject because of her name, Venus, love, and I write a lot about love in my work."—Suzan-Lori Parks (qtd. in Chaudhuri, 35)

"There are plenty of emotions in my theater, but they are things that result from this rather dry, cerebral operation of the mind, consciously and unconsciously."—Richard Foreman (*Wake Up Mr. Sleepy!*)

The 1996 world premiere production of Suzan-Lori Parks's *Venus* directed by Richard Foreman was a major event in 1990s American theatre. Much anticipated, the production on opening ignited intense interest and debate. So persuasive was this production that, in the many critical and scholarly accounts of *Venus* which have followed, the quite distinct theatrical projects represented by, on the one hand Parks's play, and on the other Foreman's production, have sometimes been conflated, inviting the question: whose work did one really see, and what went unseen? The production and its reception have influenced the status of *Venus* in Parks's oeuvre and the way the play is generally understood suggests the impact of theatrical production on the making of canons of dramatic literature and theatre history as well as the gaps and elisions inherent in these processes. Many in the theatre world (professional and academic) have taken sides in the great Foreman-Parks *Venus* debate. For some, including Parks, Foreman's *Verfremdungseffekt*-laden work, however artistically accomplished, unjustly obscured the play's intentions. For others, Foreman's *Venus* was a directorial triumph wrung from a formally simple work (by comparison with Parks's denser earlier plays) written in a style of little interest, at least initially, to Foreman. Both interpretations are valid: *Venus*'s premiere was a display of both Foreman's and Parks's particular sensibilities, yet was also characterized by a major directorial blind spot with respect to the principal dynamic of this play. That dynamic might as well be called by the same name which Parks herself has used over and over again to describe it: love. As a category for critical analysis, love presents the usual difficulties, yet given its centrality to Parks's oeuvre, particularly *Venus*, it is impossible to overlook.

Few theatrical productions involve *dramatis personae* as compelling as Parks and Foreman, two of the most important theatre-makers of their time who, artistically and personally, have everything and nothing in common, and whose work produced that rare bird: the theatrical event as occasion for complex thinking. Parks's and Foreman's artistic agreements and disagreements shed light on their distinct aims as well as their tiny, shared artistic pond: American formalist theater. *Venus*'s premiere is a story more of fruitful collision than collaboration, whose threads lead in the direction of significant artistic and social questions. What is the relationship of Africana and feminist work to Euro-American varieties of postmodern artistic theory and practice? How do the resistant differences of Africana and feminist art and art-makers make themselves known in collaborative processes characterized by asymmetrical power relations? What, if any, are the special ethical conundrums connected to representing a stereotyped body on stage? What is the function of a director in the production of a new play that is not his own? I do not aim to answer these questions definitively, of course, only to offer up the story of *Venus*'s premiere, a productive collision of seeming-opposites, as a kind of Brechtian *casus* which shows certain dynamics at work. In attempting to integrate the rather un–Brechtian matter of love into this discussion, I am aiming for another fruitful critical collision of seeming-opposites, for love is arguably the most important dynamic in Parks's theatre, and also the most neglected by scholars and critics.

Venus and the Hottentot Venus

Before *Venus*, the most significant productions of Parks's major plays (*Imperceptible Mutabilities in the Third Kingdom*, 1998-9; *The Death of the Last Black Man in the Whole Entire World*, 1992; and *The America Play*, 1994) had all been directed by Liz Diamond, with whom Parks had been closely identified both personally and artistically. The announcement of Parks's new director, chosen by the New York Shakespeare Festival/Public Theater's then–artistic director, George C. Wolfe, came as a surprise not only because of Diamond's absence but also because, as one previewer wrote, "by no means could a collaboration between these two unique minds [Foreman and Parks] be expected (Piurek F8). *Venus*'s production process followed the same model as that of *The America Play* (1994), playing first at the Yale Repertory Theatre in New Haven and then moving to the Public Theater in New York, with the difference that *Venus*'s rehearsals were held not in New Haven but in New York. At the same time, Spike Lee's film *Girl 6* (1996), for which Parks had written the screenplay, opened the week of *Venus*'s New Haven premiere. All of this, together with the pairing of Parks, still relatively unknown except among theatre cognoscenti, and Foreman, an established theatre artist of international stature, drew the interest of periodicals that had never covered Parks before: *BackStage, The Boston Herald, Harper's Bazaar, The Hartford Courant, The New Yorker, Newsday, Theatre Week, TheatreForum,* and *Essence*; and then, in turn, of specialized journals: *Callaloo, Theatre Journal,*

TheatreForum. The marketing of the production, in short, contributed to bolstering Parks's popular and cultural cachet, even among theater scholars.

Then there was the play's sensational subject: the life and death of the nineteenth-century Khoisan woman Saartjie Baartman, whose stage name was the Hottentot Venus. As Parks's play (mixing irony and empathy) shows, Baartman was exhibited as a freak before paying crowds in London, the English provinces, and Paris during the early nineteenth century, and then died in Paris in 1815 at the age of 26. Her corpse was dissected by the French naturalist Georges Cuvier (who appears in *Venus* as the Baron Docteur) in an effort to establish the "Hottentot race" as subhuman; and her genitalia, preserved in formaldehyde, were placed on display in the Musée de l'Homme in Paris. In 1982, Stephen Jay Gould's Marlowesque encounter with the Venus Hottentot's remains in the Musée's labyrinthian "innards" and "back wards" appeared in the journal *Natural History*, with the gravity and suddenness of a primal scene:

> I held the skull of Descartes and of our mutual ancestor, the old man of Cro-Magnon. I also found [Paul] Broca's brain, resting on a shelf and surrounded by other bell jars holding the brains of his illustrious scientific contemporaries — all white and all male. Yet I found the most interesting items on the shelf just above ... a little exhibit that provided an immediate and chilling insight into nineteenth-century *mentalité* and the history of racism: in three smaller jars, I saw the dissected genitalia of three Third-World women. I found no brains of women ... nor any male genitalia.... The three jars are labeled *une négresse, une péruvienne*, and *la Vénus Hottentotte* [20].

Gould was not the first to rediscover Baartman — she had also appeared in Richard D. Altick's *The Shows of London* in 1978 — but wider interest followed hard upon Gould's publication: Baartman's story subsequently appeared in the pages of *Critical Inquiry* and the *Australian Journal of Anthropology* (Brantlinger, Wiss). In December of 1995, South Africa's Griqua National Congress (whose members, like Baartman, mostly descend from marginalized Khoisan peoples) intensified its pressure on Nelson Mandela and South African legislators to secure the return of Baartman's remains from France. By the time the remains were repatriated in 2002, a process detailed by Sara L. Warner and Lydie Moudelino (among others), Baartman had morphed into a transnational postcolonial icon.

Baartman was not the first "real" historical figure to be resurrected on Parks's stage: First came "Queen-Then-Pharaoh Hatshepsut" in *The Death of the Last Black Man* in 1992. But Baartman's relative recency electrified the Frankenstein dilemmas that haunt all of Parks's history plays, which seek not merely to represent but performatively to "re-member" or reconstitute in the present an unknown past through the mechanisms of what Parks calls "the special strange relationship between theater and real-life" (1995, 4). Moreover, Baartman is not just another of Africa's many millions gone; for many South Africans, she is, in the words of one, "a metaphor for what happened to this country" (Duke A2). Baartman's death is Parks's starting point in *Venus*, and the play's most repeated refrain is "The Venus Hottentot iz dead." Parks perhaps anticipated that *Venus*'s audiences, as they learned her story over the course of the performance, would need reminding on this point, for of all of the stage figures Parks has written before and since, Baartman is the least likely to stay dead any time soon.

Baartman's story would appear to lend itself most readily to dramatic adaptation as a pitiable tragedy, an object lesson in the horrors and perversions of colonialism, and Parks doubtless recognized that many would expect *Venus* to be such a play. It is and is not. Parks's Venus is, discomfitingly for the audience, ogled, poked, and prodded again onstage, her exhibiton is reenacted, her posthumous violation is repeatedly referenced, and substantial sections of Cuvier's grim autopsy report are delivered as a lecture by Parks's Cuvier-figure, the Baron Docteur. Yet this lecture (set "in the anatomical theatre of Tübingen") is delivered during the play's intermission, outside the boundaries of the performance proper — it falls between the cracks — and the spectators, whom the lecture in effect casts as the Baron's scientific colleagues, are encouraged to walk out of the auditorium. "If you need *relief/* please take yourselves uh breather in thuh lobby," the Baron Docteur intones, even as he warns, "My voice will surely carry beyond these walls" (91–2).

This strategy of Parks's hardly lets the audience off the hook. On the contrary, it anticipates and satirizes the impulse to flee, putting the spectator in a double-bind. Neither staying nor going, the play implies, absolves anyone of the sin of complicity, a word ubiquitous in *Venus* criticism (Larson 203): complicity in voyeurism, in exploitation, in theatricality. As Glenda R. Carpio has written, the play thus effects a chiastic inversion and reversal of the interpellation "Look, a Negro!" critiqued by Frantz Fanon, recasting it as "Look, Colonizers!" (226). What the play's harshest critic, Jean Young, has called, in *African American Review*, Parks's "re-commodification and re-objectification of Saartjie Baartman" is actually committed to varying degrees by all versions of the story (even Gould applauds Cuvier's "elegant" prose) and, in a larger sense, by modernity, by history, in which we all continue to play a participatory role. Certainly nothing retold in the theatre can remain innocent of objectification and commodification: by its very nature, Parks's chosen medium, to paraphrase Brecht, "theatres" Baartman down. Parks invites critical judgment of this process by elaborately and hyperbolically calling attention to it throughout the play.

Venus does, however, test the boundaries of taste. Parks's heroine is a third-wave feminist, entrepreneurial, gold-digging sexpot who, just before her downfall, fantasizes about debating "the Negro question" with Napoleon and having her "big buttocks" perfumed and sprinkled with gold dust. History dictates she must end up a victim, but while still alive on Parks's stage she aims to oppress and impress: "Servant girl! Do this and that! / When Im Mistress I'll be a tough cookie. / I'll rule the house with an iron fist and have the most fabulous parties" (135). This Venus is "reaching for a new world" (Sellar 1999); like the Europeans who hold her in their clutches, she aims to colonize. She becomes the Baron Docteur's lover ("Do I have a choice?" she asks, in a moment that stands out in high relief) and admits that while he is "not thuh most thrilling lay" she's ever had, "his gold makes up the difference" (135). In Parks's version of the story, the love and theft are mutual.

"Most of it's fabricated," Parks admits of *Venus*. "It's questioning the history of history. The play doesn't just swallow the story whole and regurgitate it onto the stage. It embraces the unrecorded truth" (Sellar, "Making History" 37). These "truths" of Parks's invention — Baartman as a diva, Baartman as Cuvier's mistress, Baartman as a co-creator of her destiny — move the play beyond politics, beyond morality, beyond good and evil. They ask the spectator to come to know the dramatic character as the playwright has come to know her: through love, the kind of love that rejoices in Baartman's ultimate unknowability and difference, and grants her powers and rights as a resurrected figure in a stage drama which she couldn't exercise as a social actor in "real" life. Parks also grants her Venus shared authorship, dedicating the play to the unknown reader "with Love" from (among others) "Saartjie Baartman" (n.p.). Baartman's imperative at the end of the play—"*Kiss* me *Kiss* me *Kiss* me *Kiss*" (162)—can therefore be understood not so much as the desperate plea of a victim of history, but as a gauntlet thrown down before the audience by "Loves corpse," history's revenant. Parks grants her Venus the power to ogle and harass us back.

The Genius and the Girl-Genius

Knowing Richard Foreman's Ontological-Hysteric theater, founded by the director in 1968 in the East Village in New York City from his own "singular and essential impulse to stage the static tension of interpersonal relations in space" (Ontological-Hysteric Theater), one would hardly expect to find the director at any point in his career shepherding an episodic, ironic, yet deeply felt historical drama about an African colonial martyr-cum-feminist-icon. In the years before and since *Venus*, Foreman has written, directed, designed, and produced over fifty of his own intensely philosophical closet dramas for a loyal audience of fellow artists and aficionados. In its discursive structures and in its making, Foreman's theater is a solitary, bookish, introspective affair. The director has written of the influence of the theories of Jacques Lacan, Roland Barthes, and other postmodern theorists on his work, which "frustrates habitual ways of seeing, and by so doing, frees the impulse from the objects in our culture to which it is invariably linked." "Character, empathy, [and] narrative" are "straightjackets" which Foreman unmakes through a thoroughgoing integration at every step of the art-making process of literary, performative, auditory, and visual *Verfremdungseffekte*, which place the actor's body "in a state of tension" or in "positions that suggest a degree of relaxation inappropriate to the situation" (40). Alternately torqued and limp, estranged from any ostensible textual meaning (which is generally obscure regardless), actors in Foreman's theater are nothing more and nothing less than elements of the director's aggressively overdetermined *mise-en-scènes*. For Foreman, "character" (the term Foreman uses, though surely Aristotle would not approve) is a pattern of volatile, evanescent, unconscious impulses, alternately hooked and unhooked to ever-shifting objects of desire.

The empathetic identification of spectator with actor is a phenomenon which Foreman, like Bertolt Brecht, constitutionally loathes. He battles it with a juggernaut of interference: abrasive buzzers and bells, disembodied voiceovers, sound loops, hurdy-gurdy carnival music, lurching action, strings running the width of the playing space to break up the visual field and keep the spectator off-balance (all deployed in *Venus*). Foreman's plays are set in a dark Kabalistic chamber of the director's own mind, which may vary in its idiosyncratic details (fuzzy orb here, chicken headdress there) but is invariably overstuffed with the handmade souvenirs of his many journeys on the royal road to and from the unconscious. In *Venus*, these souvenirs included such typical Foremanesque scenic elements as: outsized dunce caps, semiotic pointers, candy-striped flats and floors, ladders, and, notably, placards, hanging signs and mammoth rolling set-pieces bordered with inscriptions of Parks's *dramatis personae*. ["There was nothing but my stuff on stage. It was my production. I certainly can't deny that" ("Remarks on Parks").] As Harry J. Elam, Jr., and Alice Rayner have observed, Foreman's elaborate *mise* visually entrapped the title character within the words of Parks's text: "The 'real' Baartman had fallen between the cracks in textual representation, yet the borders of text in the production contained and identified her" (273). In place of the "real" Baartman stood the actor playing Parks's version of her (Adina Porter), whose bodily presence could not, however, entirely be contained.

Foreman's theatre is hardly transparent, but the director himself is bracingly forthright about the theoretical bases of his theatre, his aims, artistic preferences, and ways of working. Parks, on the other hand, is deliberately ambiguous. She has repeatedly said that all of her writing springs from a question — Who am I? — and *The America Play* and *Venus* in particular, which dramatize the vagaries of performance as a means of making history, invite critical slippage between drama and biography. Before *Venus*, Parks spent eight years as a playwright immersed in New York–area experimental and academic theatres; she spent six of those years writing about sideshow freaks. Her Venus is a particularly poignant figure, heavy with history, a source of horror and fascination for the greasiest of citizens: the mob and academic naturalists. Yet Parks's character is also a self-conscious commodity whose self-fashionings spring from her dynamic, dangerous performances. The same is true of two other figures in Parks's *oeuvre*, both produced in the years she was working on *Venus*: the title character from *Girl 6*, Parks's screenplay for Spike Lee about a phone-sex performer (Parks once plied Girl 6's trade); and Josephine Baker, star of Parks's essay, "The Rear End Exists."

Parks has signaled her approval of the critic Stuart Klawans's interpretation of the character of Girl 6, who, Klawans writes,

> does well as a phone sex performer because she can turn herself into whatever the customers desire. She takes an actress's pride in her malleability; she profits by it. She cooperates with a world that wants her to be a cipher, and relaxes into the pleasure of cooperating, and begins to go a little mad [35].

Of Baker, Parks writes admiringly of how she "cleaved herself in two: *J'ai deux amours* was her theme song. She realized that there are two ways to couple a tattered past with a spangled present — by evolution or mitosis — and she chose mitosis" (10–11). Again and again, Parks, too, has chosen mitosis, and at the time of *Venus* was in the midst of one such transformation: from, in Foreman's assessment, "wild, experimental artist" to "more commercially acceptable artist" ("Remarks on Parks"). *Venus* stands somehow as both symptom and cause of what Foreman and many in academic theatre (including, for example, many of the drama faculty at Parks's production house, Yale) saw as Parks's artistic devolution in *Venus*.

Conscious and continuous mitosis, identity-based anti-politics, is a crucial strategy Parks employs to resist the discourses of knowledge and power that circulate around her, embracing and constricting her simultaneously. When pressed in interviews from the early 1990s, particularly when speaking to a white interviewer, Parks would connect the dense, allusive dramatic poetry of her early plays to her estranging experience as a junior high school student in Germany. In Germany, Parks told John Heilpern in 1993, "I wasn't a black person, strictly speaking. I was an American who didn't speak the language. I was a foreigner" (174). Later, Parks remembered being black in Germany in a 1996 interview with the African-American dramaturg Shelby Jiggetts, in which she connected the estrangement of looking and watching in *Venus* to her own experiences as a black woman (313).

In 1994, Parks insisted to a white male critic from *The New York Times* that she "never wanted to be a spokesperson for the race" (Richards C3) and she has frequently railed against being pigeonholed as a woman writer of color:

> It's why there are "slots" for certain kinds of plays in every season. Who believes this kind of thinking is going to sell tickets? All it does is limit the theater, and underestimate the audience, in every possible way. If you get boxed in, then you start thinking of yourself as boxed in and saying, "Hey, you gotta represent! You gotta talk about the issues!" I'm not somebody who's battling issues [Parks, personal interview, March 29, 2000].

Here we catch a glimpse of Parks the downtown New York theater person, who was much in evidence in the years before *Venus*. In 1995, in a style that recalls her early mentor Mac Wellman, Parks writes, "I'm hoping to form a sort of bulwark against an insidious, tame-looking, schmaltz laden mode of expression that threatens to cover us all, like Vesuvius, in our sleep" (6). Seven years later, in a quite different vein, Parks defended herself against charges by "certain members of the experimental theater community" that she had "betrayed [her] roots":

> Working with Harpo, Oprah Winfrey's company, to adapt *Paradise* for ABC, is me being experimental, going into areas I haven't gone into before. Some people said, "Ooh, you're writing a musical for Disney. Sellout!" To me, working with a corporation like Disney, being a woman and writing something called *Hoopz* about basketball guys is a great challenge.... There's not just one way to be experimental [37].

Parks's contradictions, her slipperiness, her insistence on playing the field, and the diversity of her dramatic subjects and forms refute categorizations of her as, for example, "a black urban woman who writes about black experience" (Malkin 156) or a member of "the Tribe of Woman" (Moore 341). Over and over again, she has successfully changed the joke and slipped the yoke.

"At the beginning, I think a lot of us saw that Suzan-Lori Parks, for all of her admirable qualities, was going to be a cult favorite," *New York Times* theater critic Ben Brantley has said (*Stage on Screen*). Predictably, as soon as Parks found a modicum of success with *Venus* in 1996 (and then more than a modicum with *Topdog/Underdog* in 2001) many in the academy and in the experimental theater lamented her apparent surrender to mainstream audiences' demand for the recognizable. After *Topdog/Underdog*, she was criticized in the *Village Voice* by her fellow playwright and early champion Mac Wellman for "distanc[ing] herself cleanly and completely from her former associates downtown" and thereby "follow[ing] the straight-arrow and time-honored road of improvement (and career)." Remaining a cult favorite constitutes an ethics, even a kind of heroism, for many in the hypermarginalized experimental American theater. Parks, like her Venus, has always been more interested in "construct[ing] a mint" (20).

For the Love of the Venus

In 1995, the year before he directed *Venus*, Foreman received a MacArthur "Genius" award. (Parks would receive her own in 2001.) In rehearsals, Parks generally went along with Foreman's choices but would sometimes tease Foreman, repeatedly answering his questions with the phrase, "I don't know, you're the genius" (Sellar, "Making History" 1996). Parks is in the business of using language strategically (her appearances in the 2002 PBS *Stage on Screen* documentary *The Topdog Diaries* are a master class in the Performance of Suzan-Lori Parks), and this is a characteristic joke-with-an-edge, a joke about power. Parks was in a new situation, working for the first time with a male director/designer/playwright, who had come bearing his own fully developed, acclaimed aesthetic. Foreman had moreover been recommended by Parks's newly acquired mentor, Wolfe, who held the future of her New York premieres in his hands. Like her title character, Parks too was reaching for new worlds, forming new alliances, and consequently sacrificing some degree of creative autonomy at the time of *Venus*'s production. Once again, one is reminded of her character's question: "Do I have a choice?"

"I hate seeing people onstage reaching across the footlights, asking for love," Foreman has written. "The results are performances that try to make the audience 'love' what they see onstage in empathetic response to the love the actors pour forth over the footlights" (38–9). Why Foreman, four years after publishing these words, would agree to direct a play the author would repeatedly describe as, quite simply, "about love" remains a mystery ("Venus to Premiere"). His reasons were not purely economic. If dramatic empathy and audience accessibility are anathema to Foreman, it is partly because unpopularity is a luxury he can afford. "I've made no secret of the fact that I couldn't have all this without the [financial] support of my parents," he said at the time of *Venus*'s premiere. "I always knew I wouldn't starve" (Arnott 25). Social class is another difference between Foreman and Parks.

Whatever the reasons, in 1996 Foreman tackled *Venus*— a play relatively straightforward in meaning and form with respect to his own drama, not necessarily amenable to his tastes, and unlike anything he had previously or has since produced. He made no secret of his reservations. "To be honest," he said at the time,

> I don't go to the theater. But I had heard about [Parks] and had read one interview with her where she credited me as one of her biggest influences.... The first time I read through the script, it bothered me. I wasn't really sure that the play's particular language came from a place that I'm usually interested in. But when I read it again, I realized there was much more there" [Piurek F8].

The remark signals the director's high-modernist disdain for conventional forms of theatricality as well as his indifference to collaboration. It also signals where he and Parks found common ground, whatever their interpretive differences: in and between the lines of Parks's weird, profane text.

Throughout the process, Foreman was unhappy with the ongoing interventions of the producer, George C. Wolfe, who wanted the play to be accessible to Public Theater audiences. As far as Foreman knew, so was Parks: "We were sort of in league against George, who was the 'commercial' producer" ("Remarks on Parks"). Yet Parks had worked closely with Wolfe for two years on revising *Venus* and had been unusually amenable, by comparison with her earlier plays, to suggestions for cuts and other changes from both Wolfe and Foreman. Successive drafts of *Venus* drafts show that these changes steadily moved the play away from the abstract realm of Parks's earlier drama towards more familiar, empathy-generating modes of dramatic storytelling and character construction.

Unaccustomed to collaboration, Foreman generally does not work with dramaturgs or playwrights or with sound, lighting, or set designers, having learned over the years "that it's easier to do these things myself" (Piurek F8). Nevertheless, Parks attended rehearsals and became close with the cast. In the press surrounding the production, Parks was ambivalent yet circumspect: "It's so hard doing a co-production. You have to work intimately on so many aspects. You try to stay flexible, try to think of how everybody loves the play and wants it to be successful" (Arnott 25). Yet she wondered in light of Foreman's stylized, estranged, idiosyncratic staging whether audiences would "think it's a play about crazy people" (Arnott 21). How did Foreman's "very strong, very specific visual sense" jibe with Parks's vision? "It's like being a dead playwright," replied Parks, who has produced perhaps the most exhaustive account of the varieties of social death in the history of the American theater (Sellar 1997, 37).

In Foreman's production of *Venus*, a red light, suspended over the stage, pulsated throughout the performance. "I haven't asked [Foreman] why it's there," Parks said. "You could say it's the heart of Venus that beats forever. It's love" (Shewey 5). This may have been a critical intervention on Parks's part: the production was many things—spectacular, bold, busy, stylized, awkward, uncomfortable, funny—but suffused with love, it was not. If any character was the object of the director's empathetic identification, it was not Venus but her lover, the Baron Docteur. Indeed, Foreman (and in retrospect, perhaps this could have been predicted) directed the play from the point of view of the Baron Docteur, that is, in a sense, from his own point of view, as he recognized:

> I had Peter Francis James playing the doctor as a sort of bumbling, shy guy, who was falling over things.... He had these little glasses, and was crumpling paper nervously in his fists.... I identified him with myself perhaps, this bumbling intellectual who does these strange things ["Remarks on Parks"].

Parks disagreed with this aspect of Foreman's interpretation. Between the New Haven and New York runs of *Venus*, Wolfe and Parks persuaded Foreman to change the characterization of the Baron Docteur from (as Foreman tells it) a "wormy little schlep" to "a distinguished English gentleman of that period who was a serious man of medicine, a little disturbed by his feelings for the Hottentot Venus but nevertheless a man of culture and determination" ("Remarks on Parks"). Agreeing to this change was Foreman's biggest regret about the production: "If I had to do it again today I would try to have the courage to make it stranger than it was. Maybe people thought it was strange, but I think it should have been even stranger" ("Remarks on Parks"). Arguably, however, the play, particularly in its operations on the complicit spectator in performance, invites the opposite interpretation: far from strange, the story of the Hottentot Venus, beloved black icon brought down by love and atomized after death, is all too familiar.

Parks also disputed the notion that the love of the Baron Docteur for Venus in her play is merely prurient or laughable. This requires us to take seriously the possibility of the Hottentot Venus's erotic appeal (which every historical source including Cuvier's autopsy report attests to) and suggests that, irrespective her spectators' capacity for nervous mockery, Baartman may have possessed — or at least that Parks's Venus character should possess — sexual presence and power in performance:

> *Venus* was more straightforward than Richard made it. He was not comfortable with the play's unseemly aspects. It is an erotic play.... The image of a little boy peeking was not the essence of Venus' draw. It was a sexual draw, it was about getting turned on [Parks, personal interview, 1999].

Whatever their disagreements, Parks and Foreman agreed immediately and unequivocally to cast Adina Porter in the role of Venus, and as every account of Foreman's production has testified, Porter was a magnetic presence, cutting through the manic stage business around her to confront the audience in ways not easily assimilated to the limits of expository prose. Part of this power was connected to the title character's repeated acts of posing which, as Elam and Rayner observe, turn the play "into a test *of* the audience, not *for* the audience" (278). In *Venus*'s economy of gazes, the title character's onstage and offstage audiences can look in only one direction, towards her, but Venus directs her gaze at both groups. Hers is an active *eros*, which both demands and accepts the audience's love.

Conclusion

"Love" is a word Parks has used incessantly, even excessively, when discussing *Venus*. In word and action, love is also ubiquitous in the play, as ubiquitous as death. A great deal of criticism and scholarship has ably parsed the play in terms of its politics, yet very little has been said regarding the dynamics of love in *Venus*, and what Parks means when she says, as she has repeatedly done, that the play is about love. A possible explanation for this critical blind spot is that most who wrote about *Venus* did so in the wake of viewing Foreman's production which, though spectacular, was largely devoid of empathy and feeling — indeed, which was actively constructed so as to short-circuit these channels of engagement.

As a corrective, in 1998 at the Wilma Theatre in Philadelphia, Parks directed her own, simpler version of *Venus*. A staged reading with four actors, each of whom read one of the Roles, one of the Chorus Members, and one of the members of the cast of the play-within-the-play, "For the Love of the Venus," Parks's staging, in its simplicity, actively sought the audience's erotic and emotional engagement with the title character. It also portrayed the affair between Venus and the Baron Docteur as fatally flawed yet grounded in genuine feeling and mutual attraction rather than, or at least in addition to, prurient curiosity on the part of the male character. Parks's reading, in short, put the love back in the Venus.

Works Cited

Arnott, Christopher. "Venus Envy." *New Haven Advocate*, March 21–27, 1996: 20–27.
Brantlinger, Patrick. "Victorians and Africans." *Critical Inquiry* 12 (1985): 166–203.
Carpio, Glenda R. *Laughing Fit to Kill: Black Humor in the Fictions of Slavery*. New York: Oxford University Press, 2008.

Chaudhuri, Una. "For Posterior's Sake." Interview with Suzan-Lori Parks. *Public Access* (stagebill). May 1996: 34–6.
Duke, Lynne. "To Whom These Bones, These Bones of History?" *International Herald Tribune*, February 9, 1996: A2.
Elam, Harry J., Jr., and Alice Rayner. "Body Parts: Between Story and Spectacle in *Venus* by Suzan-Lori Parks." *Staging Resistance: Essays on Political Theater*. Eds. Jeanne M. Colleran and Jenny Spencer, Ann Arbor, MI: Michigan University Press. 265–282.
Foreman, Richard. *Unbalancing Acts: Foundations for a Theater*. New York: Pantheon, 1992.
Gould, Stephen J. "The Hottentot Venus." *Natural History* 91.10 (1982): 20–27.
Heilpern, John. "Voices from the Edge." *Vogue*, November 1993: 174.
Jiggetts, Shelby. "Interview with Suzan-Lori Parks." *Callaloo* 19.2 (1996): 309–317.
Klawans, Stuart. Rev. of Girl 6. *The Nation*, April 29, 1996: 35.
Larson, Jennifer. "'With Deliberate Calculation': Money, Sex, and the Black Playwright in Suzan-Lori Parks's *Venus*." *Reading Contemporary African American Drama: Fragments of History, Fragments of Self*. Ed. Trudier Harris. New York: Peter Lang, 2007. 203–217.
Malkin, Jeanette. *Memory Theater and Postmodern Drama*. Ann Arbor, MI: University of Michigan Press, 1999.
Moore, Opal J. "Enter the Tribe of Woman." *Callaloo* 19.2 (1996): 340–47.
Moudelino, Lydie. "Returning Remains: Saartjie Baartman, or 'The Hottentot Venus' as Transnational Postcolonial Icon." *Forum for Modern Language Studies* 45 (April 2009): 200–212. *Oxford Journals—NERL*. Web. September 10, 2009.
Munk, Erika. "Is Playwright Suzan-Lori Parks the Voice of the Future?" *Washington Post*. February 28, 1993: G3.
Nietzsche, Friedrich. *Human, All Too Human: A Book for Free Spirits*. Trans. R. J. Hollingdale. Cambridge: Cambridge University Press, 1986, 1996.
Ontological-Hysteric Theater. Richard Foreman. 2009. Web. October 12, 2009 <http://www.ontological.com/INFO/index.html>.
Parks, Suzan-Lori. Personal interview. May 30, 1999.
_____. Personal interview. March 29, 2000.
_____. "Possession." *The America Play and Other Works*. New York: Theatre Communications Group, 1995. 3–5.
_____. "The Rear End Exists." *Grand Street* 55 (1996): 10–11.
_____. *Venus*. New York: Theatre Communications Group, 1997.
Piurek, Ryan. "Director Plots Course of Venus at Yale." *New Haven Register*, March 17, 1996: F8.
"Remarks on Parks: A Symposium on the Work of Suzan-Lori Parks, Part II: Directors." *Hotreview.org*. 2004. Web. October 15, 2006 <http://www.hotreview.org/articles/remarksparks2.htm>.
Richards, David. "Seeking Bits of Identity in History's Vast Abyss." *New York Times*. March 11, 1994: C3.
Sellar, Tom. "Making History: An Interview with Suzan-Lori Parks." *TheatreForum* 9 (1996): 37–9.
_____. Personal communication. April 1996.
_____. Unpublished personal interview with Suzan-Lori Parks. January 5, 1999. Transcript.
Shewey, Don. "An Eccentric Ringmaster Creates His Own Circus." *New York Times*, April 14, 1996: sec. 2, 5.
Smith, Wendy. "Words as Crossroads." *Publishers Weekly* 250.19 (2003): 37.
Stage on Screen: The Topdog Diaries. Dir. Oren Jacoby. New York: PBS/WNET. Videocassette.
Venus. By Suzan-Lori Parks. Dir. Richard Foreman. Perf. Adina Porter, Peter Francis James. Yale Repertory Theatre, New Haven, CT. April 1996 (several viewings). Performance.
_____. By Suzan-Lori Parks. Dir. Richard Foreman. Perf. Adina Porter, Peter Francis James. Martinson Theater, New York Shakespeare Festival/Public Theater. Theater on Film and Tape Archive, New York Public Library. Videocassette.
_____. By Suzan-Lori Parks. Dir. Suzan-Lori Parks. Wilma Theater, Philadelphia, PA. March 1989. Performance.
"Venus to Premiere at Yale Rep." *Yale Bulletin and Calendar*. March 4–18, 1996: 3.
Wake Up Mr. Sleepy! Your Unconscious Mind Is Dead! December 17, 2006. Web. November 20, 2009. <http://wakeupmrsleepy.blogspot.com/>.
Warner, Sara L. "Suzan-Lori Parks's Drama of Disinterment." *Theatre Journal* 60.2 (May 2008): 181–199.

Weaver, Teresa K. "Novelist Pens a Black Spin on Faulker." *Atlanta Journal-Constitution*, June 6, 2003: E1. *LexisNexis*. Web. August 15, 2003.
Wellman, Mac. "Up the Downtown Staircase." Letter. *Village Voice*, August 22, 2001. Web. August 30, 2001. <http://www.villagevoice.com/2001-08-21/specials/letters>.
Wiss, Rosemary. "Lipreading: Remembering Saartjie Baartman." *Australian Journal of Anthropology* 5.1–2 (1994): 11–41.
Young, Jean. "The Re-Objectification and Re-Commodification of Saartjie Baartman in Suzan-Lori Parks's *Venus*." *African American Review* 31.4 (1997): 699–708.

"A Full Refund Aint Enough": Money in Suzan-Lori Parks's Red Letter Plays

Jon Dietrick

Suzan-Lori Parks's play *In the Blood* premiered at the Papp Public Theater in New York in November 1999, directed by David Esbjornson. Critics familiar with Parks's oeuvre saw the play as somewhat of a departure from her earlier work in its move toward realism, or at the very least in its interesting blend of realism and self-conscious theatricality. Vincent Canby, for instance, noted that the world of the play is "exotic" but "never for a moment does it seem to be unreal or removed" (7), and David Krasner pointed out that while the play does make use of "nonrealistic devices," it differs from earlier plays by Parks in its use of "realistic settings and psychological characterizations" (565). *Fucking A* opened in February 2000 at Diverse Works/Infernal Bridegroom Productions in Houston in a production directed by Parks in collaboration with the company. The play was later produced at the Papp Public Theater as well (in March 2003), directed by Michael Greif. While critical response to *Fucking A* was generally less positive than it was for Parks's previous play (John Simon and Charles Isherwood found the tragic ending unconvincing, and both Simon and Ben Brantley found *Fucking A*'s use of Brechtian dramaturgy unimaginatively derivative), most reviews noted the play's mixture of Brechtian and realistic theatrical devices. Brantley, for instance, saw the play as mixing "Brechtian distance with the kind of intense social melodrama associated with Clifford Odets" (2).

While generally produced separately, the two plays have come to be grouped by critics as Parks's Red Letter plays—so named because in both plays, Parks, by her own description, "riffs" on Hawthorne's classic American novel *The Scarlet Letter*. Like Hawthorne's novel, Parks's two plays feature protagonists named Hester. In *In the Blood*, Hester La Negrita, an illiterate and destitute mother of five, interacts with various characters representing institutional forces of American society that, while ostensibly meant to help her, instead collude in her exploitation. In *Fucking A*, Hester Smith, an illiterate abortionist, is driven by an intense desire for revenge on a rich woman whose "snitching" sent her son to prison. Both plays end with the protagonist killing her own son, and while there are important contextual differences between the two killings, in each case this final act ironically underscores a tragic lack of agency on the part of the heroine. At the end of both plays, neither the heroine's own situation nor the social structures with which she clashes has changed significantly.

A less obvious but, in the view of this essay, crucial similarity between the Red Letter plays and Hawthorne's novel is the three works' interrogation of American attitudes toward the relation of the symbolic to the real. As an external visual marker of what is supposed by other characters as its wearer's "internal," spiritual state, Hester Prynne's Scarlet "A" is, among other things, an emblem of a powerful American anxiety regarding the gulf between appearance and reality. The desperate and dangerous need for fixed signs and self-evident identities that obsesses Hawthorne's characters likewise informs *In the Blood* and *Fucking A*. But Parks's plays locate the root of this attitude in economic life.

While critics almost universally acknowledge Parks's concern with the economic structures of society, and while several critics investigate Parks's obsession with the verbal and visual sign and its relation to racial, cultural, and gender identities, very little work has been done to connect these two aspects of her work.* Over the past four decades the work of "New Economic" critics such as Marc Shell, Walter Benn Michaels, and Jean-Joseph Goux has read money as a symbol of a troubling discrepancy between the symbolic and the real, or what Shell calls "material" and "intellectual currency" (1). An anxiety over this discrepancy informs Parks's work generally, but it finds its fullest exploration in the Red Letter plays.† Very early in *In the Blood*, a chorus of characters observes of the "welfare queen" Hester, La Negrita, "BAD NEWS IN HER BLOOD / PLAIN AS DAY" (7). In a similar vein, in *Fucking A*, protagonist Hester Smith would overcome the ambiguity of appearances by physically marking her son so as to always be able to recognize him. Nevertheless, the repeated and deeply tragic failures at recognition that characterize both plays undercut their characters' insistence on reliable verbal and visual signs, and in both plays money and economic thinking are shown to be inextricably bound up with this dilemma.

A need for money drives the plots of both plays: *In the Blood*'s Hester tries and fails to gain financial support from the fathers of her five "treasures"; *Fucking A*'s Hester tries and fails to earn enough money to buy her imprisoned son's freedom. More significantly, each play gives us a world in which relations between characters are transformed in disturbing ways by money. In *In the Blood*, a preacher named the Reverend D runs a "salvation business," a welfare worker says she cares about people because she is paid to, and an expectant mother plans to sell the valuable "fruit of [her] white womb" (55, 71). In *Fucking A*, the "kept woman," Canary's lover, "owns [her] exclusive rights," and unwanted pregnancies are good for the economy: "Their troubles yr livelihood," explains the abortionist Hester Smith to herself (117). In the worlds of these two plays, human life on every level has been transformed into an abstraction by the reification of money and economic relations.

---

*Elam, for example, points out that Parks "constructs complex interactions between race, sexuality, economics, and culture," but pays little attention to the relation between economics and the other three categories (117).

†Here as elsewhere I date the plays by their first public performance. The chronology of the plays as texts is somewhat more complicated. Parks has described *In The Blood* as the "alien baby" of *Fucking A*, much of it coming to her while she was in the process of completing an earlier, much longer draft of *Fucking A* (Garrett 134).

By focusing on the related examples of the too-sexually prolific "Welfare Queen" and the abortionist, Parks's scripts present us with an all-too-familiar world in which all human relations are monstrously transformed into abstractions and the money relation is monstrously transformed into the only living reality, and ultimately into a divine entity. In investigating this theme, the plays also explore the involvement of money and economic thinking in ideas concerning representation, and specifically theatrical representation. Both plays wrestle with and ultimately try to transcend what Walter Benn Michaels calls the "logic of naturalism," a logic that represses money and one that would divide life into neat categories such as words and action, the mimetic and the real. Parks's own mélange of Brechtian and naturalistic theatrical practice attempts to arrive at a synthesis of these two ideas, one that would reject the logic of naturalism by acknowledging a dialectical relation between the symbolic and the real, that returns the body to language and language to the body, that writes "in the blood."

A close reading of *In the Blood* reveals first that the world it presents is one in which all relationships between characters are mediated by money, in a way that seems to make any kind of existentially authentic relationship between characters impossible. The character called Welfare explains to Hester that she "cares" about her "because it is my job to care. I am paid to stretch out these hands" (55). The Reverend D, the preacher who fathered Hester's youngest child, runs a "salvation business" and explains at one point that most people think of God as "like the IRS. God garnishes yr wages if you dont pay up. God withholds" (73). The very antipathy felt by the general public toward Hester, the supposed "welfare queen," is testament to the dominance of money in relations between people: in the last scene a chorus demands the sterilization of Hester based on economics: "NO SMART / WOMAN GOT ALL THEM BASTARDS / AND NOT A PENNY TO HER NAME / SOMETHINGS GOTTA BE DONE / CAUSE I'LL BE DAMNED IF SHE GONNA LIVE OFF ME" (109). Parks interrogates this idea of the "welfare queen" having children so she can receive money in the form of public assistance by having Hester refer to her children repeatedly as her "treasures"—indeed, this term, repeated three times, makes up Hester's first words in the play (12). The fact that Hester means something very different than the term's monetary interpretation only underscores the way financial value has supplanted all other forms of value for the play's other characters.

Another way of describing the role of money in the lives of the characters is to say that it has transformed from the ultimate *means* to the ultimate *end,* and in doing so has transformed all other contents of life into means to the end of making money. On the face of it this may seem a rather obvious point, but Parks powerfully brings us back to the truly monstrous nature of this situation through the character Amiga Gringa, Hester's "friend" and the only definitively white character in the play. Repeatedly, Amiga justifies her real and intended actions by appealing to the idea of the "open market." When, in scene five, Hester shows Amiga the sewing piece-work she has been offered by the character called Welfare, Amiga immediately suggests they steal the fabric and sell it "on the open market," as this will surely bring them more money than Hester could earn through sewing (67). In this same scene, Amiga reveals that she thinks she may be pregnant, and proposes to sell the baby. By the logic of the "free market" Amiga's intentions are perfectly reasonable, and she challenges the audience to consider this: "Grow it. / Birth it. / Sell it. / And why shouldn't I?" she asks rhetorically (71). According to Amiga, this arrangement makes particular sense because she is white: "Do you have any idea how much cash I'll get for the fruit of my white womb?" (71). The sickness of this economic perspective — but also the horrifyingly straightforward "logic" of it — are emphasized by Amiga's frank assessment of her situation: "Little Bastards in there living high on the hog, taking up space" (70). In a world where everyone is thought to be driven purely by economic interest, a fetus becomes a parasite living off the mother in much the same way that Hester becomes a parasite living off the public. Hester is accused of having children in order to make money, and Amiga's planned abortion makes economic sense, as would bringing the child to term and selling it. The point of each example is that human life, even from the perspective of a mother toward her child, is here no more than a means to the end of making money.

In the Blood thus sets up a kind of reproductive economy, one that demands that Hester be sterilized, as she is by the end of the play, presumably because the fruit of her *black* womb does not command the same price as would a white baby. Children are similarly seen as no more than a financial liability by the Reverend D, who tells us he gave Hester money for an abortion when he learned that she was pregnant with his child, and who explains to Hester in scene six that it would be financially ruinous for him to be seen with Hester since it would likely cause his financial "backers" to withhold the funds with which he hopes to build his church (75). The relation of money to reproduction is an ancient idea, one at the heart of what Aristotle characterized as money's monstrous quality. In the *Politics,* for instance, Aristotle famously condemns interest-generating capital as an unnatural "breeding of money" in which "the offspring resembles the parent" (19), a notion that forms the crux of the Scholastic conception of interest-bearing capital as an unnatural generation from a "barren" substance, essentially the aspect of money invoked in Shakespeare's *The Merchant of Venice,* when Antonio describes Shylock's usury as "a breed for barren metal" (1.3.132).* This notion of a monstrously breeding money is key to Marx's critique of money:

> Capital appears as a mysterious and self-creating source of interest — the source of its own increase.... The result of the entire process of reproduction appears as a property inherent in the thing itself.... In interest-bearing capital, therefore, this automatic fetish, self-expanding value, money-generating money, are brought out in their pure state and in this form it no longer bears the birth-marks of its origin [385].

This same conception of breeding money informs *In the Blood*. As Amiga's comments demonstrate, in this play money reproduces itself *at the expense* of human reproduction: Amiga's baby is a parasite living off her limited financial resources — her "taking up space" comment essentially re-imagines the womb as real estate — only valuable if it can be *sold*. Similarly, the Reverend D illustrates the monstrous deformity of money's power — given his constant surveillance by his financial "backers" it makes greater economic sense for him to either eliminate his progeny (he says he has given Hester money to abort their child) or else to distance himself from Hester and refuse to acknowledge the child as his own.

---

*For a useful discussion on the history of the "barren metal" characterization of money, see Cannan et al.

The Reverend D's vigilance concerning the maintenance of what Hester calls "his image" (99) underscores a more specific—and more insidious—effect of money in this play. Repeatedly, money is shown to demand a performance; it is consistently associated in the play with the construction and constant maintenance of a kind of mask, with characters' alienation from each other and, more disturbingly, from their own actions. Amiga Gringa explains in her "confession" that the sex show she had convinced Hester to take part in was financially "lucrative" because of Hester's ability to alienate herself from her own actions. "She liked the idea of sex," Amiga tells us, then adds, "at least she acted like it." She "had the moves down," which seems to describe a rote performance more than an authentic sexual encounter—a performance that was "very sensual, very provocative, very scientific, very lucrative" (72). These four consecutive adjectives trace a phenomenology of alienation, taking us from Hester's body to self-consciousnessly regarding the effect of the sex on an audience, to the "scientific" abstraction of her actions, and finally to money. The Reverend D evinces a similar alienation from himself, and once again the root of that alienation is money. In the Reverend's case, it is his need to keep up a performance for financial backers who seem always to have him under their watchful gaze. As he explains to Hester, his patrons "want to make sure they havent been suckered, so they watch you real close, to make sure yr as good as they think you are. To make sure you wont screw up and shame them and waste their money" (75). Just as importantly, the good Reverend *is not* as good as they think he is—in the course of the play he masturbates in public, demands oral sex from Hester, and finally becomes physically abusive, calling Hester "slut," and threatens to "crush [her] underfoot" (103). The Reverend is intensely conscious of a gap between appearance and reality, and it is money that makes this gap necessary.

Given the total replacement of all value by financial value in the world of Parks's play, and given money's evocation of a troubling gap between the symbolic and the real, it is natural that so many characters demonstrate a desperate need to close this gap, or sometimes to deny that this gap exists. The chorus of people whose shouts begin and end the play demonstrate just this denial. "BAD NEWS IN HER BLOOD," they shout at Hester, "PLAIN AS DAY" (7). Philip Kolin usefully points out that blood "symbolizes Hester's sexual sins and shame" and constitutes "her biological scarlet letter" (253). The chorus's accusation paradoxically both acknowledges and denies a gulf between the symbolic and the real: an essentialist claim is made about Hester's character—her fate is contained *in her blood*—but that writing (and it is called "news" after all) may be read clearly on the surface. Thus Hester is used to allay other characters' anxiety regarding what they sense is a discrepancy between the symbolic and the real.

An important way this anxiety concerning appearance and reality in a hypercommodified world is shown in the play is through problems of identity and identification. The Reverend D, that walking symbol of this anxiety, begins his first soapbox sermon of the play with these words, "You all know me. You know this face. You know these arms. This body of mine is known to you. To all of you. There isnt a person on the street tonight that hasnt passed me by at some point" (46). These statements are highly ironic given that the rest of the sermon concerns self-transformation, his own and that which he promises to others who follow his advice. The Reverend even refers at one point to his "more recent reincarnation" (46). The latent content of the sermon then becomes the difficulty of *knowing* anyone. The very physical markers of identity cited by the Reverend — his face, his body — are highly unreliable symbols given his own admitted reincarnations and his need to maintain a false persona under the surveillance of his patrons.

In the Blood's other powerful symbol of the malleability of identity is Chilli, the father of Hester's oldest child, who returns in scene seven with a changed name. When Hester reminds Chilli that she has protected him by not letting Welfare know he was back in town, since he has avoided paying Hester any child support, Chilli responds: "Theyll never find me. Theres no trace of the old me left anywhere" (87). Like the Reverend D, Chilli has shed one self and adopted another, and as in the other man's case, Chilli's self-transformation is associated with money: "Ive seen the world Ive made some money Ive made a new name for myself," explains Chilli (89). These men whose money Hester so desperately needs (and is entitled to) have become money themselves, evincing just the break between seeming and being, face and material value, money has come to symbolize.

Chilli's behavior allows Parks to further investigate money as a site of rupture between the symbolic and the real through the character's desperate need to place his own subjective/"interior" perception in accord with "objective" reality. In his desperate need for a correspondence between objective reality and his own subjective vision, Chilli resembles *The Scarlet Letter*'s Chillingworth. When he is first introduced in the novel, Chillingworth is described as "a man chiefly accustomed to look inward, and to whom external matters are of little value or import, unless they bear relation to something within his mind" (Hawthorne 44). In Parks's play, this need for clear correspondence between subjective perception and objective reality takes the form of what Chilli says his doctor labels a "tic" that is a "sure sign of some disorder" (87): he repeatedly and obsessively checks a gold pocket watch to try to verify his own subjective sense of what time it is. Chilli desperately needs to make the "real" objective world coincide with his subjective vision of it. He longs for what Goux suggests the American gold-money of the nineteenth century promised but could not possibly deliver: the erasure of difference between the real and the symbolic, a substance that *is* the value it *represents*. In fact, the timepiece Chilli uses for this is a "big *gold* pocket watch" (67, emphasis added).

Chilli further attempts to make the real coincide with the symbolic when he dresses Hester in a wedding gown and declares, "This is real. The feelings I have for you, the feelings you are feeling for me, these are real" (92). He associates money with the denial of these feelings he wants certified as "real": he tells Hester "Ive been fighting my feelings for years. With every dollar I made" (92). As it turns out, the real is the very last thing Chilli is prepared to face. He tells Hester that he has "carried this picture of you. Sad and lonely with our child on yr hip. Struggling to make do. Struggling against all odds. And triumphant. Triumphant against everything. Like — hell, like Jesus and Mary" (96). Of course, when the actual Hester does not conform to his idealized vision, he rejects her with the explanation, "times change"— another way in fact of saying that *people* change. Chilli leaves presumably to make more money and yet another "name" for himself.

The obsession over a perceived disjunction between symbols and the real demonstrated by the characters of *In the Blood* is transcended by only one character in the play, and that is — ironically — Hester's intellectually "slow" son Jabber. In the first scene, following the opening chorus, we see two crucial and interrelated exchanges between Jabber and his illiterate mother. The first is a discussion of a word that someone has scrawled on Hester's "practice space," where she works at the alphabet Jabber tries to teach her. Hester's first words form the question as to whether it is "uh good word or a bad word" (9). The word, as the audience can see, is "SLUT," and Parks has Jabber respond with *no* words, but rather with two "Spells," those wordless moments Parks has described as "heightened and elongated" pauses wherein characters "experience their pure true simple state" (ix). Hester pushes her eldest son to say the word so that the two of them can "figure out the meaning together" (9). Jabber resists because he knows what the word means, or at least he knows that it is a "bad word." Crucially, Jabber understands the word as an *action*, one meant to have a very real effect on his mother: "They wrote it in yr practice place," he observes, "so you didn't practice today" (10).

Unlike other characters in this play, Jabber clearly understands the slipperiness of the talk/action distinction, understands, that is, that talk *is* action, that symbols are involved in the creation of the real and vice versa. A moment later when Hester tries to scribble an A in the dirt, Jabber makes a correction by using the body: "Legs apart hands crost the chest like I showd you" (11). Then Hester pushes Jabber again to "read that word out to me," and Jabber lies, saying he "cant" (11). These two exchanges — regarding the "bad" word Jabber refuses to say aloud and the method he uses to teach Hester the alphabet — are vitally related in that both refuse to recognize a hard distinction between talk and action, symbolic and real. The first registers the real effects of a symbol, and the second searches for a kind of embodied — we might even say performed — language.*

A bit later in the same scene Hester does sense that the word is a "mean ugly" one "meant to hurt our feelings" (12). In response to this, Jabber seems to deny the knowledge he has already demonstrated regarding the slipperiness of the real/symbolic distinction: referencing the old "sticks and stones" saw, Jabber insists, "Words don't hurt my feelings" (12). Then immediately the word/action distinction is revisited when Hester's daughter Bully enters, telling her mother that her brother Trouble "said a bad word" that she will not repeat: then notes, "What he said was bad but what he did, what he did was worse." We soon learn that Trouble has stolen a policeman's club (13).

An interrogation of the talk/action distinction haunts other plays by Parks, most notably *Topdog/Underdog*. This theme is revisited at the very climax of *In the Blood*, again in a scene focusing on Hester and Jabber. Crucially, this scene occurs just after the Reverend D viciously calls Hester "slut," verbalizing the written word we see near the beginning of the play. In scene eight, having heard the Reverend D's verbal abuse of Hester, Jabber admits that he could have read the word aloud to her but "didn't wanna" (103). In a nice reversal, Hester now tells Jabber not to speak, but the two have an extraordinary exchange in which Jabber reveals the depth of his understanding about the relation of the symbolic to the real. "I was reading" the word, explains Jabber, "but I was only reading it in my head I wasn't reading it with my mouth I was reading it with my mouth but not

---

*This notion of embodying language is present in most of Parks's work. See for example Louis's discussion of *The Death of the Last Black Man in the Whole Entire World*.

with my tongue I was reading it only with my lips and I could hear the word outloud but only outloud in my head" (103). Jabber explains to Hester that he "didnt wanna to say the word outloud in your head" (104). It is remarkable how the "bad" word moves, in Jabber's speech, from his own subjectivity, through his body (his mouth, his tongue), out into the air and then into his mother's subjectivity: Jabber saying the word "outloud in [Hester's] head." Jabber has a sophisticated understanding of the fluid relation between "inside" and "outside," between subjectivity and objectivity. Through Jabber, Parks replaces a hard distinction between talk and action, the symbolic and the real, with a more sophisticated understanding of the two as dialectically interrelated.

The ultimate demonstration of the involvement of the symbolic in the real is the tragic, bloody murder of Jabber by his own mother. Hester brutally slays her son to stop him saying the hurtful word. What's more, the weapon Hester uses is the policeman's club that Trouble stole at the beginning of the play (the deed his sister Bully uses to distinguish between words — the "bad" word Trouble said — and actions). That club becomes the means by which Hester would control the real by limiting the "talk" of other characters. Interestingly, by the time Jabber is murdered, the policeman's stolen club has already been involved in the play's meditations on the question of free will. In scene four, for instance, Hester twice warns Welfare, "Dont make me hurt you," the second time raising the club to hit her (57, 58). The phrase speaks to Hester's own feeling of powerlessness by denying her agency even in this imagined striking out against her oppressors. In fact, repeatedly in the play Hester's language reveals her own perceived lack of agency. "We ain't lucky," Hester declares early in the play, and she repeatedly mentions an always-elusive "leg up" that will help her children and herself, maybe even "make us rich," though she acknowledges that there is "no easy money nowheres" (12, 58, 64). "I coulda been the Queen of Sheba," Hester tells the Doctor in scene two, only "it just werent in the cards" (41). Parks is not blaming Hester for the character's own perceived lack of agency. To read the play in this way is to ignore both the notably rigid hierarchy that encompasses all of the characters as well as the play's consistent undermining of the Reverend D's manipulative, dishonest "self-help" philosophy. The Doctor who eventually sterilizes Hester does so, he says, at the behest of "The Higher Ups" (41). In fact, in the monologues called "Confessions" that punctuate the play, various characters — the Doctor, the Reverend, Amiga, Welfare — confess to their own lack of agency. "Times are tough," says the Doctor in a typical passage, "What can we do?" (44). Amiga Gringa justifies Hester's exploitation this way: "Ah, what do you expect in a society based on Capitalizm?" (72). And the Reverend D lives under the constant surveillance of his "backers." All of these characters consistently blame Hester for her own situation while all deny any agency on their part.

This sense of inevitability finds its ultimate symbol in *In the Blood* in the form of cosmic signs Hester repeatedly reports observing. In scenes five and six, she claims to have seen an eclipse, though other characters cannot verify this (66, 76). By scene seven, the eclipse has become a "big dark thing. Gods hand. Coming down on me. Blocking the light out" and even the "5-fingered hand of fate" (84). Scene eight, in which Hester kills Jabber, is entitled "The Hand of Fate" (99), and her last words — also the last words of the play — are "big hand coming down on me," repeated three times (110). None of the other characters see the hand but, as I have argued, they all seem to live with the sense of helplessness and lack of agency the hand of fate symbolizes. This is a lack of agency rooted in economic thinking. In the world of the play, what Aristotle called the unnatural "breeding of money" has been made natural, and the "breeding" of humans has been made unnatural: a baby is either a way to make money (as Amiga sees it) or a financial burden on society (as Hester is seen). Hester's "spaying" *for economic reasons* is the ultimate, monstrous end of this process of reification. The "hand of fate" that no one but Hester sees is Smith's "Invisible Hand," that force born of self-interest, competition, and supply and demand.

As in *In the Blood*, *Fucking A* presents a world in which characters seem forced to profit from each other's misfortunes. Unsurprisingly in this bloody revenge tragedy that Parks coyly refers to as an "otherworldly tale," the situation is even more vicious, the characters' sense of helplessness even more pronounced (113). In the first scene, Hester Smith describes the situation this way, referring to her abortion business: "Their troubles yr livelihood, ... There aint no winning" (117). Similarly, the character called Freedom Fund decries the loose sexual morals of the women of the town but then throws her hands up and asks "what can you do?" since "them cleaning up their act would put you out of yr cleaning business" (132). And Hester's best friend, Canary, who would have the Mayor as her husband and financial benefactor, rejoices over his troubled marriage: "Things are getting worse between the Mayor and his wife. Lets celebrate" (119). Later in the play, Canary tells Hester she has a story to tell that will "make you smile" since "its at her expense" (123). With one notable exception, which I shall discuss, the characters in *Fucking A* always and everywhere profit at each other's expense while remaining convinced of their own lack of agency.

While *In the Blood* implicates money relations in the characters' widespread lack of agency, *Fucking A* gives us what at least appears to be a more stable system of money: money is tied to gold, and there seem to be only two denominations of currency, gold pieces (presumably gold coins) and what are just called "coins," with one of the former equaling 500 of the latter. In this way the money economy of *Fucking A* resembles the gold-money economy of nineteenth-century America. Helpfully, Jean-Joseph Goux traces a vital homology between what Marx calls the three historical stages of money — measure of labor, medium of exchange, and finally means of wealth — and the psychoanalytic categories of the real, the symbolic, and the imaginary. Like Marc Shell, Goux cites the gold-money of the nineteenth century as an instance of the fantasy of bringing these three functions together in one object: "At once the *ideal* measure of value, the *symbolic* instrument of exchange, and the *real* means of reserve, gold-money brought together the functions of *archetype,* of *token,* and of *treasure* into a single object." Yet with the advent of representative money (paper, then credit cards, then electronic money), the "three functions have come asunder": "The inconvertible signifier that circulates today, that floats, that always postpones its 'realization,' guarantees the monetary function in the realm of pure symbolicity, but only by mourning the loss of the unlocatable (or floating) standard and the uncertain reserve value, secured by nothing" (114). The money system of *Fucking A* seemingly represents just the fantasy of a value that *is* what it *represents*, that gold (and silver) money represented to the "hard" money advocates of the American nineteenth century. A closer look at the play, however, reveals that as in life, the real value of money is just as relative despite its being tied to gold. We see this most clearly through Hester's attempts to buy visitation rights to her imprisoned son Boy. Each time she saves enough money to purchase a picnic with Boy, the price of that picnic changes due to further crimes Boy has supposedly committed while in prison. Hester always falls short. When she shows up with a gold coin to purchase visitation rights, she is told that because of these crimes committed by Boy, his "picnic price has doubled" (134). Though Hester's son, as we learn, likely has been involved in further crimes, the rather arbitrary and extreme changes in the cost of his visitation rights undermine any supposedly stabilizing character of the gold-money.

Fucking A goes further to implicate money in the relativizing of all other value and meaning in the world of the characters. When, in scene six, Canary is crushed to learn that even if the Mayor has his wife murdered, he will not marry Canary, the Mayor assuages her disappointment by giving her gold (153). Then after each character has a "Spell," the Mayor says, "'Wife,' 'Mistress,' what does it matter? Take the gold. Buy something nice" (153). Money erases the difference between wife and mistress. As soon as Canary has the money, she does an immediate emotional about-face, calling the Mayor "Sweetheart" and then breaking into the song "Gilded Cage" (153). Likewise, the First Lady, desperate to get pregnant for what basically amounts to economic reasons, erases the difference between two ostensibly very different people — her husband the Mayor and the escaped convict Monster (who in reality is Hester's son Boy). Happy to discover that she is pregnant with Monster's baby, and deciding to let the Mayor think it is his, she reasons: "One seed is as good as another. And when the husband resembles the lover, he wont be none the wiser" (191). The economic ends, here, constitute what is important, and they make human beings interchangeable.

As the world of *Fucking A* seems at first to have a less monstrous money form, so does that world seem to regulate semiotic exchanges through a kind of hierarchical system. To begin with, there are two different kinds of spoken English in the play: "ordinary" speech and TALK, a special language that for the most part only the women use when speaking to each other. Although Talk is a strange sort of English-German-novel language, one thing that is clear is that it is much more concrete and metaphorical than the standard English used by most of the characters most of the time. Parks provides a TALK-English translation at the back of the printed play. Menstruation is expressed in TALK as "falltimeh ma OVO" (124); and the First Lady compliments the state of her own vagina in similarly concrete, imagistic language: "Meh Kazo-say greengrass ee-sunny skies" (128). After TALK, we hear the comparatively less metaphor-rich, less concretely expressive standard English most of the characters use. Finally, there is writing, most of which is done by a character called Scribe who in one instance in the play takes down Hester's words in a letter to her imprisoned son. Hester freely admits that this letter contains lies (148), leaving us to wonder if, in the world of the play, lying becomes easier the further speech moves from the body.

Given the relationship of truth to the present, speaking body, we need to consider two further semiotic levels. The first involves identifying marks on the physical body: the marks Hester created to ensure that she would always recognize her son (two identical scars she created with her teeth, on her son's arm and on her own, "in the same place"), as well as the letter "A" that has been branded into Hester's chest (166). The next semiotic level involves the embodied/performed, non-verbal communication that Parks refers to as "Spells." If *In the Blood* began with the protagonist embodying the letter A and ended with her writing in blood, thus bridging the gap between the immediate presence of the body and the absence of writing, *Fucking A* further investigates this idea through these different semiotic levels that exist in different proximities to the physical body. Given that Parks describes a Spell as a non-verbal means of communicating a character's "pure true simple state" (ix), it is not unreasonable to assume that a continuum exists wherein the truth becomes more obscured as we move from the performing body to writing on the body, to private language (TALK), to public discourse, and finally, to writing, or words that are separated from a speaker.

While on one level it seems that Parks is setting up this hierarchy of semiotic economies, as symbols become less reliable the more removed they are from the body, the play in fact deeply complicates this hierarchy. One way this is done is through Hester's repeated failure to recognize her own son. When, in scene nine, Butcher suggests that Hester likely won't be able to identify her son, not having seen him since he was a small child, Hester reveals that she has already anticipated the problem. "Just before they took him," she explains, "I bit him. Hard. Right on the arm just there. I bit hard. Deep into his skin. His blood in my mouth" (166). Hester then bit an "identical" mark into her own arm. In this way, she resists the commodification of life to reduce all to the least common denominator, to make all interchangeable — to erase the difference between "wife" and "mistress," for example — by giving her son a distinctive mark. At the same time, however, the identical marks Hester places on her son's and her own body symbolize her refusal to see her son as a separate, distinct, existentially independent being. She would have him always be the "angel" she once convinced herself he was, and no amount of evidence of his violent acts could change her view of him. The mark by which Hester tries to make her son always recognizable is also the mark by which she tries to fix his identity to match her own ideal vision of it. The two scars are, in an intriguing way, very like the scarlet A in Hawthorne's tale, in that all three symbols try to make a supposed "internal"/ spiritual/ideal state externally visible, or all three try to place the real and the symbolic in sync. Hester Smith even says of her own scar that it "kind of looks like a heart. Like Im wearing my heart on my sleeve or something" (179). The very scar, then, that would fix Boy's identity in fact marks the dissolution of that identity in the face of Hester's idealized image of her son.

In her need for a simple and reliable correspondence between "inside" and "outside," the real and the symbolic, the Hester of *Fucking A* actually resembles Chilli from *In the Blood*. Chilli obsessed over his need to make the external world coincide with his own idealized vision of it through his compulsive game with his pocket watch and his rejection of Hester La Negrita when she refused to conform to his idealized vision of her. Similarly, Hester Smith would erase the difference between the symbolic and the real, and refuses to recognize physical reality when it does not coincide with her own idealized vision of it. When Freedom Fund tells Hester her son has committed more crimes in prison, Hester responds, "Must be a mistake. Hes a very good boy" (133). Freedom Fund's response would subtly move identity from essence to existence: "Well, yr good boys been doing some very bad things lately" (133). Yet Hester insists, "My sons an angel" (134). Butcher possesses the same essentialist view of his own daughter, except that instead of seeing her as an "angel," he calls her "rotten to the core" (160).

A powerful irony of the play is that it is just this refusal on Hester's part to let go of an essentialist view of identity that keeps her from recognizing her own son. When Canary points out that Monster, the recently escaped convict, has a scar very like Hester's, she refuses to believe this could be her son, saying "Hes an evil person" (196). When Canary reminds her again about the identical scars, Hester makes the following leap: "Which goes to show that mothers all over the world bite their sons" (196). Hester's inability to let go of her idealized image of her son makes the recognition she sought through the scar impossible. Monster's scar, insists Hester, "looks horrid. Like a gash," while hers "looks like a heart" (209). It is easier for her to believe that her son is dead than for her to accept that he is not the "angel" she repeatedly swears he is. When Monster shows her his mark, Hester responds, "I marked my *son*. He was good and then he died" (208). This narrative Hester constructs and clings to about her son denies him as a living, acting being. "He *was good*" — a description of an essential state, not an action — "and then he died."

Tragically, Hester's inability to see people as complex beings who change over time is at the very root of the revenge fantasy that drives the plot of *Fucking A*. After all, Hester holds the First Lady responsible for "snitching" on Boy "when she was a little girl." Unwilling or unable to blame the legal system for turning her Boy into a "Monster," for essentially holding him for ransom through its "Freedom Fund," Hester simply persists in blaming the person who sent Boy to prison in the first place. Importantly, money is deeply involved in Hester's obsession with the First Lady. In the first scene of the play, Hester explains that "when she was a little Rich Girl she thought she owned the world. And anything she wanted she could buy. Sent my son away to prison with a flick of her little Rich Girl finger" (124). Now, however, the First Lady is thought (incorrectly) to be infertile, and Hester takes pleasure in this fact: "She cant buy a son or a daughter now but I can buy mine. Im buying mine back" (124). Two things are significant here. The first is that, as in *In the Blood,* the money economy seems to flourish at the expense of the human reproductive economy. The "Rich Girl" has no offspring, while the financially strapped Hester does. The second is that Hester would take comfort in the very quality that makes human life convertible into money. The same money economy that grants the Mayor the "exclusive rights" of another human being (his mistress, Canary), that makes the difference between wife and mistress meaningless, that puts a price on Hester's son's freedom, also allows her the only hope she has of ever reuniting with that son. This *all-encompassing* quality of the money economy is the real tragedy of *Fucking A*. Hester is, of course, deluded in thinking she could use that money economy to get her son back, as the price of even a visit astronomically escalates. The point is that she is allowed no other option: that money is seen as the only available and always insufficient means of overcoming the very alienation that it has created.

The comfort Hester derives from the First Lady's supposed sterility dissipates when we learn that the First Lady is pregnant. When Hester has her nemesis drugged and brought to her home and then performs an abortion on the woman, she unwittingly destroys her own grandchild. If Hester had not chased her son off immediately before the First Lady's arrival, having refused to recognize him even after he showed her his "mark," this final, tragic mistake would have been avoided. In an important sense, however, Hester's insistence on revenge is a powerful rejection of the money economy and all it represents in the play. Earlier, when it is believed that Hester's son is dead, Canary advises her to just accept an offered "full refund" of all the money she has contributed over the years toward buying a visit with him, get over her hatred of the First Lady, and retire. Canary suggests they should both "take [their] bad luck on the chin" and move on, but Hester insists on having her revenge, despite Canary's sense of powerlessness ("Anyway, what can we do?" [194]). Hester refuses to be paid off in cash and rejects the lack of agency the money economy encourages throughout the play. The life of her son, Hester insists, can never be valued in money: "A full refund aint enough" (195).

At the same time as she refuses to put a price on her son's life, the very logic of Hester's revenge demonstrates her conditioning by the money economy, with its demand that all be reduced to a least common denominator. She first plans to kill the First Lady, an action she says would make them "equal" (193). Obviously this would not, in any meaningful sense, since Hester is still alive. When Hester learns of the First Lady's pregnancy, she decides to get her revenge by aborting the fetus: "Rip her child from her like she ripped mine from me" (205). Of course, the real situation is more complicated than this, and the First Lady, whatever her faults, did not "rip" Hester's child from her. This careless thinking equates two very disparate things as monstrously as money does, and the results are tragic for Hester: she unwittingly aborts her own grandson and also loses precious time during which she might have saved her son from a group of vicious bounty hunters. Hester declares that she is "not a mother" if she forgoes vengeance on the First Lady (194). In the end, she is no longer a mother *as a result of* her insistence on settling the score, on *paying back* the First Lady in kind.

Hester's last act is to slit her son's throat using a method Butcher taught her, one he uses to kill the animals which exist only as commodities for him. The most remarkable thing about Hester's mercy killing of her own son is the utter meaninglessness of it. One is tempted to read this act as at least marking Hester's agency, but that begs the question, of what use is agency such as this? Her Boy is denied dignity even in death. As the Hunters declare, there is "plenty of fun still to be had" with his body (220). The extent of the Hunters' own inability to think "outside" the money economy is evident in the First Hunter's comment to a woman who has just killed her own son: "If you think yll get any of the reward money, you got another thing coming" (220). Hester tries to sing another verse of her "Working Woman's Song," that paean to her lack of agency in the capitalist world of the play: "I dig my ditch with no complaining," the song begins (221). Hester does trail off, seemingly unable to finish the song, but in the end she *"gets up, picks up her tools and goes back to work."* No significant change, either for Hester or for any of the other surviving characters, seems to have occurred as a result of the actions of the play.

In both *In the Blood* and *Fucking A*, Hester's murdering her own son is deeply involved with her desperate attempt to escape being objectively determined by her respective society, and in each play it is the money relation that is implicated in the protagonist's sense of being objectively determined. And in both plays, the protagonist remains just as trapped and powerless as she was in the beginning. Elam is correct in seeing Hester La Negrita's murder of Jabber as a striking out against a social order that "not only restricts the roles of women and people of color, but also preordains how one's offspring will function within this system" (203). Nevertheless, as Verna Foster rightfully points out, the two Hesters ultimately harm those they love and themselves "without effecting any change in the social conditions that produced their rages" (75). Despite her son Jabber's lessons on the mutually generative relationship between human subjectivity and what we perceive as the objective world, Hester La Negrita ends succumbing to what she perceives as the "Hand of Fate." Despite her own struggle to escape the money relation and its tendency to make all interchangeable, Hester Smith is still resigned to a fate beyond her control. In this way, the Red Letter plays suggest an extremely pessimistic view of the ability of human beings to wrest control of their own lives from the market mechanisms they have created.

Yet this view of the plays as confirming their protagonists' view of their own helplessness is only possible if we ignore Parks's masterful employment of Brechtian stagecraft.* Both plays make use of Brechtian devices such as episodic plotting, single actors playing multiple roles, songs, figurative names (Trouble, Jabber, Monster, Welfare), onstage text (the Doctor's mortarboard in *In the Blood;* the "nonaudible simultaneous English translation" of the TALK passages that Parks's stage directions call for in *Fucking A*) (115). In addition, Parks's novel use of the chorus in *In the Blood* similarly creates a very Brechtian combination of distance and identification for the audience. Harvey Young claims that through her "embrace and (post)modernization of the Greek chorus," Parks uses that chorus as a "veiled critique of present-day, societal complicity in the objectification of others" (30). The audience recognizes itself in the chorus but does not like what it sees. Through all these Brechtian devices, Parks discourages our over-identification with the heroines of the two plays, rejects the classical idea of the characters' *hamartia* as responsible for their fate, and works against realism's tendency to encourage a view of the world as always already pre-constructed. The "fate" of Parks's two Hesters demonstrates the folly of looking for a solution on the level of the individual. The Brechtian stagecraft works in conjunction with the message of the plays to encourage us to work toward a structural solution to the problem the play foregrounds. And there are hints within the plays of the more human social arrangements we might choose to construct, none more powerful than the non-economic relationship in *In the Blood*. Hester and Canary may joke about the economics of their relationship — long ago Hester gave Canary an abortion on credit — but the truth of their relationship is very different. Hester calls herself "a good business woman" for placing Canary in her debt. Canary, however, upon paying Hester her "debt and then some," tells the truth: "Yr a good friend" (126, 125).

---

*Critics seem to disagree as to which of the two plays is more Brechtian. Geis, for instance, calls *In the Blood* "a somewhat more naturalistic play" than *Fucking A* (127). Schafer, however, describes *Fucking A* as "Brechtian epic theatre" and describes *In the Blood* as "classical tragedy in a contemporary setting" (182). Foster sees *Fucking A's* plot as more "classically Aristotelian" (82). In fact, both plays rely heavily on the Brechtian techniques I have outlined.

Works Cited

Aristotle. *Politics*. Translated by Benjamin Jowett. New York: The Modern Library, 1943.
Benn Michaels, Walter. *The Gold Standard and the Logic of Naturalism: American Literature at the Turn of the Century*. Berkeley: University of California Press, 1987.
Berkman, Len. "Language as Protagonist in *In the Blood*." In *Suzan-Lori Parks: A Casebook*. Edited by Kevin J. Wetmore, Jr., and Alycia Smith-Howard. New York: Routledge, 2007. 61–72.
Brantley, Ben. "A Woman Named Hester, Wearing a Familiar Letter." *The New York Times,* March 17, 2003:1–2.
Canby, Vincent. "A Side-by-Side Contrast of Solemn and Lively." *The New York Times,* Dec. 19, 1999: AR7.
Cannan, E. et al. "Who Said 'Barren Metal'?: A Symposium." *Economica* 5 (June 1922): 105–11.
Elam, Harry J. "The Postmulticultural: A Tale of Mothers and Sons." In *Crucible of Cultures: Anglophone Drama at the Dawn of a New Millennium*. Brussels, Belgium: Peter Lang, 2002. 113–28.
———. "Theatre of the Gut: Tennessee Williams and Suzan-Lori Parks." In *The Influence of Tennessee Williams: Essays on Fifteen American Playwrights*. Edited by Philip C. Kolin. Jefferson, N.C.: McFarland, 2008. 200–15.
Foster, Verna A. "Nurturing and Murderous Mothers in Suzan-Lori Parks's *In the Blood* and *Fucking A*. *American Drama* 16.1 (Winter 2007): 75–89.
Garrett, Shawn-Marie. "The Possession of Suzan-Lori Parks." *American Theatre* 17.8 (October 2000): 22–26, 132–34.
Geis, Deborah R. *Suzan-Lori Parks*. Ann Arbor: University of Michigan Press, 2008.
Goux, Jean-Joseph. "Cash, Check, or Charge?" In *The New Economic Criticism*. Edited by Martha Woodmansee and Mark Osteen. London: Routledge, 1999. 114–27.
Hawthorne, Nathaniel. *The Scarlet Letter*. 3rd ed. New York: Norton, 1988.
Isherwood, Charles. Review of *Fucking A*, directed by Mark Greif. *Variety,* March 17, 2003: 6.
Kolin, Philip. "Parks's *In the Blood*." *The Explicator* 64.4 (Summer 2006): 253–55.
Krasner, David. "Review of *In the Blood*." *Theatre Journal* 52 (December 2000): 565–67.
Louis, Yvette. "Body Language: The Black Female Body and the Word in Suzan-Lori Parks' *The Death of the Last Black Man in the Whole Entire World*." In *Recovering the Black Female Body: Self-Representations by African American Women*. Edited by Michael Bennett and Vanessa D. Dickerson. New Brunswick, N.J.: Rutgers University Press, 2001.
Marx, Karl. *Capital: A Critique of Political Economy*. Edited by Frederick Engels. Translated by Samuel Moore and Edward Aveling from the 3rd German ed. New York: International Publishers, 1967.
Michaels, Walter Benn. *The Gold Standard and the Logic of Naturalism: American Literature at the Turn of the Century*. Berkeley: University of California Press, 1987.
Parks, Suzan-Lori. *Fucking A*. In *The Red Letter Plays*. New York: Theatre Communications Group, 2001. 113–242.
———. *In the Blood*. In *The Red Letter Plays*. New York: Theatre Communications Group, 2001. ix–112.
Schafer, Carol. "Staging a New Literary History." *Comparative Drama* 42.2 (Summer 2008) 181–203.
Shakespeare, William. *The Merchant of Venice*. In *The Complete Works of Shakespeare*. 4th ed. Edited by David Bevington. New York: HarperCollins, 1992. 178–215.
Shell, Marc. *Money, Language, and Thought: Literary and Philosophical Economies from the Medieval to the Modern Era*. Baltimore: Johns Hopkins University Press, 1993.
Simmel, Georg. *The Philosophy of Money*. Edited by David Frisby. Translated by Tom Bottomore and David Frisby. London: Routledge, 1990.
Simon, John. "Expletive Committed." *New York* 36.11 (March 2003): 56.
Wetmore, Kevin J., Jr., and Alycia Smith-Howard. *Suzan-Lori Parks: A Casebook*. New York: Routledge, 2007.
Young, Harvey. "Choral Compassion: *In the Blood* and *Venus*. In *Suzan-Lori Parks: A Casebook*. Edited by Kevin J. Wetmore, Jr., and Alycia Smith-Howard. New York: Routledge, 2007. 29–47.

Does Reshuffling the Cards Change the Game? Structures of Play in Parks's *Topdog/Underdog*

Jochen Achilles

> Play becomes an attitude characterized by a readiness to improvise in the face of an ever-changing world that admits of no transcendently ordered account. — Malaby, "Anthropology and Play," 206.

Suzan-Lori Parks is arguably "the most prolific playwright in ... all African American drama" (Kolin, "Introduction" 7). With regard to dramatic style, she is primarily interested in the interplay between form and content and ridicules modes of contemporary drama which disregard form in the pursuit of message and emotional effect alone (see Parks, "Elements of Style" 6, 7–8). The new perspective of her drama, or factor x as she calls it in her essay "An Equation for Black People Onstage," intended to redefine problems of race, consists of the transformation of modes of performance, or rules of games, rather than direct political intervention (see Parks, "An Equation for Black People Onstage" 20). The factor x is not a catalyst of radical innovation or revolution, but can rather be understood as the motivating force behind gradual change. Such change may consist of negotiations and variations of personal identities, of the social and political status quo, as well as of cultural traditions and memories. In this process of transformation, Parks does not underrate the weight of the past, as her multiple theatrical variations of traumatic historical events, such as the assassination of President Abraham Lincoln by the actor John Wilkes Booth in Ford's Theatre in Washington, D.C., on April 14, 1865, in both *The America Play* (1995) and *Topdog/Underdog* (2001) demonstrate. The potentially loosening, deconstructive variations of a petrified past, leading to reconfigurations, are effected by repetition and revision, the so-called "Rep & Rev" technique — the most noted stylistic feature of Parks's plays — which she explains as "a concept integral to the Jazz esthetic in which the composer or performer will write or play a musical phrase once and again and again; etc. — with each revisit the phrase is slightly revised" (Parks, "Elements of Style" 8–9). Such variations of recurring elements are not only noticeable within Parks's plays but also among them. While *Fucking A* (2001) and *In the Blood* (2001) can be considered intertextual variations of *The Scarlet Letter* (1850), Hawthorne's most famous romance, *The America*

Play and *Topdog/Underdog*, both based on President Lincoln's assassination, are the first of her plays which clearly respond to each other (see Wetmore, "Oberammergau Thing" 125, 130, 134).

Suzan-Lori Parks's *Topdog/Underdog* and Interrelated Structures of Play

Topdog/Underdog is Parks's greatest success as yet. Its off-Broadway premiere in 2001 at the Public Theatre was followed by a run on Broadway at the Ambassador Theatre between April and August 2002. In the same year, Parks received the Pulitzer Prize for drama for *Topdog/Underdog*, making her the first African American woman dramatist to be so honored. Compared to Parks's previous work, especially *The America Play*, a continuity "in terms of performative issues, language, and themes such as ancestry, violence, and commodification" is obvious in *Topdog/Underdog* (Geis 114). Although, on account of its psychologically rounded characters and quasi-realistic plotline, *Topdog/Underdog* is more accessible than some of Parks's earlier plays, she is not falling short of her avantgardist aesthetic claims. The play's straightforward action that seems to hark back to a realistic theatre tradition is radically reshaped by the fissures that run through it and by the contexts in which it is ironically embedded, as Parks herself has pointed out in an interview (Wetmore, "Oberammergau Thing" 135).

The meaning of *Topdog/Underdog* establishes itself through the interrelations of its diverse performative scenarios and their contexts. The two-character play is not only about two black brothers, allegedly named Booth and Lincoln by their father for fun, and how they try to cope with the loss of their parents, their jobs, and their partners by living together in a seedy rooming house (21–22). And the play is not only about the rising aggression of Booth, the younger brother, motivated by his inability to win back Grace, his former girlfriend, and by his failure to make his brother Lincoln acknowledge that he is a better hustler than Lincoln is. In addition to such personal issues, the play repeats and revises the murder of Abraham Lincoln on both the simulacral level of the arcade, where the black Lincoln impersonator — complete with top hat, false beard, black frock coat, and white face mask — is shot at all day with blanks, and on the level of a very realistic re-enactment of Abraham Lincoln's assassination by John Wilkes Booth, when Booth's sexual and familial humiliations overwhelm him so that he actually shoots his brother. This realistic stage killing, like the multiple virtual ones, repeats and revises the same motif, as it unfolds in Parks's earlier *The America Play*. As opposed to the repetitive, obviously fake Lincoln shootings in the arcade, the realistic stage murder of Lincoln at the hands of his brother, which ends the play, is sufficiently mimetic to trigger reflections about the fatefulness of the brothers' lives, which ultimately seem to re-enact, or, to use Parks's terms, to repeat and revise, not only the assassination of President Abraham Lincoln by John Wilkes Booth but, more mythically still, the murder of Abel by Cain. Thus the seemingly realistic plot of *Topdog/Underdog* oscillates between ethnicity and universality, mimesis and simulation.

Structurally, *Topdog/Underdog*, developing Booth's and Lincoln's interaction in six scenes, all set in Booth's seedy rooming-house apartment and spanning one week, from Thursday night to Thursday night, is dominated by "three particular performance scenarios which are repeated and revised throughout the play" (Bush 84). They partially overlap, influence and thereby transform each other, before they finally converge. These performative scenarios are acted out as well as discussed and commented on in the interaction between the brothers which constitutes the play. They are: (1) Booth's self-stylization as a potent male and dexterous professsional card player against the background of his family history; (2) the Lincoln shootings; (3) the three-card monte con, in which the card dealer first shows, then covers up and moves around the winning card among other cards. Players must locate and identify the winning card. All three of these scenarios reproduce and hold up for inspection essential ground structures of stage plays as well as of games and play in general. The structural parallels between the three performative scenarios named and stage plays turn *Topdog/Underdog* into a meta-drama which both multiplies and thematizes its own basic constituents.

The interplay of the performative scenarios in *Topdog/Underdog* demonstrates that staged as well as lived realities partake in important ways of the nature of games and of play — an insight which can be substantiated by a comparison of the structural ingredients of Parks's play with some major findings of contemporary game theory. It is my contention that the added factor x Parks writes about in "An Equation for Black People Onstage," which, in her view, will transform and spice up the dramatic consideration of the African American situation, is most importantly embedded in *Topdog/Underdog* by her demonstration of the universality of play structures. This very universality of play both organizes and transcends interethnic conflicts and provides a platform for shifty re-negotiations of contingencies, which may turn the attitudes of Parks's African Americans into an emblem of the twenty-first century's *zeitgeist* in general. Whereas research on Parks has hitherto concentrated on other important factors, such as economic aspects of unemployment and money circulation (see Dietrick and Tucker-Abramson), history (see Achilles, Birkle, Foster, Holder, and Schmidt), masculinity (see Bush), and meta-theatre (see Wetmore, "Re-enacting"), this approach tries to highlight universalizing tendencies of *Topdog/Underdog* based on ludic elements.

Performative scenarios whose ground structures resemble those of games dominate Parks's drama from *The America Play* and *Venus* (1995) to *Topdog/Underdog*. As scenarios such as the Lincoln shootings and the three-card monte con tend to swallow up the action of the play, they suggest a growing convergence of games and play on the one hand and reality and life on the other. Beyond the concrete issues it addresses, Parks's drama demonstrates by its structural layout — multiple forms of play within play — the existence of a universe of the playful that tends to collapse the distinction between virtuality and reality and to become universal. Interestingly, this diagnosis, implied by Parks, is confirmed by game theory, which is often inspired by the current phenomenon of digitalized multiplayer online games. The findings of game theory are nevertheless relevant for the discussion of Parks's *Topdog/Underdog*, as the Lincoln killings and the three-card monte act are also multiplayer games. Computerized versions of their arcade and street scenarios are easily imaginable. The difference is a difference of medium, not of essence.

Traditional approaches to play and the ludic such as Johan Huizinga's *Homo Ludens*

(1938) and Roger Caillois's *Les jeux et les hommes* (1958) depart from a strict opposition between the realm of play and the real world. In this view, reality is an unquestionable given, while play, measurable against the norm of the real, is exceptional, idiosyncratic, and potentially negligible. Under the current impact of the digital universe, the demarcations between what is real as opposed to playful are being redrawn, however. Contemporary theorists hold that play, gesturing towards both the serious and the inconsequential, "in the fullest sense is coextensive with culture" (Ehrmann 44; cit. Motte 33). Play negotiates not only the conflict between virtuality and reality, earnestness and fun, but also between order and disorder. Games, as well as art, constitute self-constructed environments which follow their own rules and control contingency and randomness. The clear-cut distinction between ordered and rule-bound play on the one hand and disorderly, unruly real life on the other proves as unsustainable as that between reality and virtuality, however. There are games like chess which try to eliminate contingency. But there are others which invite it, such as baseball, allowing for unpredictable events, and roulette, including chance events (Morson 134–138).

The games played in *Topdog/Underdog*—three-card monte, the Lincoln act, and the familial game of systematic rule-breaking—also negotiate between the opposite poles of total control and total contingency, between Lincoln's impeccable expertise with a deck of cards and Booth's anarchic disorganization. Three-card monte can be positioned between roulette and baseball because, like baseball, it allows for more application of skill than roulette, which is based on chance alone, but is also heavily chance-dependent. As in the case of roulette, there is a statistical probability that the house, or the gang of con men, will win most of the time. Nevertheless, there is also the chance to really beat the con men either by superior power of observation or sheer luck: "Roulette and similar games are about 'beating the odds,' which is possible but by definition unlikely" (Morson 136). This is the chance Booth seeks and overrates. In the following, the negotiations between rule- and chance-dependence, between predetermination and spontaneity within the three performative scenarios which shape *Topdog/Underdog* will be inspected more closely.

Booth's Self-Stylization Against the Background of His Family History

Topdog/Underdog opens on the tentative continuation of a very unstable familial situation. Lincoln has given up his job as a three-card monte dealer, as his partner Lonnie was shot. He has accepted a job in an arcade as an Abraham Lincoln impersonator. He has been thrown out by his wife, Cookie, has moved in with his unemployed brother Booth and is living with him in his rooming house room without sink, toilet, or running water. They live on the wages Lincoln brings in every Friday and on the things Booth steals. Lincoln is in danger of losing his job to a wax doll. Booth wants to re-establish his relationship with his ex-girlfriend Grace. Obviously, neither the economic nor the intersubjective aspects of this cohabitation are unproblematic. When Lincoln suggests that he is the sole breadwinner of the two, Booth insists that he can rely on his inheritance, a remark that unfolds its destructive potential at the end of the play (15).* Nevertheless, both brothers seem to have settled into the semblance of a husband-and-wife arrangement, with Booth in the feminine role. When, in the second scene of the play, the brothers play the game of Ma and Pa on pay day, they demonstrate their awareness of this arrangement and their respective roles within it. The interaction of the brothers obviously bears traces of the same playful constructedness as the Lincoln act and the three-card monte con in which they are also involved (24). This is particularly true with regard to Booth's self-stylization, which in large parts dominates the interaction of the two brothers.

Booth's perception of the world and himself can be described as a naïve acceptance of appearances and the belief in their radiation as symbolic capital (see Bourdieu). Booth believes, for example, that he will change into an expert card player, if he simply renames himself "3-Card" (6, 17). The fact that he violently threatens anybody, especially his brother Lincoln, who may choose to ignore this new moniker, betrays the strength of his belief in the possibility of an identity change via the doubtful magic of a name: "Anybody not calling me 3-Card gets a bullet" (17). When, at the end of Parks's play, Lincoln calls Booth "Mr. 3-Card" ironically, as he has just proved to Booth that the name does not provide him with the desired identity of a card wizard, Booth makes good his threat (105). While Lincoln is earning money in bizarre ways, Booth is stealing clothes "generously" (26) in order to heighten both brothers' social prestige by polishing their outward appearances: "Booth is essentially shopping (or shoplifting) for new identities.... As he peels off each layer of stolen identity, we never see the true Booth, only more clothes" (Larson 195). Booth wants to impress his former girlfriend Grace both by the surface grandeur of his new but stolen clothes and by buying her a ring which is not quite what it seems: "Diamond. Well, diamond-esque" (8). Even the telephone, he explains to his brother, is not so important as a pragmatic means of communication but rather as a symbolic appliance, signaling financial solidity and personal independence to a woman (30). Booth's spurious claim of being reunited with Grace, who aptly studies "cosmetology" (41), is based on a fabricated reinvention of Grace's identity for his own benefit: "She wiped her hand over our breakup. She wiped her hand over her childhood, her teenage years, her first boyfriend, just so she could say that she been mine since the dawn of time" (36–37). Booth is so willing to believe in appearances that he can even accept them when he frankly admits that they are distortions.

Booth's preparations for a romantic dinner with Grace also follow this predilection for appearance over substance. The crystal and silver Booth stole for the occasion make a grand impression, just like the stolen suits. The only problem is that Grace does not appear to appreciate them (62–63). Booth cannot accept this humiliation in front of Lincoln, which obviously falsifies his optimistic reports of his relationship with Grace. In the last scene of the play, he therefore invents a rosy future of married life with Grace. Grace wants to marry him, he announces, and he wants Lincoln to move out for Grace to move in. Booth claims that Grace even wants his baby, whom, in case it is a boy, they will name after Lincoln (85). Lincoln realistically admonishes Booth to get a job to be

---

*All quotations from Suzan-Lori Parks, *Topdog/Underdog* (New York: Theatre Communications Group, 2001) are by page numbers in parentheses.

able to care for his wife (87). In Booth's game of simulated realities and make-believe identities, Lincoln is not as near-omniscient as in hustling cards, however. He sees through Booth, but not sufficiently to fathom the total fabrication which Booth's alleged reconciliation with Grace represents. In reality, Grace's lack of interest in, and indifference to, Booth becomes so unbearable to him that he kills her as a last resort to wipe out and silence the reality of her opposition (107). The overwhelming desire to keep up appearances leads to death as the only verifiable reality. In order to maintain the fabrication of Booth as successful lover and potential husband and father, which is not matched by any facts in real life, he is even willing to kill.

Booth's relationship with Grace, who significantly remains an off-stage character, is nothing but a projection screen of his rivalry with his brother Lincoln, with whom he wants to compete as a card player, but mostly as a man: "Women are completely absent from this play. They are literally signifiers, symbols of the brothers' failed attempts to achieve a stable masculinity" (Tucker-Abramson 90). Booth construes an illusionary virility for himself with Lincoln as his ambivalent role model, whom he tries to both emasculate and imitate. He drastically insinuates Lincoln's impotence and weakness and several times claims to have slept with his brother's wife, Cookie: "You a limp dick jealous whiteface motherfucker whose wife dumped him cause he couldnt get it up and she told me so. Came crawling to me cause she needed a man" (43). But he also makes sure that he, too, uses the same oversize, magnum condoms Lincoln claims to use (40). He brags to Lincoln about sex with Grace in front of a mirror, again spectacle being more important than experience (39–40). Lincoln punctuates his brother's self-congratulatory praise of his manhood by insinuating that, going by the evidence of the porn magazines under his bed, his sexual activities restrict themselves largely to masturbation. Like the aggression involved in the Lincoln shooting act, which may even be satisfied by shooting at a wax doll, Booth's love life is much more virtual than he claims. He argues that he needs "constant sexual release." Otherwise libidinous impulses will turn into sheer aggressiveness, a process that again likens him to the arcade visitors who play John Wilkes Booth: "I'd be out there doing who knows what, shooting people and shit" (43). This connection of sex and violence is also implied in the ambivalent meaning of the magnums he wants to use for sex: "through the metaphor of the penis as gun, sex too becomes a violent act" (Tucker-Abramson 92). But the reverse is also true. Grace has to die because she denies Booth sex. So he uses the other magnum. Booth's self-stylization shares many characteristics with the Lincoln act and the three-card monte game. It is also a performative scenario that resembles a play, a monodrama in this case, in which Booth never steps out of the role of his virtual maturity. If the role is no longer sustainable, he reacts violently.

For Booth, the relationship to his brother clearly continues the traumatic separation of the parents who left the brothers alone at age 13 and 16, respectively (63, 67). More than Lincoln, Booth is chained to perceptions and experiences of his childhood, which dominate his adult life and which he tries to counteract by the scenario of his imagined maturity. His interest in fancy clothes, for example, is, in the last analysis, an attempt to adopt and thereby preserve aspects of his father's presence, remembered and admired from childhood. One of the father's striking characteristics was his elegant suits: "He had some nice stuff. I would look at his stuff and calculate thuh how long it would take till I was big enough to fit it." As he believes that he will become a competent card player by adopting a name which suggests just that, Booth thinks that his father's personality will rub off on him if he wears similar clothes. Lincoln's attitude is completely different. He burns the father's clothes because they remind him of his death: "I got tired of looking at em without him in em" (27). Thereby he more realistically "both affirms and denies clothing's ability to imbue identity" (Larson 194). Booth is still ailing from the breakup of the parents two decades ago. He still wants Lincoln to care for him, as he is three years his junior (19). While Booth openly expresses his sorrow for the broken-up family, Lincoln only does so indirectly by the blues song he sings in the first scene (Geis 121). The song obliquely reflects the loss of both his parents and his wife and uncannily anticipates his death, conjuring up the atmosphere of isolation and loss that surrounds this African American family. This melancholy atmosphere may have triggered the father's gallows humor when he named his sons Booth and Lincoln, respectively.

The brothers' conscious reconstruction of their family history sets in late in the play in scene 5, when Lincoln goes through the family photograph album and begins to reminisce about a familial harmony that never existed and more realistically about pranks in which he bonded with Booth against their father. Together the brothers approach the mystery of their parents' separation. The mother left two years before the father, who seems to have waited till Lincoln was eighteen and could take care of his younger brother alone. Lincoln retrospectively senses parental desires within the prosperous and deceptively harmonious family scenario, which were irreconcilable with it and finally uprooted it: "I think there was something out there that they liked more than they liked us and for years they was struggling against moving towards that more liked something. Each of them had a special something that they was struggling against" (66). As the Lincoln act and the three-card monte scam, the brothers' family life seems determined by an instinctual dynamics of subterraneous forces which move and transform it. Both Booth and Lincoln try to make sense of this process in equally idiosyncratic ways. Booth concludes that the job routines and the upkeep of the house became insufferable for the parents. This is why he himself declines to work: "Like thuh whole family mortgage bills going to work thing was just too much. And I dont blame them. You dont see me holding down a steady job. Cause its bullshit and I know it. I seen how it cracked them up and I aint going there" (67).

As a farewell gift and inheritance each brother received the identical sum of five hundred dollars from their parents — Booth from his mother in one of her nylon stockings and Lincoln from his father in a clean handkerchief. From the almost magical symmetry of these dispensations Booth concludes that there must have been a secret understanding between the parents, although they split: "They left separately but they was in agreement. Maybe they arrived at the same place at the same time, maybe they renewed they wedding vows, maybe they got another family." Lincoln is less optimistic: "Maybe they got 2 new kids. 2 boys. Different than us, though" (68). While Booth hankers after the parents' potential reunion, Lincoln considers the family as an arrangement that can be reproduced at will with different participants. Booth cannot bear such randomness. If he cannot have his parents back, he wants to team up with Lincoln again: "I didnt mind them leaving cause you was there. Thats why Im hooked on us working together. If we could work together it would be like old times.... It was you and me against thuh world, Link. It could be like that again" (69).

Like three-card monte and the Lincoln killings, the family is a performative scenario that provides cohesion by the observance of rules and the ritual control of desire and aggression. From Booth's and Lincoln's limited infant points of view, their father's and mother's interaction must have appeared as fascinating and enigmatic as the goings on of the three card monte setup for bystanders whose curiosity draws them into the game. In this regard, Booth's urgent pleading with Lincoln to become a three-card monte dealer again and to accept him, Booth, as his partner reveals itself as a strategy to reestablish the broken familial bonds. Booth wants to reknit himself to the familial harmony of his childhood by using the system of assigned roles within the three-card monte con as a surrogate for equally clearly structured family relationships. This is possible because both the family and the con can be conceived of as sharing the ground structures of games. But Booth wants to superimpose the family solidarity based on love on the con's solidarity based on greed, which is a transformation of the latter game that must fail. From this angle it is obvious why Booth opposes his brother's involvement in the Lincoln act. There is only one role left in this binary scenario of murdering or being murdered, that of Booth, the assassin. Unlike three-card monte, the Lincoln act leaves no room for the fraternal solidarity Booth craves for.

In scene 6, the last scene of the play, Booth and Lincoln again discuss their parents and their disloyalties. While the father's episodic sprees in brothels do not challenge his marriage per se, the mother's affair with, and pregnancy by, another man leads to the parents' separation. The brothers have been influenced in very different ways by witnessing their parents' sexual exploits. Lincoln, unaware of the mother's affairs, was allowed to accompany his father to his mistresses, apparently to admire his erotic potential. But the youth experiences his own superior attractiveness and has a successful initiation into sexual independence and adulthood: "He made it seem like it was this big deal this great thing he was letting me witness but it wasnt like nothing.... One of his ladies liked me, so I would do her after he'd done her" (89). Lincoln is unexpectedly liberated by his implication in his father's affairs. By contrast, Booth's emotional dependence on his mother increases when he becomes the accidental witness of her adulterous relationship with a man who visits her on Thursdays and whom Booth therefore calls "her sideman, her Thursday dude, her backdoor man" (99). Coincidentally, Lincoln offers his brother the job of sideman in the three-card monte con so that Booth can adopt a role similar to the one he may have desired at home as a boy — the oedipal position of the successful rival of his father in gaining the favors of his mother (72). From Booth's perspective the three-card monte team of his brother, whom he sees as a surrogate father all along, emerges as a surrogate family constellation. In this context, his affair with Lincoln's wife may be a symbolic reenactment of the mother's infidelity — this time with Booth as triumphant lover. From the angle of this psycho-logic Booth's murder of Lincoln at the end of the play completes the oedipal father slaying which the mother's departure sets in motion.

At one point, the mother wants money for an abortion from her lover, perhaps to save her marriage. But he refuses and she leaves with this man for good, handing Booth the five hundred dollars, wrapped in one of her silk stockings, as an inheritance and a farewell gift. While the experience of the father's visits to prostitutes is connected with Lincoln's own sexual empowerment, for Booth the mother's affair is tied to her loss and disappearance. The silk stocking is not a container of money for him but the embodiment of the mother's ambivalent mystery. She made a precious gift to him, expressing her appreciation for her son, but at the same time left him forever. This insoluble contradiction explains Booth's synecdochic hold on the stocking which he keeps intact over the years. Booth's strong emotional reliance on Lincoln — the only person who shared his mother with him — and the desperation with which he tries to win Grace back, who left him like his mother, bespeak the trauma this farewell scene represents and may explain why masturbation is the only adequate form of sexuality for Booth. He is emasculated rather than empowered by witnessing his mother's adultery, as sexuality is coupled with irretrievable loss and sadness (99–100, 104–05). It is perhaps this Faulknerian dimension of psychological and emotional depth which is most responsible for the hitherto unique position of *Topdog/Underdog* in Parks's canon.

The Lincoln Shootings

Re-enactments of Abraham Lincoln's assassination permeate both *The America Play* and *Topdog/Underdog*. Throughout *The America Play* Lincoln is a volatile and sliding signifier. He is referred to as the "Foundling" rather than the Founding Father — occasionally also as "faux-father" or "foe-father," thus paying tribute to both the arbitrariness and aggressiveness of white settlement in America and, perhaps additionally, to the foundational significance of Derrida's *différance* (see Parks, *The America Play* 159, 184). In *The America Play* as well as *Topdog/Underdog*, the historical event of President Lincoln's assassination by John Wilkes Booth and its reverberations emerge as a conflation of plays and games. In *The America Play*, Parks intertextually plays with the universal mode of play as it were. Scenes of Tom Taylor's *Our American Cousin* (1858), the play whose performance turned into Lincoln's death scene, are being reproduced in *The America Play*, which deals with theme park recreations of Lincoln shootings, which are then repeated and revised in *Topdog/Underdog* by turning them into the life story of two contemporary African American men, allegedly jocularly named Booth and Lincoln by their father.* By signifying on the assassination of Abraham Lincoln in the sense of Henry Louis Gates's *Signifying Monkey* (1988), Parks ironically foregrounds the determining force of performative style and memorable aphorism for the ways in which historical data become forms of cultural memory which predetermine yet further re-enactments. Deborah Geis aptly summarizes these dialectics:

> As she will repeat in *Topdog/Underdog*, Parks uses tourists who want to act out the part of Booth in the assassination of Lincoln — and the complicity, even profit, of the Lincoln

---

*In *The America Play*, Parks not only repeats but also revises Taylor's *Our American Cousin*. She adds a line to Act III, Scene 2, of *Our American Cousin*: "Sir, your American talk do woo me" (Parks, *The America Play* 187; see Taylor 46–47). Parks also claims to reproduce dialogue from Act III, Scene 5, of *Our American Cousin*, but actually combines passages from Act III, Scenes 6 and 7, conflating two different characters.

impersonator — to comment on the reduction of history to a kind of cultural tourism that prioritizes the thrills of revenge and death over the real moments of bodily trauma or the political implications of the assassination itself. The tourists are would-be actors imitating the failed actor Booth, but like Booth, derive a feeling of power from 'making' history happen. The Lincoln impersonator earns money and fame from the act, but he also allows himself to be violated [Geis 104–105].

It is in this disruptive sense that *Topdog/Underdog* is a continuation of both *The America Play* and *Our American Cousin*. The both serious and inconsequential constituents of play determine the comedy of manners, African American drama, as well as political assassinations and ongoing familial tragedy. Over the centuries Parks's plays thus intertextually converse with the ancient trope of *theatrum mundi*, Jaques's famous soliloquy in Shakespeare's *As You Like It* (Act II, Scene 5) and with the play within the play in *Hamlet* (Act III, Scene 2). The audiences and readers of *The America Play* and *Topdog/Underdog* watch a theatricality which derives from both hallowed cultural traditions and the everyday life of amusement galleries and street gambling at the same time.

When Lincoln first appears in *Topdog/Underdog*, he is coming home from his job as Abraham Lincoln impersonator to his brother's rooming house, still in his Lincoln garb. Booth, taken by surprise when his brother appears behind him in his Lincoln costume, draws a gun and almost shoots him. Although this situation is realistically motivated — Lincoln is wearing his costume because he had to hurry to catch the bus — it also ironically extends Lincoln's job situation, in which he is a target, to his private sphere. Already in this initial stage of the play, Lincoln's brother tentatively steps into the shoes of the Abraham Lincoln assassin whose name he bears and practices a role which he will later play so horribly expertly (6).

Lincoln tells his brother about an experience he had on the bus home from work. An obviously wealthy schoolboy, enthusiastic about Abraham Lincoln and what seems to be his present incarnation, offers Lincoln ten dollars for his autograph. Lincoln first wants to reduce the sum to five, as the five dollar bill bears the Lincoln image. But then he asks for ten and accepts twenty as the boy only has a twenty dollar bill on him, promising that "Honest Abe" will give the change back on the bus the next day (9–10). But contrary to his promise, Lincoln spends the whole twenty dollars immediately on drinks for himself and other barflies, which brings him back a little of the acceptance that money can buy, so well known to him from his earlier gambling days. The boy is duped by Lincoln because he all-too naïvely believes that Abraham Lincoln's replica will share the historical model's proverbial honesty: "he does not know actual history from a disparate facsimile" (Larson 185). Lincoln's reaction shows that simulations can have very real and problematic consequences. He brings the same attitude to the Lincoln act as he formerly did to the three-card monte con in which he was involved. For him, games are played for profit alone. The unfeeling exploitation of the little boy demonstrates the same callousness which he later betrays in his reminiscences about his three-card monte crew's exploitation of their victims: "We took them for everything they had and everything they ever wanted to have. We took a father for the money he was gonna get his kids new bike with and he cried in the street while we vanished" (54). In another respect, Lincoln differentiates between three-card monte and the Lincoln act. When Booth suggests that the Lincoln act is a "hustle," Lincoln corrects him and argues that "people know the real deal. When people know the real deal it aint a hustle" (20). Both performative scenarios differ with regard to their comprehensibility. In the case of the Lincoln act the rules of the game are known to the players and in the case of the three-card monte con they are not. The tourists are aware, for example, that they are using blanks and that they are not really killing anybody. They know, of course, that Lincoln is not Abraham Lincoln although he is decked out in Lincoln paraphernalia.

Lincoln himself also distinguishes between the simulation and the simulator: "They say the clothes make the man. All day long I wear that getup. But that dont make me who I am" (27). And he adds: "I was Lincoln on my own before any of that" (28). While Booth believes that the Lincoln impersonation absorbs his brother's future into the national past of slavery and oppression — "way back then when folks was slaves and shit" (20) — Lincoln clearly claims an identity that may be identical in name but is different in substance. Lincoln's further claim that his Lincoln job is just indifferent to him — "sit down, you know, easy work" (31) — proves untenable, however. Lincoln's best customer, who seems to come for the Lincoln shooting very frequently and may be another (black) brother, whispers disquieting remarks in Lincoln's ear while he performs the shooting. These seemingly enigmatic remarks hit Lincoln more severely than the caps. The best customer asks Lincoln whether the show stops, "'when no ones watching or does the show go on?'" And he provides an indirect answer to this question when he tells Lincoln that he can only be himself "'when no ones watching'" (32). The implication of these statements is that one can only maintain an independent identity outside the performative scenarios one is involved in or when essential conditions that define these scenarios (the presence of customers or players; or, in the case of the Lincoln act, the presence of someone willing to adopt the role of Booth) are invalidated. Within the scenario one is not free to be outside.

But are Booth and Lincoln ever outside? The interrelations of the several scenarios of *Topdog/Underdog* generate multiple ironies with regard to one's position inside and outside of these scenarios in a dance of continual border crossings, leading back to variants of what one just left. In other words, to repetitions and revisions. Lincoln claims to have left the three-card monte scenario, for example, because his partner Lonnie was shot and he knew: "I was next, so I quit. I saved my life" (33). But this move of leaving the three-card monte scam sets Lincoln free to enter the game of the Lincoln act, in which his fear of being shot is virtualized but also routinized. When Lincoln returns home, he leaves the scenario of the Lincoln act but enters a privacy in which his brother Booth, by being Booth, automatically recreates it again. By having their father name the brothers after the historical participants of the original Lincoln shooting, which can thereby be repeated and revised both in the penny arcade and in Booth's rooming house, Parks generates an indeterminacy about her protagonists' respective identities which matches the indeterminacy of the winning card in its constant repositionings during the movements of the three-card monte con. In this sense, Parks's *Topdog/Underdog* reproduces the ground structure of three-card monte.

When Booth suggests that he might rework one of the cap guns used for the Lincoln shootings as a real gun, he is initiating a discussion about the reality or virtuality of, and the motivating forces behind, the Lincoln act: "You ever wonder if someones gonna come in there with a real gun? A real gun with real slugs? Someone with uh axe tuh grind or something?" (46). Booth thus begins to invest the performative scenario of the Lincoln act with his own fraternal rivalry. Lincoln's response, the description of the actual arcade situation, makes clear that the Lincoln act is a game to release and channel murderous instincts. In a dented fuse box Lincoln can see the reversed reflection of the customers and would-be assassins who are turned into John Wilkes Booth impersonators by the arrangement they enter: "And when the gun touches me he can feel that Im warm and he knows Im alive. And if Im alive then he can shoot me dead. And for a minute, with him hanging back there behind me, its real.... More come in. Uh whole day full. Bunches of kids, little good for nothings, in they school uniforms.... Housewives with they mouths closed tight, shooting more than once" (48).

Obviously the arcade game encapsulates the murderous instincts of its customers. Perhaps Lincoln's fear of being replaced by a wax dummy is unjustified, if the customers are really checking on the warmth of his body before they shoot. In this case, the motivation of the customers is killing somebody who is killable, i.e., "warm" and therefore alive. If so much realism is necessary, the wax dummy will have a hard time replacing Lincoln. Lincoln's description of the actual shootings raises questions as to how close the arcade experience needs to be to an actual murder. Would a computerized Lincoln shooting game also sell and render the wax doll superfluous as the last vestige of tangible realities? Like Booth who projects his unacknowledged anger against his brother for not sufficiently taking care of him into the Lincoln shooting, all the customers project their respective aggressions in similar ways. For some may be true what one critic suggests: "they are essentially becoming members of a lynch mob, lining up to kill a black man.... For they can, of course, see Lincoln's blackness. He wears only white*face* and they come from behind him, in full view of his black neck" (Larson 190). But others, like the tight-mouthed housewives who pull the trigger several times, may have their white husbands in their sights.

In order to avoid Lincoln's replacement by a wax dummy, the brothers try to intensify the Lincoln act at home, as Booth believes Lincoln can better compete by a heightened intensity, of which the wax doll is constitutionally incapable. Whereas the historical Lincoln was the spectator of a play when he was assassinated by an actor, Lincoln jazzes up his presentation of Abraham Lincoln's death by histrionic antics which expose him as an actor: "HE TAKES HIS GETUP OUT OF HIS SHOPPING BAG. HE PUTS IT ON, SLOWLY, LIKE AN ACTOR PREPARING FOR A GREAT ROLE: FROCK COAT, PANTS, BEARD, TOP HAT, NECKTIE.... HE PRETENDS TO GET SHOT, FLINGS HIMSELF ON THE FLOOR AND THRASHES AROUND" (35). Abraham Lincoln's transition from the spectator of *Our American Cousin* to the present-day representation by an actor resembles the transition of the passing-by spectator from the outside of the three-card monte game to an actor within the context of the game. Both the Lincoln act and the three-card monte scam are preconceived performative scenarios which turn all their participants into actors.

When, in Scene 3, Booth and Lincoln actually rehearse the Lincoln act together, Booth, getting carried away, seems to melt into his historical namesake: "Booth screaming 'I am the assassin!' breaks down a psychological barrier between Lincoln's life and Lincoln-the-President's life and makes the superficial costume very real" (Larson 191). As a consequence, the brothers shy away from their own deep immersion in the shooting of Abraham Lincoln which suddenly appears "too real" (50). Lincoln is afraid that he will scare away customers by this hyper-intensity, which may disturb the conventions of the petrified Lincoln reception established in history classes: "People are funny about they Lincoln shit. Its historical. People like they historical shit in a certain way. They like it to unfold the way they folded it up. Neatly like a book. Not ragged and bloody and screaming. You trying to get me fired" (50). Both Booth's identification with his historical model and Lincoln's rejection of the rehearsal's realism are indicators of the Lincoln act's mediating function between the participants' bloodthirstiness and the wish to camouflage and deny this bloodthirstiness. The Lincoln act both releases and controls the murderous instincts of the participants which they yet do not have to acknowledge. It negotiates between the sheer and anarchic desire for bloodshed and the virtuality of the arcade game which neutralizes this desire but also partially satisfies it. Precisely this intermediate status between seriousness and fun, reality and virtuality, the equilibrium between arbitrariness or messiness and order or shape is the domain of play.

When, towards the end of *Topdog/Underdog*, Lincoln has been fired and replaced by the dummy, the brothers take a look back on the Lincoln impersonation. In a sense, they historicize it, as the nation has historicized Abraham Lincoln. In both cases, historicization means sentimentalization, a nostalgic form of memory that denies and ignores the impact of the past on the present. Even Booth, who tried so hard to persuade Lincoln to give it up, suddenly decides that he will miss the Lincoln costume on his brother (89). This feeling is due to his belief that he will not have to see Lincoln in the costume again, that the past is just that. Lincoln's willingness to don the Lincoln garb for a last time to have a photograph taken has a similar motivation. The photograph will document a phase of his life that has no longer any impact on him, of which he can say: "This wasnt a bad job. I just outgrew it" (91). But Lincoln also has doubts about how the performance may yet affect his identity. He still cannot tackle the question of his best customer about where the impersonation ends and his personality begins, or whether there is no distinction between the two. On the one hand Lincoln is satisfied with having been "a damn good Honest Abe considering." On the other hand, he claims to have been just himself in a different getup: "I was just sitting there in thuh getup. I wasnt pretending nothing" (90, 91). Booth, too, rejects the option of taking over Lincoln's arcade job as he is not "into pretending Im someone else all day" (91). Ironically, Booth is continually pretending to be a successful lover and card hustler. His very identity consists of a permanent self-stylization that glosses over his inability to cope with the loss of his mother.

Topdog/Underdog raises severe doubts about the possibility of simply shedding the roles one plays and wriggling out of performative scenarios one has become part of. Lincoln puts on the Lincoln getup for a photograph that celebrates the end of Lincoln impersonation (89–90). He stays in it till the end of the play which is coterminous with the end of his life. When Booth takes the picture, the shot, of Lincoln in his garb to preserve the memory of a phase of life that seems irrevocably over, this proves as deceptive as the final disappearance of the brothers' parents, which only seemingly ends their influence on their sons' lives. Booth's conduct derives almost exclusively from the departure of the mother. By the same token, the photographic parting "shot" with the Lincoln impersonation assumes a macabre double entendre when Booth actually shoots Lincoln in the end. Like the three-card monte bystanders once drawn into the game, the brothers cannot escape their assigned roles in the Lincoln shooting scenario. Historical events may not persist as such, but they generate constellations hard to recognize and even more difficult to revise.

Three-Card Monte

In African American drama the combination of entertainment acts and gambling goes back to Loften Mitchells' play *Star of the Morning* (1965), in which the turn-of-the-century black singers Bert Williams and George Walker play a poker game whose loser has to put lamp soot on his face — a gesture as humiliating as Booth's ineptitude as a gambler and Lincoln's acceptance of whiteface for his Lincoln impersonation (Mitchell 594, 600). From the beginning of *Topdog/Underdog* Booth imagines himself as a three-card monte ace like his brother Lincoln, when he practices "HIS 3-CARD MONTE SCAM ON THE CLASSIC SETUP" alone and already renames himself "3-card" (5). Right from the start, it is clear that, for Booth, losses in gambling symbolize the loss of his parents. He wants to stake five hundred dollars, exactly the sum his mother bequeathed to him. And he fantasizes in ways which recall his own problems with his parents about the ignominious familial background of a fictitious adversary, whom he just gloriously beat in a three-card monte game he really played against himself (6). Booth's remarks appear as a projection of his own suffering and demonstrate that, for him, the scenario of three-card monte is a reanimation of the scenario of his family history. While for Lincoln, three-card monte has come to mean a threat to his life since his partner Lonnie was shot, Booth romanticizes what for him was probably a time of prosperity, when his brother brought home lots of money won by the three-card monte con. Booth suggests a new three-card monte team with Lincoln again as card dealer and himself as Stickman: "You would throw the cards and I'd be yr Stickman. The one in the crowd who looks just like an innocent passerby, who looks like just another player, like just another customer, but who gots intimate connections with you, the Dealer, the one throwing the cards, the main man" (17–18). Clearly, Booth needs his brother as a near-paternal mentor, "the main man," with whom he entertains "intimate connections." Once again, Booth conflates the reestablishment of the family he lost and his career as a con man. Even so, Lincoln refuses his offer of cooperation and intimacy. Booth does not consider that a major reason for Lincoln's rejection may be the fact that Booth suggests for himself exactly the position in the crew which Lincoln's murdered partner Lonny held (33, 54). Both brothers remain ensconced in their respective mental scenarios.

By contrast to the Lincoln act, the three-card monte con is based on a setup in which the distinction between the team of con men on the one hand and their customers, the passersby to be drawn into the games on the other is intentionally blurred. The lethal Stickman-role Booth wants to play is precisely the site of this opacity: the Stickman acts like a bystander fascinated by his luck in the game, but he is really a crew member who lures passersby into the game. In this regard, the three-card monte con depends on the obscurity of its rules. Booth, who is unable to penetrate surface impressions, does not understand this when he considers "the winning of the game as a combination of skill and luck" (Dietrick 8) and suggests to Lincoln: "We do the card game people will know the real deal. Sometimes we will win sometimes they will win. They fast they win, we faster we win" (20). By contrast Lincoln tries to make Booth understand that the game has a preconceived script with fixed roles for the crew or cast, like a play in the theatre. As this is not known to the potential victims, the scenario functions like a trap that predetermines the outcome: "Cards aint luck. Cards is work. Cards is skill. Aint never nothing lucky about cards" (33).

The performative scenarios of three-card monte as well as the Lincoln act increasingly invade Booth's rooming house room. Lincoln wants to rehearse the Lincoln act to avoid being laid off and, in order to win Booth's cooperation, offers in turn to monitor Booth's practice of three-card monte. By rehearsal and practice, forms of repetition and revision, both these scenarios increasingly reveal their prime function, the negotiation of aggression. Lincoln's promise to introduce Booth to his former three-card monte gang, if he becomes expert enough, is accompanied by the recommendation to buy a good gun. Predictably, Booth wants to steal a gun used for the Lincoln shootings in order to rework it for real bullets (48). Booth's wounded pride and feelings of inferiority triggered by what he perceives as the superiority of his brother lead to a conflation of both scenarios. The Lincoln act and three-card monte begin to converge on the basis of their common game structure but also as ritualizations of desire and violence.

Lincoln's return to three-card monte is motivated by his being fired as a Lincoln impersonator but also because cards are his addiction: "HE STUDIES THEM LIKE AN ALCOHOLIC WOULD STUDY A DRINK" (55). His renewed interest finally allows him to give in to his brother and to adopt the paternal mentor role demanded of him. Half of scene 5 is taken up by his attempt to initiate Booth into the particulars of the three-card monte game (69–81). Like a director of a play instructing the cast, Lincoln explains the roles indispensable for the scenario: "Theres thuh Dealer, thuh Stickman, thuh Sides, thuh Lookout and thuh Mark" (71). The first lesson he tries to teach Booth is the distinction between illusion and reality—a lesson Booth seems constitutionally unable to learn, addicted to make-believe as he is: "First thing you learn is what is. Next thing you learn is what aint. You dont know what is you dont know what aint, you dont know shit" (72). The dealer must always be able to make this distinction. Lincoln, who claims this position for himself, attributes to the dealer the top rank in the hierarchy of the game's crew, an omniscient, godlike position. If anybody, it is he who pulls the strings, who observes the crowd, his crew and even himself dispassionately: "Everybody out there is part of the crowd. His crew is part of the crowd, he himself is part of the crowd. Dealer always sizes up thuh crowd" (73).

Lincoln also tries to explain the psychological and perceptual dynamics of the game. The dealer controls the game by pretending to be dispassionately aloof, "although of course the Dealer has been wanting to throw his cards all along. Only he dont never show it." The dealer's pretended non-involvement functions as a foil and stimulus for the crowd's desire, which amalgamates material greed and the interest in spectacular skillfulness: "He holds back and thuh crowd, with their eagerness to see his skill and their willingness to take a chance, and their greediness to win his cash, the larceny in their hearts, all goad him on and push him to throw his cards" (73). Lincoln then points out the interplay of performance and speech that marks three-card monte as well as drama: "Theres 2 parts to throwing thuh cards. Both parts are fairly complicated. Thuh moves and thuh grooves, thuh talk and thuh walk, thuh patter and thuh pitter pat, thuh flap and thuh rap: what yr doing with yr mouth and what yr doing with yr hands" (74).

Three-card monte thus emerges as a highly complex performance that is both language- and action-based. It is driven by a mix of desires and it is a challenge to the perception of the itness of a situation, of what is real and what is not. The game, as rehearsed more skillfully by Lincoln and less so by Booth, is a parabolic demonstration that reality, meaning, and truth are as difficult to fix and nail down as the deuce of spades moving through the dealer's dexterous hands, accompanied by hypnotizing chants: "The game's great lesson is, ironically, just what Booth fears: the difficulty of reading signs, and the impossibility of the 'mark's' discerning, in Lincoln's words, 'what is' from 'what aint'" (Dietrick 8). Three-card monte thus appears as an illustration of Lacan's statement about the slippage of the signifier under the signified: "We are forced, then, to accept the notion of an incessant sliding of the signified under the signifier" (Lacan 87).

In scene 6, the last one in the play, Lincoln is back in the position of the three-card monte ace he once was, complete with lots of money and prestige among the women of his crowd: "you got it back you got yr shit back in thuh saddle, man you got back in business" (82). When Booth once again challenges Lincoln about his expertise as a card dealer, Lincoln has him set up the card table again. When he guesses the right card more than once, it is ironically Booth, otherwise not at all interested in empirical verifiability, who finds fault with the virtuality of their play situation shut away in the rooming house. It invalidates his success. Contrary to the rehearsal of the Lincoln act in his room, during which he shouts that he *is* Booth, he is worried that the three-card monte he plays with his brother does not "feel real" (96). Lincoln tells him that they will not be able to reproduce the game's usual situational context: "We're missing the essential elements. The crowd, the street, thuh traffic sounds, all that" (96). When Booth suggests that they can, nevertheless, heighten the realism of their private three-card monte game by playing for money seriously, Lincoln puts down the five hundred dollars he just won in the "real" three-card monte street hustle. Booth sets his inheritance against this sum, his mother's nylon stocking, containing the five hundred dollars she gave him when she left. Lincoln instinctively rejects the offer because he senses that too much is at stake but then deals the cards all the same.

From that moment on, three-card monte turns serious because real money can be lost. But the family history is also at stake because Booth's five hundred dollars expose and render vulnerable the memory of his mother, as well as his own identity based on this memory. Winning seriously in the decisive game when Booth cannot guess the winning card, Lincoln is not only challenging Booth's skill as a three-card monte player: "Aint yr fault if yr eyes aint fast. And you cant help it if you got 2 left hands, right?" (103). He is challenging Booth's whole sense of self as it develops out of the familial constellation of his childhood. This fundamental destabilization is signaled by the seemingly humorous banter about their brotherhood, which precedes the decisive three-card monte game.

Booth and Lincoln are certainly brothers in the sense that all African American men are. But the focus on their mother's promiscuity raises doubts as to their common paternity (103).

Lincoln can accept such uncertainties, but, characteristically, Booth wants to deny them. The child in him needs absolute trust in his mother, no strings attached. When Lincoln has won the mother's nylon stocking, he is flabbergasted that Booth never opened it to see whether there are actually five hundred dollars in it: "She coulda been jiving you, bro. Jiving you that there really *was* money in this thing. Jiving you big time. Its like thuh cards" (105–06). Lincoln does not realize that the unopened nylon stocking with its implications of intimacy without reserve is the objective correlative of Booth's need to accept his mother's integrity as sacred, even in the face of his positive knowledge of her infidelity. Opening the stocking is therefore tantamount to violating Booth's innermost being. By contrast, Lincoln suggests that the mother may just be another player of games. Like a three-card monte hustler, she may have deceived Booth, had him on. In Lincoln's view, the position of the winning card has to be empirically verified to win, as the stocking has to be cut open to actually reveal the five hundred dollars. It is not enough to believe one knows where the right card is, which is what Booth does in the decisive last game. Perhaps Booth's acceptance of simulacra of all sorts goes back to the desire to honor his mother, although he knows that she may be less than honorable. Her honor can only be preserved by not looking too closely.

Lincoln makes matters worse by informing Booth that he never had a chance to win the decisive three-card monte game, since the godlike dealer masterminds it from its very beginning: "Cause its thuh first move that separates thuh Player from thuh Played. And thuh first move is to know that there aint no winning. It may look like you got a chance but the only time you pick right is when thuh man lets you" (106). Lincoln is neither Honest Abe nor an honest brother but a player following his self-interest, as he believes everybody else is, too. He cannot understand that this is different for Booth. While Lincoln may be near-omniscient as a card dealer within the scenario of three-card monte, he is unable to grasp that for Booth three-card monte is a way of redefining his relationship to his brother in a continuation of their childhood solidarity. Describing the three-card monte game as being predetermined by the dealer, Lincoln gives Booth to understand that this transformation does not work, that the underdog is the underdog right from the beginning, and that the dealer will always be top dog. In Lincoln's interpretation of the game, Booth will always remain inferior. In this case, the father's naming the brothers Booth and Lincoln is not at all a joke; it is a statement on unmovable hierarchies. Like the murder of Abel by Cain, the murder of Abraham Lincoln at the hands of John Wilkes Booth is perhaps not a singular historical event but an anthropological pattern which can be revised but does not lose its essential contours. Both the determining power of the three-card monte set-up and of the Booth-Lincoln constellations may also be a specifically American social allegory: "White America, the play implies, is playing with a stacked deck, especially economically" (Larson 199).

Actually shooting his brother, still in his Abraham Lincoln attire, Booth steps into the actor John Wilkes Booth's shoes, as well as into the shoes of the arcade customers. Fatefully, he is also becoming himself by fulfilling what his name anticipates. Booth's motivation for thus literalizing the Lincoln act derives from its convergence with the three-card monte con in Lincoln's interpretation. Like a paternal deity, like a national hero such as Abraham Lincoln, the card dealer inevitably decides the fate of his people, the players. John Wilkes Booth may have acted out similar feelings of inferiority as the ones Booth harbors. If Lincoln's opening of the nylon stocking proved the corruption of the mother with regard to her son, Lincoln's worldview would be completely confirmed, as it is confirmed by Grace's treacherousness. Therefore both Grace and Lincoln must die.

In their deaths, the three scenarios of Booth's self-stylization against the background of his family history, the Lincoln impersonation, and the three-card monte con converge: "In that final contest all three performative elements, the 3-card Monty game, Lincoln in costume, and the stakes of the fetishized memorial object are on display" (Bush 84). The fate of Booth and Lincoln depends on their respective positions within the game structures of their family history, the Lincoln act, and the three-card monte scam. The individuals are determined by their function within these constellations, as Lacan claims their position with regard to the purloined letter determines the characters in Poe's short story: "The slightest alteration in the relation between man and the signifier ... changes the whole course of history by modifying the lines which anchor his being" (Lacan 103–104; see also Muller and Richardson). As in moments of historical and mythical catastrophe, such as the murder of Abel by Cain, Abraham Lincoln by John Wilkes Booth, Martin Luther King, Jr., by his assassin, scenarios of domination and rebellion, superiority and inferiority, topdog and underdog seem to repeat themselves ineluctably in a Hegelian dialectics of master and servant: "The 'topdog' needs the 'underdog' to continually define and redefine his dominance. The 'underdog' needs the 'topdog' to complete that ever present Davidian American narrative of the underdog rising to the top against all adversity" (Bush 76). Even in his last statement, Booth documents the insoluble persistence of the tension between, on the one hand, the wish for independent self-determination and, on the other, the desire to reconstruct the scenario of the family of his childhood. He tries to tell his dead brother that he will develop a self "that dont have nothing to do with you." But this will make him famous "like Link was" (109).

Performative Scenarios, Predetermination, and Freedom in *Topdog/Underdog*

In the course of *Topdog/Underdog*, the three scenarios of Booth's self-stylization, the Lincoln shootings, and the three-card monte con come into finally fatal contact. Contemporary game theory addresses such issues of both the interplay of ludic scenarios and the mutual influence of different sets of rules on each other. Meta-games may include challenges not only within the respective game but also to its ground rules. Such elementary challenges may necessitate a transformation of the game into a different one which can then cope with the challenge. Certain classes of video games are cases in point (Morson 140–142). In *Topdog/Underdog* the brothers' lives are determined not only by the individual games they play but chiefly by their interaction and conflation, which challenge and transform their previous ground rules. In Booth's and Lincoln's rendition, the three-card monte con as well as the Lincoln act repeat sequences of playful rehearsal and serious, consequential repetition. Parks thereby demonstrates the convergence of game and life structures, play and earnestness, also foregrounded by game theory. The control generated by the rules of an individual game evaporates, as these rules are partly invalidated and transformed by the changed rules of revised versions of the same game, or by the fact that one game merges with another.

The final three-card monte game played by Booth and Lincoln, for example, is transformed by the fact that Booth's maternal inheritance is at stake. The familial game of betrayal and loss is a game in which disloyalty as well as lack of control and order seem the only valid rules that tend to invalidate all others. It is the meta-game which dominates and modifies both the three-card monte con and the Lincoln act. The latter is tied to the family game through the thoughtless (or all too thoughtful) naming of the brothers by their father, which associates them with a doubtful prehistory. The brothers' place in the family is questionable on account of their parents' promiscuity, or rule-breaking, which makes it doubtful whether they are really brothers. Their names also link them to a normatively equally uncertain national prehistory in which a fore-, or faux-, or foe-father is killed by an actor during the performance of a comedy, which in turn has overtones of violent deaths.

While the rule-bound nature of individual games, such as the Lincoln act and the three-card monte con, leads to predetermined and therefore predictable results, the interrelations of games and scenarios produce unforeseeable consequences and unexpected, contingent results. These negotiations of seriousness and inconsequence, virtuality and reality, order and contingency by game structures raise questions as to their impact on the relationship between the freedom or predetermination of decisions and actions. The stricter the rule-dependence of performative scenarios, the less leeway remains for spontaneity. Concerning computer games, a crucial distinction can be made which sheds light on this problem. Digitalized games are organized by a deep structure of possible moves within their cosmos, an electronic ground plan. This structural layout of the game functions as a "hidden strategic map," which determines the potential of the "smooth surface game world," the fantasy landscape actually presented to the viewer (Ryan 168). As in the three-card monte scam the interested bystander and potential player is unable to gauge the degree to which the game is prearranged, the computer game player is led to believe in the openness of the smooth surface he sees on the screen, as "strategic game-space can be mapped onto a mimetic narrative space that represents a world" (Ryan 166). In the three-card monte con the perspectives of the con men and the interested bystanders are widely divergent and, in fact, the success of the game from the point of view of the con men depends upon this divergence. Similarly, the computer game designer's perspective is also fundamentally different from that of the user. The designer generates the hidden strategic map of the computer game which determines it and then hides it from view by the smooth surface game world which the player sees: "From the point of view of the designer, game worlds are discontinuous spaces structured by invisible lines that delimit the range of application of certain units of code, while from the point of view of the player, they are open territories full of opportunities for action and exploration" (Ryan 167).

Some theorists, like Katie Ryan, see in the smooth surfaces of computer games, which hide from view their more rigid strategic ground maps and suggest an open field for free play, a felicitous synthesis of the impulses shared by storytelling and game structures. Others, like David Golumbia, believe that especially multiple player online games are not games at all, as they do not allow for the looseness, let alone freedom, that should be characteristic of play. Golumbia considers the binarism of the hidden strategic map on the one hand and the soft surface on the other as the expression of an illusionary sense of freedom which camouflages what are essentially fully predetermined exercises of functional skills, useful for the labor market of a power-oriented, late capitalist, global society based on digitalization. In this perspective, the game surfaces full of opportunities are nothing but delusional window dressing for the monotonous sameness of eliminating rivals in the mindless attempt to reach a higher level of spurious prestige (Golumbia 183–90).

With her "Rep & Rev" techniques, Parks pays tribute to both tendencies of ubiquitous postmodern play: to its determinative tendencies by repetition and to the potential for free development by revision. In *Topdog/Underdog* she clearly privileges predetermination over freedom. The performative scenarios in this play are prisons and traps rather than instruments of viable self-invention. As in computer games, the smooth surface of three-card monte at first sight promises an attractive chance of winning. But the strictly choreographed, hidden strategic map of the well-rehearsed con revokes and nullifies it. The Lincoln act is devoid of freedom in different ways. It amounts to little more than a fluctuation between historical violence and its virtual repetition. By Booth's murder of his brother, violence comes into its own again. It is only temporarily relegated to symbolization before it cyclically resurges. This can also be said of Booth's game of self-invention, which is never free but tied to rebuilding the family which his parents dismantled. Booth may for a moment desperately cling to the hope that he can liberate himself by killing Grace and Lincoln. But unwittingly, he is only recreating the hidden strategic map of his childhood fantasies. In a larger historical context, he is also reenacting the both virtual and real killings of black and white Lincolns reaching back to April 1865 and beyond. The question that Parks asks from this historical, and perhaps anthropological, perspective is: Who is the card dealer or game designer of this multiplicity of games? Who is pulling the strings?

Works Cited

Achilles, Jochen. "The Synchronicity of the Modern and the Postmodern: Eugene O'Neill's Representations of Blackness and the African-American Drama of August Wilson and Suzan-Lori Parks." In *Representation and Decoration in a Postmodern Age*. Edited by Alfred Hornung and Rüdiger Kunow. Heidelberg: Winter, 2009. 211–234.

Birkle, Carmen. "Revising America, Revisioning the Past: American Drama in a Global(izing) World." In *Global Challenges and Regional Responses in Contemporary Drama in English*. Edited by Jochen Achilles, Ina Bergmann, and Birgit Däwes. Trier: WVT, 2003. 105–20.

Bourdieu, Pierre, *Distinction: A Social Critique of the Judgment of Taste*. Translated by Richard Nice. Cambridge: Harvard University Press, 1984.

Bush, Jason. "Who's Thuh Man? Historical Melodrama and the Performance of Masculinity in *Topdog/Underdog*." In *Suzan-Lori Parks: A Casebook*. Edited by Kevin J. Wetmore, Jr., and Alycia Smith-Howard. New York: Routledge, 2007. 73–88.

Dietrick, Jon. "Making It 'Real': Money and Mimesis in Suzan-Lori Parks's *Topdog/Underdog*." *American Drama* 16.1 (Winter 2007): 47–74.
Ehrmann, Jacques. "Homo Ludens Revisited." Translated by Cathy and Paul Lewis. In *Game, Play, Literature*. Edited by Jacques Ehrmann. Boston: Beacon, 1971. 31–57.
Foster, Verna. "Suzan-Lori Parks's Staging of the Lincoln Myth in *The America Play* and *Topdog/Underdog*." *Journal of American Drama and Theatre* 17.3 (Summer 2005): 24–35.
Geis, Deborah R. *Suzan-Lori Parks*. Ann Arbor: University of Michigan Press, 2008.
Golumbia, David. "Games without Play." *New Literary History* 40.1 (Winter 2009): 179–204.
Holder, Heidi J. "Strange Legacy: The History Plays of Suzan-Lori Parks." In *Suzan-Lori Parks: A Casebook*. Edited by Kevin J. Wetmore, Jr., and Alycia Smith-Howard. New York: Routledge, 2007. 18–28
Innes, Christopher. "Staging Black History: Re-Imaging Cultural Icons." In *Race and Religion in Contemporary Theatre and Drama in English*. Edited by Bernhard Reitz. Trier: WVT, 1999. 95–107.
Kolin, Philip C., ed. *Contemporary African American Women Playwrights: A Casebook*. London: Routledge, 2007.
Lacan, Jacques. "The Insistence of the Letter in the Unconscious." In *Modern Criticism and Theory: A Reader*. Edited by David Lodge. London: Longman, 1988. 80–106.
Larson, Jennifer. "Folding and Unfolding History: Identity Fabrication in Suzan-Lori Parks's *Topdog/Underdog*." In *Reading Contemporary African American Drama: Fragments of History, Fragments of Self*. Edited by Trudier Harris and Jennifer Larson. New York: Lang. 2007. 183–202.
Malaby, Thomas E. "Anthropology and Play: The Contours of Playful Experience." *New Literary History* 40.1 (Winter 2009): 205–218.
Mitchell, Loften. "Star of the Morning—Scenes in the Life of Bert Williams." In *Black Drama Anthology*. Edited by Woodie King and Ron Milner. New York: Meridian, 1986. 575–639.
Morson, Gary Saul. "Contingency, Game, and Wit." *New Literary History* 40.1 (Winter 2009): 131–157.
Motte, Warren. "Playing in Earnest." *New Literary History* 40.1 (Winter 2009): 25–42.
Muller, John P. and William J. Richardson, eds. *The Purloined Poe: Lacan, Derrida, & Psychoanalytic Reading*. Baltimore and London: Johns Hopkins University Press, 1988.
Parks, Suzan-Lori. *The America Play and Other Works*. New York: Theatre Communications Group, 1995.
———. "Elements of Style." In *The America Play and Other Works*. New York: Theatre Communications Group, 1995. 6–18.
———. "An Equation for Black People Onstage." In *The America Play and Other Works*. New York: Theatre Communications Group, 1995. 19–22.
———. "Possession." In *The America Play and Other Works*. New York: Theatre Communications Group, 1995. 3–5.
———. *Topdog/Underdog*. New York: Theatre Communications Group, 2001.
Ryan, Katie. "'No Less Human': Making History in Suzan-Lori Parks's *The America Play*." *Journal of Dramatic Theory and Criticism* 12.2 (Spring 1999): 81–94.
Ryan, Marie-Laure. "From Playfields to Fictional Worlds: A Second Life for Ariosto." *New Literary History* 40.1 (Winter 2009): 159–177.
Schmidt, Kerstin. *The Theater of Transformation: Postmodernism in American Drama*. Amsterdam: Rodopi, 2005.
Taylor, Tom. *Our American Cousin*. 1858. Online at http://www.gutenberg.org/dirs/etext02/ouamcl1.txt.
Tucker-Abramson, Myka. "The Money Shot: Economies of Sex, Guns, and Language in *Topdog/Underdog*." *Modern Drama* 50.1 (Spring 2007): 77–97.
Wetmore, Kevin J., Jr. "Re-enacting: Metatheatre in Thuh Plays of Suzan-Lori Parks." In *Suzan-Lori Parks: A Casebook*. Edited by Kevin J. Wetmore, Jr., and Alycia Smith-Howard. New York: Routledge, 2007. 89–105.
———. "It's an Oberammergau Thing: An Interview with Suzan-Lori Parks." In *Suzan-Lori Parks: A Casebook*. Edited by Kevin J. Wetmore, Jr., and Alycia Smith-Howard. New York: Routledge, 2007. 124–140.
Wetmore, Kevin J., Jr., and Alycia Smith-Howard, eds. *Suzan-Lori Parks: A Casebook*. London: Routledge, 2007.

Suzan-Lori Parks's *365 Days/365 Plays*: A (W)hole New Approach to Theatre

Jennifer Larson

"I'm a good re-writer. I think that's my talent — re-writing." — Suzan-Lori Parks, in an interview with Kevin J. Wetmore (2007)

Suzan-Lori Parks's photograph traditionally adorns the back cover of her plays. Thus, it seems remarkable that the front cover and spine of the published *365 Days/365 Plays* feature seven pictures of Parks, sometimes smiling and sometimes half smiling, in a red convertible. In addition, unsuspecting or novice Parks readers would likely assume the volume was actually entitled *Suzan-Lori Parks,* since her name towers nearly three times larger than the true title. Those who know Parks well have written at some length about her personal connections to this play-a-day collection, connections that seem inevitable based on the timeline and circumstances of its creation. For example, Rebecca Rugg, who worked with Parks as the University Network producer for the 365 Festival, discusses in her essay "Dramaturgy as Devotion: *365 Days/365 Plays* of Suzan-Lori Parks" how the collection "was inspired by Parks's ten-year *Ashtanga* yoga practice" ("Dramaturgy" 68). *New Yorker* writer Hilton Als even suggests that "Parks's rhythmic, repetitious, and poetic dialogue can be seen as evidence of her efforts to dig for the meaning of her own biography, which, out of a kind of artistic necessity, eludes her" (77). Yet those who do not know her as intimately, or who only know her through her other work, can still understand — even just judging this book by its cover — that *365/365* is as much an exploration of the writer's process and the function of revision, as it is what Rugg calls "an experiment in short form" ("Dramaturgy" 68).

Parks wrote this collection over the course of a year beginning November 13, 2002, and two years later, she and producer-friend Bonnie Metzgar decided to bring the plays to the stage, or *stages*. After much logistical fine-tuning, a network of over 700 theatres emerged to produce the year-long 365 Festival — hailed by many as the largest theatrical collaboration of all time — which began in November 2006. Theatres received a week's worth of plays to perform and were charged a $1 per day per play licensing fee. The only rule: no admission fee. *New York Times* theatre writer Campbell Robertson suggested just days before the festival's 2006 start that *365/365* "created a sort of theatrical Internet, which was the idea; ideally a tiny theater in, say, Denver that is presenting a certain week will trade ideas with a theater presenting the same week thousands of miles away" (3).

According to Debra Geis, "The willingness of theatres across the country to participate speaks volumes about the recognition of [Parks's] importance as a dramatist" (158). Parks's "experiment," however, did not meet with universal praise. Maria Beach reports in her review of the Austin, Texas, performance of *365/365*:

> Members of the Literary Managers and Dramaturgs of the Americas debated the value of the festival online for days: many felt that this project was exciting and had the potential to reinvigorate American theatre, while others either dismissed it as a "stunt," pointing out that some of the 365 scripts are not very strong, or worried that this festival would divert resources and attention away from deserving local dramatists [651].

Parks's response to such criticism was simple: in her interview with Als she asserted, "I don't care what anybody says, ... Stick to the spirit of the play and you're doing it right. It's about embracing the spirit of the text instead of noodling some idea about things" (76).

Indeed, the self-proclaimed philosophical goal of *365/365* and the 365 Festival is one of "radical inclusion," a term borrowed from Iris Marion Young's *Inclusion and Democracy*. Commenting on this central idea, Rebecca Rugg writes in "Radical Inclusion 'Til It Hurts," that

> [It] involves destabilizing the comfortable polarities of center and margin. It imagines that instead of one, there are many concentric circles of community, of imagination, of good ideas and possibility. Radical inclusion takes more work than a typical project of liberal outreach, as it is aiming for nothing less than a redrawn geography of the American theatrical landscape. To accomplish this means inclusion to the point of discomfort: inviting to the table people who are ideologically or aesthetically miles apart from one's own taste ["Radical" 58].

By Parks's and Metzgar's bringing "radical inclusion" to the stage, Philip Kolin argues that they "have used their enormous influence (as Pulitzer Prize–winning playwright and leading producer) to reclaim the popular/ritualistic heritage from which theatre emerged" (80). In short, as the festival's motto proclaims, "there's pie for everyone." *365/365*— both the festival and the written text—seeks to bring more people to the theatre and to make theatre relevant to more people while also challenging writers and performers to re-envision and re-imagine their preconceived notions about theatre specifically, and art or artistic creation in general.

Opening the printed *365/365* and reading the plays only confirms that this collection illuminates how a creative mind like Parks's "writes through" ideas. Aside from the obviously meta-theatrical entries and entries that feature a character named "Writer" or "Playwright" or "Poetess," there are those that speak overtly or subtly to the page/stage or reader/watcher dichotomy for which Parks's plays have become so famous. A few (of the many) notable meta-theatrical entries are "The Script" (June 3), "A play for the People" (September 1), and "A Play for George Plimpton" (September 26). The page/stage dichotomy is particularly problematic in plays such as "Dragon Keeper" (March 11), "The Good Cook of Szechuan" (May 20), and "House of Cards" (August 20), among many others. Overall, *365/365* has no shortage of familiar themes and characters as it often returns to the conflicts and contexts that shaped Parks's earlier works. Not the least among these are Abraham Lincoln, infanticide, sexual violence/subjugation, the plight of the playwright, and the ubiquitous and ambiguous Great Hole of History.

Taken together, the emphasis on creation and re-creation, alongside the persistent intertexuality, suggests that *365/365* is a lens through which we can discover more about the thematic and formal structures of Parks's previous work, and vice-versa. More specifically, a close reading of *365/365* grants unparalleled clarity about the Great Hole of History and reveals how this enigmatic construction shapes and has been shaped by Parks's works, especially her Lincoln plays: *The America Play* and *Topdog/Underdog*; *Venus*, and her novel, *Getting Mother's Body*.

As Rugg, Kathryn Walat, and others have pointed out, people are digging holes all over *365/365*, and the links to Parks's other plays, the Lincoln plays especially, are by no means hidden. According to Deborah Geis, Parks's frequent return to the concept "suggests the struggle to create the plays themselves: the need to keep 'digging' for more material, and the playwright's fear of having gotten herself into a 'hole' by having taken on the project" (163). Taken as whole, Geis argues, "The interest in digging and holes also evokes sexuality, death, resurrection, and history — all thrown into a kind of bottomless pit, shades of Beckett, that forces a new kind of archaeological practice, a new way of 'digging' the past to look at the world" (163).

Viewing *365/365* as a meditation on the evolving significance of the Great Hole of History allows readers to more meaningfully connect these self-revisionary moments, perhaps best called "re-visitations," in keeping with the spiritual tone cited in previous scholarly discussions of this collection. In addition, this (w)hole-istic reading underscores *365/365*'s importance as a text about writing — and thus, simultaneously, the importance of the written text — as it takes the reader on a daily aesthetic journey, a journey that is simultaneously linear and circular, temporal and spatial, personal and communal.

In order to explore the Great Hole of History's evolution in *365/365* and connect this evolution to Parks's previous work, this essay will focus on representative examples from the dozens of plays that specifically mention holes. In some examples, *365/365* reinforces the Great Hole of History's original meaning; in others, the volume directly challenges that meaning. All the examples, however, use a hole or holes to engage one or more of Parks's previous works and offer a compelling re-imagining or revision of the Great Hole of History's function in that text. The malignancy of Parks's earliest version of the Great Hole stems from its inability (or unwillingness) to preserve identity, but the holes in *365/365* do not always erode identity or reflect a history that does; at times, *365/365*'s holes liberate, or bring people together. They are sometimes inherently feminine, and sometimes they just exist. At times they are Great Holes of capital-H written history, while at other times, they are Great (or not-so-great) Holes of small-h personal history.

Early in the volume, for example, Parks gives us a play that — like *The America Play*— provides us with a definitive exploration of the concept. During November 27's simply titled "Hole," we meet a man digging a hole "with great relish" (27). He "digs up" a woman with a suitcase (28). The woman watches him dig and inquires about the hole's purpose. The man responds, "The hole? Its just a job. It isnt my hole, Im digging it for a fella. A rich fella. He's got money to burn and — yeah, he's living high, lemmie tell you"

(29). But he proceeds to tell her about the "road" that led him to hole digging and how "digging holes creates the need to dig holes" (30). The woman then takes a bag from her suitcase, throws it in the hole, and asks the man to "cover it up" (30). According to the closing stage directions, he does so, and the couple goes to a motel to have intercourse after the man's hole-digging shift. The stage directions then reveal that "it was her fondest memories that were in that bag. She and the rich man were lovers once. Years ago" (31).

Similarly, in *The America Play*, the Great Hole of History begins as a very literal and generally malignant hole (dug in the ground) that doubles as a theme park. One of the play's main characters, Lucy, describes the Great Hole of History, where she honeymooned with her husband, the Foundling Father, an Abraham Lincoln impersonator. She explains of the hole:

> You could see the whole world without goin too far. You could look intuh that whole and see your entire life pass before you. Not your own life but someones life from history, you know, someone who'd done something of note, got theirselves known somehow, uh President or somebody who killed somebody important, uh face on a postal stamp, you know, someone from History. *Like* you, but *not* you. You know: *known* [196].

According to Haike Frank, "All of history amalgamates in this theme park; difference is erased by the all-comprising myth of greatness" (17–18). The Great Hole of History is a void in which history's important moments, those that have had the most potent impact on the world, are contained. Visitors who have otherwise been excluded from capital-H written history can use the hole to put themselves, although only superficially, into that history.

The hole(s) of "Hole" are reminiscent of the original Great Hole of History in *The America Play* because they are tangible. The man digs holes; he moves earth. Yet, those tangible holes — in both plays — hold and/or create deeply metaphorical, almost supernatural, elements: a theme park and the unearthing of a woman with a suitcase. The woman in "Hole" can also bury "her fondest memories" in a bag in the hole, and "cover it up." In so doing, she adds her individual history to a collective American consciousness not unlike that which visitors access when they look into the Great Hole of History to "see your entire life pass before you."

The "hole" in *365*'s "Hole" and the Great Hole of History also share an emphasis on compulsion. In *The America Play*, the Foundling Father and The Lesser Known crave notoriety; they want to be "known" so badly that they abandon their families, and even their individual identities, in the quest to find fame. In "Hole," the digging man desires — and indeed feels compelled — to dig more holes. Although his need is less public, it is no less intense. The digger initially asserts that digging holes is "just a job," but he soon reveals that "digging holes creates the need to dig holes" (30). Both holes reflect an inherent need to participate in history, to make a mark — literally and figuratively — on the earth. Since both "Hole" and *The America Play* connect their respective holes to wealth and power, these two Parks's works suggest that a least part of the task of creating a place in history for oneself involves working both for and against those power structures.

While these similarities illustrate key elements of the Great Hole of History's enduring significance, the divergences between "Hole" and *The America Play* also illuminate significant features of both plays' holes. For example, while the Great Hole of History already exists and the characters merely visit it to try to become a more significant part of History, the digger in "Hole" actively participates in the creation of his holes. And while he does this work for the "rich fella"—thus participating in a traditional power dynamic that privileges wealth and power—he also does this work, a least in part, for himself. He explains to the woman that while travelling on "the road," he "met a guy over there who was digging a hole and it looked so—right" (30). He later adds, "I said to myself that if I ever get back, you know? I said if I ever get back thats just what Ima do. Dig a hole" (30). The hole for him represents redemption, survival, and, ultimately, resurrection, for the woman rises out of one of the holes that he digs. Each of these features is inherently personal, rather than social like the theme park in *The America Play*.

In fact, the man lies about his past at first, actively trying to exclude himself from the communal history (or rather, communal tragedy) "the road" represents. When he tells this lie, he does not specifically mention the hole that he is digging but instead centers his description around the concept of his "whole life."

> MAN: See that road there? The wide one? Squint yr eyes up and yll see it.
> WOMAN: I came down that road once.
> MAN: Everybody does. Comes down it or goes up it. Comes in on it or leaves out that way. Me, Im the exception. Ive never been further than this side of the road proper. In my whole entire life. Some would call that a rut. But some would call that road a rut and both would be right or wrong. Alls I know is that the whole world has passed by me and Ive never felt the need to join it. Ive spent my whole life right here.
> WOMAN: Thats not what I heard [29].

In the ideal, fabricated history, man has "spent my whole life right here," that is, digging holes. Thus, the play links a wholeness, a suggestion of a full and complete life, to the act of digging a hole. This association implies that Parks's new holes of *365/365* are by far more redemptive than their ancestor, the Great Hole of History—which showed a visitor his "entire life," but only as much as it could be superimposed on the life of someone more famous.

But even this new type of hole has its complications, and these complications are familiar, for they focus on writing (or otherwise recording experience) and the difference between the written and the performed text. Man unearths Woman, and they do develop "a closeness" (31). However, the play reveals this element of their relationship only in the stage directions, and thus only fully to the reader, for "closeness" would be a difficult concept to perform. Earlier in the play, the man underscores the importance of written/recorded history versus spontaneous performance or casual interpersonal communication when he places emphasis on the need to record his thoughts about "the road." He tells the woman, "You better write this down or tape-record this or document this in some fashion, take pictures or film it or—cause Im only gonna say it once" (30). The man wants his story to be a part of recorded History, but he also wants to forget it. This dichotomy, together with the written-only emphasis on the couple's "closeness," suggests that even these new holes, with their focus on "wholeness" rely on both written and performed expression to fully capture the nuances of human experience.

Written history plays a particularly important role in *365/365*'s revisiting of the

Great Hole of History and its implications. Not surprisingly, these issues first appear in a "Lincoln" play: November 26's "Mrs. Keckley and Mrs. Lincoln." In this play, Mary Todd Lincoln and her dressmaker/confidante Elizabeth Keckley discuss what dress Mrs. Lincoln should wear to the theatre — to the performance that the historically-aware reader/audience knows will be the site of her husband's assassination. The women also talk about the Civil War, the size of Abraham Lincoln's genitalia, and why Mrs. Lincoln wants Mrs. Keckley to call her by her first name.

"Mrs. Keckley and Mrs. Lincoln," like Parks's *Topdog/Underdog*, enacts the timelessness of the trauma and violence that characterize the Great Hole of History. As Mrs. Lincoln is getting dressed, "there is a sound of a gunshot" (27). When Mrs. Lincoln inquires about the sound, Mrs. Keckley responds that it was "just the sound of a car backfiring" (27). Mrs. Lincoln questions this response, and Keckley backpedals, as if in an attempt to hide her anachronism. For the reader/audience, though, this attempt only highlights that Keckley seems to exist outside of time and insinuates that the scene could have just as easily occurred "here" and "now" as happens in *Topdog/Underdog*.

The gun shot, especially when read as a foreshadowing of the gunshot that would inevitably kill president Lincoln later in the evening, underscores *365/365*'s connection to the Great Hole of History in general and to *Topdog/Underdog* specifically. However, the fact that Keckley seems to understand and work within the play's historical paradigms while Mrs. Lincoln appears naive and ignorant suggests an inversion of the Great Hole of History's identity politics: no more is a black man looking at the hole to see a historical misrepresentation of himself, a misrepresentation authored by white hegemonic power structures. Instead, we find a black woman with a clear knowledge of history — past, present, and future.

The Great Hole of History is, of course, never explicitly mentioned in *Topdog/Underdog*, but in a 2006 interview, Parks suggests an inherent connection between the Great Hole and the bullet hole in Lincoln (the president) that undoubtedly transfers to Lincoln (the character):

> WETMORE: So you're writing, looking for a particular conjunction of alignment.
> PARKS: Right, right. Like the hole in Lincoln's head and the (w)hole of history, and they line up and all of a sudden, through that (w)hole hole comes meaning [130].

The hole that marks the site of intra-racial violence against both Lincolns is related to the Great Hole of History because, like the literal hole in *The America Play*, this hole represents how the culmination of personal and social frustration has very destructive potential, especially vis-à-vis African American identity. In *Topdog/Underdog*, identity remains almost entirely fluid. Booth becomes Booth-the-Assassin because he succumbs to "the myth of greatness," the idea of becoming "*known*."

Indeed, the one-room apartment that contains the entire play becomes a Great Hole in itself, a type of black-hole-like vacuum,* a site of temporal and spatial stasis wherein Lincoln and Booth re-enact the arcade/theme-park history reminiscent of that seen in the original Great Hole from *The America Play*. Essentially, then, Lincoln and Booth have

---

*My thanks to Andrew Daub for pointing out these "black holes" in *Topdog/Underdog*.

fallen into the Great Hole of History, and they cannot escape, just like the unnamed character who falls into "a deep hole" in *365/365*'s "Analysis" (I examine this play in more detail below). Since *Topdog/Underdog* is set in the "here" and "now," the play implies that these brothers are not the first, nor will they be the last, to do so (2).

Indeed, Mrs. Keckley and Mrs. Lincoln appear to be in the same "hole." The title of "Mrs. Keckley and Mrs. Lincoln" even sets up an ambiguous dominant/subordinate dichotomy like that in *Topdog/Underdog*. Parks labels Lincoln topdog and Booth underdog, but as the play twists and turns, these designations destabilize. Likewise, Mrs. Lincoln and Mrs. Keckley are white employer and black employee, respectively. Yet Keckley seems to have the upper hand. Mrs. Lincoln frets and needs Mrs. Keckley to feed her narcissism, to call her by her first name so she can "feel young," all the while Keckley remains almost aloof as she calms and compliments the first lady, even when Mrs. Lincoln turns the conversation to war and racial politics (25). In these moments, Mrs. Keckley speaks volumes through her silence. When Mrs. Keckley tells Mrs. Lincoln, "We wouldn't want to keep yr president waiting," she responds, "He's yr president too" (27). Mrs. Keckley does not offer a verbal reply, but the text shows:

MRS. KECKLEY
MRS. KECKLEY
(Rest) [27].

This "Spell" and "(Rest)" amount to a substantial break in the action, an uncomfortable silence — even if a director fills it with physical action. As in all her plays, Parks defines "(Rest)" and Spell, in "From the Author's 'Elements of Style'" at the beginning of the volume as "(Rest)" is where the reader/performer should "Take a little time, a pause, a breather; make a transition" (ix). The spell is "An elongated and heightened (Rest). Denoted by repetitions of figures name with no dialogue.... This is a place where the figures experience their pure true simple state. While no action or stage business is necessary, directors should fill this moment as they best see fit" (ix).

Keckley's choice to remain silent again demonstrates her understanding of the historical complexity of Mrs. Lincoln's assertion. Keckley may indeed believe that Abraham Lincoln is "a fine man"; however, her disconnection from the American political process that elected him president, and his somewhat inconsistent approach to civil rights, complicates this claim. Mrs. Keckley understands that history as Mrs. Lincoln sees it, and as the Great Hole of History would represent it, does not reflect her life and her struggles as a nineteenth-century black domestic worker — just as it does not reflect Lincoln and Booth's lives in the "here" and "now."

In *365/365*, some of the most enigmatic and revealing hole plays feature women as the primary actors, and many of the plays simultaneously engage sexualized agency or women's roles, just as Parks does in *Venus*. In March 8's "Holey," for example, two women discuss what to do when one drops her "ego," clearly a euphemism for sexual agency, into a hole (34). And August 30's "Holey Moley" describes a woman's obsession with the hole outside her house (304). Both plays are short (½ and ¾ of a page, respectively), but both, nevertheless, offer substantial insight into their holes, specifically their effect on femininity/sexuality and their connection to personal relationships.

"Holey," a dialogue between Woman 1 and Woman 2, opens not with explanatory stage directions, but with a question: "what?" (146). The exchange that follows reveals that a woman has dropped what she calls her "ego" into what we can assume, based on the title, is a hole, for the "ego" is "down there," apparently out of reach (146). The women wait for "a Returner" summoned by the blowing of a whistle. However, Woman 1 explains, "It usually takes them — a day or 2 sometimes. Once there was this guy — I wont bore you with it. Well, 2 weeks it took. He couldnt do his thing for 2 whole weeks" (146). After Woman 2 tries to whistle again, and again, the stage directions explain that "Woman 1 gets bored and goes on her way" while Woman 2 waits alone, "very much in vain" (147).

The quotation marks around "ego" serve, as they do with the word "slut" in Parks's 1999 play *In the Blood*, to complicate a term and all it represents. Ego traditionally signifies self worth, but deeper psychological readings, including but not limited to Sigmund Freud's conception of an "ego" that checks the passions and balances desires, suggest a myriad of possible interpretations. In any case, the dropping of the "ego" into the hole renders the dropper impotent, be it physically or metaphorically, such that the term naturally lends itself to more sexualized readings.

In *Venus*, Parks more closely examines how women's lives and experiences relate to the Great Hole of History. Here, as in *Topdog/Underdog*, the Great Hole of History can be traced to a bodily site of violence as well as linked to a figurative, identity-complicating reading of history. Under the heading "sex" in the extended version "from Elements of Style" that appears in *The America Play and Other Works*, Parks writes, "People have asked me why I don't put any sex in my plays. 'The Great Hole of History'—like, duh" (16). This assertion suggests that the Great Hole of History has inherently feminine characteristics, pointing to the female genitalia, especially as a locus for the violence and subjugation that characterize the Great Hole's account of the past. In addition, reading *Venus* through the lens of the Great Hole highlights how women are especially susceptible to being written out of history and only superficially put back.

Venus follows The Venus (the fictionalized Sartjee Baartman) as she leaves her native South Africa hoping to be famous and make "a mint" as a stage performer in England (20). This quest for fame, of course, recalls the Foundling Father's in *The America Play*; however, questions of agency and complicity haunt *Venus* and its creation and thus put a uniquely feminized spin on the Great Hole of History's function in this play. Since Parks's Venus is based on, but is not a true representation of, Baartman, she is, to paraphrase Lucy, "like Sartjee, but not Sartjee," so the protagonist begins with a fragmented, ambiguous identity. Then, even within the play, The Venus and others struggle with whether to label her the victim or accomplice in her own tragedy. The play thereby demonstrates how History fails to represent the complexity of women's lives and their compounded oppressions.

A hole's ability to negate sexuality channels the connection between the holes in *365/365* and the femininity of the Great Hole of History in *Venus*. In "Holey," though, the hole is more "equal opportunity." Both men and women can drop their egos into holes and be rendered impotent. Yet, as in *Venus*, only an external authority (in *Venus* it is the court; here, the "Returner") has the power to restore that sexual agency, and again, as in *Venus*, that authority fails. The courts rule The Venus complicit in her own exploitation, and the Returner never comes to help Woman 1. No one, in fact, helps Woman 1, not even Woman 2, for while she is initially supportive in commiserating with Woman 1, she abandons her distressed sister in the ending stage directions simply because the situation no longer interests her. "Holey," therefore, highlights a failure in feminine community, vis-à-vis this sexuality, that also occurs in *Venus*. There, Mother Showman, Venus's boss, puts the young woman on display, and even allows her to be raped, in order to increase the profits of her travelling performance.

Later in *365/365*, however, Parks gives us "Holy Moley," a play in which a positive, redemptive relationship does seem to exist. This relationship, though, is between a man and woman. In "Holey Moley," one of the last major "hole" plays of the *365* volume, Man tries to coax Woman away from the door where she stares anxiously at "The hole" (304). Between her paranoid observations —"Its out there," "its turned onto its side," "its calling to me," "it wants me to cross the threshold"— he talks to her about tomatoes (304–5) until suddenly he exclaims, "Look! The holey mole!" The following exchange ends the play:

WOMAN: Outside?
MAN: Inside.
WOMAN: Holey Moley! Where?
MAN: Its small, come see.
The woman comes to look. He points to nothing. She smiles. He smiles too [305].

"Holey Moley" thus at first seems to be almost a complete departure from Parks's earlier work. In this one-act, the woman is "saved" by a supportive male companion, rather than abandoned by a selfish lover (as seen in *Venus*), and the hole here takes on unparalleled animation: in addition to "calling to" the woman, at one point it "turn[s] onto its side" (304). In no previous Parks play has the Great Hole of History ever rolled over. Yet, as with the original Great Hole of History, the promising surface belies a potentially insidious subtext. While he speaks to her, the man nibbles on cherry tomatoes that the woman has grown, praising her for their quality (304). While certainly not the apple that Eve gave Adam, these cherry tomatoes nevertheless suggest a similar "fall" from the ideal. The man tells her, "you could win a ribbon if youd just believe in yourself," thereby asking her to measure her worth by the quality of her domestic production in general, and specifically her ability to cultivate fruit — a thinly veiled metaphor for child-bearing (304). As he devours the tomatoes, the fruit of her vine, he does not take her paranoia seriously. He does admit that the hole "is always out there," but he doesn't address why she is afraid or obsessed; he simply tries to distract her with a discussion of how she could bake the tomatoes into a pie, yet another traditionally domestic act (305).

Even in the final moments of the play, when both smile at the invisible "Holey Mole," he has used subterfuge and trickery — rather than legitimate emotional connection — to draw the woman away from the door. The woman, however, seems at least temporarily happy and at ease, drawn away from a consuming and likely unhealthy obsession with the personified hole. Plagued by this nagging duality, the hole in "Holey Moley," like the Great Hole of History, remains an identity-complicating site for women.

Parks takes a similar look at holes and relationships, with particular focus on the relationship between The Great Hole and the writer, in July 10's "Two Writers Digging

Bach." In this play, as the opening stage directions explain, "2 writers: a woman who could be mistaken for / Suzan-Lori Parks (but not) and a Man who could be mistaken for / William Faulkner (but not)" are "both digging the same hole" / "They take turns passing the shovel back and forth. / There is some Bach music playing: Cello Suites by Pablo Casals" (250). As in *Venus*, the simple presence of someone that is "like you, but not you"— in this case, like Parks and like Faulkner, but not them — immediately channels Lucy's description of the Great Hole of History from *The America Play*. Plus the play on words in Bach/back suggests that the hole that these writers dig is connected, at least tangentially, to the past.

In "Two Writers," however, the hole is not a single space nor is it an artistic vacuum. Instead, it is almost like a tunnel, a route to a destination — in this case, "back." And as with the definitive "Hole," the actors participate in the Hole's creation. In case of "Two Writers," this creation, and the exchange that occurs during the creation, dominates the action. While they are digging, which both seem to enjoy since they each ask to take their turn at it, Walter (Faulkner, but not Faulkner) sings and waxes poetic, dropping quotables such as "Gray skies are candy" (250). Meanwhile Simone (Parks, but not Parks) spontaneously composes a poetic statement about racial expression, "My people we dig too. Dig?," that Walter labels a haiku (250).

Since Parks and Faulkner are digging together in "Two Writers," the play directly channels Parks's novel, *Getting Mother's Body*, which is based on Faulkner's *As I Lay Dying* and *Light in August*. In *Getting Mother's Body*, there are both literal holes, as in *The America Play*, and figurative holes, as seen in *Topdog/Underdog* and *Venus*. The novel's heroine, Billy Beede, describes the metaphorical "Holes" her mother Willa Mae taught her to see in others. She explains, "It's like a soft spot and everybody's got one. Mother said she could see The Hole in people and then she'd know how to take them" (9). Willa Mae herself speaks from beyond the grave to further clarify the concept. For her, the Hole is "not just the lack" of something, but also the "craving" for it: "A Hole-in-the-heart person craves company and kindness, not no book" (31). This craving, of course, is deeply reminiscent of the compulsion that fuels the Foundling Father, the Lesser Known, The Venus and many of the other characters we have seen in *365/365*.

The more literal hole, perhaps ironically, is Willa Mae's actual gravesite, which Billy, her friends, and her family all dig up near the novel's end. Not unlike the Great Hole of History, Willa Mae's grave represents the convergence of all the characters' personal histories. Her infamy and her death have scarred all of them, and her resurrection (and her possible buried treasure) brings potential relief from the lingering pain of her absence. Yet *Getting Mother's Body* stands out from the other works discussed thus far, not only because it is a novel instead of a work written specifically for the stage, but also because it is the work in which Parks most closely engages another writer. Other plays address literary and cultural history on the thematic level, but *Getting Mother's Body* very closely signifies on both the form and context of William Faulkner's texts. As such, this novel, like *365/365*, can be read as a text about writing as well as a text about history — personal and communal.

By the time we get to "Two Writers" in *365/365*, then, holes are generally positive; the malignancy that characterizes the Great Hole of History and even the holes in "Hole" has given way to an almost exclusively productive potential. Simone and Walter agree that the hole digging is "hard work," especially in the heat, which likely represents the critical gaze that comes with fame (250). However, Simone later concludes, "Not much in life that beats digging a hole, huh?," a question/statement to which Walter responds, "I'll drink to that"—and he does (250). They then laugh together.

Such a shift in Parks's view of holes, however, must not be misunderstood as a shift in her appraisal of the destructive potential of the hegemonic power structures that created the more malevolent earlier holes. In fact, immediately following "Two Writers" is the bluntly entitled "I Cant Help the Mood Im In, but Right Now Im Thinking That the Narcissism of White America Knows No Bounds," in which a white person stares at and repeatedly asks "The Other" some variation on "You thinking of me?" (251). This type of narcissism, one could argue, lies at the core of the Great Hole of History's corrosive impact on individual black identity, i.e., white folks want to be the most important (perhaps even the only) players in their own Histories.

Plus, Parks examines her own relationship with these power structures by writing herself into the play. Since Simone could be Parks, but is not, Parks positions herself within the original Great Hole of History's identity complicating paradigm, but then inverts its value judgment (she is "Parks, but not Parks"). Since Parks herself is famous and "known," those looking into a Great Hole would, in theory, see her—but instead, the play gives Simone, the unknown, this role. This new "lesser known" thus occupies the privileged historical position in the Great Hole's reflection, and Parks the playwright derives artistic identity from this new more democratic, more radically inclusive, model.

Parks privileges another "lesser known," the homecoming soldier, in her most prominent recurring "play" of *365/365*: "Father Comes Home from the Wars." This 11-part cycle follows a man and his family when the man returns—usually without notice—from a nameless, indistinct war with a nebulous timeline. This structure and timeline alone, reminiscent of the vacuum-like hole in "Mrs. Keckley and Mrs. Lincoln" and *Topdog/Underdog*, connects the Father cycle to the Great Hole of History tradition in general, but each part of the cycle also connects to the specific elements of the Great Hole that Parks explores in her other works and in other *365/365* entries.

The Father plays suggest that the individual soldier, his family, and perhaps even all of the world, have fallen into a hole or a rut, not unlike the stifling societal expectations that plague Lincoln and Booth or the artistic chasm that Geis describes Parks fearing throughout the *365* collection. In February 10's Part 2, for example, a painter works on a portrait of the family, but then, the stage directions explain, "Soldier Man arrives, dressed in battle dress. It does not matter from which war: the Trojan war, WWI, American Civil, Iran-Iraq, Napoleonic, Spanish Civil, Crimean, Zulu, ANC against the Powers that Were, whatever, the Chinese-Tibetan conflict, the War of the Worlds, whatever, it does not matter" (119). Similarly, in September 5's Part 9, we find out that the "war" need not be a physical conflict with a formal declaration of hostilities. Instead, the Fathers in Part 9 are simply men in some kind of uniform: "a Soldier, a Sailor, a Janitor with a broom, a Security Guard with a badge and a gun, a Mechanic with an oily rag and a wrench, a Businessman with a suit and a briefcase, maybe an Astronaut even. They are all young-looking, fresh-faced, and firm-limbed; but very, very old-acting in the most typical of ways: forgetful, passive, paranoid, sad, weak, infirm, angry" (310). Even though the soldier and the sailor dominate the discussion, the others chime in, and at the end they all, together, "strain their necks downstage to get a better look" at the "war" (311).

Since time and place "does not matter" (even stated twice for emphasis) in these Father plays, the characters, like Mrs. Keckley in her plays, exist in a kind of temporal stasis. War — literal or metaphorical — and the effects thereof become a black hole, or vacuum, in which these characters exist — able to know the past, present, and future, but nevertheless still destined to repeat it. This message clearly culminates in the final play of the cycle, November 4's "Father Comes Home from the Wars (Part 11: His Eternal Return — A Play for My Father)." Written exclusively in a stage direction, this play begins with a "war news-in-brief soundtrack backed with military band music that's played a slower than normal speed" (368). A group of servicemen walk on stage; wives run out of the audience to greet them; then, children run out to greet them. This happens again, and again, again. The directions, in fact, indicate that:

> The action repeats eternally. Long after the audience has emptied of Women; long after the Men have grown out of the desire to be hugged and kissed and welcomed; long after the Children have become less cheerful and more sensible and taken up trades, like accounting or real estate or politics; long after the Children's Children have outgrown joy and have all grown-up and moved away. Forever [368].

Even when there is no one left to fall into it, the hole lives on, waiting for new participants.

This black-hole-like space, as in "Mrs. Keckley and Mrs. Lincoln" and *Topdog/Underdog*, also complicates racial and social identity. Part 2's Father is "only a father figure," holding the place in the photograph for the actual father, Soldier Man (119). As the play winds to a close, Soldier Man breaks from his portrait pose and asks the family, "Let's have a sing-along, shall we?" before beginning a minstrel-like dance to a Puccini aria. According to the stage directions, "He reaches out to the Family. They cringe and shrink from his touch. He can live with it. He dances around. It's clear he's missing an eye, a leg, an arm — he sings and dances, quite beautiful, though, all the same. The Family watches him with mounting horror, spoiling the portrait" (199). Here, not only can the veteran Father be replaced with a stereotypical substitute, but the Father himself has become a locus of fear for the family. Disembodied by his wounds, the meaning of his beautiful dance is lost in the tragedy of the circumstances, so he is ultimately unable to express either his pain or his love for his family.

Thus, in *365/365*'s Father plays, the Great Hole is again a site of violence as well as social and personal frustration. In June 18's Part 8, "Father enters dragging an enormous bloody sword" (232), and in November 3's Part 10, Father declares, "I'm home but I still got the taste for killing, you know?" (366). He is "home," but he has brought the war home with him, and so it continues to torture him without reprieve. In March 9's Part 3, for example, Father is surrounded by "his soldiers," who want to talk about the war with him, but he refuses, exclaiming that all he wants to do is "watch some goddamn game shows" with his son, Junior (146). However, Junior explains, "All thats on is war movies," for which the soldiers provide the sound effects (146). Even "home from the wars," then, the father has no space for personal and familial healing. And as they watch,

Junior adds, "I'm gonna be a soldier just like yr a soldier, right, Pop?" The son will likely repeat/relive his father's choices and his father's pain, again reinforcing that the hole is timeless: cyclical and enduring.

The Father plays, however, are just as much about the Mother as they are about the Father (or the soldier), and this theme links the Father cycle and its holes to the Great Hole of History at work in plays such as "Holey Moley" and *Venus*. In November 14's Part 1, for example, Mother greets the unexpected Father with surprise; she makes him leave and come in again. This surprise entrance and its visceral effects on the wife are reminiscent of the husband's shocking return in Kate Chopin's "The Story of an Hour," in which a frail woman who has just come to terms with — and even sees the possible benefit of — her husband's death in a train accident dies of shock when he walks in the door, alive and unaware of the previous false report.

In Part 2, we learn that the wife has been having an affair (an affair that the husband names but to which the woman herself only alludes), and the stage directions tell us that she considers killing him, twice, in an "Almost murder" (6). This violent reaction to her husband's return suggests that she preferred his absence, an absence in which she was still able to find sexual fulfillment. She also clearly used this absence to sequester herself from any possible connection to him: leaving letters and the phone unanswered (5). Therefore, as with the couple in "Holey Moley," there no evidence of true emotional connection between the Mother and the Father.

Even when that connection seems to exist, as it does in April 8 and 9's Parts 5 and 6, in which husband and wife (now Joe and Lovey) are at a "very stylish" dinner party, the mother finds herself in a tenuous middle ground between Joe's pain and others' expectations. In Part 5, Joe "hugs Lovey too hard" as he talks with the Host and Hostess about his desire to eat raw meat (172). She must then downplay this seemingly savage inclination for the party goers while also reminding him that he is, indeed, "home now" (172). Then, when Joe goes back to "the Front" in Part 6, Lovey must defend him, decline sexual advances from the Next Door Neighbor, and reassure her audience and herself of Joe's love for her, confirmed by her "whole room full of letters and theyre all love letters" (173). Father may come home and go back to the wars, but Mother must always face the consequences.

Less than a week later, however, in April 15's "Mother Comes Home from the Wars," Parks reverses the roles. Here a woman returns after being "freed" (178). She tells the man how "The National Publisher wants to buy the rights to my story" and how her picture was in the paper (178). Near the middle of the play, the couple has the following exchange:

WOMAN: Hon?
MAN: What.
WOMAN: What are you looking at?
MAN: God
WOMAN: You'll go blind [178–9].

He then pretends to already be blind, and when she realizes he's kidding she says, "Yr such a joker. I could have you shot. I had a lot of men shot. They were all just like you." He nevertheless welcomes her home and "they embrace. We can see that their embrace, while warm and passionate, causes them both excruciating pain" (179).

The woman's "selling" of her story immediately channels *Venus*'s story as well as the black woman writer's experience in the literary marketplace. It becomes especially significant, then, that the following dialogue mirrors closely an exchange from the film adaptation of Zora Neale Hurston's *Their Eyes Were Watching God*, for which Parks co-authored the teleplay. In the film, however, it is Janie, the strong female protagonist, who responds that she is "watching God" when someone asks her why she gazes at the sky. Giving Janie's lines to the Man in "Mother Comes Home from the Wars" signals a dramatic shift in power dynamics that is underscored by the woman's threat to kill the man for joking about his blindness. This shift and the woman's reaction to it again point to an identity-compromising and corrosive version of the Great Hole at History at work in the Father cycle. And even as the man and woman cling to each other at the end of the play, there is no end to the pain that separates them.

In the midst of all this familial and relational pain, however, there is a potential for productivity not unlike that proposed by "Two Writers Digging Bach." In May 13's "Playing Chopsticks (Father Comes Home from the Wars, Part 7)," Father, now called "Soldier Dad," tries to teach his son how to use chopsticks to carry grains of rice across the stage while someone plays chopsticks on the piano in the background. The son feels both "awe and anger" when he witnesses his father's proficiency at this task, and the son's initial failure frustrates Soldier Dad, even to the point of making him doubt his son's paternity (206). The son catches on, however, and soon, "each is amazing at moving the rice. And they are enjoying themselves. It is horrible to see them enjoying themselves doing such a pointless task. But they are building a monument together — and this monument will be a fortress against the future pain. And the music, playing all the while, seeps into the walls of the fortress, seeps in and holds it like stone" (207). Therefore, even the Father plays, with their connections to the worst elements of Parks's original Great Hole of History, manage to find some hope for a healing and solidarity that can be found through repetition, culmination, and a little bit of music.

The final hole plays of the volume, October 11's "Measure and Walk Away" and its next-day companion "Analysis," continue this movement away from the problematic Great Hole of History and toward less destructive, more historically redemptive holes. Indeed, the holes in these plays are neither overtly malignant nor overtly benign; they simply exist, and characters can exist within them, filling the "space" as desired.

In "Measure and Walk Away," two people find a hole, measure it, and label it with a sign that says, "Another Deep Hole;" after they measure, "they go" (351). While both players initially revel at the sight of this hole, neither pays it much attention ultimately. As such, this play suggests that holes now only have that power that their diggers/observers/patrons give them. Holes may be worthy of note because — as Parks writes in her annotated table of contents at the end of the volume — "Every great gap should get a sign," but this simple notice may suffice (351). After that, anyone can just "walk away." In "Analysis," though, someone has fallen into a hole. Whereas in *Topdog/Underdog* this fall has disastrous consequences for Lincoln and Booth, in this late moment of *365/365*, being at the bottom of a "deep hole," while regrettable, comes across as only mildly disturbing. The person in the hole still has the wherewithal to take "a sample" of the hole and give it to his companion, who declares that the hole is made simply of "space," a nothingness, a blank canvas waiting to be filled (352). Halfway through this short play, music starts. The stage directions explain, "Interludey music plays. / Something from the soundtrack of the 70s, / or something mushy and very recognizable, or maybe something / *deep* like a cut from *Miles Davis in Stockholm*" (352, emphasis added). Linking Miles Davis's art and the hole through the word "deep" suggests that the deep hole has unlimited artistic potential and may even be the locus of some artistic expression. Just as not–Parks and not–Faulkner creatively engage each other over hole digging, being in a hole "deep" can allow the "space" for unparalleled self reflection.

Both "Measure and Walk Away" and "Analysis" also speak subtly to the art/critic relationship. Again, holes are the perfect theme for such an examination, since the Great Hole of History ranks among the most critically engaged elements of Parks' works. Parks's previous comments on critics and literary criticism have hinted at a slightly contentious relationship. In her 1996 *Callaloo* interview with Shelby Jiggetts, for example, she reports that she had not read any reviews of her work since 1990 and says, "I get really nervous when people I don't like talk about my work" (315). But this conflict seems to find at least partial resolution here: labeling and analysis, just a few of the tools at the critic's workbench, find some acceptance. Just as the holes in *365/365* are a more inclusive version of the Great Hole of History, so too is *365/365* itself a more inclusive examination of the critical gaze.

365/365 as a "whole," then, is a bringing together, and not simply in performance or its move toward what Parks and her collaborators have called "radical inclusion." As many texts made one, *365* stands as a fitting formal metaphor for its re-envisioning of the Great Hole of History. The volume not only describes the convergence of art and text, it enacts and embodies it. It allows the written and the performed text to exist not in a bitter dichotomous battle, but in symbiotic harmony. As Philip Kolin concludes, there will likely never again be an occasion that will allow all 365 plays in the volume to be performed at once—at least not on the traditional stage, so its future likely lies in "cyberspace, or digital theatre, a theatre of virtual performance(s)," in which "each *365* play or group of plays might be envisioned as a link connecting readers/audience to yet another link, whether it be a day's or a week's or a month's work of performances by theatres/performance groups/independent artists nationwide" (81). Readers, however, can take in the volume, from cover to cover, at any time—and when they do, they will see Parks's seven pictures smiling back at them.

Thus, the written text preserves the "whole," extending "radical inclusion" beyond the stage to the page, and then to the writer as well. In so doing, the Great Hole of History, most notably characterized by its inability to represent identity, can be replaced by more productive holes designed to create rather than destroy, include rather than exclude.

Works Cited

Als, Hilton. "The Show-Woman: Suzan-Lori Parks's Idea for the Largest Theatre Collaboration Ever." *The New Yorker*, October 30, 2006: 74–81.

Beach, Maria. "Performance Review: *365 Days/365 Plays* (Week 1)." *Theatre Journal* 59 (2007): 649–51.

Frank, Haike. "The Instability of Meaning in Suzan-Lori Park's *The America Play*." *American Drama* 11.2 (2002): 4–20.
Geis, Deborah R. *Suzan-Lori Parks*. Ann Arbor: University of Michigan Press, 2008.
Jiggetts, Shelby. "Interview with Suzan-Lori Parks." *Callaloo* 19.2 (1996): 309–17.
Kolin, Philip. "Redefining the Way Theatre Is Created and Performed: The Radical Inclusion of Suzan-Lori Parks's *365 Days/365 Plays*." *Journal of Dramatic Theatre and Criticism* 22.1 (2007): 65–83.
Parks, Suzan-Lori. *The America Play and Other Works*. New York: Theatre Communications Group, 1995. 158–199.
_____. *Getting Mother's Body*. New York: Random House, 2004.
_____. *365 Days/365 Plays*. New York: Theatre Communications Group, 2006.
_____. *Topdog/Underdog*. New York: Theatre Communications Group, 2002.
_____. *Venus*. New York: Theatre Communications Group, 1997.
Robertson, Campbell. "What Do You Get If You Write a Play a Day? A Lot of Premieres." *The New York Times*, Nov. 10, 2006, 3.
Rugg, Rebecca. "Dramaturgy as Devotion: *365 Days/365 Plays* of Suzan-Lori Parks." *PAJ* 91 (2009): 68–79.
_____. "Radical Inclusion 'Til It Hurts." *Yale Theatre* 38.1 (2008): 53–75.
Walat, Kathryn. "These are the Days: Suzan-Lori Parks's Year of Writing Dangerously Yields 365 Plays." *American Theatre* (2006 November): 26–27, 81–83.
Wetmore, Kevin J. "It's an Oberammergau Thing: An Interview with Suzan-Lori Parks." In *Suzan-Lori Parks: A Casebook*. Edited by Kevin J. Wetmore, Jr., and Alycia Smith-Howard. New York: Routledge, 2007. 124–40.
Young, Iris Marion. *Inclusion and Democracy*. Oxford: Oxford University Press, 2000.

Parks and the Traumas of Childhood

Christine Woodworth

In Suzan-Lori Parks's opus *365 Days/365 Plays*, the play written on January 6 titled "The Birth of Tragedy" features Tragedy as a four year old, celebrating his birthday. The Midwife, Herald, Chair Man, and Dignitaries treat the day with reverence while Tragedy simply behaves like any typical four year old. "I want my cake!" Tragedy demands. At the end of the brief play, however, Tragedy orders, "And—kill the dignitaries" (Parks, *365* 80). The majority of the child characters in Parks's dramas embody this duality or seeming contradiction: innocent playfulness, marked by darker adult overtones. Yet much of the scholarship on Parks has overlooked the children in her plays. Verna A. Foster observes that "a disturbing feature of the literature on motherhood, whether traditional or feminist, has been the absence of any developed treatment of children as autonomous beings who might themselves influence the experience of motherhood" (85). In a footnote, however, Foster notes that Harry J. Elam's analysis of the multi-racial children in *In the Blood* is one exception (85). Philip Kolin has also addressed *In the Blood* and the multi-faceted symbolism of the title as it pertains to Hester and her children. In this essay, I will study Parks's depiction of children and how they inform the larger concerns of her dramaturgy.

Children are inseparable from the troubled families they come from. For Parks, the family is a complexly woven, yet fractured entity. The children in Parks's dramas, though playful and unaware at times, are confronted with challenges that prove destructive even to the adult characters. Poverty, murder, war, and absent fathers often push children into adulthood. Yet the sense of innocent childhood—however fleeting—persists. Parents are estranged from their children in plays such as *Fucking A* and the "Father Comes Home from the Wars" series within *365 Days*. Children are also alienated from their parents as in *Topdog/Underdog*, *In the Blood*, and *Imperceptible Mutabilities in the Third Kingdom*. Yet even through these examples of familial rupture, there is a sense of connectedness and a focus on the cyclical nature of family. Deborah R. Geis asserts that Parks's own childhood may have contributed to the construction of these narratives of absent parents as she was the daughter of an army colonel and "felt profoundly the effect of her father's being gone for long periods of time" (3). Indeed, "from her perspective, her father 'died' in those periods only to be reborn upon return" (Geis 3).

Parks's use of cycles also reflects her treatment of history, as several critics have observed. Geis, in her discussion of *The America Play*, claims that "history perpetuates itself through simulacra, and ... each generation is called upon to imitate the previous one without questioning the nature of the falsehoods or performances involved" (109). Similarly, Shawn-Marie Garrett highlights the inevitability of history in *Imperceptible Mutabilities*, noting that "the self is less an invention of one's own making than a result of historical forces" (10). The "perpetuation of history" or convergence of "historical forces" is inscribed on the child characters in Parks's plays. I will focus on her treatment of children by dividing them into several categories: the Mythographer Child (children who declaim or transcend childhood to be historians of their family); the Ghosted Child (adults who are haunted by their childhoods); the Sacrificial Child (children who are sacrificed for being black and poor); and the Child of the Mise-en-Scène (children that are seen and not heard or heard and not seen). In each of these categories the child characters function to some extent as performative genealogies of their family histories or larger histories, highlighting the cyclical nature of Western literary traditions and Parks's reworkings of those traditions. Parks does not always indicate whether child characters are to be played by child actors or adult actors (though there are exceptions as we will later see). Regardless of whether or not the child characters are played by child actors, the impact of childhood is writ large on the adult characters and the worlds of her plays.

Parks's influences are varied and include Greek tragedians; modernist writers such as Virginia Woolf, Gertrude Stein, William Faulkner, and Samuel Beckett; African American playwrights including August Wilson, Ntozake Shange, and Adrienne Kennedy; and countless others.* Parks's use of cycles positions her within larger canons of literature that represent children. She reworks classical mythology including the stories of Oedipus and Iphigenia, canonical plays such as *The Tempest*, American literary classics such as *The Scarlet Letter*, even the traditional Dick, Jane, and Spot characters from early reader books, specifically refracting them through the experience of African Americans. This focus on the experience of African Americans connects Parks to August Wilson, whose Pittsburgh Cycle or Century Cycle plays dramatize the experiences of African Americans in each decade of the twentieth century. Stylistically, Wilson and Parks are radically different as Wilson primarily employed a realistic approach, albeit one that was poeticized. Parks's dramaturgy overall remains decidedly abstract, with the exception of *Topdog/Underdog*. Whereas Wilson gave voice to African Americans within specific moments in twentieth century American history, Parks expands her focus chronologically and geographically. She reworks pieces from the canon of Western drama, situating black characters into the narratives where previously they were not represented. Parks can also be situated alongside other African American female writers such as Toni Morrison, Alice Walker, Sonia Sanchez, and Gwendolyn Brooks, whose fiction and poetry have represented children as central or marginal yet significant figures.

---

*For a full discussion of her influences, see Deborah Geis's *Suzan-Lori Parks* as well as Kevin J. Wetmore, Jr., and Alycia Smith-Howard's *Suzan-Lori Parks: A Casebook*. Additionally, Parks has enumerated her influences in several notable interviews. In an essay in *Yale Theater* (1999) entitled, "Tradition and the Individual Talent" she states, "No need to snub a writer because she is not similar to you in color, gender, or age: there is no such thing as an 'old white fart,' just as there is no such thing as a 'marginal colored writer'" (27).

Although Parks's canon is varied in terms of form, style, and subject matter, tropes connect her work. Principal among them is her technique of "Rep & Rev" or, as Kevin J. Wetmore, Jr., writes, "Do it again; do it differently" ("Introduction" xvii). This process of "Rep & Rev" serves, according to Heidi J. Holder, to "unmoor images and sounds from their expected context" often leading to "repetitions and revisions [that] are frequently nonsensical and impossible" (19–20). Wetmore, in his interview with Parks, then adds a third component to her formula: "Rep & Rev & Ref," highlighting Parks's tendency to craft intertextual resonances among and between her own works ("Interview" 129). Joseph Roach describes Parks's technique as the "cyclical process of forgetting" which "reveals the attraction exerted by the future on the return of the past" (309). Significantly, the child characters in Parks's plays serve as the locus for the simultaneous "return of the past" and the movement forward into the future, highlighting the inevitability of history.

Parks's "Rep & Rev" of history draws attention to the "Great Hole of History" not just in *The America Play* but in each of her works. Debby Thompson asserts that "Playfully signifying on American and Western history through African American accents, Suzan-Lori Parks performs archaeologies and genealogies on contemporary racial discourses and identities" (167). Parks self-identifies as an African American playwright, noting that "there is no single 'Black Experience,' there is no single 'Black Aesthetic' and there is no one way to write or think or feel or dream or interpret or be interpreted" ("Equation" 21). Ten years after writing this essay, Parks offered a follow-up commentary entitled "New Black Math" where she again troubles pat designations of what constitutes a "black play." Among the numerous characteristics that she offers, Parks asserts that "a black play has studied, conducts discourse, and, on certain days of the week, can be found living in the big house of tradition" (578). This "big house of tradition" has previously offered troubling representations of African American children. Using "racist kitsch figurines" as one example of the negative depictions of African American children, Tavia Nyong'o offers an excellent genealogy of the performing black child (375), studying characters such as Topsy from *Uncle Tom's Cabin*, the Little Black Sambo character, as well as many children from *Our Gang, The Little Rascals* as reflective of similar racist sentiments that enabled the creation of racist ceramic figurines. African American playwrights such as Lorraine Hansberry and August Wilson have also crafted child characters that not only resist such negative stereotypes but draw attention to the larger societal institutions that perpetuate racist constructions.

Parks's *The America Play* directly confronts the mis/dis/remembering of history as a means of resistance to racist historical narratives. This play is also emblematic of the ways in which Parks's child characters often serve as the mythographers of their families, writing and re-writing their inherited legacy. As Parks wrote in her essay "Possession," "Through each line of text I'm rewriting the Time Line—creating history where it is and always was but has not yet been divined" (5). The act of "rewriting the Time Line" dominates the lives of the characters in *The America Play*. The first half of this script features the Foundling Father (a play on the notion of a founding father as well as a foundling or orphan) digging the "Great Hole of History" and making plans for his wife and son. By the second half of the play, the Foundling Father is gone and in his place his son Brazil continues to dig, under the guidance of his mother Lucy. Brazil desperately tries to piece together or re/member his past and his father. As Sanja Bahun-Radunović explains, "Searching for the remains of the father who left him when he was five years old enables Brazil to recover his lost origins, or, at least, their traces" (461). *The America Play* makes literal the act of digging into history and listening for echoes of the past that still reverberate. For Brazil, this act of digging is deeply personal. He looks for traces of his father but also traces of the larger arc of history. By knowing more of his father, he is better able to determine his own place in the world. As his mother listens to various echoes of his history, Brazil states, "My faux-father. Thuh one who comed out here before us. Thuh one who left us behind. Tuh come out here all uhlone. He's one of them ... He's one of them. All of them who comed before us — my Daddy" (184).

Not having seen his father in thirty years, Brazil has only vague recollections and his mother's stories to fill in the gaps in his memory. As he continues to dig, Brazil relates the story of his mother and father, embellishing much like a child. His mother admonishes, "Keep your story to scale" (180). This parent-child exchange is repeated throughout the course of the play. Although Brazil is now an adult, his childhood comes into sharp focus in his conversations with his mother as the boyish elements of his demeanor are evident. They even play a child-like game in which they challenge each other with the state capitals (189). Indeed, in his review of the 1994 New York Shakespeare Festival production, David Richards asserted, "Mr. Potts, as the son, ricochets broadly from one adolescent extreme to another" (C3).

Brazil follows his father through the act of digging. His mother gives him his father's spade, which is his inheritance, telling him how much he resembles his father. "We could say I'm his spitting image," Brazil states. "We could say that," Lucy replies. "We could say I just may follow in thuh footsteps of my foe-father," claims Brazil (190–191). Indeed, the parallel construction of the first and second halves of the play support that assessment as the actor playing Brazil finds himself in the same place, going through the same motions as the actor playing his father in the previous section of the play.

Brazil's legacy is shaped largely by Lucy, as her memories serve as the basis for Brazil's images of his father. She discusses both the physical residue that shapes her memory as well as "My re-memberies — you know — thuh stuff out of my head" (194). These re-memberies of the Foundling Father are at once ephemeral and ever-shifting and made physically manifest in the body of her child. Likewise, Brazil's own re-memberies of his own childhood are inscribed on his body and memories and ever-present in his dialogues with his mother. Brazil seems trapped in the act of digging, thus illustrating the legacy left by his father as well as the impossibility of disrupting the familial and historical cycles.

In a similar vein, Parks's *Topdog/Underdog* illustrates the difficulty in breaking fully away from the patterns of childhood. In the case of the brothers Booth and Lincoln, the patterns of their ghosted childhood feature a relationship that is at once loving and fraught with competition and distrust, ending in the destruction of their tenuous family unit through Booth's murder of Lincoln. For Parks, a ghost is "a person from, say, time immemorial, from, say PastLand, from somewhere back there, say, walks into my house" ("Elements" 12). For the men in *Topdog*, these ghosts of their childhood seem ever-present. There is a strong sense of the history of the brothers' relationship in every discourse. At one point, Lincoln pulls out a photograph album and reminisces about their childhood before their parents abandoned them. Booth initially resists engaging in the reminiscence.

> LINCOLN: There we are at that house. Remember when we moved in?
> BOOTH: No.
> LINCOLN: You were 2 or 3.
> BOOTH: I was 4.
> LINCOLN: I was 9. We all thought it was the best fucking house in the world.
> BOOTH: Cement backyard and a frontyard full of trash, yeah, dont be going down memory lane man, yll jinx thuh vibe I got going here. Gracell be walking in here and wrinkling up her nose cause you done jinxed up the joint with yr raggedy recollections [68].

Lincoln's "raggedy recollections" are a nostalgic attempt to rewrite the brothers' history. He fondly re/members, "We had some great times in that house, bro. Selling lemonade on thuh corner, thuh treehouse outback, summer spent lying in thuh grass and looking at thuh stars." Booth abruptly responds, "We never did none of that shit." Lincoln concedes, "But we had us some good times" and then relates the mischievous destruction of their father's tires. Booth engages in this memory and the audience glimpses the adoration the younger brother felt for his older sibling. He exclaims, "I was sure he was gonna find us out and he woulda whipped us good. But I kept glancing at you and you was cool, man. Like nothing was going on. You was cooooool" (68–69).

The relationship between Booth and Lincoln is not that of good-natured brotherly love. Instead, it is marked by jealousies and resentment, suspicion and rivalry. When their parents abandoned them, one at a time, each gave one brother an "inheritance," or $500. These inheritances symbolize their childhoods, which were marked by poverty, crime, and Lincoln's role as the big brother and surrogate parent, a legacy that they fail to escape until the violent death of Lincoln. At the end of the play, Lincoln concedes to play three-card monte with his younger brother, with their inheritances as the stakes. Lincoln ultimately wins, due largely to his ability to distract his brother. "You think we're really brothers," he asks (107). After taunting his brother for losing, Lincoln attempts to give back his winnings, but Booth becomes enraged.

> LINCOLN: Ima give you back yr stocking, man. Here, bro—
> BOOTH: Only so long I can stand that little brother shit. Can only take it so long. Im telling you—
> LINCOLN: Take it back, man—
> BOOTH: That little brother shit had to go—[112–113].

Finally, Booth shoots Lincoln. Although their childhoods continued to haunt their lives, their actions had very adult consequences. Geis asserts that "a key theme of *Topdog* that echoes Parks's earlier works is one of legacies and inheritances, lineage and recording (and sometimes misremembering) of history" (120). Booth and Lincoln are metaphorically and literally destroyed by their inability to break free from the cycles of poverty and betrayal inherited from their parents.

Topdog/Underdog and *The America Play* feature characters whose childhoods emerge as ghosts that haunt their adult lives. Or, as Parks writes, "History is time that won't quit" (Parks "Elements" 15). *Fucking A* also demonstrates the ways in which an adult character is haunted by a childhood that ultimately destroys him. *Fucking A*, one of Parks's Red

Letter plays which adapt Hawthorne's *The Scarlet Letter*, also features a character who is marked by his lineage, though in a more literal sense. Hester, the abortionist at the center of Parks's play, has bitten her young son as the police take him away. She also bit herself to have a matching scar. When he is old enough to be released from prison, Hester plans on using the marks to identify her son, Monster. Brazil in *The America Play* had the spade and the act of digging to connect him to his father. Lincoln and Booth had their inheritances as physical reminders of their parents in *Topdog/Underdog*. The scar on Monster's arm also serves as the physical reminder of his lineage. The mark that Hester makes on her son eventually becomes a valuable symbol because the prison initially tries to convince her that Jailbait, another prisoner, is her son. Reviewing the play, Ben Brantley claimed, "Suzan-Lori Parks scholars — and such a breed surely already exists — will find much to ponder. There is, for starters, her poetically disciplined patterns of imagery, especially the allusions to scars and mutilations of the flesh" (E1).*

Monster, unaware that Hester is his mother, breaks into her house to steal from her. The stage directions indicate that "as he takes the money from her he sees her scar. He takes a good long look, then plays it off" (169). In the final scene, Monster returns to Hester to convince her that he is her son. "Look. My mark. *(Rest)* You marked me years ago. Its just like yours. Look" (208). She sends him away but he returns with the Hunters close behind. He pleads with Hester to kill him. She agrees, slicing his throat the way that Butcher has taught her for the painless slaughter of an animal. Mother and son are united by their identical scars. Their blood ties and future lineage are severed when Hester mercifully kills her son and vengefully aborts the First Lady's pregnancy. Her actions terminate the future genealogy of her family.

Like Brazil, Monster has few recollections of his childhood. While Brazil attempts to piece together the re-memberies of his father, Monster bears the literal inscriptions of his childhood in the form of his scar. The blood that connects him to his mother is ultimately spilled, thereby connecting mother and son to a larger context, that of the sacrificial child. According to Elin Diamond:

> This stage blood is more than a representation of real blood; it is an emblem of the unseen networks of global migratory labour in which women and their offspring are merely functional and conveniently anonymous. When blood is spilled, when the mothers themselves slaughter their children, both the system *and* the suffering can be glimpsed, and in that glimpse, recognised, and in that recognition, resisted [20].

Both Hester and Monster are oppressed by society. Hester is branded for her role as an abortionist, and Monster is imprisoned following the false accusations of the First Lady. Hester granted her child a merciful death, knowing that he would have been executed regardless. Through the termination of her bloodline, Hester's act once again brings into focus the literal inscriptions of childhood on the body of her adult son. As he dies, "She holds him in her lap" until the Hunters come and take him away (220).

Fucking A reworks Hawthorne's *The Scarlet Letter* in a Brechtian-feminist manner, reflecting both past and present. The setting is a somewhat ambiguous totalitarian society

---

*In addition to the twin bite marks inflicted by Hester, she wears a weeping "A" that has been burned into her chest to signify her occupation.

that serves as an allegory for today. Adultery no longer holds the same stigma as in the world created by Hawthorne. However, the role of abortionist in contemporary society seems an apt parallel. In Hawthorne's original, Pearl recognizes her mother by the letter "A" pinned to her bodice. Similarly, Monster recognizes his mother through the matching scars on their arms. Unlike in Hawthorne's novel, however, Monster is sacrificed. Parks indicts the penal system and corrupt government officials. Much as she did in *Topdog/Underdog* and *In the Blood*, Parks demonstrates the ways in which those trapped in cycles of poverty and violence—further amplified by racism—can rarely break free. Hester in *Fucking A* sacrifices her child as a gesture of mercy and a symbol of her own perpetual sacrifice as a mother. In Parks's other adaptation of Hawthorne's novel, *In the Blood*, Hester sacrifices her child for very different reasons. Both plays, however, illustrate the ways in which institutional oppressions impact the lives of children and subsequently haunt their adulthoods.

In the Blood features Hester La Negrita as an impoverished and homeless mother of five. Although Hester remains the central figure, various characters step out of the world of the play to interact with her. While Hester in *Fucking A* kills Monster in order to spare him from a more brutal death, Hester La Negrita kills her oldest son in a fit of rage at the end of the play. Yet, as Verna A. Foster asserts,

> The rage of Parks's two Hesters and their literary foremothers is not directed at the child or children whom they kill but at what the child represents, what society has made of the child or will do to the child. In killing their children, the contemporary Hesters destroy not those who have harmed them but those whom they love, those who are in some sense part of themselves, without effecting any change in the social conditions that produced their rage [75].

Similarly, Harry J. Elam describes the moment when Hester beats Jabber to death as an "act of indirection and transference," as Jabber stands in for his father whom Hester cannot confront.

The cast of *In the Blood*, according to Parks's stipulations, requires six adult actors. One plays Hester throughout the piece, while each of the five children doubles as an adult character. Some such as Jabber also play the character that fathered them. In this way, Parks sets up the cycle of oppression and disenfranchisement that is perpetuated through Hester's children. Caryl Churchill does the same thing in her casting parameters for *Cloud 9*, having the adult actors strip away the innocence from the child characters. Because of the circumstances of their lives, Hester's children have been forced to prematurely age. Elam asserts that *In the Blood* "stages the fluidity of race and underscores the problematic nature of racial categorizations" through the multiracial casting of Hester's children (black, white, and Latino) (117). Elam elaborates:

> Within the theatrical conventions of performances like *In the Blood*, one can seemingly escape the visible markers of the body—an adult can portray a child—even as the action or content of the performance reinforces the power and meanings of the visible body. One can perform but also subvert conventional cultural roles. Thus, with her portrait of these children and of Hester's world, Parks questions what is "in the blood." Hester's problems simultaneously involve and obscure race [117].

By extension, age is also "involved and obscured" through the way children are cast. As Barbara Ozielbo points out, "Such cross-age doubling decenters identity and emphasizes the relativity of emotions and actions" (56).

Through her Brechtian-feminist aesthetic, Parks problematizes the stereotype of the black welfare mother by foregrounding the societal conditions that shape her experience. As Lisa M. Anderson asserts, "The juxtaposition of Hester from *The Scarlet Letter* with contemporary welfare queens suggests that we are not far removed from early eighteenth-century Americans in their condemnation of children born out of wedlock" (66). In addition to playing the children and the corollary adult characters, the ensemble also comprises the chorus. For Carol Schaefer, this triple casting parallels the use of the chorus in ancient tragedy. She writes, "These characters personify institutions similar to the way that masks in tragedy personify emotional attributes" (190). These institutions — religion, welfare, and medicine — have all exploited Hester and her children in some manner. Even Hester's so-called friend Amiga Gringa has exploited her. Although the triple casting of the children allows for a sense of alienation from the characters, in rehearsal Parks was adamant that each of the roles be approached in a complex and nuanced manner. She informed the actors, "None of these people are cardboard characters. They're all trying to figure out their past" (Letzler Cole 97).

Each of the five children has a distinct personality. Their names — Jabber, Trouble, Bully, Beauty, and Baby — illustrate the almost allegorical function of each figure as they behave according to their names. Jabber is the oldest and the most favored. He has been slowly teaching his mother to read and tries to protect her from the slurs that have been written on the wall of their home under the bridge. In spite of society's claims that she is "SHIFTLESS/HOPELESS/BAD NEWS" (as vocalized by the chorus in the prologue), Hester is a selfless and caring mother to her children (*Blood* 6). Referring to them repeatedly as "My treasures. My 5 joys" (21), she constantly deprives herself in order to provide for her children. The life of deprivation and struggle is not without cost, as Hester is ultimately driven to beat her eldest to death.

Rather than Hester wearing the scarlet letter, as in Hawthorne's novel, the signifier is ever-present on the wall of her "home." By opening the scene with the graffiti rather than with Hester's letter, Parks essentially translates the symbolism of the letter "A" and its significance to Hester's circumstances. By placing the image on the wall, rather than on Hester's body, Parks shows that Hester's marginalization impacts her entire family. The brand that society has given her informs every action of the play. Jabber, woken in the middle of the night by the confrontation between his mother and the Reverend D, confesses that he was able to read the slur that had been written at the beginning of the play. Jabber says, "I didnt wanna say you the word. You wanna know why I didnt wanna say you the word? You wanna know why? Mommie? ... It was a bad word" (104). Jabber reveals that the word was "slut" and although he asks his mother for a definition, he eventually concedes that he knows what the word means. Hester repeatedly tells Jabber to stop saying the word but he persists. Parks indicates that "the word just popped out, a childs joke" (106). Jabber, like so many of Parks's child characters, possesses a seemingly contradictory duality. He displays a sense of maturity and protectiveness towards his mother by attempting to shield her from the brand on the wall. Yet his immaturity is illustrated through his uncontrolled repetition of the word "slut." Hester eventually snaps and beats Jabber to death in the presence of three of the other children. She then uses his blood to write an "A" on the ground, just as Jabber had been teaching her at the start of the play.

Hester's act of murder renders her even more powerless, as she is immediately imprisoned and forcibly sterilized. The murder of Jabber was not prompted by his naughty behavior. Rather, the murder was the result of escalating desperation brought on by the exploitation of Hester at the hands of those who were supposed to be helping, the abandonment of the children's fathers, and the starvation. Foster asserts, "*In the Blood* and *Fucking A*, then, can be taken as showing that killing one's child is at once the ultimate form of maternal autonomy and of the victimization of both mothers and children, who are deprived of all autonomy" (85). Through the sacrifice of their children, both Hesters in these adaptations of *The Scarlet Letter* also sacrifice themselves.

The fathers of the five children in *In the Blood* are at once absent and present through the doubled nature of the casting. *Imperceptible Mutabilities* also utilizes doubling in its casting, allowing for echoes and resonances to weave among and between the various sections of the piece, through the actors. As Garrett asserts, "A cyclical history is built up over the course of the play through the bodies of the five actors, who circulate through all four sections and all twenty roles in the play" (7). Part Four (or the Slugs) features the Smith family. Mr. Sergeant Smith is deployed to some distant land, waiting for his "Distinction" so he can return home triumphant (58). Meanwhile, Mrs. Smith waits at home with her daughter Buffy. Much as Lucy and Brazil collectively re-member the Foundling Father, Mrs. Smith and Buffy retell the story of Mrs. Smith's visit to the Sergeant following a long bus ride. Buffy learns from her mother, much like Brazil learned from Lucy, how to perform the tasks of the family mythographer.

As the Smith family appears in subsequent scenes, it increases in size so that it eventually includes another daughter named Muffy and a son named Duffy. It is clear that Buffy, the oldest, has aged as well and is helping to care for the younger children in the family. Muffy asks her sister, "Mind if I yo-yo, Buff?" She replies, "Be careful, K?" (66). When Sergeant Smith does finally return home, his children are unfamiliar to him. "Who're you uhgain?" he asks upon seeing Duffy, but the boy assures him, "I'm your spittin image. Did you bring my airplane?" Mr. Sergeant Smith replies, "I was uh fine lookin man — like you — once. I got pictures. Uh whole wallet full. There. That's me." Duffy corrects him, "Nope. That's me. We look uhlike" (69). Although his children may be strangers to him due to his absence, they find their own lineage to be unmistakable. The cost of his absence is greater than a sense of unfamiliarity, however. Over the course of the play, the "men from thuh Effort" continue to come by and take pieces of furniture, and, eventually, Mrs. Smith loses her eyesight. As Mel Gussow observed, "His family at home extols him in his absence, maintaining a happy façade while falling into blindness (literally, in the case of the sergeant's wife)" (C24). The cycles of departure and return emerge in a number of other Parks works. The families left behind make do the best they can, all the while their physical world is disappearing from around them. Buffy's role as the surrogate parent also illustrates the ways in which children grow up too fast when their parents are absent, as do the brothers in *Topdog*.

Part 3: Open House of *Imperceptible Mutabilities* also features children separated from their parents. This section of the play brings together a number of categories of the representation of children: children as mythographers, children haunted by their childhoods and children of the mise-en-scène. This part of the play focuses on Aretha, whom

Garrett describes as "a dying slave nanny who hallucinates her way to the present day, where she continues to haunt her former charges" (7). Anglor and Blanca, the white children she cared for, appear initially as children, played by adult African American actors in whiteface. Hence, Anglor and Blanca stand in stark contrast to the children of the Smith family. Their "whiteness" has afforded them privileges not granted the Smiths. While the Smith family watches their home being dismantled piece by piece, Anglor and Blanca acquire additional trappings of their bourgeois heritage at the expense of others, namely, Aretha. Although the Smith family maintained a "happy façade," Anglor and Blanca cannot be coaxed into smiling, not even for a family photograph.

In the first scene in which they appear, a slideshow of images shows pictures of the two children with Aretha while the actors speak in semi-darkness. As Aretha attempts to get the children to smile for their portrait, they refuse to mind her. Anglor cries, "I want my doll. Where is my doll I want my doll where is it I want it. I want it now" (41). Later, the brother and sister reappear, as a husband and wife who are looking to purchase the apartment that Aretha has been living in. Their childhood ghosts them as Anglor recognizes Aretha. "Haven't I seen her somewhere before?" he asks. Blanca humorously replies, "Anglor Saxon!— He's always doing that. When we met he wondered if he hadn't seen me somewhere before. And he had!" (49). When Anglor and Blanca reappear as adults, their own children appear as part of the *mise-en-scène*. Anglor introduces them: "Meet our children: Anglor and Blanca. They're so nice and quiet they don't speak unless they're spoken to they don't move unless we make them" (50). Anglor and Blanca are at once like the characters in *In the Blood* who play their own children and are like the figures in *The America Play* and *Topdog/Underdog* whose own childhoods are inscribed on their adult lives. Additionally, Anglor and Blanca's relationship with Aretha connects them to the larger history of African American oppression created by slavery and servitude. Similarly, the portrayal of the characters in whiteface connects this piece to other plays by Parks, namely *The America Play* and *Topdog/Underdog* in which Parks uses her "Rep & Rev" style to critique traditions of minstrelsy.

Although *Imperceptible Mutabilities* is one of Parks's early plays, it bears many striking similarities to one of her more recent works. *Imperceptible Mutabilities* and the "Father Comes Home from the Wars" series in *365 Days/365 Plays* both feature children whose fathers are absent. In each of these pieces, however, Parks dramatizes the anticipation of and perpetual return of the father from war. Both stage the cycles of perpetual returning and the fractured nature of the families to which the fathers (and in one instance in *365 Days*, the mothers) return. Just as Brazil tries to re-member his father by digging in the "Great Hole of History" and Lincoln crafts his "raggedy recollections," the families in these plays must re-member their lineage when father ultimately returns.

365 Days/365 Plays functions as a microcosm of Parks's oeuvre to date and includes representations of children in each of the categories I have set forth. This voluminous collection of short plays features familiar characters, plot structures, and thematic trends. Rebecca Rugg writes:

> It's a rhizomatic structure, a root system holding together the cycle as one whole thing, brought together by the calendar year. The cycle does not put forth a worldview in the service of a single politics or any one legible worldview. It could be called fractured, and in

some sense, yes, postmodern — and yet thoroughly humanist in the way it values, earnestly, the ideal of radical inclusion ["Radical Inclusion" 74].

Parks's notion of "radical inclusion" deals primarily with the staging of the *365 Plays* cycle, which took place over the course of a year at sites throughout the United States. Including actors of all races and levels of training (or lack thereof), and taking place in traditional and non-traditional performance venues, *365 Days* exploded traditional performance conventions. In a separate article, Rugg describes the staging process as something of a "spiritual geography" ("Dramaturgy" 69), due to the disparate nature of performing venues and producing companies. Kolin goes so far as to describe *365 Days* as "panotoptic" ("Redefining" 66) and argues that the multiplicitous approach to production "democratizes theatres by linking them locally and nationally" and disrupts privileged notions of theatre-going (67).

The series of short plays within *365 Plays* entitled "Father Comes Home from the Wars" continuously dramatizes the return of the father from a distant land, connecting explicitly to the Smith family in *Imperceptible Mutabilities* and implicitly to all of Parks's plays in which a parent or parents is/are absent. In each case, there is a sense of unfamiliarity with the family at home, reflecting Parks's own experiences with the perpetual departure and return of her military father. In the first instance of Father's return, the children are either not there or do not yet exist. "Where are the children?" Father asks. "What children?" Mother replies. In some respects, this is an inversion of the actions in *Imperceptible Mutabilities*, when the father returns home and fails to recognize his children. In Part 2 of the series, the family sits for a family portrait with a different man standing in for the Father/Soldier Man. The children (silent as in many of the plays in *365 Days*) fidget until "Mother eyes them or slaps them on their hands and they do their best to keep still." Eventually, the "real" father returns and "Soldier Man taps the Father of the Family on the shoulder, relieving him from duty. The Father was only a father figure, and, very graciously bows, clicks his heels and leaves." Yet this Soldier Man is frightening to the family who do not seem to recognize him. He puts on a Puccini record and implores the family, "Lets have a sing-along, shall we?" When he reaches out to the Family, however, "They cringe and shrink from his touch." The family notices the Soldier is missing various pieces of his body and their recognition and horror get in the way of the portrait. When the Painter admonishes them "Oh, this will never do!" they "snap back into polite alignment" and as the Soldier Man continues dancing, "the Family, very bravely, you understand, holds very very still" (119). This play illustrates the darker side of family members returning from war. In the case of the Smith family, the father's return (or ever-anticipated return) was celebratory. Although they had adapted to life without him, his homecoming was welcome. In the case of the family in Part 2, the return of the father is not romanticized. Rather, the years of absence make him strange to the family. The horrors of war have been emblazoned on his body, constant reminders of the perils he endured. The final image of the family holding "very very still" symbolizes their sense of duty and obligation, in spite of their fear.

In Part 3 of the series, Father comes home and brings the war with him in the shape of the fellow soldiers that stand at the door. As he tries to return to his everyday life by watching television with his son, the soldiers "make loud war noises." As with the obvious wounds in the previous play, the soldiers represent the ways in which war is carried home to the family and is inescapable for the soldier. Just as Duffy was the "spittin image" of his father and Brazil "follow[s] in thuh footsteps" of his foe-father, Junior also wants to be like his dad. "Im gonna be a soldier just like yr a soldier, right, Pop?" This causes Father to take a Spell before replying, "You betcha" (147). The Spell may symbolize the father's dread at the thought of his child entering into war. In a later section of the series, "Playing Chopsticks (Father Comes Home from the Wars, Part 7)," Soldier Dad teaches his son to use chopsticks, to the accompaniment of "Chopsticks" on an unseen piano. The father and son move grains of rice from one pile to another. As Soldier Dad attempts to teach his son this skill, he is also evidently testing to see if the boy is, in fact, his child. At the end of the play Soldier Dad exclaims, "Chip off the old block after all. I was worried. I'd been away for so long and you — you couldnt do the rice thing. *(Rest)* It was the only thing I brought you back and you couldnt do it and I was worried. But you can do it. My Kid's my Kid!" (207). In all of these plays, as with *Imperceptible Mutabilities*, *Fucking A*, and *In the Blood*, there exists anxiety on the part of the parents (mostly on the part of the fathers) as to the authenticity of their parenthood. The children are asked either implicitly or explicitly to prove their blood ties to the rest of the family.

By Part 8 of the series, the children are no longer present. Echoing the first "Father Comes Home from the Wars" play, Father asks again, "Where are the children?" Mother replies, "Grown up and moved away." (232). There is a somewhat chronological or narrative arc that unfolds over the course of the "Father Comes Home from the Wars" plays that feature children or the mention of children. From the first scene in which the children are evidently yet to be born, to their unfamiliarity with their absent father, to their attempt to know and be like him, to their own exit into adulthood, the children are defined through their relationship to their father. In the final offering of the series, "Part 11: His Eternal Return — A Play for My Father," Parks crafts a piece that is entirely stage directions, demonstrating the child of the mise-en-scène. Instead of one family whose father returns, Parks creates an epic scene in which a "neverending loop of action" shows the return of group after group of servicemen. As the soldiers return, wives and children greet them with joy. As Parks writes:

> The action repeats eternally. Long after the audience has emptied of Women; long after the Men have grown out of their desire to be hugged and kissed and welcomed; long after the Children have become less cheerful and more sensible and have taken up trades, like accounting or teaching or real estate or politics; long after the Children's Children have outgrown joy and have all grown-up and moved away. Forever [368].

This sequence, along with all of the "Father Comes Home from the Wars" plays, illustrates the legacies of war and its impact on families. The effects of war and absent Soldier/Fathers are inscribed on their children as well as future generations. The families demonstrate great joy at the return of the Soldier/Fathers. Yet this sense that the cycle will persist into eternity also suggests that war itself and the residual effects on children and families will also continue. Although there is happiness within this particular scene, taken with the other "Father Comes Home from the Wars" plays, the ultimate message is much darker. In both Part 4: Greeks (or the Slugs) of *Imperceptible Mutabilities* and the "Father Comes Home from the Wars" series, the wars are vague, epic, and therefore broadly applicable to any specific conflict. The children who grow up with a father at war are somewhat unmoored from their genealogies and work to reconnect to the man who returns a stranger.

Although *365 Days* borrows from some of Parks's previous techniques, the dramaturgy of this piece is markedly different from her other plays. One of the elements that sets this collection of pieces apart from her other works is her emphasis on stage directions in many of these short plays. Among many of her stage directions is a sense of the peopled nature of the landscapes she crafts. She moves between designating the specific characters and types required to vaguely suggesting who might comprise the various throngs of people on her stage. Occasionally, these peopled landscapes include characters that are specifically designated as children. Most often, these characters are part of the stage picture and do not speak.

Some of these landscapes are epic in scale and address matters of war, as previously discussed. In "The History Lesson," Napoleon and Wellington are accompanied by "their vast armies" which include "men, women, boys and girls, all in uniform and bearing arms" (50). Others are more contained and depict images of family structures. For example, in "1000 South Kelly" a seemingly perfect family eats dinner. When the father asks "Seconds?" the son gets up and exits. As he does so, "we see that he has shackles on his feet and hands, and he wears a prison uniform." At the conclusion of the play, "they continue eating as before, but with no food on their plates, theyre just going through the motions" (56). Implicit within this piece is a critique of a society and judicial system which has imprisoned far too many young black men, thereby estranging them from their families. Other plays within this collection begin in a contained manner and expand into epic proportions, such as "Something for Mom." In this piece a child (Parks notes, "You could even cast an actual child") presents his or her mother with a bunch of flowers and the mother, in turn, "showers love." This repeats several times, adding additional mothers and children until "'Mothers' and 'Kids' are mutating and expanding to include all of us, filling the stage, the theater, and the world, as the action continues and repeats forever. Even during peacetime" (163). This play stands out as somewhat utopian in contrast with much of Parks's darker writing. The intergenerational dynamic is healthy and affirming and offers a potential alternative to the negative familial cycles of estrangement, abuse, and poverty found in some of her other plays. These plays overall illustrate the ways in which the actions of adults impact the lives of children. Though not given an opportunity to voice their reactions, their silent, persistent presence implicitly draws attention to their place within family and societal structures. Whether bleak (as in "The History Lesson" and "1000 South Kelly") or beautiful (as in "Something for Mom"), the role of children in these plays in purposeful.

In contrast to the images of silent children that run throughout *365 Days*, several plays feature children that are heard but not seen. In the darkly comic "Photos with Santa," Parks indicates that "a Woman comes onstage backward, wagging her finger at an Unseen Child." The mother yells, "YOU ARE GOING TO SIT THERE AND SHUT UP AND STOP CRYING AND WAIT FOR SANTA OR I AM GONNA BREAK YR PRECIOUS FUCKING NECK. DO WE HAVE AN UNDERSTANDING?" (63). Although potentially comical, this brief scene stands in stark contrast to the "showers of love" in "Something for Mom." The violent language of the mother could belie a larger cycle of emotional and physical abuse. Or, perhaps more likely, "Photos for Santa" dramatizes the often imperfect act of mothering. Frustration and impatience can often lead to thoughtless yet hurtful comments directed towards children.

Later in the collection, "Goodbye, Children" features a number of unseen children whom we hear playing. A Woman waves goodbye to them with her whole body until "the sound of the children fades into the distance." An exchange between the Woman and a Man indicates that though these children are gone, others will come to take their place. Indeed, the play ends with the stage direction, "Sound of the playing children builds again, getting louder as the children come nearer. The Woman and Man, horrified, cover their ears as they resist the urge to flee" (209). In each of these pieces, we see the effects of the children on the adult characters. While the particulars of the dynamic between adult and child(ren) are vague, the toll the relationships take on the adults is evident. The Woman in "Photos with Santa" demonstrates her aggravation as she yells at the Unseen Child. Similarly, the Woman in "Goodbye, Children" indicates that her interactions with the children are strenuous. In response to the Man's assertion that other children will return, she states, "Less of me will be here to greet them, Im afraid" (209). The source of the Man and Woman's horror is unclear. Are the children menacing? Or are the adults perhaps exhausted from the effort of maintaining a good-natured front that enables the children to continue to play, blissfully unaware of what may be happening around them?

The children in *365 Days* that are seen and not heard or heard and not seen reflect Parks's evident interest in "radical inclusion." The worlds that she creates in *365 Days* are not merely worlds inhabited by adult characters. The child characters that people her dramatic landscapes (either visually or aurally) reflect the human diversity within this set of plays. As Parks wrote in "an Equation for Black People Onstage," "We should endeavor to show the world and ourselves our beautiful and powerfully infinite variety" (22). Yet the intergenerational dynamics revealed in these plays in which children are part of the mise-en-scène calls attention to the often marginal place of children in society. Children, it seems, are still often seen yet not heard. Those that are heard, on the other hand, evidently have the potential to negatively impact the adults in their lives.

These examples are not an exhaustive list of the instances in which children appear in the plays of Suzan-Lori Parks. Indeed, they appear in a number of plays in *365 Days/365 Plays* including in scenes with teachers and students, which address the role of children outside family structures. Additionally, as in the piece that this essay opened with, "The Birth of Tragedy," there are several plays that blend humor with dark subject matter and utilize children as central or secondary figures, including "We Are Fresh Out of Canned Laughter," "Get Some Off the Television," "The King's Head," and "For Sale by Owner."

Much of the scholarship on Suzan-Lori Parks has addressed her reworking of history in order to recover, reflect, and rewrite African American experiences. Unquestionably, she has forged a unique and ever-evolving dramaturgy that playfully yet poignantly reimagines history, literature, and contemporary identities. As Andrea J. Goto observes:

> Reversing or revising ideas such as "whiteness" and "blackness," "truth" and "fiction," or the ever-confounding notion of an "American Identity," the playwright treats them as malleable, dynamic concepts rather than as fixed ones, thus exposing the layers that compose an African

American identity and challenging her audiences to rethink racist assumptions and in its place see the human experience [107–108].

I would argue that Parks also treats notions such as "child" and "adult" as equally malleable, as the examples in this essay suggest. Histories, in the form of epic conflicts of war or the smaller genealogies of family lineage, are inscribed within the figures in Parks's plays. The children in these plays are sometimes seen but not heard (or heard but not seen), ghosted on the bodies of their adult selves, or connected to the larger webs of historical legacies. As Steven Drukman aptly notes in his description of Parks's work, "Identities (including, but not limited to, racial) are performed, reinhabited, reimprinted ... but never for the first time" (353). The presence of children in Parks's canon underscores the cyclical, and traumatic, life of families and, by extension, history.

Works Cited

Anderson, Lisa M. *Black Feminism in Contemporary Drama*. Urbana: University of Chicago Press, 2008.

Bahun-Radunovi, Sanja. "History in Postmodern Theater: Heiner Müller, Caryl Churchill, and Suzan-Lori Parks." *Comparative Literature Studies* 45.4 (2008): 446–470.

Brantley, Ben. "A Woman Named Hester, Wearing a Familiar Letter." Review of *Fucking A* by Suzan-Lori Parks, directed by Michael Greif. *The New York Times*, March 17, 2003: E1.

Diamond, Elin. "Bloody Aprons: Suzan-Lori Parks, Deborah Warner and Feminist Performance in the Age of Globalisation." In *Staging International Feminisms*. Edited by Elaine Aston and Sue-Ellen Case. New York: Palgrave Macmillan, 2007: 9–22.

Drukman, Steven. "Suzan-Lori Parks and Liz Diamond: Doo-a-diddly-dit-dit." In *Re:direction: A Theoretical and Practical Guide*. Edited by Rebecca Schneider and Gabrielle Cody. London: Routledge, 2002: 352–365.

Elam, Harry J. "The Postmuticultural: A Tale of Mothers and Sons." *Crucible of Cultures: Anglophone Drama at the Dawn of the New Millennium*. Bruxelles: P.I. E. Peter Lang, 2002: 113–128.

Foster, Verna. "Nurturing and Murderous Mothers in Suzan-Lori Parks's *In the Blood* and *Fucking A*." *American Drama* 16.1 (Winter 2007): 75–89.

Garrett, Shawn-Marie. "Figures, Speech and Form in *Imperceptible Mutabilities in the Third Kingdom*." In *Suzan-Lori Parks: A Casebook*. Edited by Kevin J. Wetmore, Jr., and Alycia Smith-Howard. New York: Routledge, 2007. 1–17.

Geis, Deborah R. *Suzan-Lori Parks*. Ann Arbor: University of Michigan Press, 2008.

Goto, Andrea J. "Digging Out of the Pigeonhole: African-American Representation in the Plays of Suzan-Lori Parks." In *Suzan-Lori Parks: A Casebook*. Edited by Kevin J. Wetmore, Jr., and Alycia Smith-Howard. New York: Routledge, 2007. 106–123.

Gussow, Mel. "Identity Loss in *Imperceptible Mutabilities*." Review of *Imperceptible Mutabilities in the Third Kingdom* by Suzan-Lori Parks, directed by Liz Diamond. *The New York Times*, Sept. 20, 1989: C24.

Holder, Heidi J. "Strange Legacy: The History Plays of Suzan-Lori Parks." In *Suzan-Lori Parks: A Casebook*. Edited by Kevin J. Wetmore, Jr., and Alycia Smith-Howard. New York: Routledge, 2007. 18–28.

Kolin, Philip. "Parks's *In the Blood*." *The Explicator* 64.4 (Summer 2006): 253–255.

_____. "Redefining the Way Theatre Is Created and Performed: The Radical Inclusion of Suzan-Lori Parks's *365 Days/365 Plays*. *Journal of Dramatic Theory and Criticism* 22.1 (Fall 2007): 65–83.

Letzler Cole, Susan. *Playwrights in Rehearsal: The Seduction of Company*. New York: Routledge, 2001.

Nyong'o, Tavia. "Racial Kitsch and Black Performance." *The Yale Journal of Criticism* 15.2 (2002): 371–391.

Ozielbo, Barbara. "The 'Fun That I Had': The Theatrical Gendering of Suzan-Lori Parks's 'Figures.'" In *Suzan-Lori Parks: A Casebook*. Edited by Kevin J. Wetmore, Jr., and Alycia Smith-Howard. New York: Routledge, 2007. 48–60.

Parks, Suzan-Lori. *The America Play*. In *The America Play and Other Works*. New York: Theatre Communications Group, 1995. 157–199.

_____. "An Equation for Black People Onstage." In *The America Play and Other Works*. New York: Theatre Communications Group, 1995. 19–22.
_____. "Elements of Style." In *The America Play and Other Works*. New York: Theatre Communications Group, 1995. 6–18.
_____. *Fucking A*. In *Red Letter Plays*. New York: Theatre Communications Group, 2001. 113–225.
_____. *Imperceptible Mutabilities in the Third Kingdom*. In *The America Play and Other Works*. New York: Theatre Communications Group, 1995. 23–71.
_____. *In the Blood*. In *Red Letter Plays*. New York: Theatre Communications Group, 2001. 1–110.
_____. "New Black Math." *Theatre Journal* 57.4 (December 2005): 576–583.
_____. "Possession." In *The America Play and Other Works*. New York: Theatre Communications Group, 1995. 3–5.
_____. *365 Days/365 Plays*. New York: Theatre Communications Group, 2006.
_____. *Topdog/Underdog*. New York: Dramatists Play Service, 1999.
_____. "Tradition and the Individual Talent." *Yale Theater*. 29.2 (1999): 26–33.
Richards, David. "Seeking Bits of Identity in History's Vast Abyss." Review of *The America Play* by Suzan-Lori Parks, directed by Liz Diamond. *The New York Times*, March 11, 1994: C3.
Roach, Joseph. "The Great Hole of History: Liturgical Silence in Beckett, Osofian, and Parks." *The South Atlantic Quarterly* 100.1 (Winter 2001): 307–317.
Rugg, Rebecca. "Dramaturgy as Devotion: *365 Days/365 Plays* of Suzan-Lori Parks." *PAJ* 31.1 (January 2009): 68–79.
_____."Radical Inclusion 'Til It Hurts: Suzan-Lori Parks's *365 Days/365 Plays*." *Theater* 38.1 (Spring 2008): 52–75.
Schaefer, Carol. "Staging a New Literary History: Suzan-Lori Parks's *Venus*, *In the Blood*, and *Fucking A*." *Comparative Drama* 42.2 (Summer 2008): 181–203.
Thompson, Debby. "Diggin the Fo'-fathers: Suzan-Lori Parks's Histories." In *Contemporary African American Women Playwrights: A Casebook*. Edited by Philip C. Kolin. Ann Arbor: University of Michigan Press, 2007. 167–184.
Wetmore, Kevin J., Jr. "Introduction: *Perceptible Mutabilities*—The Many Plays of Suzan-Lori Parks/The Many Suzan-Lori Parks of Plays." In *Suzan-Lori Parks: A Casebook*. Edited by Kevin J. Wetmore, Jr., and Alycia Smith-Howard. New York: Routledge, 2007. xvii–xix.
_____. "It's an Oberammergau Thing: An Interview with Suzan-Lori Parks." In *Suzan-Lori Parks: A Casebook*. Edited by Kevin J. Wetmore, Jr., and Alycia Smith-Howard. New York: Routledge, 2007. 124–140.

Demeter, Persephone and Willa Mae Beede: Suzan-Lori Parks Gets Mother's Body

Glenda Dicker/sun

> Hey everybody, wontcha gather round
> Roll up yr sidewalks
> Lay yr red carpet down
> Cause I'm here.
> This gal is here.
> This town, it's all mine,
> I'm the gal with the shine, and I'm here.
> — Suzan-Lori Parks, *Getting Mother's Body*

> My mother made those footsteps.
> She made those prints for me.
> — Traditional

> Christ warned us by his life and death,
> so who am I that I should not warn my daughter by my life?
> — Yula Moses, *Drysolongso)*

Suzan-Lori Parks claims that she has been writing novels since the age of five. In 2004, Random House gave us her first published one, *Getting Mother's Body*. The novel concerns the family and acquaintances of Billy Beede, a young African American woman in rural Texas. Willa Mae Beede, Billy's dead mother, whose jewels are supposedly buried with her, becomes the focus of a journey to dig her up. The novel is clearly informed by Parks's dramatic sensibility. "The dialogue ricochets with the rhythm, panache, and physical attention to sound that Parks's plays have" (Geis 142). But this is indeed a novel; a novel about place, race and history. Billie Beede's story begins in a town which will sound familiar to readers of her plays: Lincoln. It takes place in 1963, before the Kennedy assassination and in the early years of the civil rights movement, which is alluded to several times, as these characters with colorful names (Laz Jackson, June Flowers Beede, Roosevelt Beede, Dill Smiles, Alberta Snipes, Fat Junior Lenoir, Mr. Israel Jackson) live their colorful lives.

Parks tells interviewer Vicki Curry about why she chose to do this project as a novel: "I knew it wasn't a play, you know, because it's about place. It's very much about landscape. It's very much about the interior thoughts of the characters, which you can get in a play from a soliloquy, but it's really not the same" (qtd. in Geis 142). And in another interview she said, "When you write a play, your writing constructs a doorway, and through that door will enter the audience, the actors, the director, the people who will create your play onstage. Writing a novel, you still write a doorway. But it's a different kind of doorway — because they don't need to bring a novel to life and walk in and inhabit it as they would a play" (Wetmore 134).

As a novelist, she acknowledges her debt to the modernists and, yes, there is a passing similarity to William Faulkner's *As I Lay Dying*. Let's get that out of the way up front. Parks's novel does share certain features with Faulkner's. They both take place in small, rural towns (Mississippi and Texas respectively). Like Faulkner, Parks presents different points of view, each chapter narrated by one character. In chapters titled only by their narrators' names, the characters are developed gradually through each other's perceptions and opinions. They both feature seduced young women in need of an abortion. Both are told in stream-of-consciousness style. Both stories unveil as a road trip. In both, a matriarch speaks from the dead, Faulkner's Addie Bundren ominously in only one chapter, Willa Mae Beede lusciously throughout in blues songs. Their burial dresses feature prominently: Addie's fanned out in her reversed coffin; Willa Mae's hem hiding her treasure. In both, a child(ren) is profoundly affected by her (their) relationship with Mother. Parks has said that Faulkner is her favorite of the modernists and that

> Virginia Woolf's novel re-membered me — it put me back together because it reminded me of what I love. [She was] fascinated with what they were allowed to do ... what Joyce was allowed to do or what Joyce allowed himself to do, what Beckett allowed himself to do, what Faulkner allowed himself to do, Woolf ... what they got away with [Drukman 72].

So the debt that the book owes to *As I Lay Dying* is obvious. As she did with Hawthorne in her Red Letter plays, in this novel Parks continues a move toward critical rewritings of the classic American canon. But Ms. Billy Beede is a good deal more complicated than the ironically named Dewey Dell Bundren. "Black women's writing re-negotiates the questions of identity; once Black women's experience is accounted for, assumptions about identity, community and theory have to be reconsidered" (Davies 3). *Getting Mother's Body* takes up many of Parks's favorite themes and in so doing becomes an altogether original story, grounded in issues of duality, culture, memory and gender. Billy Beede's journey, her quest, is both liberatory and transformative. Through her stage characters Parks makes a critique of present day, societal complicity in the objectification of others and in so doing centers and reframes the black, female protagonist within each play. In *Getting Mother's Body*, a novel populated with hot, wild women smelling of Dixie Peach, she continues her loving exploration of the complex and complicated body of the "bad" woman. In centering a new black female transgressive voice as the guide to the tale, Parks follows in a tradition of black women's poetics of "wicked excess," as explored in Ajuan Maria Mance's "Re-locating the Black Female Subject: Lucille Clifton." Clifton, she suggests, uses poetry as a forum for depicting black female subjects in flagrant disregard of the boundaries that have traditionally limited their visibility. "When Clifton and other

African American poets collapse the distinctions between history and myth, sorcery and science, conjuring and creativity, they assert — mischievously, unabashedly, self-indulgently, and with pleasure — their newly reclaimed power to define the limits of their own subjectivity" (Mance 135). Willa Mae Beede is just such a black female subject, living wickedly in excess, enjoying willful transgression. In explanation of her use of the term "myth play," Mance posits "identity as fabrication in progress; rather than a fixed position, identity is a process" (136). This is a perfect description of Billy Beede's odyssey to self-hood, to stepping out of her mother's shadow. The novel could as well be called *Becoming Billy*.

Billy Beede is her own confessor and has her own chorus. In an interview, Parks promises, "If the character is very rich when you meet her — then the trip is incredibly intense, very visceral" (Sova 32). And for sure, *Getting Mother's Body* takes us on an intense, visceral trip. As with *Venus*, her "angle is this: History, Memory, Dis-memory, Remembering, Dismembering, Love, Distance, Time, a Show" (*Venus* 166). It is a novel "about locating the ancestral burial ground, digging for bones, finding bones, hearing the bones sing" (Parks, "Possession" 4). As with her plays, here the black female body is constructed as "the discursive site of restoration for black subjectivity" (Louis 141). Hortense J. Spillers argues that "the 'Great Long National Shame' of slavery and its aftermath have 'marked' black women as stereotypes, even as they have erased their true names" (60). Hardheaded black women like Willa Mae Beede are generally constructed as the supreme "other": the dark, dangerous, unruly presence against which normalcy is defined. This hardheaded woman rails against her invisibility like a virago, wanting to be seen, demanding to be heard. She is prolific and fecund, signing her experience in a loud, honest voice. She is uncompromising in her vision and in her negotiation with the powers that would muzzle her voice. She is the bad, bad, bad presence, exoticized, exploited, but rarely celebrated. Suzan-Lori Parks is having none of that. Like President Barack Obama, who is fond of saying to his critics "I get it," Suzan-Lori Parks "gets" Mother's body. In her novel, Parks continues her quest to rewrite notions of Hawthorne's "wild woman" and society's "bad girls." The plays, she says (speaking of her play-a-day series), are "strung together like beads with grace as the string" (Wetmore 125). The novel of Beedes is as deceptively short and simple as a blues song. Parks's quest here can be said to privilege an exploration of the black female desiring subject. Her guides in this quest are as varied and eclectic as her body of work. As influential as the modernists may have been, she owes a debt of gratitude to the Mother Novelists who came before her: Zora Neale Hurston, Alice Walker, Toni Morrison, and others.

Parks has a direct connection to Zora Neale Hurston. In 2005, Parks wrote the television screenplay for Hurston's 1937 novel, *Their Eyes Were Watching God*, which starred Halle Berry. Hurston presents us with an early portrait of the black female desiring subject in her novel. Her protagonist, Janie, comes to occupy progressively larger physical spaces in her quest to become a speaking black subject. Henry Louis Gates describes Hurston's rhetorical strategy as

> a profoundly lyrical, densely metaphorical, quasi-musical, privileged black oral tradition on the one hand, and a received but not yet fully appropriated Standard English literary tradition on the other hand. The quandary for the writer was to find a third term, a bold

and novel signifier, informed by these two related yet distinct literary languages. This is what Hurston tried to do in *Their Eyes*. The sign of this transcendent self would be the shaping of a strong, self-reflective voice: "Ah wanted to preach a great sermon about colored women sittin' on high, but they wasn't no pulpit for me" [181].

In a letter to Carl Van Vechten, Hurston wrote: "I love myself when I am laughing. / And then again when I am looking mean and impressive" (Walker 1). In this revolutionary beyond-what-it-appears-on-the-surface little statement, Hurston opens up a space for the smiling good girl, as well as the mean and impressive one, equally proud to be both. That Hurston trusted her own self-valuation in the face of a world of white and male supremacy is a testimony to her genius and her faith. "While Parks is more obviously a stylist in appropriating vernacular language and storytelling (including minstrelsy) she is playing off the legacy of Hurston in creating new histories (or new ways of telling history) that implicitly or explicitly critique the dominant ways of telling" (Geis 7). Hurston died penniless and was buried in an unmarked Florida grave, but before she did she left a legacy which opened door(way)s for Suzan-Lori Parks.

Alice Walker, following in Hurston's tradition, made her own way in her artistic expression of our history and culture (it was Walker who placed the headstone on Hurston's grave). "But you're up against a hard game if you have to die to win it, / and we must insist that dying in poverty / is an unacceptable extreme" (Walker 4). In *The Color Purple*, Walker's protagonist Celie moves from silence and invisibility to a recovery of her own history, sexuality, spirituality, and a voice fully her own. As in *Getting Mother's Body*, characters in Walker's novel break the boundaries of traditional male or female gender roles: Sofia's strength and sass, Shug's sexual assertiveness, and Harpo's insecurity. This blurring of gender traits and roles sometimes involves sexual ambiguity, as we see in the sexual relationship that develops between Celie and Shug. Shug's confident sexuality and resistance to male domination cause her to be labeled a tramp. She has a reputation as a woman of dubious morals who has some sort of "nasty woman disease," and refuses to allow herself to be dominated by anyone. Shug has fashioned her identity from her many experiences, instead of subjecting her will to others and allowing them to impose an identity upon her. Like Shug, Willa Mae in *Getting Mother's Body* is an extravagant sexual presence, even down to her bisexuality.

Toni Morrison's Sula, a character engaged in the construction of a radical black female subjectivity, is somebody potent, dangerous and different. Like Hester LaNegrita in *In the Blood*, "SHE'S A NO COUNT SHIFTLESS/HOPELESS/BAD NEWS/BURDEN TO SOCIETY/SLUT!" (6–7). She refuses to be a colonized body, a body without prerogatives. Unlike the historically colonized black female body, Sula's body will not be the object of confinement, limitation, and clichés that not only "deny the concept of individual or nonnormative bodily experience and purge the deviant woman from representability," but also "eras[e] the potential for adventure" (Michie 89). When Sula returns to Medallion from college, she returns to live the life of an irrepressible jazz body, one given to variation and experiment. As Parks later does with the character of Willa Mae, "Morrison gives Sula a postmortem textual resilience. Morrison textually extends Sula's body, relocating it, bringing it out of the lacuna to which the word 'dead' would normally have consigned Sula" (Dickerson 208). The now-dead Sula can still feel her face smiling. In Parks's reconfiguration, Sula could be Willa Mae's mother and thus Billy's grandmother, musing at their lives with a smile on her dead face.

But Sula is not Parks's only inspiration from the beyond. Her abiding concerns with digging, death, repetition and revision (her "Rep & Rev"), resurrection, and re/membering, bring to mind more ancient myths, those of Isis and Osiris and Demeter and Persephone. Both tales are about duality, identity, ritual, searching and digging, death and resurrection.

Osiris is perhaps the most famous of the gods of ancient Egypt. As lord of the afterlife, he is often shown in coffin art. Isis was the sister and wife of Osiris and the mother of the god Horus. As with much of the ancient Egyptian mythology, there are various versions of the story of Isis and Osiris, but basically it runs as follows. Osiris was an earthly ruler who was popular with his subjects. His brother Set was jealous of this popularity and plotted successfully to kill Osiris and send his body down the Nile in an intricately carved coffin. Isis was devastated at the loss of her husband and searched for the casket throughout Egypt and then overseas. She eventually found it and returned the coffin to Egypt for a proper burial. Unfortunately for Isis, Set found the casket and was so enraged he chopped the body of Osiris into pieces, and scattered the parts throughout the land of Egypt. Eventually Isis found all the parts except one (the penis), reassembled Osiris and wrapped him in bandages (the first mummy). Isis fashioned a phallus out of gold and sang a song around Osiris until he was resurrected. So it was that Isis conceived Horus, who became lord of the living. Being simultaneously alive and dead Osiris, a life-death-rebirth deity, became lord of the dead and the afterlife, residing in the underworld.

Willa Mae Beede is also simultaneously alive and dead. While she resides in a grave until the very end of the novel, she is not really in an underworld. Rather she exists in her own otherworld. As Billy says, she *still* wants to sing. She sings herself to life in the minds and memories of Parks's other characters, particularly her daughter Billy. Like Isis, she fashioned her own sort of golden phallus for Dill Smiles and sang her song around Dill as long as she pleased. But because she is a contrary woman, she resurrects not her lover, but herself. Each day Horus escorts the sun across the sky in his boat and each night he hands it off to Osiris to nestle in the netherworld. Billy Beede's journey spans a Thursday-to-Thursday week, seven times for Horus to float across the sky, or for a Biblical world to be born.

In Greece, the Demeter-Persephone death-resurrection myth was similar to the Egyptian one and began at a similar time. It is perhaps even more important to our deliberations here. Persephone, daughter of Demeter, goddess of the earth's fertility, was kidnapped by Hades, the king of hell. She fell down through a horrific hole in the ground opened by his rising chariot. Demeter threatened eternal winter on the earth if her daughter were not returned. What mother cannot sympathize? What mother would not blanket the world with snow, stopping spring dead in its tracks, would not go to hell and back to rescue her missing child? Backed into a corner by Demeter, Hades agreed to let Persephone return to earth. But before her release, he slyly gave her sweet pomegranate seeds to eat, eternally trapping her to spend time in hell with him. Thus Persephone spends half the year above ground and half the year in hell as queen. Each year when Persephone returns to her mother, we get our springtime. But there is a twist to this tale that has more to do with *Getting Mother's Body* than it might at first seem. Popular myths of the Mother God (Ishtar, Demeter, Isis, the Virgin Mary, and all their permutations) picture them spending their time seeking and searching, yearning and lamenting. They cannot pull themselves together. They are in need of heroes to rescue them from the underground, from devastation, from their own dark desires. But when we scrape the surface of each myth, from Yemaya to Corn Mother, lo and behold, what do we find but a self-defined woman. One who is not ripped to pieces or nailed to the cross by her father to save their people, but one who willingly rips her body apart to fertilize the ground, unafraid of blood and gore, detritus and parturition. "One violent hell of a bitch" (Parks, *Mother's* 90). This sounds more like Willa Mae and the be-coming Billy Beede.

Willa Mae needs no hero to rescue her from her dark hole; she is not devastated by or afraid of her dark desires. Billy is searching for her own identity, but she is not lamenting. Like Demeter, Willa Mae could stop spring dead in its tracks if she just put her mind to it. "I'm the gal with the shine, and I'm here" (91). Like Persephone, Billy resents her mother for seeming to abandon her, and doesn't mind cursing her even in her grave. Billy and Willa Mae are both "bad" girls; hardheaded, contrary, self-centered and dangerously beautiful. Before Persephone falls down beneath the ground, she is all innocence and bliss, gathering flowers with her friends. But legend has it that even as Persephone disappeared, screaming for her mother to save her, already her face began to take on the cold demeanor befitting a queen of hell. For her time in the netherworld, she rules willingly alongside the dark hellish king, since above ground is her mother's domain. This fearless woman frightens us because she is not a good girl, yet she won't stay in her bad girl corner. If we emulate this woman, we think we emulate the Fathers; and perhaps we do, as we have come to know them. Emulation of Father behavior makes us afraid of being too warlike, like Artemis, the warrior goddess; too imperious, like Nzinga, the warrior queen; too cold, like Persephone, Demeter's kidnapped child. We are ashamed to aspire to Persephone's double mask: the bitch goddess who is yet some mother's sweet springtime child. But Parks has her own thoughts about the "fo-foe-faux-fathers" in *The America Play* (see Debby Thompson's "Diggin' the Fo'-fathers" for a full discussion) and she is not ashamed or afraid. Parks brings her protagonists out from the Father's shadow and sets them loose, thinking with their vaginas. Vagina Thinking can cause unseemly behavior in a good girl world, like the bitch-goddess behavior of Demeter when she curses the earth, or the behavior of Sula:

> Nell also finds that Sula's betrayal is not like anyone else's. When Nell catches Sula in a sexual posture with her husband Jude, what Nell sees indicates that indeed Sula is beyond any hackneyed arrangement of bodies, any traditional notion of friendship: "They had been down on all fours naked, not touching except their lips.... Nibbling at each other, not even touching, not even looking at each other" [Dickerson 205].

Or still yet the behavior of Oya: In the 21st century season, they call her Katrina. They call her Hurricane Rita. But it is Oya, willful, tempestuous, temperamental Orisha of the storm and seas; unafraid to throw her weight around. Mythologically accomplished before Shango was named, Oya created the River Niger from a black cloth "She Tore" (Gleason 5). Or even artist Chris Ofili's controversial *Holy Virgin Mary*. The piece which shows a woman's figure decorated with a clump of elephant dung and cutouts from pornographic magazines was part of a larger exhibit titled "Sensation: Young British Artists from the Saatchi Collection" which opened at the Brooklyn Museum in 1999. The exhibit featured other artists who designed art which contained pickled cow parts, human blood and a melding of live maggots and a cow's head. Ofili, who is Catholic, was accused of Catholic bashing. Live maggots and dissected pigs floating in formaldehyde are less disgusting to his critics than the Holy Mother depicted with a broad black face and a visible vagina. What they hate more than maggots are "other" women, with their wild transgressions and their blood mysteries. Mary's conception may have been immaculate, but with birth come blood, sweat and tears.

It is in this fertile, fruitful, ferocious, bad-girl ground that Suzan-Lori Parks is thinking her Vagina Thoughts and stringing her necklace of Beedes. As the story begins, Billy Beede is clearly thinking with her vagina, not only in the wicked, excess, bitch-goddess sense, but also in the sense that black women from the beginning of time have been seduced by dangerously handsome men. Whether it is Tea Cake in *Their Eyes* or Ajax in *Sula*, these men are destined to leave in the end, through death or simple caddishness. The black woman talking subject is a sucker for a golden phallus: "Snipes thought it would be hard to get her. But it was easy" (Parks 11). Snipes swipes her virginity like Hades whispering sweet nothings in Persephone's ear. He swings her around "just like Harry Belafonte woulda" and describes his intricately carved line of coffin art, including a "pharaoh-style one too" (5). The baby in her belly is already five months along. "They say your mama went into the ground with gold in her pockets," he signifies. Billy retorts, "And I say Willa Mae Beede was a liar and a cheat. Getting locked up in jail every time she turned around. Always talking big and never amounting to nothing" (9). When he is through enjoying the intimacies of unmarried intercourse, "going at it, scootching her head up against the door handle" (3), Snipes turns his back on her, highlighting his clean shaven face, cheekbones sharp as razor blades, preparing to leave her on the side of the road a mile from home. Variously described as wild, as fast, as tempting, as a narrow dusty hussy, as a speck coming down the road, she is a fabrication-in-progress; a sexy, wanton, conflicted figure. Thus enters the panty-less Ms. Billy Beede in the springtime of her youth, clopping along in her ill-fitting shoes, walking into her future.

By and by along comes Laz, sniffing around trying to penetrate her tempting blood mysteries; a potent potion concocted from (virginal) blood, (Snipes's) sweat, and Billy's eager fecundity. Already, to his mind, she trails her wicked excess like a heavy smell. Laz(urus), a man born not breathing, signals this will be a tale about death and resurrection. As she clops, Billy comes upon him beside the road, flat on the ground with his hands, like those of Osiris, "acrost his chest, all laid out to rest," claiming to be dead. He sits up, "rising from the dead." "Being dead don't bother me none," he advises Billy. "There's more dead in the world than there is living," he solemnly intones (14–15). In his pocket he has secreted Billy's lost panties, symbol of her "downfall." His father, Mr. Israel Jackson, proprietor of Jackson Funeral Home, says the funeral home is about making people happy, but his wife has never seen anyone smiling at a funeral. Mrs. Faith Jackson will come to sell Billy an elaborate white wedding dress, false symbol of her transformation. The Jacksons divide life into two basic parts for Laz, Life and Death. "Why was you born, he asks himself: to find Billy Beede's panties by the side of the road" (17).

Now comes Dill Smiles, "bulldagger" pig farmer, walking down the steps one at a time, six feet tall and looking like a man, sour as a pickle, not smiling despite her name. She/He brags about his "good sow," lying with her litter in his own bed. The sow is sacred to both Isis and Demeter and one of Isis's aspects is actually a sow, "The Great Sow of Heliopolis." However, Dill's sow is cleverly named Jezebel, lest we forget this is a tale of wanton women. Dill has a fist like Shango's dual-edged sword, a symbol of gender ambiguity. She knocked down someone with that fist once. They didn't get up for two days. Looking like an Indian nickel, she is unable to stop touching what she thinks is the diamond ring in her pocket, symbol of Willa Mae's false promises, "promises I made, but ain't been keeping" (219). Willa Mae lived with Dill for ten years, raising Billy as Dill's own child; but one day she up and left him. She and Billy set out for Hollywood in her convertible, but death claimed her along the way. Willa sent for Dill and asked to be buried with her pearl necklace and her diamond ring. Dill took Billy back to Lincoln, but refused to continue caring for her. Thus did Billy come to live with Willa Mae's brother and his wife.

Most days, June and Teddy sit out front and watch the sunset. Just before Horus hands off the sun to Osiris, June calls out "goodbye." One-legged June Flowers Beede may owe something to Eva Peace in Toni Morrison's *Sula*. Teddy Roosevelt Beede, lapsed preacher, lost his faith when he got turned around by not taking his new wife to California as he had promised. He has his own thoughts about Billy when she is acting "ugly":

> Billy Beede and Billy Beede's bad luck: father-she-aint-never-knowd run off and dead probably; mother run wild and dead certainly; young bastard girl child tooked in by dirt-poor filling-station-running-childless churchless minister Uncle and one-legged crutch-hopping Aunt. Don't favor Willa Mae, but she's got her mother's heart and ways [48].

"I ain't no Willa Mae," Billy tells June defiantly. Having sent her virginity to hell to answer her letter from love, she hopes to find her own domain, away from her mother's rule. The dead mother Willa Mae rules the earth. The scarlet woman sings her siren song from the grave, luring her daughter and her chorus to her side. Most of Willa's chapters are in the form of blues songs. Parks tells Curry that she included songs in the novel "because there are parts in the characters' lives where regular language will not express what they're feeling" (Geis 144). Like Laz, being dead don't bother Willa Mae none. She croons her blues song with an insouciance that would have made Sula proud. Billy calls her not Mother but Willa Mae, because she likes being called her name. Willa Mae sashays into town in her red-hot dress, on her own red carpet, heading her own parade, able to wake the dead. She is sashaying, but she is fast as lightning all the same. Jails tried in vain to contain the hot, wild woman. Dill Smiles could not confine her in a good girl corner. She remembers seeing her daughter Billy walk behind her in the sand, "putting her feet prints where my feets had already made a mark. Good Lord, I thought, my child's following in my footsteps. But I tried not to worry. The way I see it, you can only dig a hole so deep" (247). Like Hester's in *Fucking A*, Willa Mae's black womb (her initials WMB almost spell the word) lacks value and proves itself threatening to society. Also like Hester she is an abortionist, but hers is self-induced and lethal. It leads to her death. Existing in both the land of the living and the land of the dead, Willa Mae directs the action of the novel and pervades the memories of every character who knew her, from her lover Dill to her daughter Billy. She is re-membered through her songs, but also serves as a sort of narrator when she speaks about her relationship with Dill (225), and as something like a griot when she gives a list of Old Daddy Beede's and Willameena Drummer's sixteen children, all named "after presidents and philanthropists ... [and] after words they liked saying" (246). Everybody's got a Hole, she teaches Billy, singing her "Big Hole Blues." Bitch goddess Willa, capable of stopping spring dead in its tracks, knows how to find the Hole. One of Willa's legacies to Billy is the ability to recognize the Hole in someone, which she says everyone has: "Soft spot, sweet spot, opening, blind spot, Itch, Gap, call it what you want but I call it a Hole" (30–31). To figure out another person's Hole is to figure out what he or she is missing, or longs for, and to exploit that knowledge. "The Hole is a place of creation (a womb) and intuition, but it also echoes the Great Hole of History in *The America Play*: it is a space within which a legacy is enacted, a space where history is passed on, significantly in this case from mother to daughter" (Geis 145).

Armed with Snipes's proposal of marriage and her mother's ability to spot the Hole, Billy runs through the town to claim her bride's gown. Rushing towards her coming subjectivity. Racing to eat the seed of her gold-eyed Hades. Her face taking on the cold demeanor of Persephone on her way to hell, Billy gets Mrs. Jackson to lower the price on the wedding dress in her window. She takes advantage of Mrs. Jackson's memory of her own wedding day and her sympathy that Billy has lost her mother. Even though she thinks Billy is hot trash, Mrs. Jackson looks at her in the wedding dress and tells her she's just as pretty as she can be. When Billy returns home with her ornate wedding dress and blinding white shoes, she finds a letter waiting for her. The letter is from Candy Napoleon, guardian of Willa's grave. The letter advises that The Rising Bird Development Corporation with headquarters in Phoenix has its tractors treacherously perched on the edge of Willa's grave, ready to dig on the next Thursday. "I think you should consider resurrecting Willa Mae," Candy writes, "but of course the final decision is up to you." But Billy has other plans and has no time for digging. She is planning to marry a man whose name she does not know. She calls him Clifford, not Clifton, as those who know him do. Riding a bus with her white wedding dress box in her lap, she follows Snipes's instruction to come up on Thursday to be married on Friday. Standing in his yard, facing his pregnant wife (Snipes had snuck off to the circus with his other stair-step children in tow), she discovers that he is indeed a cad. Billy journeys back to Lincoln with her useless wedding dress crumpled into a ball.

Going to a sort of death on her pallet underneath the filling station counter, she sinks unmoving for a whole day, looking up at her name scrawled in the wood. Finally, piecing together, processing toward, the fabric of her true undaunted being, she rises from the dead with a new plan and a new self. Billy decides she will travel to Arizona to reclaim her mother's treasure from the ground where it and she are buried. With it, she will purchase herself an abortion. She does not ask anyone's permission. Lacking bus fare, she steals Dill's truck and heads off in the dead of night. June and Teddy come along to help Billy dig. Like Damocles's sword hanging over their heads, Mr. Sanderson, owner of the filling station, will be waiting to evict them if they are not back by Wednesday for his weekly inspection. (Willa Mae told Mr. Sanderson to kiss her behind instead of getting off the sidewalk for him to pass.) June takes her map of the world along because they might not come back. June Flowers Beede, true to her name, names the flowers as they go, and later Teddy pulls them up by their roots for her garden back home. "We'll be able to visit family along the way," she says. "Estelle, Big Walter, and they boy Homer; Blood and Precious, Cornelius and them wives they got" (124–5). The invocation of "the boy Homer" signals that this is going to be an odyssey, not a simple road trip.

Esther, Homer's faithful, refined, Penelope-like mother, has risen above what she calls Beedeism. "Treasure in the ground. That's Beedeism for you," she sniffs. Her son, with his Louisiana French, archeological-sounding name — Rochfoucault not Beede — later realizes what she means: "Jewelry buried in the ground. Gals needing husbands. Bulldagger with pistols. That's Beedeism" (231). The widowed Esther "Star" Beede Rochfoucault gives them leftover smothered chicken for breakfast and sends them on their way. Homer goes along with her reluctant, refined blessings. The now two-car caravan enters into an epic journey full of "sanctified situations." They all come along to help Billy dig.

> Don't do whatcha see me do
> don't walk nowhere I lead
> my middle name is Trouble
> First is Sin and last is Greed
> Wise up, child, turn yrself around (246).

Ms. Billy Beede, marching toward her selfhood, determination like flint in her eyes, presides over Mother's resurrection; her mother who taught her daughter to cut her eyes like knives that could cut a throat from ear to ear. Mother, who owned her own pressing comb, bequeathed Billy a real talent for hair. She works her hair magic on the black woman's unruly, untamed, misbehaving locks. Her daughter's initials, BB, make her sound fast, though not lethal, like a pellet pistol. In search of Willa Mae's treasure she is, like any Beede, able to bear the unbearable. In her unstoppable quest she engages other Beedes, Precious and Blood, in a ring scam she learned from her mother. Parks does not neglect to mention the Strange Fruit of the time with several references to lynching. Billy's mother, after all, named her for Billie Holiday.

When Dill discovers Billy's treachery, she enlists Laz to drive her to Arizona in his hearse, vowing to shoot Billy Beede on sight in order to prevent any digging of any sort. Dill and Laz travel straight through, unwittingly passing the Beede caravan on the way. They arrive at the grave site before the Beedes and are greeted by an unexpected character: Candy Napoleon, a gold-toothed cowgirl who can ride a horse standing straight up in her saddle, mail-order wig cascading down to her shoulders, owner of the Pink Flamingo Motel. Following in her mother's footsteps is her God-got-Even-with-me daughter, training to ride bareback like her mother. Dill Smiles with her dual, double-sided self is reunited with her diminutive mother, but not favoring her at all. Out back is Willa Mae's Dill-dug grave. Willa Mae, lying in state with her buried treasure.

Upon the arrival of Billy's caravan, Dill defends the grave with her straight as an arrow pistol shots. When Homer starts trash talking she knocks him to the ground with her Shango fist. Candy, who knows Dill better than Billy does, decides to get her drunk with Blood Beede's homemade brew. Crouched beside Willa Mae's grave, Dill and Candy drink through the night from souvenir glasses named for all the states in the Union.

> It's a cold cold lonesome hole
> I made my bed
> Now I'm laying in it all alone [218].

But she is not alone. Down there with her are Osiris's bright sun, Demeter's wintry demeanor, Shug's sass and Sula's smile. Drunk Dill, guarding the grave with her long body stretched out atop it, knows Willa Mae is not dead: "Willa Mae, six feet underneath the top of the ground, unfolds her hands from where I laid them crosst her chest and, with a smile, takes me in her arms" (244). Willa Mae is resurrected. Aided by Mother's siren song, Billy finds the Hole in Dill's heart and warns her that the tractors will scatter Willa in pieces across the land if they do not save her. Dill curses Willa aloud for the way she went through the town bellowing that she weren't no man. Then, miraculously, she helps Billy dig. "I hear the sound of digging. A sound I know pretty well cause I done heard it so many times. You hear a lot of digging sounds in my line of work" (250). Dill and the Beedes all take turns digging, looking to Laz to see how best to respectfully behave. When Laz unfolds the tattered folds of her burial shroud, the Beedes do not look at her body, but at him. When Billy finally looks down at her mother's body, there are no pearls (Dill has sold them all), there is no diamond ring (Dill thinks it is in her pocket). For the first time she weeps tears (the last ingredient in the blood, sweat, tears recipe for birth), loud snotty tears of anger, betrayal, desperation and separation.

And then the resurrected Willa for the last time sings her siren song from the grave to remind Billy what she taught her. Billy's quick eye falls upon the hint of hem peeping out from the new quilt/shroud that Candy's daughter Even has lovingly provided. Remembering her mother's extravagant ways, Billy excavates Willa's treasure from the hem of her rended garment. As she claims the treasure, Billy comes to understand that all the "wicked" things we think we hate about Mother are sometimes only the things we fear. The ability to embrace our fears and integrate them into our own bad selves is how we be-come who we are. Become w(hole)y ourselves, become our holy selves. "When I seen her bones I knew what we all knew, that we's all gonna end up in a grave someday, but there's stops in between there and now" (257).

The adventurous little caravan that set out to get Mother's body returns in something like triumph, with Billy's belly sitting in front of her. Laz, her soon-to-be-husband, sedately drives his hearse, with Mother's body celebrating inside. They might as well have been returning from a New Orleans funeral, brass blaring, white handkerchiefs waving overhead. Going back home, Billy tells us, they made good time. She is speaking of the future from the present "now": She tells us that June gets her new leg, purchased with a portion of Willa Mae's treasure, and takes her first steps on the same day as Billy's baby. And maybe, she tells us, there is a marching band in the future funerals of Blood and Precious Beede who — blood talking to blood — helped Billy dig in their own way. Five years from now, she says, "Laz gives me Mother's diamond ring back.... There's lots of things between now and them bones" (257). Billy chooses her own future.

When she agrees to marry Laz, is she marrying Hades or Osiris or Harpo in *The Color Purple*? We will never know. But what we do know is that she is not domesticated by marriage nor is she cowed by her circumstances. She is a Beede and Beedes can bear the unbearable. As a child she lurked like a little ghost in a dark corner of the Pink

Flamingo Motel, hiding from the blood seeping from her mother's womb. In Billy Beede's *Odyssey* she emerges from that corner and becomes her own (vagina) thinking self. No longer yearning for Snipe's sweet, sweaty smile, for Mrs. Jackson's ornate wedding dress, or Willa Mae's begrudging attention. No hero, she nonetheless could rescue her mother from the insatiable hole of her grave and reclaim the buried treasure(s) that Willa bequeathed her. Product of wicked excess, participant in wicked excess, she is Her Self. Fulfilled, rewarded with treasure(s), satisfied, she wears her bespoke fabricated-identity (red?) dress.

Within the generous, big-butt body of the hardheaded black woman coalesce all the tropes of the dreaded "other": the "bad" which makes "good" glitter like gold; the wanton sexuality which makes piety so pure; the dark which makes the light shine bright, the black against which white is defined. But Willa Mae and Billy Beede's lives don't have to be like that. Parks allows them to be hardheaded, stubborn women who refuse to stand as definition for anybody. They can be both the bitch goddess Demeter and the two-faced Persephone, loving themselves when they are laughing and then again when they are looking mean and impressive. Stepping in the footprints Willa Mae Beede left in the sand long ago are all the hot, fast, wild women Parks writes about in her plays; and of course her own daughter, Billy Beede, with her baby belly. Suzan-Lori Parks gets Mother's body.

Works Cited

Davies, Carol Boyce. *Black Women, Writing, and Identity: Migrations of the Subject*. London: Routledge, 1994.

Dickerson, Vanessa D. "Summoning Somebody: Toni Morrison." In *Recovering the Black Female Body: Self-Representations by African American Women*. Ed. Michael Bennett and Vanessa D. Dickerson. New Brunswick, N.J.: Rutgers University Press, 2001.

Drukman, Steven. "Suzan-Lori Parks and Liz Diamond: Doo-a-diddly-dit-dit." *TDR* 39.3 (Fall 1995): 56–75.

Gates, Henry Louis. *The Signifying Monkey: A Theory of African-American Literary Criticism*. Oxford: Oxford University Press, 1988.

Geis, Deborah. *Suzan-Lori Parks*. Ann Arbor: University of Michigan Press, 2008.

Gwaltney, John Langston. *Drylongso, A Self-Portrait of Black America*. New York: Random House, 1980.

Hurston, Zora Neale. In *I Love Myself When I Am Laughing and Then Again When I Am Looking Mean and Impressive*. Ed. Alice Walker. New York: Feminist Press, 1979.

Louis, Yvette. "Body Language: The Black Female Body and the Word in Suzan-Lori Parks's *The Death of the Last Black Man in the Whole Entire World*." In *Recovering the Black Female Body: Self-Representations by African American Women*. Ed. Michael Bennett and Vanessa D. Dickerson. New Brunswick, N.J.: Rutgers University Press, 2001.

Mance, Ajuan Maria. "Re-locating the Black Female Subject: The Landscape of the Body in the Poems of Lucille Clifton." In *Recovering the Black Female Body: Self-Representations by African American Women*. Ed. Michael Bennett and Vanessa D. Dickerson. New Brunswick, N.J.: Rutgers University Press, 2001.

Michie, Helena. *The Flesh Made Word: Female Figures and Women's Bodies*. New York: Oxford University Press, 1987.

Parks, Suzan-Lori. *Getting Mother's Body*. New York: Random House Trade Paperbacks, 2004.

———. "Possession." In *The America Play and Other Works*. New York: Theatre Communications Group, 1995. 3–5.

———. *The Red Letter Plays*. New York: Theatre Communications Group, 2001.

———. *Venus*. New York: Theatre Communications Group, 1990.

Sova, Kathy. "A Better Mirror: An Interview with the Playwright." *American Theatre* 17.3 (March 2000):32.

Spillers, H.J. "Mama's Baby, Papa's Maybe: An American Grammar Book." In *The Women and Language Debate: A Sourcebook*. Ed. Camille Roman and Suzanne Juhasz. New Brunswick, N.J.: Rutgers University Press, 1994.

Thompson, Debby. "Diggin' the Fo-fathers: Suzan-Lori Parks' Histories." In *Contemporary African American Women Playwrights: A Casebook*. Ed. Philip C. Kolin. New York: Routledge, 2007.

Walker, Alice, ed. *I Love Myself When I Am Laughing and Then Again When I Am Looking Mean and Impressive, A Zora Neale Hurston Reader*. New York: Feminist Press, 1979.

Wetmore, Kevin J., Jr. "It's an Oberammergau Thing: An Interview with Suzan-Lori Parks." In *Suzan-Lori Parks: A Casebook*. Ed. Kevin J. Wetmore, Jr., and Alycia Smith-Howard. New York: Routledge, 2007. 124–40.

The Unconscious and Metaphors in Suzan-Lori Parks's Screenplays of *Girl 6* and *Their Eyes Were Watching God*

Charlene Regester

Suzan-Lori Parks, who is most well known as an award-winning dramatist and less well known as a playwright, is establishing her reputation as a screenwriter of note in view of her screenplays for *Girl 6* (1996) and *Their Eyes Were Watching God* (the 2005 movie made for television based on Zora Neale Hurston's popular novel). This essay examines these films to deconstruct Parks as a screenwriter whose dramatic productions might have influenced her screenplays and to assess her talent as a screenwriter. The film production of *Girl 6* was released during the year that Parks received an Obie Award for Best New American Playwright for *Venus* (1996), which in fact premiered at the Public Theater in New York that same month. These are two similar works that both reconstruct the dilemma of the exploited heroine (Geis 147). Nearly ten years later, Parks provided the screenplay for *Their Eyes Were Watching God*—a film that was released one year prior to the production of her *365 Days/365Plays* (2006).

As she made the transition from dramatist to screenwriter, Parks's screenplays brought to fore some of the very issues that prevail in her plays. For example, she addresses issues such as the construction of identity, reclamation of history, white colonialism, marginalization of blackness, resurrection, time and space, memory, racism and prejudice that is internally as well as externally imposed. While Parks addresses these issues in all of their complexity, at the same time she brings a novel approach to her works, particularly as they compare to traditional ways of reading race. For example, Parks declared, "There is no single 'Black Experience,' there is no one way to write or think or feel or dream or interpret or be interpreted" (qtd. in Shannon 603). Deconstructing Parks as a dramatist and examining how she treats race in plays such as *The America Play* (1994) and *Topdog/Underdog* (2001), Sandra Shannon claims that Parks "features characters whom she strategically casts as African Americans but whose racial identities become dramatic devices—not racial or cultural signifiers" (604).

Developing a unique approach to her dramatic productions allowed Parks to emerge as a dramatist of distinction, but equally important are her contributions as screenwriter, particularly when we consider that she has tackled some of the more complex and convoluted issues of race, gender, and sexuality as is the case in her screenplays for *Girl 6* and *Their Eyes Were Watching God*. Because of the parallels between her plays and screenplays, Parks deserves study for her work in film. In fact, Deborah Geis proclaimed that "Both works [*Venus* and *Girl 6*] critique a black woman's being objectified for the purposes of entertainment and consumption" (148). Parks's screenplays and plays often speak to the search for freedom, as in *Their Eyes Were Watching God*, which Parks described as "the story of anyone who claws away at external boundaries to figure out who they are and what they want.... 'We Americans as a people haven't freed ourselves from the burdens of our history.... When you write about somebody trying to free themselves from the constraints of their society, it's what's going on next door. It's white guys trying to get free of the roles imposed on them, too'" (Lee L:5).

While these screenplays share a similarity to Parks's plays, they are also significant in their own right because of the way in which she tells these stories through the utilization of the flashback; presents women who contend with their past, present, and future; unveils their journeys to locate themselves — a self with whom they are often in conflict; and skillfully juxtaposes the internal with the external self to produce an experience that can be universally shared. It is this skill and talent that she brings to her works and that speaks to her significance as a screenwriter.

Parks's debut as a screenwriter came when she was introduced to Spike Lee by a mutual friend, and he proposed that she write about phone sex, in view of her own prior experience as a phone-sex operator (Williams 1). Parks revealed in *Essence Magazine* that "'I actually was really good at phone sex. I have a good phone voice and a very good imagination. That's why when Spike asked me to write the screenplay I knew that I could do it'" (Morgan 74). This meeting launched Parks's screenwriting career. Several years later when she heard that Oprah Winfrey planned to bring Hurston's work to the screen, a work which she read and enjoyed in college at Mt. Holyoke, she eagerly embraced this opportunity. In fact, Geis claims that "Hurston, who traveled through much of her career as an anthropologist studying black folklore and dialects, fed Parks's interest in creating a stage language that pays close attention to sounds and that reflects the punning, inversions, creative substitutions, and metaphor that can be witnessed in Hurston's work" (7).

Although Parks has exhibited uncontestable talent as a dramatist, her skill as a screenwriter has not garnered the same level of acclaim. For example, *The Los Angeles Times* surmised that "Spike Lee's *Girl 6* sounds better than it plays, which is kind of poetic justice for a film about phone sex.... Sometimes the wrong person tries to tell the right story, and the result is very much like *Girl 6*: baffling, sketchy and unsatisfying" (Turan F14). Less critical, Janet Maslin of *The New York Times* stated that "*Girl 6* ... strains harder to sound serious notes, as with a little girl whose fall down an elevator shaft is linked to Girl 6's psyche. The film isn't sure what to make of this, or of the romantic attentions of Girl 6's ex-husband ... or even of Girl 6's hopes for an acting career" (C3). Stanley Kauffmann of *The New Republic* criticized the screenwriter rather than filmmaker and stated, "[Parks has] accomplished so little in this more conventional mode. She wrote a series of episodes about a young attractive black woman trying to make her way in the world, using her sexual self socially without physical involvement. But Parks has added nothing to our perceptions. She has simply rearranged quite familiar material, then presented it in quite familiar ways" (26). Commenting on the combined efforts of Parks and Lee, Stuart Klawans of *The Nation* wrote, "I assume Lee helped shape the script; but the themes, the psychological insights and the theatrical language all seem Parks-like to me" (35). As for Lee's contributions, Klawans continued, "Lee has always been exceptionally free in his camera placement and in the way he relates figure to frame from shot to shot; you don't find a lot of conventional master shots plus cross-cutting in his movies, but you do get graphic impact. Sometimes, too, you sense that Lee is straining to make an effect — but not in *Girl 6*, in which, apparently assuming his own mastery, he simply let himself have a good time. The result: a movie that, at its best, makes a grindingly sad subject feel as buoyant as a Minnelli musical" (36).

Enduring a similar fate in the press, *Their Eyes Were Watching God* received lukewarm reviews even though it became the "most-watched movie on any [network] in more than five years" (Kissell 1). Virginia Heffernan of *The New York Times* declared, "The movie forgoes many of the regionalisms and much of the dialect that make the novel both irregular and stimulating.... In its place are forgivable but joyless anachronisms; these do little to offset the impression that the film is less a literary tribute than a visual fix of Harlequin Romance..." (E3). Heffernan continued, "If it's too gauzy, it's also dull at times" and she characterized the film as "philosophically thin" (E3). *USA Today* claims that the film "never helps us to understand what it is about Janie we're supposed to emulate, other than her ability to survive her own bad decisions" (Bianco E9).

Whatever criticism these films received, these productions demonstrate Parks's undeniable skill and talent as a screenwriter and, interestingly, speak to how the unconscious and metaphors manifest in screen representations explore black female subjectivity. The present essay intends to read Parks's screen adaptations to interrogate the role of the unconscious in *Girl 6* and investigate Parks's insistent preoccupation with metaphors in *Their Eyes Were Watching God*. Studying Parks as a screenwriter based on these two productions, we have to understand that these screenplays were still under directorial control and so may clearly have been influenced by their directors.

Girl 6: Not Just a Phone Sex Operator but an Actress Who Impersonates an Impersonation

Girl 6 features a protagonist (played by Theresa Randle) who becomes so disillusioned with the exploitation of the acting industry when she is required to remove her top to bare her breasts before a director (played by Quentin Tarantino) that she returns to her agent to express her frustration. Her white male agent (played by John Turturro) becomes so annoyed with her inability to conform that he urges her to abandon both his agency and the industry. Girl 6 then turns to her black female acting coach (played by Susan Batson) who is engaged in "her own narcissistic melodrama" and who similarly exhibits a strong reaction to Girl 6's inability to compromise her standards to meet industry demands in view of its sexual and racial exploitation (Geis 148). The acting coach similarly dismisses Girl 6. Following this rejection, she pursues work as a motion picture extra for a major studio production, but when she is denied access to use the bathroom, she seeks alternative venues to pursue acting, thus leading her to become a phone sex operator. Girl 6 rationalizes that becoming a phone sex operator by creating sexual fantasies requires acting as much as standing before the camera. Initially, she is apprehensive and unskilled but soon becomes quite talented. With this success, unfortunately, she becomes hooked and burned out, and later commits one of the most prohibited acts in the business — she becomes attached to a client by agreeing to meet him outside the confines of the work environment. When the male client fails to appear, she realizes that she has become overwhelmed with working in this business and begins to falter at work, resulting in her dismissal.

In an effort to continue working, Girl 6 contacts another service that requires her to make calls from home (operated by pop singer Madonna). Geis contends that "a pivotal scene occurs when Girl 6 — sitting across from [her ex-husband] at a diner — acts out one of her phone calls, then becomes furious when he gets sexually excited. 'I was just playing with you,' she says, but to him there is no such distinction. The boundaries she draws between her performances and real life break down in disturbing ways as she begins moonlighting with another phone sex agency..." (150). Yet when she is confronted by a psychopath and begins to fear for her life, she comes to the realization that creating sexual fantasies is not really acting and decides to reconnect with her neighbor, Jimmy (played by Spike Lee) and ex-husband (played by Isaiah Washington, who is a shoplifter), both of whom have supported her dream to become an actress. The film ends when she embraces her ex-husband prior to her departure to Los Angeles and phones drop from the sky around them. Finally, Girl 6 is shown returning to another audition in Los Angeles for a director (played by Ron Silver), but this time she remains true to her ideals by refusing to be exploited for her sexuality and walks out of the interview.

That Girl 6's sexual encounters as a phone sex operator become an embodiment of her subconscious is plausible and calls for an examination of Freud's views on sexuality, because of the film's focus on sexuality, fantasy, and maybe even voyeurism. According to Freud, "Psychoanalysis ... shows that symptoms do not by any means result at the expense only of the so-called normal sexual instinct ... but they represent the converted expression of impulses which in a broader sense might be designated as perverse if they could manifest themselves directly in phantasies and acts without deviating from consciousness" (574). Because Girl 6 is engaged in the phone sex business, which is not considered the norm, her actions in and of themselves warrant a critique of Freud's views on sexuality. In fact, during Girl 6's training session, which incidentally is conducted by an older black woman, Lil (played by Jenifer Lewis), perhaps designed to legitimatize the business, Girl 6 is reassured by her instructor that working in this business is not just sex. These men are lonely, divorced, she says, and those with wives, or wives who are restrained when it comes to sex, as well as cross-dressers, need these fantasies because they are therapeutic. Lil then gives the women an identity and informs them that as role players, all of them are white unless the callers have other requests, as white women are envisioned as objects of desire. The female workers then construct an identity based on the number which they are given and Girl 6 thus assumes her name based on her assignment to the number six. Commenting on Girl 6's name, Geis observes that "much like

Saartjie, popularly known as only Venus (and no one knows her African name), the protagonist of this film ... is known only as Girl 6 or by one of her pseudonyms, Lovely" (147).

Following the declaration of her name, Girl 6 receives her first call: "Hi there, how are you doing, I am right here baby — where are you calling from — Texas — it's hot down there." From here she describes herself as having dark hair, dark eyes, and a really great figure with a thirty-eight DD breast size. The caller reveals that he is a businessman and that he made a million dollars by selling one company to another. Girl 6 then capitalizes on this business transaction and relates it to a sex act. She states, "I am getting excited just thinking about how you made the money." After imitating a sex act, she is applauded by her peers for her good performance and the instructor gives her a corsage to commend her on her introduction to the business and proclaims, "You broke the cherry." That Girl 6 has succeeded in her first encounter is a testament to her ability to create sexual fantasies by nearly becoming an exhibitionist, and reflects the male client's desire to engage in an act of voyeurism. According to Freud, "He who in the unconscious is an exhibitionist is at the same time a voyeur" (575). This is a testament to how both the creator of the sexual fantasy and the participant in the sexual fantasy are voyeurs and products of their own psychodynamics. Moreover, Girl 6's first encounter with this businessman then becomes indicative of her subconscious desire to become self-sufficient and economically independent.

Gaining experience in the business, Girl 6 engages in another telephone call; however, this time she talks with the owner of a beach house. The caller identifies himself and claims that whipped cream is in the refrigerator. She responds to his call by revealing that she is making slow soapy circles while scrubbing the linoleum floor with a brush on her knees, admitting that because she is scrubbing the floor, a woman's work is never done. In this instance, because she is positioned in the domestic sphere and a-not-so traditional sexual position, then perhaps this caller reminds her of the domestic space that either she seeks to avoid, secretly desires, or wants to escape. Therefore, it is conceivable that this second caller becomes an embodiment of her unconscious desire or thoughts surrounding the domestic sphere in that either she intends to avoid this sphere because it might restrain her — in much the same manner that the protagonist is caged in *Venus*— or she may secretly desire this sphere since she is thrust into the work world, or she desires to escape domestication through the pursuit of an acting career.

Receiving a subsequent call, Girl 6 is greeted by a male caller, Bob Regular from Tucson, Arizona, who informs her that he does not intend to engage in sex talk but instead is interested in talking about his mother, who is dying of cancer. He expresses the guilt that he feels for never publicly telling his mother that he loved her. Although the conversation ends, this could be interpreted as an embodiment of Girl 6's subconscious relationship with her own mother, who remains absent from the film. Because of this absence, the caller's fantasy could then stand in for her absent mother. While Girl 6's mother is never mentioned, and the only maternal figures seen in the film are her supervisor and the mother to the little girl who accidentally falls down an elevator shaft, this reference to the mother reflects or signifies Girl 6's unconscious desire for her own mother. It is also noteworthy that this is the only caller with whom Girl 6 decides to meet. Girl 6's fascination for the mother is better understood when we consider Freud's position that some people "go through in their childhood a phase of very intense but short-lived fixation on the woman (usually on the mother) and after overcoming it, they identify themselves with the woman and take themselves as the sexual object; ... they look for young men resembling themselves in person whom they wish to love as their mother has loved them" (560). This explanation could speak to both Girl 6's desire for her mother, the male client's projection of his desire for his mother onto Girl 6, or Girl 6's affection for this male client with whom she seeks a mother's love in the absence of a mother figure.

Although Girl 6 engages other calls involving her co-workers, she single-handedly responds to a call received from a baseball player practicing in his underwear (or jock strap) who hits the ball out of the park, an act that becomes synonymous with a sexual climax. The fact that a baseball player calls is perhaps a reflection of her subconscious thoughts regarding her neighbor, Jimmy, who is a collector of baseball cards and memorabilia and who desires to become independently wealthy from his collection. While Girl 6 pursues a sustainable acting career, Jimmy is in pursuit of becoming financially self-sufficient as a collector; unfortunately, when he realizes that his dream is long-term, his goals begin to fade. On some level, Jimmy could represent Girl 6's alter-ego, because while they both have goals that are beyond reach, Jimmy constantly forces her to question her decision to become a phone sex operator rather than a real actress. Therefore, it is conceivable that her encounter with this baseball caller becomes a reflection of her subconscious thoughts regarding Jimmy, with whom she shares dreams that remain unfulfilled. Freud affirms "that the dream actually has a secret meaning, which proves to be a wish-fulfilment" (225). Thus, dreams and wish fulfillment are interconnected for Girl 6, Jimmy, and the baseball player as well.

While Girl 6 becomes a participant in male fantasies, she similarly creates these fantasies or acts them out through role playing — recreating herself as another person. In fact critic bell hooks suggests that "the black female who wishes to 'make it' in that cultural sphere ... where glamour, beauty, sensuality and sexuality, desirability are always encoded as white ... [she] must be prepared to disidentify with her body and be willing to make herself over" (14). Because role playing is a more active rather than passive behavior (Girl 6 alters her physical appearance and transforms herself into someone else rather than imitating fantasies over the phone where she is more complicit), we can argue that this act of imitation where she becomes, rather than seems to be, an imitation is regarded as being more powerful and thrusts her into a position of power. Thus, when she engages in role playing she is given some degree of control and power as when she re-enacts Dorothy Dandridge in a scene from *Carmen Jones* (1954). Dandridge, who became an object of the gaze on screen, achieved some degree of success in the cinema world and is idolized by Girl 6. Her fascination with Dandridge is apparent when her ex-husband gives her an issue of *Life Magazine* with a cover featuring Dandridge. By role-playing Dandridge, she vicariously experiences what it might be like to be an accomplished actress as well as experiences the power embodied by Dandridge in a scene where she is empowered while the male character is disempowered. Re-enacting Dandridge in this scene is indicative of Parks's style as a screenwriter who draws upon historical moments from the past to inform the present. As Parks admits, "if you believe that history is in the present, you can also believe that the present is in the past" (Jiggetts 317).

Girl 6 further engages in role playing when she transforms herself as Foxy Brown, an icon from the 1970s black exploitation era popularized by Pam Grier and Tamara Dobson, women who became action heroines when more defiant and assertive black males were paraded on the screen. Grier, whose big Afro, statuesque appearance, and physical ability to ward off her enemies became signifiers of the prevailing black defiance, resorts to violence to take on a range of primarily male opponents and enemies. By re-enacting Grier, Girl 6 becomes empowered in an arena where, because of her race and gender, she normally would be disempowered.

Less violent and more domesticated, Girl 6 re-enacts Thelma's characterization (from the 1974–79 television show *Good Times*) as a hypersexualized teenager who is the daughter of the black patriarch, George Jefferson. (He was from *The Jeffersons*, 1975–85, a popular television show that presented a stereotypical black upper-middle-class family who "moved up" from the lower to the upper east side of New York.) As Thelma, she wears Afro-puffs and a short miniskirt and engages in a phone conversation of a sexual nature from an admiring suitor. Her dad, George Jefferson (played by Spike Lee), becomes irate after overhearing her conversation and, disturbed by the caller, hangs up the phone. Yet when the caller phones again, Jefferson takes his rifle and destroys the telephone. This time, Thelma/Girl 6 is not empowered in the way that she was presented in the previous two scenes, because she is protected by her class position as well as the black patriarch; therefore, she does not appear to be as vulnerable to the exploitation she endures as a phone sex operator. bell hooks contends that "all of these roles still require that she shape her sexuality in response to the eroticism of the patriarchal phallic imaginary. For that imaginary controls the world of media images — of representations" (14). However, these role playing re-enactments are a testament to her acting talent as she embarks on her dream of becoming a serious dramatic actress.

Finally, despite the fantasies appropriated by the film, Girl 6 is in conflict with her own image as a mature woman who is no longer a child. Yet it is her fascination with the little girl who has fallen down the elevator shaft that reminds her of her girlhood and innocence that she once possessed but no longer embodies. hooks claims: "Lee suggests that individuals who are psychically wounded are trapped in infantile states. Addiction to fantasies begins in childhood as a way the self is nurtured when there is no nurturance, when life is without substance or meaning" (15). This infantile state is not one assumed by the protagonist but it is also assumed by the white males in the industry who are equally "stuck in infantile stages of development" (15). Girl 6, preoccupied with this little girl for whom she has sympathy and who is healing, recognizes that the little girl's recovery coincides with the recovery of her own injured spirit. Because the little girl makes such a remarkable recovery, Girl 6 decides to return to her own dream of pursuing a serious acting career. Freud suggests that "the wish manifested in the dream must be an infantile wish" (500). Therefore, Girl 6's struggle becomes indicative of her fragile and infantile state as she returns to her dream — a dream that becomes linked to the infantile wish of the little girl who attempts to regain her health.

The ending of the film is best described by Geis, who speaks to the combination of Parks's style as screenwriter and Lee's talent as director. She notes that Girl 6 "walks across Dorothy Dandridge's star on the Walk of Fame and heads toward a marquee that announces *Girl 6*. But the self-referential gesture is never explained: is this another fantasy sequence? Is she now starring in a film about her own life story as a phone sex worker? Is this a metafilmic moment in which we the audience see her walking into the same film we have just been watching? ... The cyclicity we have seen in many of Parks's works combines with Lee's predilection for seemingly upbeat endings that force the viewer to make choices" (151). Thus, Lee and Parks have combined their talents to recreate a black woman's search for self and subjectivity.

Their Eyes Were Watching God: Janie's Meta-Discourse in Her Search for Subjectivity through Metaphors

Parks as a screenwriter constructs a different woman's story with the production of *Their Eyes Were Watching God* (2005) but one that, nevertheless, resembles *Girl 6*. First, both scenarios center the black woman in these productions; both depict black women who are on a journey or quest for self; both position women whose journey is frequently defined by or contingent upon their interaction with men; and both position women in conflict with themselves as well as with the gender and racial politics that prevail. Like *Girl 6*, *Their Eyes Were Watching God* employs strategic devices that Parks utilized in dramatic productions, such as introducing complex metaphors. In fact, with *The America Play*, Parks introduced stage metaphors "which give few concrete answers, but which produce layer upon layer of complex inquiry" (DeRose 409). I now turn to examine the metaphors Parks employs to adapt Hurston's complicated novel of Janie's search for subjectivity to the screen.

Both the novel *Their Eyes Were Watching God* and film (directed by Darnell Martin) open when Janie returns to Eatonville following Tea Cake's untimely death at her hands. In the film, Janie's bare feet touch the ground as the earth crunches beneath and the voice-over narration says that there are two things that most people have to learn about in life — they've got to find out about love and living. To convey Janie's experience and sincerity in her love for Tea Cake, Hurston declares, "Love is lak de sea. It's uh movin' thing, but still and all, it takes its shape from de shore it meets, and it's different with every shore" (191). While this sentiment comes at the end of Hurston's novel, it occurs at the beginning and end of Parks's film. That Parks selects this passage to introduce Janie's experience while Hurston placed it after Janie's homecoming comments on how Parks utilized various strategies for adapting this novel to the screen, and more importantly, signals how Janie has come full circle in both the novel and film, with both conveying her return to Eatonville. These strategies also speak to how Parks plays "off the legacy of Hurston in creating new histories (or new ways of telling history) that implicitly or explicitly critique the dominant ways of telling" (Geis 7).

In the film, Janie (played by Halle Berry) walks through the main street, worn and weary, with her face covered in muck and mud, yet with a determination to return to her former home, yet not to her former self. She re-enters the town with the camera facing her back, whereas when she left the town, the camera was facing her front. Though downtrodden as the result of life's unrelenting trials and tribulations, she is not defeated. Janie's coming full circle in both the novel and film is a theme that Alice Rayner and Harry J. Elam, Jr., suggest that Parks employed with *The Death of the Last Black Man in the Whole Entire World* (457): "History in *The Death of the Last Black Man* refuses to be linear or sequential; history is *round*" (457). Parks shares this strategy of coming full circle with Hurston.

The story unfolds through one long flashback when Janie returns to her former home and tells Pheoby (Nicki Micheaux) about her life experiences and most of all about her love for Tea Cake. Janie's return is also poignantly enveloped by the voices of her former neighbors who are inquisitive about what happened in her absence and whose discourse reveals as much about Janie as it does about themselves. They engage in double-talk. While they condemn Janie, they secretly envy Janie for leaving her space and place of comfort. In fact, Robert Burgoyne's critique of *Glory* comes to mind. He refers to identity being constructed "from across" as well as being constructed "from above" (16–21). As it relates to the sounds of Eatonville, the townspeople seemingly speak in voices that define themselves "from above" as though they set the standard by which Janie should be compared. Yet they define themselves "from across" in terms of how they see themselves as similar to and different from Janie. Yet "the film aspires to have the spectators 'go there tuh know there,' identifying us with Pheoby as empathic listeners, yet its visual and other sensory details do not get us close to Janie as the novel does" (Geis 153).

Most intriguing in the film is Parks's preoccupation with metaphors — evident when Janie begins to tell her story and hangs clothes on the line with a white blossomed pear tree appearing in the background, and a voice-over narration begins to tell her story. The camera in slow motion zooms in on the pear tree and brings the blossoms into focus. Janie moves toward the blossoms and her face peers beneath the bloom to watch a bee hovering over the bloom. Janie's delight at watching the bee is interrupted by a man in a straw hat who walks in the distance and is revealed to be Johnny Taylor (played by Jensen Atwood), her first object of desire. That Taylor's introduction coincides with the pear tree seems to suggest that the tree is the bearer of happiness, love, and sexuality for Janie. Thus, fruit becomes a metaphor that is associated with desire, affection, and happiness. The fruit metaphor is further apparent when Janie eats an apple shortly after meeting Tea Cake (played by Michael Ealy) for the first time. The apple becomes a signifier of the forbidden fruit that he might represent. When strawberries fill Tea Cake's handkerchief as a sign of his genuine desire for and acceptance of Janie despite their age difference, fruit becomes a metaphor; and when lemons are shared between the two as they indulge in lemonade and becomes a sign of their togetherness, fruit is again strategically introduced as a metaphor. Affirming the significance of food in general as a metaphor in *Their Eyes Were Watching God*, Geis suggests that it becomes "emblematic of problematized versions of nurturing.... Tea Cake, whose name itself implies a treat ... rubs lemon on her lips, they eat fish right out of the skillet, Janie places shrimp between Tea Cake's lips as they dance together and eat other delicacies..." (154).

Though Janie meets Taylor, the first object of her desire, while peering through a pear tree, their meeting is brutally interrupted by the screams of her grandmother, Nanny (played by Ruby Dee), who fears that this distraction might lead Janie on a similar destructive path to the one her mother pursued, and she insists that it is time for Janie to get married. Resisting her grandmother but then later acceding to her wishes, Janie reluctantly marries Logan Killicks (played by Mel Winkler), who owns 60 acres of land, who is much older than she, who signifies the class position to which her grandmother aspires, and who becomes the brunt of her resentment for the duration of their marriage. With the dissolution of her first marriage, Janie embarks on a second marriage when she sees Joe Starks (played by Ruben Santiago-Hudson) walking down the road in front of the house that she shared with Killicks. Eager to escape this marriage, she introduces herself and flees her former life to become Starks's wife, as well as pursue his dream of becoming a landowner in the all-black town of Eatonville. It is in this second marriage that Janie's quest for self becomes more visible and the divide becomes more rigid between her second spouse and herself—a divide that is rendered metaphorically through the use of doors and windows. For example, once the two build their home and general store/post office, Janie stands at the doorway to revel in their accomplishments and remind herself that she has achieved her grandmother's dream by ascending to the class status desired. The camera focuses on Janie leaning on the frame of the doorway as she peers into the streets of Eatonville, full of activity and promise as an all-black town. The doorway to the store becomes a site of conflict as Starks sits on the inside conducting business, while Janie stands on the outside with those playing checkers. Starks peers through the doorway, assuming that his wife is becoming more involved with common folk than he is willing to permit and exits the private space of his store to enter the public space of the checkers game. He orders Janie inside and they engage in a verbal exchange. He reminds her of her place and castigates her for disrupting his perception of her class position, thus signaling the decline of their relationship. Later, the voice-over narration reveals her inner thoughts. "Every morning, I flung open the window to a new day and every day had a new story. I wasn't petal open any more. I had an inside and an outside now and I knew how not to mix them.... Twenty years passed and while I was living a good life, it was Joe's life and not mine." Thus, doors and windows become evidence of this divide and speak to Janie's recognition of this warring struggle between the inside and outside. The doorway/window signifies the divide that exists between Janie and Starks, represents the inside world of restraint and the outside world of freedom, and in some instances symbolizes protection from the outside world, as when Janie is subjected to the criticism of her condemning neighbors.

In the aftermath of Starks's death, Janie finally achieves the freedom that she desires and the subjectivity that she longs for when she meets Tea Cake—who views her as an equal, who does not deny her a voice, who loves her unconditionally, and who allows her to live life on her terms. This union and period of her life cannot be disconnected from the water that surrounds them when they move to the Everglades of Florida and thus, water becomes another important metaphor in the film. In fact, because these are among the happiest times for Janie as she achieves a sense of self, the water serves the symbolic function of liberation, salvation, cleansing, happiness, and escape. However, ignoring the warnings of the impending hurricane finds Janie and Tea Cake overwhelmed and consumed by the storm. The water rushes into the cabin and submerges them as they both struggle to stay afloat, yet are torn apart by the force of the water. Although the two survive, Tea Cake is later bitten by a rabid dog. Because the hurricane disrupts their life, the meaning of water is altered and now represents devastation, danger, and death. This shifting symbolism becomes an extension of the fluidity of water that is ambivalently constructed, because while it signifies liberation, escape, happiness, and contentment, it also signifies its antithesis by representing danger, destruction, doom, and death.

Following Tea Cake's death, Janie returns to Eatonville to tell her story to Pheoby and admits that the only way the town saw her was as Mrs. Mayor Starks. This admission reveals that Janie was not seen as herself by others but instead was seen as the former mayor's wife, and that she was intent on constructing her own visibility and identity. Therefore, eyes/vision become another metaphor that is utilized in the film and speaks to the protagonist's ability to see or gain vision, to be seen or become visible, and to see inside herself. For example, in the film, Janie makes reference to the fact that she is watching God. Such references underscore the film/novel's theme that black women are given visibility — a visibility that they are denied, an invisibility that is sometimes imposed by others as well as self-imposed, and a visibility that she constructs for herself because of her dissenters. At the film's end, when Janie is forced to kill Tea Cake, she asks him, "Can you see me?"— a question posed because of his delirious state and her belief that at this point in his illness, he was not really seeing the Janie that he loved but some other enemy brought on by his deliriousness. The camera focuses on one of his eyes while the other eye remains in darkness, suggesting that he is no longer himself but has been transformed into something else. Janie is forced to kill the love of her life by leveling a fatal shot.

As evident in both screen productions, Suzan-Lori Parks as screenwriter and dramatist brings to her work a fascination for constructing visibility, seeing, being seen, and looking. In fact, Parks's own interest in visibility and looking was revealed in an interview she conducted regarding her play *Venus*, where she stated: "The most exciting thing about watching theater is that people are watching, and I think that's fascinating. That's why I get nervous when I go outside. There's so much watching going on. People are watching you, you are watching people.... So, it's all this kind of looking. There's a whole lot of looking going on" (Jiggetts 313). She further conveys a persistent preoccupation with space, particularly with inside/outside space, evident when she revealed, "The more I think about plays, I think plays are about space.... Plays are about space, and, say, fiction is about place. I think that one of the things that led me to writing plays is the understanding I have inside about space, because I moved around so much when I was younger" (Jiggetts 309). Parks also returns to the past to bring meaning and to inform the present, a technique that distinguishes her style as screenwriter and playwright. *Girl 6* and *Their Eyes Were Watching God* both focus on the past of their protagonists and demonstrate how the past informs the present. Returning to the past is evident in *Venus*, where Anne Davis Basting proclaimed, "The past is not behind us — in the sense of gone forever. In *Venus* the past is, quite literally, Venus's and our own individual and collective behinds — carried with us as we step into a future more aware of the deadly effects of colonialism, gazing, and racially and sexually marked standards of beauty" (225). Parks comes full circle when at the end of a production she returns to the beginning as in both *Girl 6* and *Their Eyes Were Watching God*— a strategy that marks her style. For example, Jean Young observed that "Parks ends *Venus* as it began, with the death of Baartman" (706). As a screenwriter and playwright, Parks similarly constructs vertical imagery in language — where she juxtaposes those who have ascended the economic ladder with the rhetoric of "up," "down," and "leg-up," as noted by David Krasner in Parks's *In the Blood* (565). This strategy is most apparent in *Their Eyes Were Watching God*. Finally, metaphors are strategically used to give meaning to her productions, as seen in *Their Eyes Were Watching God* and *The America Play*.

Most unique to her style as a screenwriter and dramatist is that Parks foregrounds issues of black female sexuality within a patriarchal culture and discourse, and this is what distinguishes *Girl 6* and *Their Eyes Were Watching God* while making them so fascinating. Parks has gained distinction as a screenwriter in much the same manner that she has garnered a reputation in the drama world. Her talent has contributed to other films such as *The Great Debaters* (2007), where she worked with screenwriter Robert Eisele, and a play entitled *Ray Charles Live!* (2007) that evolved from the movie *Ray*, based on the life of Ray Charles. With her indisputable talent, if she continues to bring to the screen what she has brought to the world of drama, the cinema will never be the same and can expect to be transformed cataclysmically.

Works Cited

Basting, Anne Davis. "Review of *Venus* by Suzan-Lori Parks." *Theatre Journal* 49.2 (May 1997): 223–225.
Bianco, R. "*Their Eyes* Lacks Sparkle, Inspiration." *USA Today*, March 4, 2005, E9.
Burgoyne, Robert. *Film Nation: Hollywood Looks at U.S. History*. Minneapolis: University of Minnesota Press, 1997.
DeRose, David J. "Review: *The America Play* by Suzan-Lori Parks." *Theatre Journal* 46.3 (October 1994): 409–12.
Freud, Sigmund. *The Basic Writings of Sigmund Freud*. Ed. A.A. Brill. New York: Random House, 1938.
Geis, Deborah R. *Suzan-Lori Parks*. Ann Arbor: University of Michigan Press, 2008.
Heffernan, Virginia. "A Woman on a Quest, Via Hurston and Oprah." *The New York Times*, March 4, 2005, E3.
hooks, bell. *Reel to Real: Race, Sex, and Class at the Movies*. New York: Routledge, 1996.
Hurston, Zora Neale. *Their Eyes Were Watching God*. New York: Harper Collins, [1937] 1998.
Jiggetts, Shelby. "Interview with Suzan-Lori Parks." *Callaloo* 19.2 (1996): 309–17.
Kauffmann, Stanley. "Books & The Arts: Stanley Kauffmann on Films-Found Wanting." *The New Republic*, April 29, 1996, 26–27.
Kissell, Rick. "Lots of Eyes Watch *God*." *Variety*, March 8, 2005, 1–12.
Klawans, Stuart. "Films: Candy-Colored Sadness." *The Nation* 262 (April 29, 1996): 35–36.
Krasner, David. "Review of *In the Blood* by Suzan-Lori Parks." *Theatre Journal* 52.4 (December 2000): 565–567.
Lee, Felicia R. "A Woman's Journey toward Herself." *The New York Times*, March 6, 2005, Sec. 13, L:4–5.
Maslin, Janet. "Film Review: Finding a Career in Telephone Sex." *The New York Times*, March 22, 1996, C3.
Morgan, Joan. "Wondering Who Flipped for the 'Girl 6' Script? Meet Playwright Suzan-Lori Parks." *Essence* (April 26, 1996): 74.
Rayner, Alice and Harry J. Elam, Jr. "Unfinished Business: Reconfiguring History in Suzan-Lori Parks's *The Death of the Last Black Man in the Whole Entire World*." *Theatre Journal* 46 (1994): 447–461.
Shannon, Sandra. "What Is a Black Play? Tales from My Theoretical Corner." *Theatre Journal* 57.4 (December 2005): 603–605.
Turan, Kenneth. "*Girl 6*: Spike Lee's *Girl 6* Taps Into Baffling, Bizarre World." *Los Angeles Times*, March 22, 1996, F14.
Williams, Monte. "At Lunch With: Suzan-Lori Parks." *The New York Times*, April 17, 1996, C1, 1.
Young, Jean. "The Re-Objectification and Re-Commodification of Saartjie Baartman in Suzan-Lori Parks's *Venus*." *African American Review* 31.4 (1997): 699–708.

An Interview with Suzan-Lori Parks

Shawn-Marie Garrett

I first met Suzan-Lori Parks in 1994 in New Haven, Connecticut, in connection with the premiere of *The America Play* at the Yale Repertory Theatre and have since interviewed her several times. She gave me this interview in the offices of the New York Shakespeare Festival, Public Theater on 30 June 2009. Having just moved back to New York from Los Angeles, Parks was unusually busy, even by her own standards. Two days earlier, she had given her last performance, narrating, playing guitar, and singing original songs in the Public Theater LAB production of *The Union of My Confederate Parts* and *The Way We Live Now*, the first and eighth installments of her forthcoming multimedia epic drama, *Father Comes Home from the Wars, Parts 1–9*.

A collaboration between the Public and LAByrinth Theater Company, Public LAB offers bare-bones workshop showings of developing work from emerging and established playwrights for $10 a ticket. After the enormous undertaking of *365 Days/365 Plays*, Parks was attracted to the simplicity of the LAB and spoke of returning to New York and the Public Theater after living in Los Angeles as a homecoming. Parks had been close to the Public Theater's former artistic director, George C. Wolfe, whom the Public's current artistic director, Oskar Eustis, has criticized in the press; nevertheless, Parks at the time of the interview had jumped with both feet into the new milieu of the Public under Eustis's direction, and appeared more integrated with the day-to-day life of the Public than ever.

At the same time, she spoke on the record for the first time of her feelings of isolation, which had come hand-in-hand with success, as well as of the ongoing struggle of writing, which she felt had if anything become harder. This time, though, Parks was not just writing for a living: for several years, she had been writing and performing songs, accompanying herself on guitar. Always animated in interviews, Parks displayed a deeper-than-ever sense of herself as a performer, and of language as a performative act, which is why I have tried here, at the risk of redundancy, to preserve or at least approximate the patterns and rhythms of her speech. Her discussions of her own self-inscriptions (her tattoos) also resonate, it seems to me, with imbrications of the body, writing or discourse, and action, which she continues to explore in her work.

Minimally staged and rehearsed, *Father Comes Home from the Wars, Parts 1 and 8* (*Part 9* was performed on the first night and then dropped, as Parks describes) ran for 23 days in June and was closed to reviewers. It was directed by Jo Bonney with a cast including (in addition to Parks) Nicole Beharie, Seth Gilliam, Patrice Johnson, James McDaniel, Joan MacIntosh, Lucas Papaelias, and Frederick Weller. Mr. Papaelias also contributed underscoring for guitar which Parks, seated downstage right, played as an accompaniment to the unfolding action. The press release described *Father Comes Home from the Wars* as a

> tale about slavery, war, freedom, and the difficulty of family ties. Part I tells the story of Penny, a slave, awaiting her husband's return from the Civil War while resisting her own desire to flee with a band of runaway slaves. Parts 8 & 9, set in present day, follow a Poet-General struggling with the reality of his impending death while he plans his annual celebration for the army troops.

Parks said that, like other pieces she has written, *Father Comes Home from the Wars* is inspired by the time she spent in Odessa, Texas, as a child with her mother, siblings, and maternal grandmother while her father, a career Army officer, was away on tours of duty in Vietnam.

Of the two parts, *The Union of My Confederate Parts* (*Father Comes Home from the Wars*, Part 1) was more fully realized in performance. Onstage throughout, Parks played the role of bard. The event began with Parks setting the scene (Juneteenth, 1865, in "far west Texas.... Almost springtime") and offering a brief account of the history of Juneteenth before performing two original songs, including "Bronze Star," an ode to a military father. Parks continued to play quietly under the text through the ensuing action. The scene opened with a group of slaves, including Penny and Homer (Penny's lover, whose crippled foot has kept him from the war) sitting on the front porch of a simple cabin. In meditative, rhythmic language evocative of Greek choral exchanges, the characters debated fleeing ("Slavery aint got nothin to do with the master") and pondered the fate of Penny's husband, the Poet-General, named Hero. Eventually Hero, arriving on a long, slow cross supported by video images of a lonely road, did return, together with a newly acquired wife, Alberta, and his dog, Odyssey, whom Parks had granted not only speech, but also a sense of humor. "Faithful comes extra," Odyssey observed of human beings. "Like speech comes extra to me."

Juneteenth is a day, or perhaps an existential crisis, which Parks had dramatized before. Imbued with a sense of tragic irony and near-misses, *The Union of My Confederate Parts: Father Comes Home from the Wars*, Part 1 resonated with Parks's earlier Juneteenth dramas: Part 3 of *Imperceptible Mutabilities in the Third Kingdom* (1989) and the several short plays that share the title, *Father Comes Home from the Wars,* in her collection, *365 Days/365 Plays* (2006).

Soon after the LAB production, the Public Theater announced Parks as the inaugural recipient of its Master Writer Chair position, funded by a three-year grant from the Andrew W. Mellon Foundation and inspired by the university model. The Chair includes a Visiting Arts Professor appointment at NYU's Tisch School of the Arts in the Rita and Burton Goldberg Department of Dramatic Writing. The position is also associated with the Public Theater's Writers Initiative, which nurtures the work of playwrights in all stages of their careers. At the time of the announcement, Parks spoke in the press of her excitement at being "invited to participate in the full artistic life of the theatre. I'm impressed by the course that Oskar Eustis has charted for The Public," she continued, "and I look forward to helping to support his vision in any way I can."

The day after announcing its inaugural Master Writer, the Public released more news about Parks, this time in relation to the casting of another new play, *The Book of Grace* (formerly entitled *Snake*). Scheduled to open at the Public on March 16, 2010, under the direction of James Macdonald and featuring Elizabeth Marvel as the character of Grace, *Book of Grace* is a three-character family drama described in press materials as

> a family portrait shattered by issues of rage, revenge, power and betrayal. When a young man returns home to South Texas to confront his father, everyday life erupts into a battle for personal survival. At once fiercely intimate and explosive, *The Book of Grace* weaves the story of three people bound together by love and longing, passion and ambition.

At the time of this writing, Parks is slated to direct a forthcoming Broadway revival of August Wilson's *Fences* and is writing the book for a forthcoming Ray Charles musical.

GARRETT: When you were first starting out, people used to talk a lot about the canon. And in your early essay "Possession," you refer to the "History of History" and "the History of Literature." Now that you've presumably secured a place in theater history, have your feelings about "History," about "Literature," changed?

PARKS: They're not talking about the canon anymore? I feel strongly that it's o.k. to carve people like Plato, Aristotle, Shakespeare, in stone because their ideas are still alive. Funny how, at the moment we feel that someone will live forever, we carve them in stone. Stone = eternity, although we should remember they're not fixed. History and the historical are mutable, right?

I love Shakespeare. And Shakespeare (still living, immortal) loves me back. In 1998 and 1999, when I was writing *Topdog/Underdog*, *In the Blood*, and *Fucking A*, I re-read all of Shakespeare's plays. A few years later at CalArts I taught a class called Shakespeare Read-through. I wrote down all of the titles of his plays and put them in a hat. Then we passed around the hat and each student picked one. We read all the plays that were chosen in the order in which the students wanted to read them, with the exception of the historical plays. We read those in chronological order — that made it easier to follow the lineages. I didn't assign any papers. I only asked everybody to read the plays, show up, be ready to talk about them, and read aloud. There were no right or wrong answers, no dumb or smart comments. The students got really excited because they felt they'd been freed from having to regurgitate conventional thought and they felt that Shakespeare was allowed to live again. And I had fun too! *Henry VI, Parts 1, 2,* and *3*—those are my favorites.

GARRETT: What do you take from Shakespeare for your own work?
PARKS: Everything that's there.

His characters have heart and brains in a very balanced combination. Which means they have soul, and that's what shines forth.

A lot of playwrights write with brain power, there are a lot of Ideas out there, and you feel like you're being lectured to, at least I do, because I'm not of the camp, not of the tribe, that likes a lecture. When I go to see a play: it's playtime! (Which can sometimes be some deep serious shit.) Then there are other plays that have a lot of heart, a lot of *oooooooh*, a lot of feeling. The very academic play with a lot of great ideas, or the Hallmark-Movie-of-the-Week play. Those are the extremes. Shakespeare's plays have soul, with the mind and heart in perfect balance. That's what I love about his work, and that's what I seek to emulate. Those are the footsteps that I'm working to follow in.

GARRETT: I'm glad you brought up the question of soul because your plays are, among other things ... "spiritual" is perhaps not the right word...

PARKS: I don't mind. I'm not offended. Look, at my arm (gesturing to three identical Sanskrit tattoos on left arm), possible translations: "Follow God," "Submit yourself to your Essential Goodness," or "Go with the Flow." There was a man at the farmer's market the other day, a gentleman who was selling — I don't know if he was a *gentleman*, he was a lovely man — who was selling green vegetables. And I purchased my snap peas and he looked at me and I thought "Oooo" — you know that moment where, someone is looking at you with great curiosity and all yr thinking is "woops, I must have made a mistake." In this case I'm thinking "I didn't give him the right amount of money." I have difficulty counting. So I'm looking at him, what does he need? Another dollar? And he's staring at me with this expression, and he's darting glances down at my arm, and I'm thinking, I need to give him more money, and he's looking at me, looking at me, and he says, "Your arm. *Îśvara*." He was reading my arm. Awesome! That's my favorite phrase, *îśvara-praṇidhânâd vâ*, which is from the yoga sutras, chapter 1, sutra 23, or sutra 1-2-3, easy as A-B-C, god bless Michael Jackson.

GARRETT: Speaking of which ... any thoughts?

PARKS: Yeah, MJ passed away about a week ago. I do feel like we let him down. And by letting him down, we let ourselves down. And every time people would laugh at him ... they were laughing at that part of themselves — maybe not all of us have it, but that part of us that felt like we were never "in," and wanted so much to belong, never were accepted. He was brilliant and admired and could never feel the love. And I so wanted him to have a comeback because I believe in ... the Resurrection. God bless MJ. So sutra number 1-2-3, easy as A-B-C, *îśvara*, which means "Go with the Flow," and I have it on my arm three times, each time larger and larger.

GARRETT: Do you still practice yoga two hours a day?

PARKS: I practice as much as I can. I've been to India twice, I studied Ashtanga yoga with Sri K. Patabi Jois, who we call Guruji; he passed away about a month and a half ago. Recently I've switched gears and I'm enjoying Bikram yoga. It's an experience.

GARRETT: You were raised Catholic...

PARKS: My religion these days ... it's like a buffet. There are so many good things to choose from. I admire the spirits and the gods and the healers and the saints. Ganesh I wear around my neck, and I think Jesus is great, and often misunderstood, just like Michael Jackson, and Mohammed laid down some great things too. And then the modern-day folks like Mother Teresa and Gandhi and Martin Luther King. I think they're all manifestations of our possibility. And that's what theater does too. Beautiful imitations of God. We all are. The saints are great imitators of God. Shakespeare is a great imitator of God. Not God the guy with the beard who sits in the clouds, or who's painted on the

Sistine Chapel ... I mean God must look at that and say, "Nice! Very nice!" Like you would say to a child who presents you with a drawing and says, "Look Mommy, this is you!" And you say, "Beautiful! Good job! We're gonna put it on the fridge!" That's what I think God says when he looks at the Sistine Chapel: "Beautiful! Good job! We're gonna put it on the fridge!" I think it's the same kind of adoring, "How sweet! Doesn't look a thing like me. But glad that you did good in school."

The more I do, the more the God-stuff comes out. It's creepy. It's unsettling in a way. It's not hard to talk about, but it's hard to live it. The more I work, the more it goes in that direction. Almost as if—hmm, as if I'm doing the art so that I can be given an opportunity to talk with people about the Spirit—instead of the other way around.... With each work it's more and more. My new play, we go into rehearsal in Jan 2010—it's called *The Book of Grace*.

I try ... there's part of me that's trying very hard to fit in. You know, just trying to write a normal play. But the more I listen, the more I hear, and then I go and get this "Follow God" this "go with the Flow" tattooed on my arm three times, and I can't help but hear it more. The more I write, the more it's going in that direction. Writing *365 Days/365 Plays* was a devotional act. Or like with *The Union of My Confederate Parts: Father Comes Home from the Wars, Part 1,*—I saw every performance of that play. There was such a "wyrdness"—w-y-r-d—the wyrdness of that play. I would sit onstage and watching it and I'd sometimes be thinking, "Who wrote this?"

What I love about Ganesh is, he's the transcriber of the Vedas. He's a writer! And he rides around on a mouse—that's my kind of god, right there. I've always felt this, but as time goes on I feel more and more that I'm transcribing. It's a powerful feeling, and yet, as Emerson writes, "I am a god in Nature, / I am a weed by the wall."

GARRETT: Do you still write every day?

PARKS: Sometimes "Follow God" isn't about writing every day. That's the thing about God, you have to listen. You can't make up your mind. God doesn't work so great if you set your idea of God in stone. God is mutable, change, right? And completely constant too—at the same time. So I work to roll with that. Several years ago, I could say, "Follow God, that means writing every day," but now I know that Follow God means Follow God. Sometimes I can't write every day. Over the years, it's become more difficult. It's getting wyrder and wyrder and wyrder and wyrder. People who climb Mount Everest get up there and need oxygen tanks and get dizzy—people who dive deep get the bends— it's like that. I'm walking a path where, sometimes you have to slow your steps, measure your breathing. "Writing every day" for me sometimes means "embracing the scary unknown and having compassion." I played guitar so much in this show [*The Union of My Confederate Parts: Father Comes Home from the Wars, Part 1*], so some days writing would just be about that, or just reading a little. Or sleeping late, or reading about Michael Jackson—maybe that's what I'm supposed to do today. Maybe that's what the day was about: doing a good show; remembering the words to the songs and the chords too. Writing used to mean just "writing" but now maybe writing can include RIGHTING. Get right. Be right. Right. Write. Write on. Right on. These days I'm a little more flexible. That's the thing about yoga, it makes you flexible.

GARRETT: You've expanded the range of your activities: you've appeared in an independent film, you're slated to direct *Fences* on Broadway, you have a new play, *The Book of Grace*, opening at the Public in March of 2010, you wrote a poem for President Obama, "U Being U"...

PARKS: It made me very happy to write that. To give him a gift of love when he was just starting out. NPR put it on the radio. We need to remember that "yes we can" is a daily promise. We all have to live that mantra if it's going to work.

GARRETT: The image of the Foundling Father from *The America Play* almost seems to anticipate...

PARKS: That's what a lot of people are saying.

GARRETT: The Lincoln connection.

PARKS: The Lincoln link. The Lincoln link. And Obama is a foundling. He knows his parents, but he is orphaned now as our leader. The Foundling Father in *The America Play* was parentless. And nameless. When I wrote *The America Play* it was like the guy walked in the room and started talking to me, so I knew he existed. He is present in the universe. And so he manifests himself on stage, and he manifests himself in the White House.

GARRETT: Do you see your work differently, or do you think it will be interpreted differently, in the wake of Obama's election?

PARKS: I don't really think about that. That's the thing about doing the kind of work I do, writing the way I do, it doesn't leave room for looking back.

Krishna and Arjuna are riding in the chariot in the Bhagavad Gita, and Arjuna is talking to Krishna like he's just some guy, and Krishna turns to him and opens his mouth and shows him the entire universe. And Arjuna's like, "Dude! So that's who you are!" I'm just staring into the mouth of God. It doesn't leave any room for thinking about the significance of a play I wrote in 1994 ... and not that it's not important but ... I'm thinking more about guitar chords.

GARRETT: Are you going to cut an album?

PARKS: If I get my courage up. I've written six new songs for *Father Comes Home from the Wars*.

There was a long time when I couldn't play one of the songs, "Bronze Star," without crying. That was the trouble I was having at the beginning of rehearsing this show. I really had to play the song a lot to be able to play it in public.

GARRETT: The title *Father Comes Home from the Wars* also appears in *365 Days/365 Plays*. Any relation?

PARKS: "Oh I know this girl, her name is Jill, and she lives in Mexico..." "Oh I know a Jill! But she lives in New York." "Oh I know Jack! He's married to a Jill." "But that's another Jill..." "Oh her." It's like that. They're related in title. They're related in (*operatic tone*) "Theme." Or is it "Subject?"

GARRETT: Might the fourth part of *Imperceptible Mutabilities* be a third cousin? There's another father who comes home from the wars.

PARKS: Those are some of the biggest memories I have, of my father coming home from the war.

GARRETT: There are some plans in the works for you to direct August Wilson's *Fences* on Broadway.

PARKS: Yes. The production was delayed because of the economy and because we want to make sure we can do it with the actors we really want to do it with. The producers want to keep the play in the 1950s, in the time it is set, but also really make it resonate with younger audiences today. I shared my ideas with them, and they liked them, and so we started working on it. Then the producers wanted to do it this spring, but I'd already committed to doing my play *The Book of Grace*. So they reassembled the team.

I enjoy directing. I enjoy being in the rehearsal room from day one. I enjoy being in tech. I enjoy talking to actors. I love creating pictures on stage. I've also enjoyed being in *Father Comes Home...*, although I don't think I was acting. I was just being. I was just up there being me. And playing the guitar along with the action, working with the actors. That was good scary fun.

GARRETT: *Father Comes Home from the Wars, Part 1* was underscored, almost like a melodrama.

PARKS: Lucas Papaelias wrote the underscoring. I threw in some Robert Johnson licks. And it was really fun to play. We might do a cabaret together.

GARRETT: Is there anything about your success, about being a Pulitzer Prize winner for example, which has surprised you?

PARKS: I have to say, it's very isolating. Wonderful Lynn Nottage has won the Pulitzer now, which is awesome. For me, for a long time, to be The Only One, I mean, the Only Black Woman winner in drama. To be The First One, the First Black Woman — and to have won it for a play that is so ... it's a right-down-the-middle play. It's very lean and it does not apologize and it's just ... right between the eyes. The play came down like that (*claps*) and it really does burn ... it's like lightning, it burns the ground, the Earth, my own ... psychological Earth, if you will. It was such a powerful experience. And that's what I mean about writing like I do now, it happens over and over and over. I have developed the muscles to deal with it, but at the same time, I keep waiting for it to be an easier process, a more gentle birth, but ... they always seem to come like that, like "Whoooooaaah! Heeeeere's anooother one!" (*Squeals in mock-horror.*) So the writing and the winning for me were isolating, in a way. But that's just what happens when you walk a path, that's just what happens.

GARRETT: Then with *365*, you opened yourself up in the most generous possible way.

PARKS: Again, that was the right thing to do. Why did I choose the most intense gesture, why did the most intense gesture choose me ... well thank you is all I can say because I guess that's what I'm supposed to be doing. Choose the most intense gesture and do it. That was the next thing. People said, "Why not do another Broadway play?" We did *365 Days/365 Plays* everywhere *but* Broadway! We did it everywhere! We did it in Beijing! We did it in Kenya! We did it in South Africa and Berlin and Moscow! We did it in places like Seattle and L.A. and Chicago and Minneapolis and Atlanta and Texas and New England and Colorado and Old England — more than 700 theaters were involved. We were spreading the love and we were world-wide with it.

What good can this award, the Pulitzer Prize, do? What is it for? It affords the winner (and by extension, the community) some possibilities. So I wrote a play a day and then gave them away. We had a core production team of 4 people: Bonnie Metzgar, Rebecca Rugg, David Myers and me. We joined hands with awesome theatre artists from all over and we made it together. It wasn't even a thought, it was just the right thing to do: fling yourself open and say, "Let us play." To offer people a part. And how is that different from doing a play on Broadway, a play with $70 tickets, a play with Equity contracts? We had a big free-for-all. Which was the only right thing to do after the Pulitzer, after you climb the tower and hoist the flag and "Yaaaay!" and then you fling yourself into the pit of people and say, "Let us play," and somehow that was the only right thing to do. And what was the next right thing to do? I come to New York, and I wanna be in Public Lab, which is 2½ weeks rehearsal time, no budget to speak of, a $10 ticket, run for a very limited time, no reviews cause it's a workshop production, plus I'm in the show playing guitar and singing … And what's the next right thing to do? I'm not even thinking about that … it's just "Ahhhh!" It's a little intense. And it does make it hard to … it makes it wonderful to be around people but it's also difficult.

GARRETT: Might there eventually be *Father Comes Home from the Wars, Parts 1, 2, 3 … through 9*?

PARKS: God willing, yeah, that's the plan, that's the plan. There might be more. Who knows now cause now that I've seen Part 1 over and over and over, the whole cycle might change. I'm allowing myself to be flexible, which is very important. If my plan for a "9-part cycle" is too limiting, I'll change it up. If it's not what it's supposed to be then I'll go on and let it go.

Originally it was nine parts. I had it all blocked out, I had drafts of each one, a big draft of Part 9, which was like a 2½-hour play. But now watching it every night it's changing, it's actually changing. So who can know?

GARRETT: You had originally planned to stage Parts 1, 8, and 9 but ended up staging only Part 1, is that right?

PARKS: Yeah. Yeah. We put on Part 9 one night, and I sat there and then I talked to Jo Bonney and Oskar (Eustis) afterwards, and I said we have not had enough time to rehearse Part 9, we have eight hours of rehearsal left, we have to stop, we have to stop. We have to say thank you to the wonderful actors who put in time on Part 9 but … it was too much to try to do in Public Lab. We only had three days of tech. Three days of tech to tech … Part 1 was an hour, Part 8 really is 45 minutes if we were to do it fully because it's a lot of structured improvs, and I'm performing during in the intermission, and it's a live intermission, and I'm doing a lecture during the intermission, and then there are six songs, and then this big play at the end … But Part 9 isn't ready so let's just put it aside for now, let's just focus on Part 1, it's only an hour, let's only do two songs, and scale way back. So it was an hour of really well done theater. Eventually we'll do the rest. Cause the families come together in the end, the two families that you see in Part 1, there's a rupture, and we track them through the whole thing, and then they come together in the end.

GARRETT: In the present?

PARKS: In the present-day.

GARRETT: One family tree is…

PARKS: Penny and Homer. And then the other family tree is Hero and Alberta. And both family trees produce 2 different men, both named Smith. A Lincoln-Lincoln, Jill-Jill kinda thing. Or the Hester-Hester kinda thing. So both family trees produced a man named Smith. And one is a poet. And one is a critic.

GARRETT: The George Bernard Shaw-type of critic, or the consumer-reports-thumbs-up-thumbs-down-type?

PARKS: I don't know. Right now he's more of a fan.

GARRETT: The Greeks seem to be circulating around this play, the *Odyssey* in particular…

PARKS: I named the character Penny because I have a friend named Penny who died. Penny Lincoln. Really. Go figure. I named another one Homer because he stays home. You know me, there's not a lot of front-loaded thought. I don't think one has to have read any of those great Greek works to understand this story. And even when the characters refer to those old, old stories, they tell you the stories. It's not like *Finnegans Wake* where you have to be in the know.

GARRETT: The weight of homecoming was a palpable presence in this performance.

PARKS: Like I said, it's from my dad. My dad came home. From the Wars. That's what it's about. For me. It starts with that. I'm just talking about something I know, something which I can really only emotionally understand by looking at it through a play, through the framework of the big picture.

Different writers have different methods — all of them valid and good. I don't get to my plays through thought. "Thought" in the conventional sense. I don't get to my plays through ideas. I think writing them would be easier if I did. Because ideas and thought, they're verbal, and I think my plays are preverbal. From my guts.

GARRETT: In a way, you've always been writing songs.

PARKS: Thanks! All my writing is more like songs, cause in a song you're in the ocean, the ocean of emotion, and you're moving around, and you're trying to breathe, and that's what it feels like, trying to write. That's what I try to do. I try to sing to people.

GARRETT: And when you lay it down on the page…

PARKS: A play is the road. You're giving an actor or a director the path. And the way a word is … if you put a word in the middle of the page, that's very different than if you put it on the side, and if you put a character's name in a line, that's very different than if you put it in the middle, with parentheses. Or italics, which can be very vigorous if used sparingly, like saffron. Italics are like surprises. Punctuation marks are jewels. With every letter I hold my breath and think, "Is it this or that? What best communicates the energy that's gonna course through the language, that's gonna tell an actor — whose instrument is finely tuned — how to shoot that energy through to the audience night after night, so they can ride that wave of language. It's very, very, very important to me how it is on the page, how it lies there. How it lies there in its grave. You lay them out right, and they can be continually and beautifully resurrected.

Space. The rhythm of the words. Repetition. How the character is saying what she's saying. Each choice should indicate a specific emotional thing. Which can vary in color night after night after night as the actor continues making it anew. Is it y-o-u-r or y-r? With y-o-u-r there's more room. See what it feels like in your mouth, in your tongue, in your body. Allow the language to inform the choices. Read the words, and *feel*. My plays *beg* for feeling. They *beg* for the gut response. Let the stomach-brain, let the heart-brain, inform your head-brain, and not always the other way around. Because then we're getting to some deep stuff. And it's frightening. But it's also healing.

Garrett: Do you read criticism or scholarship of your work?

Parks: I read what I feel will most help my process. Scholarship is important but for me — reading it doesn't help me write. Reading scholarship about the works of "Suzan-Lori Parks" would take me outside the work. And I need to keep myself inside it, I need to be deep up in it, not outside intelligently observing, not at arm's length. Staying deep up in it: that's the best way for me to write my next thing.

A Parks Remix: An Interview with Liz Diamond

Faedra Chatard Carpenter

One should expect that an in-depth study of Suzan-Lori Parks's canon would, eventually, turn its attention to Liz Diamond. After all, it was Liz Diamond's direction of Parks's *Imperceptible Mutabilities in the Third Kingdom* in 1989 that first brought Parks to national attention — a collaboration that earned Suzan-Lori Parks an Obie Award for Best New American Play and Liz Diamond an Obie Award for Best Direction.

In the two decades since that time, the many articles and interviews that address the recurring partnership of Parks and Diamond reveal common thematic threads: Diamond's great appreciation of Suzan-Lori Parks's poetic, yet playful, language, and the director's ingenious stagings of Parks's distinctive visual and aural cues. While Diamond credits Parks's plays with teaching her invaluable lessons about directing poetic language and imagery, it must also be noted that Diamond helped shape Parks's dramaturgy in its formative stages. As a passionate and informed questioner and respondent, Liz Diamond facilitated the development of Parks's early plays and, just as significantly, helped audiences receive them by bringing Parks's texts to life. Diamond's layered contributions to Parks's canon were not lost on *New York Times* critic Alvin Klein when he aptly acknowledged that the acclaimed director's role extended beyond her production title: "As much a collaborator and orchestrator as a director, Liz Diamond stages the sounds and the reverberations of Ms. Parks's words with the lyric flow of a visual poem."* Such recognition makes it clear that the American theatre is indebted to Diamond not only for directing some of the most notable incarnations of Parks's work, but also for empowering audiences in their ability to see — *and hear* — the fullness of Parks's artistry.

Following the success of *Imperceptible Mutabilities*, the partnership between Diamond and Parks fostered the development of several other notable projects and served as a model for fruitful playwright/director collaborations. Diamond not only re-staged *Imperceptible Mutabilities* in 1991 at the New City Theatre in Seattle, but she went on to direct foundational productions of other plays by Parks: *Betting on the Dust Commander* (Working Theater, 1991), *The Death of the Last Black Man in the Whole Entire World* (Yale Repertory Theatre, 1992) and *The America Play* (Yale Repertory Theatre in 1994 and The Joseph

---

*Alvin Klein, "Yale Rep Offers 'America' Premiere," *The New York Times*, 13N, p. 17. January 30, 1994.

Papp Public Theater in 1994). And most recently, Diamond directed pieces from *365 Days/365 Plays* for Yale Repertory Theatre and the New York Theatre Workshop.

Diamond's career, like that of Parks, continues to proliferate with honors and opportunities. In addition to the Obie Award, Diamond won the Connecticut Critics Circle Award for Outstanding Direction and has received a number of fellowships and grants for her work, including awards from the Ford Foundation, the National Endowment for the Arts, the New York State Council on the Arts, the Asian Cultural Council and the SDC Foundations. While Diamond's directorial accomplishments in regional theatre, Off-, and Off-Off-Broadway are critically acclaimed and manifold, she is also distinguished by her important leadership roles at the Yale School of Drama (where she serves as the chair of the directing program and as a resident director for the Yale Repertory Theatre) and the Shanghai Theatre Academy (where she serves as a visiting professor).

It has been 20 years since the original pairing of Diamond and Parks, thus it seemed particularly appropriate to include the thoughts and reflections of Liz Diamond in an anthology dedicated to the work of the esteemed playwright. While the following interview covers new ground, in the spirit of "Rep & Rev" it also offers a "remix" of queries previously addressed to Diamond. In particular, this timely conversation invokes the 1995 *TDR* interview, "Suzan-Lori Parks and Liz Diamond: Doo-a-diddly-dit-dit," conducted by Steven Drukman. Drukman's notable interview not only offered a revealing account of how Diamond and Parks worked together, but it also offered insightful dramaturgical readings of Parks's texts and their musical sensibility. Taking up where the *TDR* conversation left off, this 2009 interview expounds on Diamond's philosophies towards dramaturgical research and elaborates upon her strategy of approaching Parks's work like a "musical score."

Although benefiting from retrospection, this discussion takes its own course, venturing further on the topic of musicality and revealing Diamond's insight into the polyrhythmic nature of Parks's work as well as her own preference for using "soundscapes" to help sculpt the texture of Parks's plays. As an educator as well as an artist, Diamond also shares her pedagogical perspectives, offering both practical and philosophical ways to approach Parks's work in and beyond the classroom. Moreover, this contemporaneous interview is particularly unique in that Diamond addresses provocative and timely issues (such as cross-cultural casting) in an era in which a black man is not simply "playing a president"—but *is* our president. In revisiting past assertions and considering new possibilities, "A Parks Remix: An Interview with Liz Diamond" discloses nuanced ways of understanding and contextualizing both Parks's dramatic canon and Diamond's own directorial vision.

This interview was conducted on the telephone and through e-mail between Maryland, Connecticut, and New York, September 21–November 14, 2009.

CARPENTER: First of all, I'd love to revisit a notable anecdote I came across: early in Suzan-Lori Parks's career you clearly recognized her brilliance, proven by the fact that you even contributed some of your own money to produce *Imperceptible Mutabilities* [*in the Third Kingdom*] at BACA in New York. Now, that certainly speaks to your commitment! Reflecting back on that time, was it something about Parks's work—or perhaps something about the artist herself—that garnered that kind of commitment? How did you know that she was going to be such an important voice?

DIAMOND: It was the writing itself; it was the strangest, newest, most enticing playwriting I had ever read. And then it was hearing the writing out loud. Suzan-Lori and I read her work out loud together. I had never heard language like that, theatrical poetry like that. I felt that I was in the presence of a completely new sound in the theatre. And I felt Suzan-Lori was writing about relationships, life, the specific experience of being African American, and more generally the experience of feeling oneself to be "other," in a way that no one had written about. I found her writing extraordinarily capacious in its themes, political concerns, psychological insight, and its passion. I was equally compelled by the artist herself. When I direct a writer's work, there's got to be an emotional connection. I was drawn to Suzan-Lori herself—to her absolutely fabulous sense of humor and her fierce sense of her own gifts as a poet and playwright. I think Suzan-Lori realized, at a very early age, that she was in possession of a unique poetic gift. Early on, when so many were finding it difficult to enter her work, she did not cave or become confused, but had the ego-strength and clarity about her own voice to, essentially, wait for people to catch up with her. That quiet, fierce strength was hugely attractive to me.

CARPENTER: I know that you've said that working with Parks's plays taught you a lot about poetry and metaphor. That her work has helped you discover, and I'm quoting now, "the ways in which a text is a three-dimensional thing."* You've also likened your reading and staging of her plays to the process of reading the script like a "musical score." In learning how to shape her plays, are there lessons you've learned that are transferable to others? Do you ever use her work to teach and, if so, how do you communicate the ability to read her work to your students?

DIAMOND: I find Suzan-Lori's work powerful in teaching directors how to read a play. My students and I read scenes aloud. We put the language in our own bodies, and, putting a brake on our impulse to infer, we try to discover what the language is doing to us. If you say "the" with a long "e," it's quite different from "thuh" pronounced with a short "u" sound. The sound affects your body, your face, your posture, your energy. All of which starts to send you information about who a character is, what they are doing. And we examine the text on the page. When you are learning to direct you have to relearn how to read. To read a play for action and event, a director has to slow down every aspect of her response. Take nothing for granted. Not word choice, not word sound, stylistic device, not even the blank space on the page. Moment to moment events are embodied in the sound and shape of the words. In Parks's texts, stage directions are embedded in the dialogue itself—much like Shakespeare and the Greeks. It's all there, but you can't be a lazy reader. And that's why these plays are great for student directors—you have to actually accept the text itself and suppress the impulse to "translate" the play. If Suzan-Lori places her play in something called "the Great Hole of History," for example, chances are that's exactly where it takes place.

*Steven Drukman, "Suzan-Lori Parks and Liz Diamond: Doo-a-Diddly-Dit-Dit: An Interview," *TDR* Volume 39, no. 3 (Autumn, 1995), p. 59.

CARPENTER: I've never worked with a Suzan-Lori Parks piece in production, but I recently used *In the Blood* in class and was sharing with my undergraduates how you've expressed this idea of approaching the script as a musical score. I was hoping you could expound on that. I was trying to articulate what I thought you meant, but then the question came: does one have to have a musical sensibility to use that approach? Is it about finding *the musical score* or *a* sense of musicality in the work of Suzan-Lori Parks?

DIAMOND: I think all I was trying to say was that when you read a play—whether a verse or prose play—it's crucial to look for its rhythmic patterns. And the best way to do that is to say it out loud. Look and listen for its unique "sonic" features. There's an exquisite passage in *IMP* [*Imperceptible Mutabilities in the Third Kingdom*], for example, where Mrs. Smith and her daughters engage in a kind of call and response: "You were just as proud." "I was just as proud." "You were just as proud?" "I was just as proud...," etc. It's a lyrical, exuberant passage that builds, thanks to the repetition of those big open vowel sounds in "proud." Parks makes each word its own unique object. And the content is entirely bound up, made manifest, in the form. Anna Deavere Smith feels that rhythm in speech patterns is the thing that most reveals character. I think that's right, and it certainly applies to Suzan-Lori's characters.

CARPENTER: In pushing this idea of music, does Parks's work draw you to any particular forms of music? Have you used music or song in Parks's work that can be distinguished from the way you've incorporated these elements in other plays you've directed?

DIAMOND: I don't use a lot of musical underscoring in a text as richly poetic and musical as Suzan-Lori's. But soundscapes — textures, riffs — can sometimes help the language reverberate. Suzan-Lori is herself a musician. She was teaching herself the harmonica when I first met her, and she got really good very quickly. She took up the guitar a while ago, and plays well enough to have played the guitar, and sung her own songs in the workshop production of her latest play at the Public this past year. So, the musicality in the plays is part of Parks's makeup. When I directed *Imperceptible Mutabilities in the Third Kingdom*, I listened, at Parks's urging, to a lot of Ornette Coleman — the complex, almost jagged edges of his sound helped me embrace the radical tonal shifts that occur from tych to tych. *IMP*, which Parks calls a "tetraptych," is made up of 4 distinct plays that function together to make a striking — at times deliberately discordant — composite portrait of a people caught, as the play's "third kingdom image" suggests, in the middle passage, somewhere in that watery, dangerous limbo between Africa and America. Much of the language in the play is quite lyrical, lush. But the entire assemblage, like Coleman's music, is discordant, disturbing, angular. I didn't use Coleman's music in the show. That wasn't the point — but Coleman gave me the vibe...

On *The Death of the Last Black Man in the Whole Entire World*, I brought on Dan Moses Schreir, who composed music and created the soundscape for the show. He created a beautiful score, using jazz riffs with horns and sax, deep thrumming sounds, and voices. We created a whispering chorus of "ghosts" that played as the audience entered the theatre and took their seats. These were the voices of all those "figures" from the past, arriving and naming themselves, as they gather to teach the history of the Black Man, to get us to face it, own it, and "write it down." Dan's soundscape for the final chorus of the play —

synthesized instruments whose sounds were bent and stretched — underscored the sense of awe that grows in the play as Black Woman and Black Man together recognize the enormity, the comic and cruel ironies and tragic grandeur, of their past.

CARPENTER: These reflections on musicality make me think about how a playwright may have a particular "voice." For example, the way that Kia Corthron uses language suggests a particular sense of rhythm to me. When I read her work, I think: "Oh, this is very Kia-esque." And so I was wondering, I suppose, if there is any identifiable rhythm in Suzan-Lori Parks's work?

DIAMOND: Parks's work might be described as polyrhythmic. She uses all kinds of rhythms and plays them off one another in her work. Her writing is playful and its rhythmic patterns — tempi, silences, torrents of language, alliteration, onomatopoeia, punctuation — change from play to play, and character to character. I suppose I can see some patterns in how Suzan-Lori deploys these tools, these strategies; I guess that recognition might be called having a "feel" for a writer's voice, but I want to approach every play as if encountering the voice for the first time. Take nothing for granted. A great writer's voice is not fixed.

CARPENTER: Well, imagining the productive challenges Suzan-Lori Parks's work presents for young directors makes me also think about how her work challenges audiences. I love what you said earlier about Suzan-Lori letting "people catch up with her." Do you think our theatre audiences have become more sophisticated since you first directed *Imperceptible Mutabilities* in 1989? Has the increased complexity of our society — for example, our fuller recognition of the intersecting identities of race, culture, sexuality — enabled us to embrace her work more readily than we did 20 years ago?

DIAMOND: You mean, is the younger generation fundamentally better equipped to embrace formal experimentation, and ambiguity? Quite possibly. To some extent, I'd say it's more that Parks's recent work has been more classical in form. *Topdog/Underdog* is a much more classical play than *Imperceptible Mutabilities*. It is structurally simpler. It's not episodic, it's essentially a continuous rising action with a great big catharsis at the end. It's beautifully built, and sweeps us into the terrifying, un–inevitable madness of that last gunshot. *IMP*, written years earlier, is more formally complex, and its formal complexity is in direct proportion to the complexity of the ideas Parks is exploring. What *IMP* explores is a deeply disturbing idea — that history is not the ramp up envisioned by the Enlightenment. In *IMP*, through four discrete stories, the characters evolve. But, in opposition to the way Darwin's theories are traditionally understood, their evolution doesn't necessarily signify progress. The adaptations to their realities that they are forced to make distort them in profound ways. The characters are snails, or worse, slugs, as Mr. Smith declares, shapeless little organisms with no protective shell. *IMP* gets under your skin — it's intensely funny and dramatic, and does what great theatre is supposed to do: Rock you. Invade your heart and mind.

CARPENTER: That actually leads me to another question I had about Suzan-Lori Parks's canon, and how it's changed. From my position — as someone who has tried to follow her work and bring Parks's plays into the classroom — it seems to me that her work has gotten much more accessible. I don't know if that reflects a shift in her explorations, or if it's a matter of what is being selected and highlighted for consumption — do you have any insight into that?

DIAMOND: I don't think Suzan-Lori, in her early career, set out to prevent audiences from understanding what she was about. I think she wrote out of necessity and she continues to do so. She is always searching for the form that will carry the content roiling around inside her. You know, Faulkner is one of her favorite novelists. She loves the subversive wit of Gertrude Stein, especially to be found in her early plays, which challenge our ideas about dramatic action itself. She loves Adrienne Kennedy's lush expressionism, and the deeply personal nature of her writing. But she loves classical Greek tragedy as well. And she loves comedy. I don't think she wants to be constrained by what you might call "traditional rules of dramaturgy." But she will use them when they serve her purposes. I think with *Topdog/Underdog* she wanted to write a play that would be a genuine, absolute sucker-punch. I think the story that she was telling in that play *required* a classical structure; *required* a kind of lean, cruel, dramatic build, catharsis — I think the *form* of that play entirely suited the content. Suzan-Lori has always assumed that form and function go hand in hand and she looks for the form that is going to carry the thing she's trying to do. *The Death of the Last Black Man in the Whole Entire World* required a ritual form; she was writing a requiem for the *last black man in the whole entire world* after all! That story takes the form of a kind of mass, or passion play, and contains within it a dramatic narrative, a dramatic action, that must be remembered, and passed on. It memorializes, in fact, teaches, the absolute importance of the act of remembering — whereas *Topdog/Underdog* is an excruciating, at times, violently funny play about this tragic, consumptive, jealous love between two brothers — it's a Cain and Abel story. And it needed to be one, clean, long, straight dramatic action. Like the bullet that ultimately goes through one brother's head.

CARPENTER: You mentioned Faulkner and Gertrude Stein as early influences on Parks's work. Those references bring to mind the Drukman interview you did in 1995 with Suzan-Lori —

DIAMOND: — oh yeah, the funny one!

CARPENTER: — Ah, it was so much fun to read, yes! And very revealing — a lot is revealed about how you and Suzan-Lori work together in that interview. In fact, one thing that is discussed is the intertexuality in Suzan-Lori's work. That is, the idea that a text may "talk" to, or about, another text — the way in which her plays use the textual histories that preceded them by repeating and revising certain elements. How much dramaturgical research does a director need to do in order to do justice to Suzan-Lori's work? How aware does a director need to be of these various influences?

DIAMOND: I don't think you have to go out and read all of Gertrude Stein's plays in order to direct Parks's plays, but look: knowledge is power and the more a director contextualizes the work of a writer, the more deeply he or she will understand the soul of the work. I do believe, to quote Peter Brook, "preparation is crucial." You prepare, you read as much as you possibly can about the author, you read as much of the author's work as you can, you read around the play, about the social and political and economic histories that may inspire it, you listen to music, look at art, photographs, and you take it all and somehow fold that into your spirit as you enter the rehearsal process. You don't enter a rehearsal process and deliver seminars. It's just going to fertilize your work...

As for the ways Suzan-Lori's plays "talk" to one another, and to other texts and stories — a director does need to discover these playful, artful remixes and homages and parodies that are to be found all over Suzan-Lori's work. It is useful, for example, for the actor playing Prunes and Prisms to know that this phrase she repeats over and over, "Prunes and Prisms," is spoken by a character in Joyce's *Ulysses*, as a cure for fat lips. It offers the actor ways of imagining this character; it suggests all kinds of things about who Prunes and Prisms is and what she wants. There is, as Alisa Solomon has written about Parks's work, "'Signifyin' on the Signifying" going on throughout these plays, and if you don't know what the sources are, you can't play the joke.

CARPENTER: Right. I'm thinking about Sandra L. Richards's concept of "the absent potential" — the idea of taking time with the work, creating moments that are not necessarily written on the page — a concept that is inherent in Parks's work as signified by her strategic use of "spells" and the architectural structure of her scripts.

DIAMOND: I don't know about "absent potential" in Parks's plays. In the example you cite, the "spells" of *The America Play*, the action called for is in fact very precisely written on the page. When Suzan-Lori creates a series of lines with no speech — just alternating silences exchanged by characters — THAT is the action. It is a moment electrically charged between two people who are using silence on one another in very specific ways. The plays are plenty roomy for actors and directors to make choices, but they are not open fields either.

CARPENTER: In taking up the topic of "directorial choices," I'm wondering about your interest in looking back at your own work with Suzan-Lori Parks's plays. Because her work is so capacious and layered it seems that the possible stagings and presentations of it, even from a single director, could be endless. So with the passage of time, are there any works you would love to revisit and do you have a particular "re–vision" you would want to bring to them?

DIAMOND: I would love to do *The Death of the Last Black Man in the Whole Entire World* again. I think it's a great play, a masterpiece, frankly. I think it's stunning, stunning. I think *Venus* would be fabulous to do. While I know *Venus* well, I've never directed it. *Black Man, Venus* and, absolutely, *The America Play*, and *Betting on the Dust Commander*, a play I adore.

CARPENTER: When you think of those things that you'd like to go back to, for example, with *Death of the Last Black Man* or *The America Play*, do you have a new artistic vision or is there something, specifically, that you'd want to articulate or bring forward a second time around? Is it the love of those particular texts or is there something that you would be sure to do differently?

DIAMOND: I'd be interested to see what would resonate differently for me the second time around. And for all of us. A black man is now our President. This has not ushered in the longed for "post-racial" utopia, but I would say that the conversation about race has entered a new phase—the history of African Americans is being vividly "written down." We have, for example, Mrs. Obama's family history—a history marked by the agony of slavery—published in the paper and talked about on radio, TV, the Web. So the experience of the play will be different. Histories like hers are at last being included in the Big Huge History of all of us. Will this make the play more elegiac, or more celebratory? I can't really say at this point ... but everything—design and other features of the production—would be impacted. *(laughs)* I'm a different person and we are a different country. *(laughs)*

CARPENTER: I wanted to jump here a bit. I'm curious to know if you think there is a "Parks Effect." Meaning, as you encounter younger or emerging playwrights, do you see them being notably influenced by Parks?

DIAMOND: Yes, yes, I do. I think that many young writers are attracted to the wordplay in Suzan-Lori Parks. To her sly, subversive messing with the language, her repetition and revision—the "Rep & Rev," as she calls it. And the punning and the playful use of white space on the page. I think all of that has found its way into the plays—good, bad, and indifferent—of younger writers. And to no small extent that has to do with their exposure to her in universities and conservatories. The academy has embraced Parks, big time—she's on every syllabus. So, in one way or another, her voice is getting into the groundwater of our culture. The theatre is not taking the lead in this—it's the university. I deplore that more major, regional theaters in this country have not taken on her writing. It's just plain scandalous to me that two masterpieces, *The America Play* and *The Death of the Last Black Man in the Whole Entire World*, haven't been done in major revivals. But that will change. That is changing, and I think, in no small measure, due to the kind of groundwork—the "diggin'" *(laughs)*—by teachers and students.

CARPENTER: In your estimation, do these masterpieces—*The America Play* and *The Death of the Last Black Man in the Whole Entire World*—offer unique gifts or challenges for directors?

DIAMOND: Among many things, they require the director and actor to fully embrace a non–naturalistic theater. These plays do not take place in an illusionistic space. There is no kitchen or sofa in either play. The plays require the director to embrace and to embody allegory. When you direct these plays, the question, "Where are we?" is huge. In *The America Play*, we are somewhere "Out West" ... in a place referred to as "The Great Hole of History," and "The Hall of Wonders" ... a place where the Foundling Father is lost and found. Maybe we show his lonely little sideshow booth, the site of what will become, in Act 2, an archeological dig by a son for his father. But the space is also a place that's strange and mysterious—history's hole ... ghosts appear, echoes reverberate and mix up what happened with what we might dream happened. Its atmosphere resonates with clues that add up to a great, tragicomic disappearing act...

These plays of Parks invite the director and actor to inhabit a theatrical landscape where past and present are conflated. Who is Ham in *Black Man*? The cursed son of biblical fame, the keeper of the history, the aged warrior, a Philoctetes who's hung onto every betrayal ever perpetrated on his people or by his people. He's the raving homeless prophet who names your secret, whose life holds eons of history to pass on, and has no one to talk to. How do you show that? What do you tell a costume designer? These are the kinds of questions Suzan-Lori gives her collaborators to dig into and finding answers that give the actor something specific and concrete to play, to inhabit—and that are as reverberant, as expansive as the writing—is the challenge.

CARPENTER: In thinking about universities and the promise they hold in terms of acquainting students to Suzan-Lori Parks's plays which, hopefully, will lead to more of her plays receiving professional productions, I'm wondering about the demographics of many universities and their ability to cast Parks's work. So, my question is really about cross-cultural casting and Suzan-Lori Parks's work. Do you think cross-cultural casting necessarily works against Parks's artistic vision?

DIAMOND: Is *The Last Black Man* subverted if Black Man with Watermelon is played by a white actor? For me, right now, yes. Because the performance of that action by a black actor carries a tragic resonance that still seems crucial. There is a truth and reconciliation action underway in that play that is still meaningful as an action to be performed by black actors and for all people. I'm not sure I'd be ready to cast the play with people referred to in the text as "them" just yet. There is enormous richness in seeing the roles of Suzan-Lori's that were written for African American actors, performed as written. These characters, these plays, open the spectator's mind and soul to ideas that are really important. And there are great, great African American actors to play these roles.

CARPENTER: I'd like to continue with this idea of "cross-cultural" productions, but this time in relation to directing. Specifically, as a white female director directing the work of Suzan-Lori Parks, I'm curious to know how the dialogue of race has come into play for you during rehearsals.

DIAMOND: Faced with a white director, it was reassuring to the African American actors in these productions that Suzan-Lori chose me to direct the plays. It was significant for them that she and I so clearly trusted each other, and had a warm, easy relationship as collaborators. But some were not always sure I fully understood what was embedded in this material, whether in terms of culturally specific language and gestures, or history. Conversation about these things, and more generally about the gap between my experience of life in the U.S. as a white woman and the experience of the actors as black men and women, was an essential feature of our creative and collaborative process. And, frankly, for me, it was one of the most rewarding aspects of the work.

CARPENTER: I think it's wonderful when you have a director willing to have that dialogue. I was recently at an LMDA [Literary Managers and Dramaturgs of the Americas] conference and Morgan Jenness was talking about how sometimes you have to "wade through the mud" of racial dialogue in order to get to the other side. I really loved that idea.

DIAMOND: I think there's a lot of mud often because white people want to believe ourselves to be far more evolved in matters of race and cultural identity than we are. The whole conversation scares us because of what it may reveal to us, about us. It's very hard for white people in this country to just shut up and listen; to really think about, be conscious of, our personal experience of race, of whiteness, let alone step into the shoes of a black person. But these are essential tasks.

CARPENTER: But I'm also wondering about the dynamics of interculturalism within the theatre. Were there profits — or challenges — that you encountered when directing Parks's work?

DIAMOND: One of the ways interculturalism worked in my rehearsals on Suzan-Lori's plays was that the actors, in order to make sure I got things right, would freely correct me or teach me on a point of history or cultural expression. And this was a really valuable thing for the quality of the work, and a healthy thing for the process itself. Any rehearsal process is strengthened when the actors take responsibility for the whole show — not just their roles. It was also exciting and interesting when the actors discovered, as they did from time to time, that the cultural references in the work didn't always conform to more Afro-centric tropes or styles. In *The Death of the Last Black Man in the Entire World* some actors were very concerned that the tone of the chorale at the end of the play had more to do with the cool, high-church sound of Roman Catholicism than the jubilant, participatory elements of—

CARPENTER: — the black Baptist or Pentecostal church —

DIAMOND: —Yes, exactly. It really upset a few of the actors at first. They very much wanted the gorgeous choric passage at the end of the play to be a hot, call-and-response kind of ending. At first I thought perhaps we should embrace that idea. But Suzan-Lori said, "No, no, no, no no — that's not the tone at all. It's cool. Think High Mass. Think Requiem." That was a challenging, difficult thing for the actors.

CARPENTER: I have to admit, it's interesting that you highlight that experience because when I was reading the 1995 *Bomb* interview in which you were talking about directing *The Death of the Last Black Man*, I was immediately struck by the discussion.* I was like, "Oh, that's different — Roman Catholicism?!" And then I had to remind myself, okay, this *isn't* James Baldwin and we're not talking about *The Amen Corner;* this isn't August Wilson and we're not talking about *Joe Turner's [Come and Gone]*. Which goes back to what Suzan-Lori has articulated clearly in and through her writing, the idea that there is no single African American experience or any standard way of representing African American experience*s*.

DIAMOND: There certainly isn't. When we cooled that passage down into cadences more reminiscent of the Latin Mass, that "Hold It" became a hushed prayer, and all of us felt it was right. That Latin Mass doesn't belong to white Europeans only, after all.

CARPENTER: Thinking of not being "fixed" and of utilizing a wealth of dramaturgical strategies, I wanted to close by asking about Parks's ingenious blending of humor with the more serious, social-political commentary in her work. How much of your ability to pull that humor out of the work is facilitated by your own sense of humor and your repartee with Parks? Is missing the humor a misstep that is too easily made with her work?

DIAMOND: Well, we do love to laugh — dumb jokes, sly jokes, dirty jokes — you name it. I suppose people can get a bit too reverential and serious in the presence of a writer whose work has been dubbed "groundbreaking" or "the voice of a new generation." That's

---

*Marc Robinson, "Liz Diamond," *Bomb* 51 (Spring 1995).

the problem with becoming an iconic writer in your own time. I think it was Heiner Müller who said something like: "In America it's when you have your first hit that the tragedy of your success begins." *(laughter)* So I think any director working with Parks's material should — as Lucy in *The America Play* says — "keep it to scale." You know, keep it to scale, look for the jokes, have fun, look for the puns. As I said earlier, it's in the wordplay where the truly devious, subversive humor lies.

A Production History of the Works of Suzan-Lori Parks

Richard E. Kramer

The Sinner's Place
- Première: Amherst, MA, 1984
- Reading: New Play Festival, Hampshire College, Amherst, MA, 1987

Fishes
- Reading: International Women Playwrights Festival, 1987

Betting on the Dust Commander
- Première: The Gas Station [makeshift bar in East Village garage], New York, NY, 1987; directed by S.-L. Parks
- Company One Theatre, Hartford, CT, 3–13 October 1990; directed by Liz Diamond
- Working Theatre, New York, NY: "Working One Acts '91," 13 June 1991; directed by Liz Diamond

Imperceptible Mutabilities in the Third Kingdom
- Première: BACA Downtown [Brooklyn Arts and Culture Association], Brooklyn, NY, opened 14 September 1989; directed by Liz Diamond
- New City Theatre, Seattle, WA, 9 (?)–27 October 1991; directed by Liz Diamond
- Yale School of Drama, New Haven, CT, 9–13 May 1995; directed by Kaia Calhoun
- MIT Dramashop, Cambridge, MA, 8–10 and 15–17 February 2007; directed by Thomas F. DeFrantz

Greeks
- BACA Downtown (at Manhattan Theatre Club's Downtown/Uptown Festival of alternative performances): Fringes, New York, NY, 21 April 1990; directed by Liz Diamond

The Death of the Last Black Man in the Whole Entire World
- Reading: New York Theatre Workshop, New York, NY, 2 October 1989; directed by Beth A. Schachter

- Première: BACA Downtown, 13 September 1990; directed by Beth A. Schachter
- Yale Repertory Theatre: WinterFest (16 January–7 March 1992), New Haven, CT, 22 January–7 March 1992; directed by Liz Diamond

Anemone Me (screenplay, with Bruce Hainley)
- Apparatus Productions and Zeitgeist Films, 1990; directed by Parks and Hainley; shown at Millenium Film Workshop, New York, NY (10, 11 & 13 December 1990), Los Angeles International Gay and Lesbian Film and Video Festival (11–20 July 1991), New York International Festival of Lesbian & Gay Film (4–14 June 1992)

The Third Kingdom (radio play)
- Commissioned by New American Radio, 1990

Pickling (radio play)
- Commissioned by New American Radio, 1991
- Stage production: Scenic Route Productions and Queen's Company at Mint Space, New York, NY: "She Keeps Time" (2 one-acts; 1–17 August 2000); directed by Allison Eve Zell
- Stage production: Cherry Lane Theatre, New York, NY: Black History Month, 20 February 2002; directed by Allison Eve Zell

Devotees in the Garden of Love
- Commissioned by Actors Theatre of Louisville, Humana Festival, Louisville, KY, 1992
  - Actors Theatre of Louisville (at Victor Jory Theatre), 16th Annual Humana Festival, 18 February–22 March 1992; directed by Oskar Eustis

Locomotive (radio play)
- Commissioned by New American Radio, 1991

The America Play
- Rehearsed reading: New Dramatists, New York, NY, 23 July 1991; directed by Liz Diamond
- Commissioned by Theatre for a New Audience, New York, NY, 1993
- Arena Stage, Washington, DC: PlayQuest Workshop, 24 February 1993; directed by Peter Wallace
- Workshop: Arena Stage, Washington, DC, and Dallas Theater Center, Dallas, TX, 1994
- Première: Joseph Papp Public Theater (Martinson Hall), New York, NY; co-production among New York Shakespeare Festival, Yale Repertory Theatre, and Theatre for a New Audience, New York, NY, 22 February–27 March 1994; directed by Liz Diamond
  - Yale Repertory Theatre Company, 20 January–5 February 1994
- American Repertory Theatre, Cambridge, MA, 31 March–10 April 1994; directed by Marcus Stern

Girl 6 (screenplay)
- 40 Acres & A Mule Filmworks, 22 March 1996; directed by Spike Lee

Venus
- Commissioned by The Women's Project, New York, NY, 1995
- Première: Yale Repertory Theatre (co-production with Joseph Papp Public Theater/New York Shakespeare Festival), 14–30 March 1996; directed by Richard Foreman
- Joseph Papp Public Theater, 16 April–19 June 1996; directed by Richard Foreman
- Yale School of Drama, 27 February–3 March 2007; directed by Jessi Hill

In the Blood
- Première: Joseph Papp Public Theater/New York Shakespeare Festival, 2 November–19 December 1999; directed by David Esbjornson
- Guthrie Theater, Minneapolis, MN, 20 April–13 May 2001; directed by Timothy Douglas
- Next Theatre, Evanston, IL, 31 January–9 March 2003; directed by Lisa Porter

Fucking A
- Première: DiverseWorks Art Space (co-production with Infernal Bridegroom), Houston, TX, 24 February–18 March 2000; directed by S.-L. Parks
- Joseph Papp Public Theater (Anspacher Theater), 16 March–6 April 2003; directed by George C. Wolfe

Urban Zulu Mambo [S.-L. Parks one of several contributors; conceived by Regina Taylor]
- Signature Theatre Company, New York, NY, 25 February–25 March 2001; directed by Henry Godinez

Topdog/Underdog
- Staged reading: Joe's Pub, Joseph Papp Public Theater: "New Works Now!" 19–29 April 1999
- Première: Joseph Papp Public Theater/New York Shakespeare Festival (Anspacher Theater), 26 July–2 September 2001; Ambassador Theatre, Broadway, 7 April–11 August 2002; directed by George C. Wolfe
- Royal Court, London (Public Theater production), 6–20 August 2003; directed by George C. Wolfe
- Hartford Stage (co-production with Steppenwolf Theatre Company and Alley Theatre), Hartford, CT, 14 April 2004; directed by Amy Morton
  - Steppenwolf Theatre Company, Chicago, IL, 21 September–2 November 2003
  - Alley Theatre, Houston, TX, 16 January–15 February 2004
  - Dallas Theatre Center, 26 February–21 March 2004
- Seattle Repertory Theatre, Seattle, WA, 8 September 2003; directed by George C. Wolfe
- Philadelphia Theatre Company, Philadelphia, PA, 15 October 2003; directed by Leah C. Gardiner
- Mark Taper Forum, Los Angeles, CA, 2 February–28 March 2004; directed by George C. Wolfe
- Luna Stage, Montclair, NJ, 28/30 April–22 May 2005; directed by Eric Ruffin

Getting Mother's Body (novel)
- Random House, New York, NY, 6 May 2003

Their Eyes Were Watching God (teleplay, with Misan Gagay and Bobby Smith; adapted from Zora Neale Hurston novel)
- Harpo Films (Oprah Winfrey); ABC-TV, 6 March 2005

"Welcome Me" (song)
- World première: Curious Theatre Company, Denver, CO: "The War Anthology," 11 March–29 April 2006; directed by Bonnie Metzgar

365 Days/365 Plays
- Theaters nationwide (over 700), 13 November 2006–12 November 2007

The Great Debaters (screenplay, with Robert Eisele)
- Harpo Films, Marshall Production, Road Rebel, Weinstein Company; 25 December 2007; directed by Denzel Washington

Ray Charles Live! (musical play; adapted from 2004 film *Ray*)
- Pasadena Playhouse, Pasadena, CA, 31 October–9 December 2007; directed by Sheldon Epps
- Broadway première: See below, *Unchain My Heart, the Ray Charles Musical*

Father Comes Home from the Wars (Parts 1, 8 & 9)
- Public LAB (co-production of Joseph Papp Public Theater and LAByrinth Theatre Company), 5–28 June 2009; directed by Jo Bonney; Parks appeared in the cast

The Book of Grace (formerly titled *Snake*)
- Première: Joseph Papp Public Theater (Anspacher Theater), 17 March–4 April 2010; directed by James MacDonald

Unchain My Heart, the Ray Charles Musical (formerly titled *Ray Charles Live!*; see above)
- Scheduled Broadway première: undetermined Shubert Organization theater, scheduled to open spring 2011; directed by Sheldon Epps

Paradise (screenplay, adapted from Toni Morrison novel)
- Oprah Winfrey's Harpo Productions; in development (for ABC television miniseries)

Act V (screenplay; from Ira Glass's *This American Life*, Chicago Public Radio)
- Plan B Entertainment for Warner Brothers; produced by Brad Pitt, Jennifer Aniston, Brad Grey with Plan B Entertainment; in development

Cabrini Green (screenplay, with Angelo Pizzo)
- Todd Wagner & Mark Cuban's 2929 Productions, produced by Judge and Amy Reinhold (A Barking Catfish Productions); in development

About the Contributors

Philip C. Kolin, University Distinguished Professor at the University of Southern Mississippi, has published more than 40 books on African American drama, Tennessee Williams, Shakespeare, and business and technical writing. Among them are *Williams: A Streetcar Named Desire* (2000); *Othello: New Critical Essays* (2001); *The Tennessee Williams Encyclopedia* (2004); *Understanding Adrienne Kennedy* (2005); *Contemporary African American Women Playwrights* (2007); *The Influence of Tennessee Williams: Essays on Fifteen American Dramatists* (2008); and *Successful Writing at Work*, 9th ed. (2009). His more than 200 articles have appeared in *African American Review, American Drama, Journal of Dramatic Theory and Criticism, Michigan Quarterly Review, Modern Drama, Southern Cultures, Tennessee Williams Annual Review, Theatre History Studies, University of Texas Library Chronicle*, etc. Kolin was the founding co-editor for *Studies in American Drama, 1945–Present* as well as guest editor for special issues on Tennessee Williams for the *Southern Quarterly, Mississippi Quarterly*, and the *South Atlantic Review*. A poet as well, he has published books on poetry and is the publisher and editor of *Vineyards: A Journal of Christian Poetry*.

Jochen Achilles is professor and chair of American studies at the University of Würzburg, Germany. Prior to that, he taught at Mainz University, Germany, for many years and was a visiting professor at Georgia State University in 1992/93. His books include a study on the development of Sean O'Casey's plays in the context of modern drama and a book on the interface between the gothic tradition and psychological fiction, focusing on Sheridan Le Fanu. He has also co-edited a volume on contemporary Irish dramatists (1996), another one on transformations of cultural identity in the English-speaking world (1998), and *Global Challenges and Regional Responses in Contemporary Drama in English* (2003), plus a book on representations of evil in literature and film (2009). In addition, he has published numerous articles in American, Irish, and German journals on American and Irish fiction and African American drama.

Faedra Chatard Carpenter is an assistant professor in the Department of Theatre at the University of Maryland, College Park. Her teaching and research interests include contemporary African American performance and dramaturgy. Carpenter's publications include articles in *Theatre Topics, Text and Performance Quarterly*, and *Women & Performance*. Also a freelance dramaturg, she has worked at the Kennedy Center, Center Stage, Arena Stage, and Crossroads Theatre Company.

Glenda Dicker/sun is professor of theatre and head of the African American theatre minor at the University of Michigan. She is the author of *African American Theater: A Cultural Companion* and recently completed an educational 2-disc DVD, *What's Cookin' in the Kitchen: A Global Portrait 2001–2004*, which documents her Kitchen Prayers Performance Dialogues on

9/11 and global loss series. Her recent essays include "Let the People See What I've Seen: In Praise of Mamie Till" for the *Southern Quarterly* and "Katrina: Acting Black/Playing Blackness" in *Theatre Journal*. Dicker/sun is currently working on: *Anabel's Brush*, an oral history of Georgia Sea Island descendants of African slaves; and a book, *The Saga of Lily Overstreet: Rhodessa Jones and the Spectacular Review*.

Jon Dietrick is an assistant professor of English at Babson College. He is a contributor to *Critical Insights: Death of a Salesman* and has also published articles in *American Drama, Twentieth-Century Literature,* and the *Journal of International Women's Studies*.

Rena Fraden is the dean of faculty and vice president for academic affairs and the Keith G. Funston Professor of English and American Studies at Trinity College, Connecticut. She has written two books, *Imagining Medea: Rhodessa Jones and Theater for Incarcerated Women* with a foreword by Angela Davis (2001), and *Blueprints for a Black Federal Theater, 1935–1939* (1994). Her articles on Parks have appeared in *The Massachusetts Review* and *Journal of American Drama and Theatre*. She is currently working on a book-length manuscript about Parks, tentatively entitled *To Be Possessed: Suzan-Lori Parks and Literary Tradition*.

Shawn-Marie Garrett is an assistant professor of theatre at Barnard College, Columbia University, and a contributing editor for *Yale Theater*. Her publications include an essay in *Performance Studies: The Key Terms*, edited by Gabrielle Cody and Charles O'Malley; and an essay, "Figures, Speech and Form in *Imperceptible Mutabilities in the Third Kingdom*" in *Suzan-Lori Parks: A Casebook*, edited by Alycia Smith-Howard and Kevin J. Wetmore. She is currently revising her monograph on the use of stereotypes by Parks and other contemporary artists for publication.

Richard E. Kramer is an actor, director, and dramaturg/literary manager. He has written extensively on contemporary American drama for a number of essay collections as well as for such journals as *Theatre History Studies*, the *Drama Review, Studies in American Drama, 1945–Present,* and the *Tennessee Williams Literary Review*. Since March 2009, Kramer has written and edited a blog entitled "Rick on Theater" (http:rickontheater.blogspot.com).

Jennifer Larson teaches literature, writing, and film at the University of North Carolina at Chapel Hill. She is the assistant editor of *Reading Contemporary African-American Drama: Fragments of History, Fragments of Self* (2007) and authored two essays on Parks for that collection. Her work has also appeared in *Women's Studies* and the *South Carolina Review*.

Nicole Hodges Persley is an assistant professor of theatre at the University of Kansas. Her most recent publications include an essay, "A Singer of Urban Tales: Jay-Z's Freestyling of an Afro-Homeric Oral Tradition," in Julius Bailey and Cornel West, eds., *Jay-Z: A Critical Reader of the Artist, the Man, and the Visionary* (2010); and "A Hip-hop History Timeline" in *Icons of Hip-hop: An Encyclopedia of the Music and Culture* (2007). She has also published performance reviews on African American theatre in *Theatre Journal*. Her current book manuscript explores the impact of African American cultural production in Hip Hop on theatre, conceptual art, and dance practices of non–African American artists.

Charlene Regester, an associate professor in the Department of African and Afro-American Studies, University of North Carolina–Chapel Hill, has published *African American Actresses:*

The Struggle for Visibility, 1900–1960 (2010); *Black Entertainers in African American Newspaper Articles, Vol. 1: An Annotated Bibliography of the Chicago Defender, Baltimore Afro-American, the Los Angeles Sentinel, and the New York Amsterdam News, 1910–1950* (2010); and *Black Entertainers in African American Newspaper Articles, Vol. 2: An Annotated Bibliography of the Pittsburgh Courier and the California Eagle, 1914–1950* (2010). She has also published essays on early black film stars and filmmakers in *Film Literature Quarterly*, *Popular Culture Review*, *Western Journal of Black Studies*, *Studies in American Culture*, *Film History*, *Journal of Film and Video*, and *Screening Noir*. She is an editorial board member for the *Journal of Film and Video*.

Jacqueline Wood is the director of African American studies at the University of Alabama at Birmingham. She has published essays on Sonia Sanchez and Adrienne Kennedy and her interview with Sanchez was published in *African American Review*. Her edition of Sanchez's plays is forthcoming from Duke University Press.

Christine Woodworth is an assistant professor of theatre history at the University of North Carolina–Greensboro, where she also serves as departmental dramaturg. Her articles and reviews have appeared in *Theatre Symposium*, *Theatre Journal*, *Theatre Annual*, *Theatre Topics*, *Text and Presentation* and the Theatre Library Association's *Broadside*. Her essay "The Abject of My Affection: The Erotics of Stepmotherhood in Sarah Kane's *Phaedra's Love* and Wooster Group's *To You, The Birdie (Phèdre)*" is included in *Essays and Scripts on How Mothers Are Portrayed in the Theater: A Neglected Frontier of Feminist Scholarship*, edited by Anna Andes and Beth Osnes.

Index

acting methods 81, 80
African American identity 20, 34, 35, 36, 38, 39, 40, 41, 43, 65, 66, 67, 68, 69, 70, 71, 72, 73, 74, 75, 78–79, 81, 183, 195
African Diaspora 59
Afrika Bambaataa 67
Albee, Edward 55
allegory 57, 58
Ambassador Theater 104
America Play 13, 14, 15, 31–32, 46, 47, 48, 49, 56, 65, 66, 67, 72, 74, 75, 77, 81, 103, 104, 111, 112, 126–129, 131, 133, 141, 142–143, 144–145, 149, 161, 169, 176, 180, 181, 186, 191, 197
American history 31–32, 65, 69, 72, 75, 140–141, 142, 153–154
Amos 'n' Andy 58
Anemone 9
Aristotle 24; *Politics* 91
Armstrong, Louis 35
As I Lay Dying 133
As You Like It 112
Atlick, Richard D. 78
audience 34, 35, 38, 40, 43, 195–196

Baartman, Saartje 76–87, 131
BACA Downtown 45, 52, 57, 192
Baker, Josephine 81
Baldwin, James 9, 22, 200
Barthes, Roland 80
Baston, Susan 171
Beats 65, 66, 68, 74
Beckett, Samuel 11, 20, 34, 36, 141
Belafonte, Harry 162
Berry, Halle 176
Betting on the Dust Commander 9, 17, 21, 34, 35, 36–39, 41, 43, 191, 197
black women 35, 36, 37, 39, 40, 41, 42, 43, 158, 159, 161, 165, 166, 167
Blood 103

Bonney, Jo 182, 188
Book of Grace 183, 185, 186, 187
Booth, John Wilkes 103, 119, 120
Borges, Jorge 20, 21, 29
Brecht, Bertolt 11, 20, 34, 38, 77, 79, 80, 88, 90, 101; Brechtian-feminist aesthetic 145–147
Brook, Peter 196
Brown, Foxy 173
Buchenwald 60

California Institute of the Arts 8
Callois, Roger 106; *Les jeux et les hommes* 106
Canby, Vincent 88
capitalism 91, 94–95
Casals, Pablo 133
casting 141, 146–148, 152, 192
Charles, Ray 9, 67, 180, 183
Chekhov, Anton 11
Cheng, Meiling 66
children (in Parks's plays) 50–53, 56, 57, 60–62
Chopin, Kate 136
Churchill, Caryl 146
Coleman, Ornette 194–195
colonialism 78, 79, 80
comedy 10, 53, 55
creation myths 26
cross-cultural directing 199
cyclical structure of time 36–38, 67, 68, 75

Daily Daily 9
Dandridge, Dorothy 174
Davis, Miles 38
Death of Last Black Man 12, 16, 21, 27, 46, 50, 56, 65, 67, 68, 69, 70, 72, 74, 75, 77, 78, 94, 177, 191, 194, 196–197, 200
Dee, Ruby 177
Demers, Joanna 67
Demeter 160, 161, 162, 164, 167
Derrida, Jacques 111
Devotees 15, 34, 35, 42–43, 50, 56
Diamond, Liz 45, 47, 56, 65, 77, 191–192, 193–201
Dickens, Charles 71

dig(ging) 21–22, 66, 68, 124–139
digital theater 25, 138
DJ(s) 66, 67, 68, 69, 70
DJ Kool Herc 67
DJ Spooky 65, 68
Drukman, Steven 28–29, 30, 67, 192, 196
Dubois, W.E.B. 71

Ealy, Michael 177
Eastern religions 11, 22
Elam, Harry, Jr. 57, 69, 101, 140, 146
"Elements of Style" 21, 28, 103
"An Equation for Black People on Stage" 26, 103, 105, 142, 153
eros/erotics 84–85
Esbjornson, David 88
essentialism 26, 29
Eustas, Oskar 181, 183, 188

fabricated absence 68, 72
Fanon, Frantz 79
Father Comes Home from the War 8, 13, 29, 61, 134, 181–182, 185, 186, 187, 188
Faulkner, William 11, 20, 30, 31, 133, 141, 157, 196; *As I Lay Dying* 133; *Light in August* 133
feminist icons 77, 79, 80, 91, 170
Fences 183, 187
Foreman, Richard 27, 76–77, 80, 81–84, 85
free market conditions 90–91
Freud, Sigmund 172, 173, 174, 175
Fucking A 11, 30, 50, 88–102, 103, 140, 144–146, 148, 151, 163

game theory 104–106, 120–122
Gates, Henry Louis 158, 159
Geis, Deborah 37, 49, 55, 65, 66, 140, 170, 171, 172, 173, 175, 176
gender issues 34, 40, 41, 43
Germany 9, 81–82, 97, 187

Getting Mother's Body 8, 30–31, 57, 126, 133, 156–157
Girl 6, 8, 77, 81, 169–180
Glory 177
Good Times 175
Gould, Stephen Jay 78
Goux, Jean-Joseph 89, 93, 96
Great Hole of History 32, 46, 72, 126–138
Grief, Michael 88
Grier, Pam 175
Griot 68, 75
Guggenheim Fellowship 9

Hall, Stuart 67, 71, 73
Hamlet 11, 53, 112
Hannaham, James 30
Harpo Productions 82
Harris, Trudier 67
Hatshepsut 70, 78
Hawthorne, Nathaniel 11, 30, 88, 89, 92, 93, 98, 103, 145–146, 147–148, 157, 163
Henry VI 183
Hinduism 24–25
Hip Hop 65–75
hooks, bell 174, 175
Hughes, Langston 35
Huizinga, Johan 105
Hurston, Zora Neale 10, 37, 137, 158, 159, 169, 170, 176–180

identity: and the body 92–93, 97–99, 126, 129; as fabrication in process 158, 162, 167
Imperceptible Mutabilities 9, 12, 13, 16, 18, 27, 45–64, 77, 140, 141, 148–152, 182, 186, 191–192, 194–195
In the Blood 9, 16, 18, 30–31, 56, 88–102, 131, 140, 145–148, 149, 151, 180, 194
interculturalism 200
intertextuality 196
Isherwood, Charles 88
Isis 169, 161, 163

Jackson, Michael 184
Jam Master Jay 69
jazz 17, 34–43, 65, 66, 67
The Jeffersons 175
Jenness, Morgan 199
Les jeux et les hommes 106
Jews 60
Jiggets, Shelby 29, 82, 174
Joyce, James 20, 71, 189, 197
Juneteenth 56, 182

Kafka, Franz 52
Keckley, Mrs. Elizabeth 129–130, 134–135
Kennedy, Adrienne 11, 13, 15, 20, 47, 54, 56, 66, 70, 141, 196

Kennedy, John F. 156
Kentucky Derby 37
King, Martin Luther, Jr. 66, 120, 184
Kolin, Philip C. 10, 12, 25, 35, 67, 92, 125, 138, 140
Krasner, David 88
Krishna 24, 186
Kundera, Milan 46

Lacan, Jacques 80, 118, 120
language 16, 17, 36, 37, 41, 42, 43, 51–52, 53, 61; talk/action distinction 94–95, 97
Lee, Spike 8, 77, 81, 170, 171, 172, 175
Lewis, Jennifer 172
life-death-resurrection 160, 161, 162, 163, 164, 166
Light in August 133
Lincoln, Abraham 13, 72, 73, 74, 103, 111, 112, 114, 119, 120, 126, 129–130; impersonations 104, 110, 111–116
Lincoln, Mary Todd 99–100, 129–130, 133–135
love as theme in Parks 76–77, 79–80, 83–84, 85, 186
lynching 50, 53, 54, 56, 58, 61

MacArthur Foundation 9
malapropisms 57
Mandela, Nelson 78
Martin, Darnell 176; *Glory* 177
Marx, Karl 91
Mbiti, John 31
Medea 10
memory as technique 3, 35, 36, 38, 39, 41, 46–47, 49, 51, 57, 58, 61, 69, 115, 157
Merchant of Venice 91
meta-games 121–122
Metzgar, Bonnie 18, 25, 124
Michaels, Walter Benn 89, 90
Middle Kingdom 62
Middle Passage 53
Midsummer Night's Dream 7, 8
Miles Davis in Stockholm 138
Miller, Paul 65, 68
minstrelsy 58, 149
Mitchell, Loften 116
money 88–102; monstrosity 91
Morris, Steve Leigh 26
Morrison, Toni 27, 141, 159
Mother Teresa 184
Mount Holyoke College 7, 9, 23, 170
Müller, Heiner 201
music and musicality 17, 20, 65–75, 181, 194
Mutual of Omaha, *Wild Kingdom* 54

Namib 55
Naturalism 90
Negro College Fund 49
Neologisms 35, 41
"New Black Math" 26–27, 142
New York Shakespeare Festival/Public Theater 67, 77, 83, 143, 181, 182–183, 188, 191–192
New York Theater Workshop 192
Non-naturalistic theater 198
Nottage, Lynn 187

Obama, Barack 158, 186, 197–198
Obama, Michelle 158, 186, 197–198
Oberammergau 11
Obie Award 62, 169
Odets, Clifford 88
Ofili, Chris 161
O'Neill, Eugene 29
Ontologic-Hysteric Theater 80
oral narratives 66, 67, 75
Oscher, Paul 17, 66
Osiris 160, 163, 166, 168, 169
Our American Cousin 111, 112, 114

Papp, Joseph 67, 88, 191–192
paratext 60
Parks, Suzan-Lori: *America Play* 13, 14, 15, 31–32, 46, 47, 48, 49, 56, 65, 66, 67, 72, 74, 75, 77, 81, 103, 104, 111, 112, 126–129, 131, 133, 141, 142–143, 144–145, 149, 161, 169, 176, 180, 181, 186, 191, 197; *Anemone* 9; *Betting on the Dust Commander* 9, 17, 21, 34, 35, 36–39, 41, 43, 191, 197; biography 22, 140; *Blood* 103; *Book of Grace* 183, 185, 186, 187; childhood 62; *Daily Daily* 9; *Death of Last Black Man* 12, 16, 21, 27, 46, 50, 56, 65, 67, 68, 69, 70, 72, 74, 75, 77, 78, 94, 177, 191, 194, 196–197, 200; *Devotees* 15, 34, 35, 42–43, 50, 56; "Elements of Style" 21, 28, 103; "An Equation for Black People on Stage" 26, 103, 105, 142, 153; *Father Comes Home from the War* 8, 13, 29, 61, 134, 181–182, 185, 186, 187, 188; *Fucking A* 11, 30, 50, 88–102, 103, 140, 144–146, 148, 151, 163; *Getting Mother's Body* 8, 30–31, 57, 126, 133, 156–157; *Girl* 6, 8, 77, 81, 169–180; *Imperceptible Mutabilities* 9, 12, 13, 16, 18, 27, 45–64, 77, 140, 141, 148–152, 182, 186, 191–192,

194–195; *In the Blood* 9, 16, 18, 30–31, 56, 88–102, 131, 140, 145–148, 149, 151, 180, 194; "New Black Math" 26–27, 142; *Pickling* 34, 35, 39–41, 43; "Possession" 22, 142; *Ray Charles Live—The Musical* 9, 66, 67, 180; *Their Eyes Were Watching God* 137, 169–171, 176–180; *365 Plays/365 Days* 7, 10, 12, 23–25, 61, 124–138, 140, 149–153, 169, 181, 182, 185, 186, 187, 192; *Topdog/Underdog* 12, 14, 23, 31, 32, 83, 94, 126, 129–131, 133–135, 137, 140, 141, 143–145, 146, 148, 169, 183, 195–196; "Tradition and the Individual Talent" 29–30; *Union of My Confederate Parts* 181, 182, 185; *Venus* 9, 12, 15, 27–28, 47, 49, 76–85, 126, 130–133, 136–137, 158, 173, 179, 197
Pearce, Michelle 32
Perkins, Marlin 54–55
Persephone 160, 161, 162, 164, 167
Peterson, James Braxton 69, 70
Phi Betta Kappa 9
Pickling 34, 35, 39–41, 43
Plimpton, George 125
Plumpp, Sterling 52
Poe, Edgar Allan 120
Politics 91
polyrhythmic 192, 195
Porter, Adina 81, 85
"Possession" 22, 142
post-racial world 197
Public Theater 9, 88, 104
Pulitzer Prize 9, 187, 188
punctuation marks 189
puns 48, 49–61

radical inclusion, concept of 22, 23, 25, 32, 125, 149–150
Randle, Theresa 171
rap/rappers 73
Ray Charles Live—The Musical 9, 66, 67, 180
Rayner, Alice 69
Reconstruction 50
religion 21, 22, 24–25, 184
Re-membering 35, 38, 39, 40, 43

remixing 67, 68, 75
Rep & Rev techniques 17, 35–36, 39, 41, 43, 47, 51, 57, 58, 66, 67, 103, 116, 122, 142, 149, 160, 198
reproduction and money 91, 99
Richards, Sandra L. 197
Roach, Joseph 22, 73
Roman Catholicism 22, 162, 184, 200

sampling 66, 67, 68, 70, 73, 74
Sanchez, Sonia 141
Schafer, Carol 66
Schloss, Joseph 68
Schreir, Dan Moses 194
Sertima, Ivan van 71
sexuality 92, 130–132
Shakespeare, William 7, 20, 21, 29, 32, 91, 141, 183–184; *As You Like It* 112; *Hamlet* 11, 53, 112; *Henry VI* 183; *Merchant of Venice* 91; *Midsummer Night's Dream* 7, 8
Shakur, Tupac 69
Shange, Ntozake 9, 11, 66, 141
Shaw, George Bernard 189
Shell, Marc 89, 96
Signature Theater 9
signifying 34, 36, 39, 41
Silver, Ron 172
Simon, John 88
Smalls, Biggie 69
Smith, Anna Deavere 194
Solomon, Alisa 29, 197
Sonic 66, 67, 68, 70, 75, 194
Spells 7, 17, 41, 67, 68, 74, 94, 98, 130, 197
Spiller, Hortense 158
staging 15–16, 29, 56, 57, 58, 82–85, 149
Stein, Gertrude 38, 141, 196
stereotypes 67, 69, 70, 142
Stowe, Harriet 142

Tarantino, Quentin 171
Taylor, Tom 111
tetraptych 194
Their Eyes Were Watching God 137, 169–171, 176–180
theology 184–85
Thompson, Debby 28

Three-Card Monte Con Game 110, 112, 113, 114, 116–120
365 Plays/365 Days 7, 10, 12, 23–25, 61, 124–138, 140, 149–153, 169, 181, 182, 185, 186, 187, 192
time 34, 35, 36, 37, 40, 43
Topdog/Underdog 12, 14, 23, 31, 32, 83, 94, 126, 129–131, 133–135, 137, 140, 141, 143–145, 146, 148, 169, 183, 195–196
"Tradition and the Individual Talent" 29–30
Turturro, John 71

Union of My Confederate Parts 181, 182, 185

Venus 9, 12, 15, 27–28, 47, 49, 76–85, 126, 130–133, 136–137, 158, 173, 179, 197
Viet Nam 61
Virgin Mary 161, 162

Walker, Alice 141, 159, 166
Walker, George 116
Washington, George 58
Washington, Isaiah 172
Wellman, Mac 82
White Wild Kingdom 58
"wicked excess" 157, 158, 162, 167
Wild Kingdom 54
Williams, George 116
Williams, Tennessee 10, 26
Wilma Theater 185
Wilson, August 141, 183, 187, 200; *Fences* 183, 187
Winfrey, Oprah 82, 170
Winkler, Mel 178
wisdom 31–32
Wolfe, George C. 9, 77, 83–84, 181
Woolfe, Virginia 141, 157

Yale Repertory Theater 67, 77, 81, 191–192
yoga 22, 25, 124
Young, Jean 27–28
YouTube 25

Zen 22

www.ingramcontent.com/pod-product-compliance
Lightning Source LLC
Chambersburg PA
CBHW060300240426
43661CB00060B/2844